STATES, SOCIAL KNOWLEDGE, AND THE ORIGINS OF MODERN SOCIAL POLICIES

STATES, SOCIAL KNOWLEDGE, AND THE ORIGINS OF MODERN SOCIAL POLICIES

Edited by Dietrich Rueschemeyer and Theda Skocpol

PRINCETON UNIVERSITY PRESS
PRINCETON, NEW JERSEY

RUSSELL SAGE FOUNDATION
NEW YORK

Published by Princeton University Press, 41 William Street,
Princeton, New Jersey 08540
In the United Kingdom: Princeton University Press, Chichester,
West Sussex

Library of Congress Cataloging-in-Publication Data

States, social knowledge, and the origins of modern social policies /
edited by Dietrich Rueschemeyer and Theda Skocpol.
p. cm.
Includes bibliographical references (p.) and index.
ISBN 0-691-03444-3 (cl : alk. paper). — ISBN 0-691-00112-X
(pa : alk. paper)
1. Social policy. 2. Knowledge, Sociology of. I. Rueschemeyer,
Dietrich. II. Skocpol, Theda.
HN28.S79 1996
361.6'1—dc20 95-17924 CIP

This book has been composed in Galliard

Princeton University Press books are printed
on acid-free paper and meet the guidelines
for permanence and durability of the Committee
on Production Guidelines for Book Longevity
of the Council on Library Resources.

Printed in the United States of America by Princeton Academic Press

10 9 8 7 6 5 4 3 2 1

(Pbk.)
10 9 8 7 6 5 4 3 2 1

Contents

Preface

THE INTELLECTUAL conversations that led to this book started years ago under the auspices of the Committee on States and Social Structures at the Social Science Research Council. The Committee had already commissioned conferences that culminated in the volumes *Bringing the State Back In,* edited by the two of us along with Peter B. Evans, and *The Political Power of Economic Ideas: Keynesianism Across Nations,* edited by Peter A. Hall. A focus on social knowledge and the origins of modern social policies seemed a good way to further explore the sorts of questions that had been taken up in these earlier projects, and especially in the one coordinated by Peter Hall. With funding from the Spencer Foundation, meetings of social scientists and historians were convened and papers were drafted and revised. After some years interrupted by other demands on academic schedules, this collection came together. By the time it was ready for publication, the SSRC Committee had moved to the Russell Sage Foundation, to become the Working Group on States and Social Structures.

Over the course of work on this book, we have accumulated many debts. All of our colleagues on the original Committee on States and Social Structures had a hand in planning this project, and for that we thank Peter Evans, Albert Hirschman, Ira Katznelson, Peter Katzenstein, Stephen Krasner, and Charles Tilly. We also appreciate the work done by SSRC staffers Martha Gephart and Yasmine Ergas. And we are very grateful for the support given to the workshop meetings and preparation of the book by the Spencer Foundation. Martin Bulmer, Stephan Liebfried, and Giovanna Procacci made valuable contributions to meetings on this project, contributions which have intellectually enriched the book as well as the group discussions. For help with publication, we are grateful to Lisa Nachtigall at the Russell Sage Foundation, Malcolm DeBevoise at Princeton University Press, and the anonymous scholarly reviewers who made valuable suggestions in response to the first version of the manuscript. We would also like to acknowledge Margie Towery for the meticulously prepared index. Finally, we wish to thank our spouses, Marilyn Rueschemeyer and Bill Skocpol, for the help and encouragement they have offered in many ways.

STATES, SOCIAL KNOWLEDGE, AND THE ORIGINS OF MODERN SOCIAL POLICIES

Introduction

THEDA SKOCPOL
AND DIETRICH RUESCHEMEYER

THE MODERN social sciences took shape in close interaction with early attempts by national states to deal with the social consequences of capitalist industrialization. From roughly the 1850s to the 1920s, such social policies as regulations of the industrial labor process, pensions for the elderly, unemployment insurance, and measures to educate and ensure the welfare of children were enacted into law in many industrializing capitalist nations. This was also the period in which the modern social sciences emerged, taking on intellectual and institutional characteristics still recognizable today. The emerging social sciences can be examined as social groups and as modes of knowing about the social world. In both senses they influenced, and were influenced by, the making of early modern social policies.

This book uses a focus on the origins of modern social policies to explore the interrelations of states and social knowledge. The chapters examine how the social dilemmas of industrialization changed the ways in which knowledge about social and economic life was created—and how, in turn, new knowledge and newly constituted knowledge groups influenced the substance and direction of governmental policies. Looking at the emerging social sciences in relation to governmental policymaking enhances our general understanding of the cultural accompaniments and intellectual bases of state action.

We can examine in a fresh and informative way matters which, heretofore, have been de-emphasized in scholarly debates about the development of national states and their social policies. Previous scholarly debates about the origins of modern social policies have focused almost exclusively on class and political conflicts, de-emphasizing the equally important contributions of ideas, of knowledge-bearing groups, and of knowledge-generating institutions. Most previous research has likewise not explored as fully as possible the impact of varying national government institutions and social policies on the outlooks, institutional arrangements, and civic impact of the emerging social sciences.

Although this book looks at its own distinct time period and set of substantive questions, its comparative-historical and institutionalist approach resembles the theoretical and methodological approaches used in

Communities of Discourse: Ideology and Social Structure in the Reformation, the Enlightenment, and European Socialism by Robert Wuthnow, and in *The Political Power of Economic Ideas: Keynesianism Across Nations,* edited by Peter A. Hall.[1] Both of these works, and this collection as well, investigate intellectual transformations in the modern world—asking about the social locations of the proponents of new ideas, and about the institutional conditions that have influenced the spread, transformation, and policy successes or failures of the ideas and their carriers. This book, like the other two, concludes that historically changing and cross-nationally varying institutional configurations—interrelations among states and social structures—have much to do with the development and deployment of systems of ideas, including scientific ideas as well as political or moral ideologies.

In the remainder of this brief introduction, we do two things. We first note the broad epochal transformations that form the backdrop for all of the chapters in this volume, pointing to the special relevance of partially autonomous elites and groups making claims to new kinds of knowledge about the social world in the nineteenth and early twentieth centuries. Then we introduce the three major parts of the book, discussing how the chapters included in each part address a particular subset of issues about states, social knowledge, and the origins of modern social policies.

Social Knowledge and Modern Social Policies

Leaders of states in the modern world have concerned themselves with social order and with at least the external conditions for the smooth functioning of markets and production processes. Modern social policies of the more specific types we are considering in this volume were developed by or through the national states of industrializing capitalist countries in the later nineteenth and early twentieth centuries. These state interventions aimed at giving working people and their dependents, or members of the "respectable poor," minimal protection against the economic hazards of injury, illness, family breakup, old age, and unemployment. In time, the earliest social policies established by industrializing nations were expanded and knit together into what have been labeled, since World War II, "modern welfare states." Governments became involved in social life in unforeseen and unprecedented ways.

Creators of modern social policies responded to a number of master trends set in motion by the rise and success of capitalism. Class interests, both new and old, became more openly antagonistic, and they expressed themselves with an unheard-of starkness in collective organization and collective action. At the same time, there occurred what Karl Mannheim called the "fundamental democratization" of society—the empowerment of subordinate groups and classes formerly excluded from political influence and participation. Together these two developments raised the specter of nations irreparably divided: politically and economically disruptive class conflict loomed as a realistic possibility. And a third development gave a special urgency to these threats to social order and economic efficiency. As English dominance of the international economy gradually gave way to an increasingly harsh competition among nationally organized political economies, authorities within each nation had geopolitical as well as domestic reasons for attending to the problems raised during the course of capitalist economic development.

Who, then, defined such transformations as political challenges, and then devised ideas about how to respond to them? The obvious answer may seem to be: the political representatives of dominant class interests facing challenges from the subordinate classes. Yet this answer does not take account of major transformations at the apex of the industrializing capitalist political economies.

It does not take into account, in the first place, the rise in many places of bureaucratic states whose power was structurally separated from the economic power of landlords and of capitalist entrepreneurs. Power grounded in the ownership of land no longer, in and of itself, conferred governmental authority; and neither did power grounded in the ownership of other capital assets. Increasingly effective in their internal workings, bureaucratizing state apparatuses became—at different times and in varying degrees in different countries—more important as sites for official actors who were potentially autonomous from dominant economic groups. And so did political parties devoted to mobilizing groups for (more or less democratic) elections. Thus, even in the United States, where bureaucratized agencies of government emerged only slowly and in piecemeal fashion, powerful political organizations—in this case, patronage-oriented political parties, along with state and federal courts—exercised some relatively autonomous authority in relation to social classes and class conflict.[2]

Also obscured by a simple class analysis are the new uses of knowledge and the new roles of knowledge-generative institutions and knowledge-bearing elites. Throughout Western Europe and North America, schools, academies, universities, and scholarly societies were reconstructed or newly created on a large scale. The rise of capitalism and of modern national states created many new practical uses for social knowledge. Set off to some extent from religious leaders as well as from economic owners and established political authorities, knowledge-bearing groups and intellectual elites acquired a new authority based on their claims to effective secular knowledge. While the new knowledge-bearing elites probably never had (nor ever will have) the dominant impact on society that was ascribed to them by the eighteenth-century French philosophers—not to mention by such present-day theorists of "post-industrial society" as Alvin Gouldner and Daniel Bell—they did gain considerable social and policymaking influence.[3] Just as the state cannot be collapsed into capitalism or class conflict, neither can knowledge-generating institutions or knowledge-bearing groups and their ideas be analytically collapsed into capitalism or the state.

This said, of course, the role of experts and intellectual elites was markedly greater when and where they served the knowledge needs of other powerful actors—above all interests understood and acted upon by agencies of modern national states. In historical actuality, the rise of bureaucratically organized government and the new role of secular knowledge were not unrelated. Not unjustifiably did the seminal social theorist and comparative-historical analyst Max Weber view bureaucratization and the increased governmental use of social knowledge as twin aspects of a more comprehensive process of "rationalization" associated with capitalism from its earliest beginnings.

The major actors in the initiation of modern social policies were not, in fact, simply class-based groups. The bourgeoisie and the industrial working class were without doubt of great importance; their relations shaped much of the context within which knowledge-bearers and policymakers operated. Yet, in any immediate sense, neither bourgeois capital owners nor industrial workers played the leading roles in social reform. In fact, both business and working-class organizations took either oppositional or reserved and ambiguous positions in the debates about such policies as social insurance for workingmen and their dependents.[4] Working-class organizations, such as unions and early social-democratic political parties, often constituted an apparent threat to the established order; and without this threat the formulation of proposals for the first modern social policies is hardly conceivable. Yet challenges from below had an effect on social reform primarily through the perceptions and interpretation of elite actors powerfully situated in or around the state.

In the later nineteenth and early twentieth centuries, the primary forces behind policy innovations were often what one might call "third" parties (presuming that capital and labor are considered as the two main parties to many underlying conflicts). The "third party" role could be played by such central political figures as Britain's Lloyd George and Winston Churchill, and Germany's Chancellor Bismarck. As well, civil servants often had a critical part in the design and in the political realization of social reform measures. Similarly, intellectual elites reshaped educated opinion and advised governments on social problems and social policy.

The historical record and the chapters of this volume show that various sorts of ideas and different sorts of knowledge-bearing elites have played distinct parts in various countries, and in relation to specific kinds of policy issues. But amidst the variation, there is one constant: intellectual expertise and authority invariably left their imprint on the formation of early modern social policies. We need to understand more deeply both the ideas and the socio-institutional locations of the bearers of new knowledge about society who figured so importantly in the origins of early modern social policies.

Looking Ahead

All of the authors in this volume engage themselves in historical comparison, undertaking the difficult task of exploring policy changes and the generation and use of knowledge across national borders. Inevitably then —and we think, valuably—the chapters cut at different points into complex webs of interrelationships, all parts of which need to be explored if we are to better understand states, social knowledge, and the origins of modern social policies. We have chosen to cluster the essays not by country or by time but according to how each set cuts into the empirical interrelationships at issue here. In this way, the findings and arguments of these chapters can be seen to resonate with, and build upon, one another, leading toward more sophisticated and grounded generalizations than one could achieve by theoretical deduction alone.

The nature of modern social knowledge as it took historical shape in industrializing Europe is the concern of the chapters collected into Part I, "The Emergence of Modern Social Knowledge." As Ira Katznelson points out, scholars often move too quickly to asking about the instrumental purposes of intellectuals—"knowledge for what"—before adequately exploring "knowledge about what." In Katznelson's view, there emerged in modernizing Europe a quest for knowledge about the relationships of postfeudal political authorities to citizens of more and more participatory nation-states. A "new liberal" intelligentsia, Katznelson argues, focused thought and research on the changing linkages among states, markets, and citizens. These intellectuals had faith that empirical and rational analysis would lead toward scientific solutions of ethical and policy problems. The bulk of Katznelson's chapter discusses in detail the ideas of certain English "new liberals," chiefly John Stuart Mill, Alfred Marshall, and H. L. Beales. Variants of the same ideas, and reactions against them, have in Katznelson's view "shaped and limited" Western social science from the nineteenth century to the present.

Anson Rabinbach also writes about the substance of social knowledge in modernizing Europe, about the emergence of the general belief that society develops in lawlike ways and that behavior and public policies can rationally be made to conform to social laws. Specifically, Rabinbach examines ideas embodied in late nineteenth-century French and German discussions about industrial accidents. Two "novel ideas" gained currency and prestige at the end of the nineteenth century, he tells us. Society came to be seen as having an obligation to reduce risks and inequities for individuals. And the notion developed that "social responsibility can be grounded scientifically and demonstrated by statistical laws." Because of the emergence of such ways of thinking, issues about industrial accidents that were once centered directly in immediate employer-employee relationships were "displaced" into realms of jurisprudence and statistical and medical expertise. Industrial "work" became subject to social-scientific investigation, as did other aspects of economic and social life. This did not, however, end class conflict. Rather, it led to the "politicization" of knowledge, as conflicts based in class and other interests came to be carried out in the guise of disputes among scientific experts, situated within new institutional locales, and using new forms of discourse.

Neither Katznelson nor Rabinbach pay great attention to the causes of cross-national variations in ideas or public policymaking. To be sure, Katznelson notes the limits of his focus on English intellectuals; and Rabinbach discusses in considerable detail the contrasting sorts of industrial accident policies and political coalitions that held center stage in France versus Germany at the end of the 1800s. But both Katznelson and Rabinbach are chiefly interested in similar trends in the contents of modern social knowledge as it emerged in nineteenth-century Europe. In contrast, the third chapter in Part I, by Björn Wittrock and Peter Wagner, stresses the need for, and analytical advantages of, comparative studies of variations across the nations of industrializing Europe.

Wittrock and Wagner have written a synthetic "think piece" that reflects on findings in all of the chapters in this book. The origins of modern social policies in Western nations coincided, these authors point out, with the emergence of modern universities and professions as the institutional settings for the production and deployment of new kinds of social knowledge. Yet no single master evolutionary path of change was followed, and scholars cannot understand these intertwined changes either in terms of socioeconomic reductionism or simply the internal logic of ideas as such. They must, instead, explore and seek to explain cross-national variations, with a focus on the diverse institutional configurations that tied together political institutions and knowledge-producing institutions.

Wittrock and Wagner argue that key differences are to be found between "statist" European nations that had bureaucratic-absolutist political systems prior to industrialization, and "non-statist" nations, such as England, that lacked such pre-modern institutional arrangements. Yet Wittrock and Wagner do not reify this as the only comparative-historical distinction that matters. They go on to show that differences among governmental institutions within the "statist" and "non-statist" categories also matter for the purpose of making sense of cross-national variations in ideas and politics.

Wittrock and Wagner's chapter marks an appropriate transition to Parts II and III of this book, where their call for careful cross-national analysis of actors within varying institutional configurations is put into practice. Each chapter in Part II, "Reformist Social Scientists and Public Policymaking," features a close comparison of analogous groups of policy-oriented reformist intellectuals in two nations. Actors with ideas and reformist policy goals thus become the entering point of discussion, rather than the content of idea systems as such. Likewise in Part III, "State Managers and the Uses of Social Knowledge," actors remain at the center; these chapters look at groups of officials in parallel governmental agencies of two or more national states. The authors of each of the chapters in Parts II and III move "outward" from the groups of actors they have chosen to juxtapose, toward an analysis of the cultural, social, and institutional conditions that explain cross-national similarities and differences in intellectual and policy developments.

Germany and Great Britain were among the first Western nations to use national social policies to address the insecurities of the industrial working class during industrialization; and the German Verein für Sozialpolitik and the English Fabian Society were groups of reformist intellectuals centrally involved in the social investigations and policy debates that shaped these pioneering welfare states. In the first chapter of Part II, Dietrich Rueschemeyer and Ronan Van Rossem compare the sociopolitical contexts within which these two knowledge-wielding nations emerged, operated, and changed over time. Both the content of authoritative social knowledge and the nature of knowledge-bearing groups are shown to depend on larger socio-institutional patterns.

The authority and effectiveness on public policymaking of the German Verein was originally grounded in the status and bureaucratic structures of the Imperial German "Kulturstaat," Rueschemeyer and Van Rossem argue. As Germany partially democratized, the Verein's distinctive fusion of cognitive and moral-political authority dissolved, putting the emerging German social sciences on a new academic trajectory. Meanwhile in Britain, the nature and modes of operations of the Fabian Society depended equally on the porousness of the British state, social status structure, and emerging moderate labor movement. As the liberal British oligarchy of the nineteenth century gradually democratized, the Fabians' "amateur" empiricist style of social research persisted through its incorporation into a wing of the Labour Party.

Reform-minded British social investigators also figure in Libby Schweber's chapter which seeks to compare them to their counterparts in the late nineteenth- and early twentieth-century United States. Schweber analytically revisits a historical paradox first noted by the historical sociologist Philip Abrams, who argued that there was an elective affinity between the persistence of amateur social inquiry and the early emergence of a national welfare state in Britain and the converse turn toward academic, professional social science, while early efforts at national welfare-state-building were failing in the United States.[5] Schweber introduces both greater complexity and more analytical specificity into this comparative insight. She traces in detail the modes of politics used, more or less effectively, by reformist social scientists promoting new governmental responses to industrial unemployment in Britain and the United States. In order to explain the differences she notes in the involvements of intellectuals in policy formation, Schweber brings together a historical and institutional account of transformations in political institutions, and changes in universities in relation to states and social structures.

The final chapter of Part II takes us further into North American history. John Sutton is fascinated by early developments in an area of modern social policy, child welfare policy, where the United States, even at the national level, actually took earlier programmatic steps than did other nations, including Canada. Canada has often been seen by scholars as closer to the pioneering welfare states of Europe, while the United States has been considered an extreme laggard in modern social policy, but in the area of child welfare policy this overall pattern does not hold. Sutton analyzes two federal-level governmental agencies—the U.S. Children's Bureau and the Canadian Council on Child Welfare—both of which grew out of social-reform movements spearheaded by women's groups wielding new research methods and ideas about families and the needs of children. After noting a series of telling differences between the reform movements and the agencies, Sutton relates them to differences between the U.S. and Canadian colonial experiences and constitutional and party structures. He argues, moreover, that especially in "weak" states such as Canada and the United States, nonofficial groups serve as crucial intervening agents in the setting of policy agendas and the definition of the modes of research and information that can influence state policymaking. The exact characteristics, capacities, and proclivities of those groups may have a great deal to do with the substantive evolution of a policy area such as child welfare.

Taken together, the chapters of Part II suggest that the social composition, ideas, and favored modes of research and argument of knowledge-bearing groups are profoundly influenced by the social-status arrangements and the political institutions of their respective societies. In turn, these larger contexts influence whether and how (that is, through what kinds of knowledge-claims) policy-oriented intellectuals can have influence within national politics. The chapters show, as well, that national contexts are not unbreakable, essentialist entities; there can be important, analytically explicable differences across groups and policy areas as well as nations and epochs. This point is especially well driven home for the nations that appear in more than one chapter in Part II: Britain, which figures in similar yet slightly different ways in the findings of Reuschemeyer and Van Rossem versus Schweber, and the United States, about which clearly different aspects are highlighted in the respective arguments of Schweber and Sutton.

In Part III, governmental agencies and officials who create or mobilize social knowledge for policy purposes come to the fore. The chapters by Stein Kuhnle and Sheldon Garon also expand the comparative and theoretical scope of this volume by focusing on nations beyond the core European and North American "great powers." The state and intellectuals tied to it emerge in these essays as pivotal, not only to the management of intranational social conflicts, but also the handling of international relations, including the spread of models of social policymaking from one country to another.

Stein Kuhnle builds his analysis around a pair of precise questions about Scandinavian social policy innovations in the 1890s. Why, he asks, did Denmark, Norway, and Sweden all enact new social insurance or income maintenance programs in that decade; and why were there significant variations in the kinds of programs first established? Neither sheer levels of industrialization nor the simple imitation of policy models from Bismarck's Germany can explain the Scandinavian patterns, Kuhnle argues. He shows that the prior development of state agencies with certain capacities to collect and analyze official social statistics was a key variable contributing to the timing and forms of Scandinavian social programs. The point is not only that governmental leaders were themselves influenced by the problem-definitions and data offered by agencies that had collected statistics. They were. Yet Kuhnle also points to other influences. Ties had been established between official statistical agencies and societal actors, including emerging economics professions and politically active groups and social movements.

Official statistical capacities afforded technical supports for certain kinds of legislation and administration, and they also helped to make extra-state actors comfortable with the idea that government should actively address social problems. Thus, as Kuhnle puts it, the prestigious foreign model of German social insurance became available at a juncture when officials and groups in Scandinavian countries were politically and intellectually "prepared" for "state social action," albeit of different particular types in each country. The German model helped to stimulate social policy innovations in Scandinavia, but the contents of those innovations depended on prior governmental capacities and varying social needs and political alliances in each nation.

A concern with international policy modeling mediated by active and partially autonomous governmental officials also figures in Sheldon Garon's essay, comparing the role of official experts in shaping and reshaping the industrial relations of Japan and Great Britain. Despite their many differences—in social structure, political institutions, and the timing of industrialization—Garon points to certain similarities of official involvement in social policy innovations in these two nations. He highlights the roles of the Labour Department of the Board of Trade in Britain, and of the "social bureaucrats" of various Japanese national ministries, particularly the Home Ministry. Officials in both countries were concerned with handling labor unrest and, initially, both sought to incorporate organized labor into public policymaking. But Garon also underlines the different ultimate outcomes: pro-labor social policies were enacted in Britain, and the labor movement was incorporated into a democratizing national polity, but in Japan, social bureaucrats eventually abandoned incorporative efforts, turned toward authoritarian foreign models, and played a central role in the 1930s dissolution of the Japanese labor unions.

To elucidate "how bureaucratic innovation and the application of social knowledge could produce such contrasting results," Garon explores the different kinds of social knowledge—including shifting foreign models in the Japanese case—to which civil servants had access. Even more, he underlines the need to examine the overall contexts within which partially autonomous state interventions emerge and play out, including relations between employers and employees, the political relations of national state authorities to labor and employers, and societal attitudes toward state intervention. These contextual factors differed greatly between Britain and Japan, and over time in Japan. "In the Japan of the 1930s," Garon concludes, "we witness a case of what can happen when relatively autonomous bureaucrats deal with crises by relying on social knowledge that is divorced from actual conditions in civil society."

Sheldon Garon's chapter is an excellent concluding piece for this volume. Because of the cross-cultural and temporal boldness of his comparative analysis, he is able to underline the need to avoid "whiggishness" in historical understandings of the intertwined development of states and social knowledge. From a European historical perspective it may look as if state-building, the growth of modern social knowledge, and socially ameliorative public policymaking all go together. But, as Garon points out, the history of modern Japan highlights the darker possibilities of state controls over the development and mobilization of social knowledge, as well as the danger of hyper-bureaucratic autonomy married to "runaway social knowledge."

In the Conclusion, we offer reflections on generalizations that may be drawn from all of the studies assembled here, considered against the backdrop of previous contributions to the literature on states and social knowledge. As this Introduction has tried to convey, however, each of the chapters to come is compelling in its own terms, and there are many crosscurrents among them. Singly and together, these chapters raise fascinating analytical questions and develop historically rich hypotheses about states, social knowledge and the origins of modern social policies.

Notes To Introduction

1. Robert Wuthnow, *Communities of Discourse*. Cambridge, MA: Harvard University Press, 1989; and Peter A. Hall, ed., *The Political Power of Economic Ideas*. Princeton, NJ: Princeton University Press, 1989. Hall's collection, like this one, was sponsored by the Committee on States and Social Structures, which was originally based at the Social Science Research Council and moved in the early 1990s to become the Working Group on States and Social Structures of the Russell Sage Foundation.

2. Theda Skocpol, *Protecting Soldiers and Mothers: The Political Origins of Social Policy in the United States*. Cambridge, MA: The Belknap Press of Harvard University Press, 1992, chap. 1.

3. See the discussion in Dorothy Ross, "American Social Science and the Idea of Progress." In *The Authority of Experts*. Thomas Haskell, ed. Bloomington, IN: Indiana University Press, 1984, pp. 157–59.

4. Quite plausibly, August Bebel claimed that without the socialists' political presence, Germany's social insurance legislation would not have come about. At the same time, the SPD (German Social Democratic Party) was both hostile to an enterprise designed to undercut its appeal and participated in parliamentary revisions of the legislation. See Gerhard A. Ritter, *Sozialversicherung in Deutschland und England: Entstehung und Grundzuege im Vergleich*. Munich: Beck, 1983, pp. 49–52, esp. p. 50.

5. Philip Abrams, *The Origins of British Sociology*. Chicago, IL: University of Chicago Press, 1968.

Part I

THE EMERGENCE OF MODERN SOCIAL KNOWLEDGE

1

Knowledge about What? Policy Intellectuals and the New Liberalism

IRA KATZNELSON

FROM ROUGHLY the middle of the nineteenth century through the early decades of the twentieth, scholars, in tandem with activists, state officials, and politicians, developed fresh ways to talk about public affairs and the role of the state in Western Europe and North America. They also helped create new institutional forums to initiate, debate, and refine such ideas. As key actors, these intellectuals were not just traditional wise thinkers. They composed a new type whose claims to professionalism and recondite understanding about public policy demarcated them as a group from broadly comparable predecessors. The knowledge they produced—organized in disciplines and based on claims to rationality and science—become a leading feature of public life. Concurrently, public reasoning about complex social problems became a hallmark of both democratic and authoritarian politics and a defining influence on social science scholarship.

To help think about these entwined developments, I propose a reorientation of perspective. Studies that inquire after the instrumental purposes of intellectuals (that is, those that ask the question Robert Lynd made famous, "knowledge for what?") too often take for granted the content of policy-relevant knowledge. A stress on "for what?" at the expense of "about what?" moreover, has characterized the two dominant approaches to social knowledge within the social sciences: the *Marxisant* sociology of knowledge, associated with such seminal thinkers as Karl Mannheim and Alvin Gouldner, which locates producers of ideas either within, or aside, the capitalist stratification system, and the Weberian alternative, which identifies the growth of social knowledge with a hunger for usable information by states with enlarged managerial capacities and ambitions. Whether scholars who work in these traditions deem expertise, ideas, and policy advice to be mere rationalizations of conduct or a primary impetus for action (issues I believe to be situational and contingent),[1] they tend to treat the macroscopic environment and the subject matter of social knowledge in terms of bulky and seemingly self-evident categories like the industrial revolution, modernization, and capitalist development. These background assumptions are unfortunate. The purposes of social knowledge necessarily remain underspecified in the absence of a finely targeted identification of the substantive objects of social knowledge.

With these considerations in mind, I should like to inquire after the central elements of the macroscopic context which both summoned and shaped the emergence of the new social knowledge. What, precisely, was this body of thought about? Which aspects of large-scale processes did its producers and practitioners concern themselves with? In pursuit of these puzzles, I treat policy intellectuals in terms of their relationship to the ties that bind states, markets, and citizens in capitalist and democratic societies. In so doing, I claim the period's social knowledge can best be understood as a constitutive aspect of revisions to liberalism's doctrines, institutions, and policies. These innovations sought to make liberalism capable of apprehending and managing the social and political tensions inherent in societies premised simultaneously on commodification and mass political participation. This "New Liberalism" (labeled as such in late Victorian Britain), including its American Progressive variant, grappled with the analytical and political space between pre-modern conservatism and Spencerian laissez-faire, on the one side, and the wholesale rejection of liberal markets and citizenship, on the other. We know, of course, that since the Second World War it has been just this political zone that has come to define the location and legitimate limits of public policy in the European and North American democracies. Conservatives and socialists alike have been co-opted into a politics based on liberal institutional foundations.

I address these subjects by looking primarily at nineteenth- and twentieth-century Britain (principally England). In so doing, I run the risk of distortion. Certainly the ties between social knowledge and state institutions were less developed there than in Germany or France. The British knowledge community was more humdrum and pragmatic in cast than, say, the Austrian, where a militantly conservative strand within neoclassical economics confronted a creative Marxism. By contrast, it also was more expansively ideological than the American. There, after a flirtation with socialism by leading figures of the academic generation of the 1870s and 1880s (including Richard Ely, Henry Carter Adams, and John Bates Clark, who played a leadership role in the founding of the American Economics Association), this tendency petered out and what became the Progressive impulse remained contained within the new social liberalism. Quite unlike Britain, socialism in America was left "without a respectable intellectual base."[2]

The British case also is distinctive in what it meant to speak of the state as compared to countries on the continent and in North America, and in such features of its state as parliamentarism and the utilization of expertise lodged in civil society (especially in the ancient universities of Oxford and Cambridge). Nonetheless, the British example exhibits some of the principal tendencies that have characterized the relationship joining knowledge and policy in settings where politics has been concerned more with defining the character of liberalism than with securing its presence. For all its specificities, the development of social knowledge in Britain proved exemplary of the architectonic role taken by policy intellectuals in the marking of the "new liberal" welfare state and of the substantive objects of their work. During the period assayed in this book, Britain and other broadly liberal settings confronted immensely significant practical and normative choices concerned with how the state should transact with markets and citizens. For more than four generations, these concerns have defined the main axis of democratic political conflict in the West, and so they remain at the center of the public sphere.

Property and Sovereignty

Neither of the great macrostructures of modernity, those of national states and capitalism, was new to the nineteenth century. They were grounded in the postfeudal separation of property from sovereignty. Even before the age of constitutionalism, states in early modern Europe that centralized sovereignty and shattered the power of autonomous authorities (who, under feudalism, had controlled property rights as well as political authority simultaneously at a local level) constructed new relationships with the governed. These ties were not just instrumental and strategic. They nestled within conceptions of the public interest and the general welfare. These embraced not only specific roles and obligations, "but also the residue of the traditional ethical mission which perforated the limits of state activity and called for loyalty transcending the appeal of interests."[3] Thus, the national states that were shaped between the thirteenth and sixteenth centuries had both an instrumental and a moral dimension. Each possessed: sovereignty, based on law, and with it legitimate force within a distinctive territory; an ensemble of institutions; and a vision and articulation of the common good. With these attributes, the state emerged as a calculating actor vis-à-vis other states, the newly separated economic sphere, and a newly distinguishable civil society.[4]

Modern capitalism, like the modern state, also was the product of the postfeudal division of property and power. In his 1914 article on stages in the history of capitalism, Henri Pirenne drew our attention to the towns of medieval Europe, especially the Italian city republics of Venice, Florence, and Genoa, to argue that "capitalism is much older than we have ordinarily thought it."[5] Such may be the case, but the key break point in the development of capitalism as the dominant framework for economic development in the West came only with the concentration of sovereignty, the liberation of the political order from direct control of production relations, and the establishment of an authoritative framework for property rights and economic transactions on a large scale. Capitalism prospered and urbanization (as well as rural proto-industrialization) accelerated once capitalist development began to move in tandem with the new national states that centralized sovereignty. As Douglass North and Barry Weingast have argued in the case of England, this political envelopment of capitalism as a consequence of the dissociation of property and political power helped secure property rights and their less arbitrary enforcement. The result was a more entrenched capitalism, blessed by a reduction in the burdens of specifying and enforcing contracts and in realizing the gains from these exchanges. These reductions in transaction costs proved a prod to dramatic gains in investment and productivity, and with these advances the various national states enhanced their capacities to raise revenues for their own purposes through tax collections.[6]

What was fundamentally new about the postfeudal relation of polity and economy was the emergence of a state that was not merely extortionist, but which shared an interest in creating the conditions required to organize independent market transactions. Whereas early medieval face-to-face exchanges had taken place in towns whose existence depended on grants of autonomy from local lords, thus creating insecurities outside this tight embrace, by the sixteenth century, kings, in exchange for revenue, protected towns and traveling merchants on a much larger scale. Within the framework of law and enforcement mechanisms that developed in some of these states, "sophisticated forms of organization, efficient capital markets and trading systems evolved with the encouragement and support of the State."[7]

With states providing a framework for capitalist development and not acting merely as rent-seekers, as in the public choice vision, the linkage between the economy and the polity was utterly transformed into a new kind of strategic game. States will not ensure just any structures of property rights, but only those consistent with state interests; capital will not give obeisance to any state, but only to those that secure its economic activities. The terms of this relationship thus became the first of two fundamental pivots of modern domestic politics in the West.[8]

The second was the hinge between the state and civil society. Separated from property, and concentrated in authority, the states of postfeudal Europe had to forge new, and uncertain, ties to civil society. If the hallmark of the possession and the centralization of sovereignty is "the final assertion of authority within a territory,"[9] one of the problematical correlates is a set of contestable questions both about the range of activities over which the state will have such authority—that is, the extent of its *hubris* in penetrating and regulating civil society—and about the ways in which members of civil society will be able to affect the activities of the state. From one vantage point, this pivotal issue of modern politics appears as that of the autonomy of the state: the extent to which it will be capable of imposing its will by ignoring other actors, but this is an entirely misleading perspective. With the breakup of the tightly knit juridical, economic, and social units characteristic of feudalism, states could not simply impose their will by despotic imposition. Instead, it was a condition of their effectiveness that they transact with society and coordinate aims with other "private" power holders, to develop what Michael Mann has called infrastructural capacity. Building on this insight, John Hall and John Ikenberry note that it was the curbing of despotism, and the emergence of a politics based on a widening sphere of consent that made the growth of infrastructural state capacity possible. Taking the example of eighteenth century England, they observe that "the presence of the state was accepted because it was recognized that the state could be trusted, not least because its actions were subject to control. The state had the capacity, in other words, because it represented society." State-society relations become reciprocal; over time, the very ability of the state to utilize its authority to intervene in society "may eventually lead to commitments and obligations that bind the state in subsequent periods of decision."[10]

Both of the pivots of post–sixteenth-century domestic politics—transactions between states and economies and between states and societies—thus were marked by a reduction in arbitrariness. The terms of these exchanges became the objects of political struggle and the subjects of expert consideration by political theorists and by political economists. Hobbes, Locke, Montesquieu, Rousseau, Millar, Steuart, the Physiocrats, and Adam Smith, amongst a cast of many, mostly lesser, others, theorized these relationships and sought to find rules of interested engagement between the relevant parties.[11] At stake was both the scope of responsibility of states for economic and moral situations and the ways in which the actions of states could be shaped by people, interests, and values outside the state itself.

To speak of transactions between the state and the economy and the state and society is not, of course, to imply equal exchange or a stable set of abilities. It is to suggest bargaining relationships in which all the actors possess resources the others require. At critical moments, the rule-governed and institutional *terms* of these transactions become the subjects of the most fundamental kind of political struggle.[12]

Liberal Markets and Citizenship

The period with which this book is concerned was just such a formative moment. Coming at the junction of the decline of mercantilism and the ascent of a new kind of interventionist state, state-economy and state-society transactions experienced a fundamental restructuring.

Mercantilism had produced a powerful recipe for state-building and for rules to govern the transactions between the state and the economy and between the state and civil society. Its main aspects included "regulation of the economically strong, support and direction for the economically weak, and the state's own enterprise where private initiative is wanting."[13] As Perry Anderson, among others, has stressed, at its early moments mercantilism was put to use for the conservative purposes of buttressing a social order in crisis; later, under the initiatives of Charles Colbert, mercantilism went hand in hand with the protection of property rights and the reduction of transaction costs to provide a dynamic basis for capitalist economic development. Both facets were integral to the process of state-building from the fifteenth to eighteenth centuries in which

> regional rulers utilized provisions for welfare as well as force to extend their control over all the inhabitants of their realm. Indeed, it was precisely the need for such a politics of welfare over a larger area when the old local welfare arrangements were being broken down that went far to establish the ruler as the head of the state.[14]

During the first half of the nineteenth century, the mercantilist formulas for state-economy and state-society transactions could not withstand "The Great Transformation." Karl Polanyi has stressed the ways in which independent labor markets with more than local and regional scope came to be a pivotal institution of industrial capitalism. With the introduction of market mechanisms to allocate people to jobs and set wage levels, capitalism entered a new, liberal, phase. Now, as labor markets joined markets in capital and land, the conventions and moral impulses of economic markets became so powerful as the governing rationales of capitalist societies that they no longer seemed to be objects of human action.[15] Yet, Polanyi stressed, at the very moment when markets prevailed over mercantile regulation, they "implied a start utopia" because they "could not exist for any length of time without annihilating the human and natural substance of society; it would have physically destroyed man and transformed his surroundings into a wilderness." For just this reason, it was inevitable that "society took measures to protect itself" by invoking the state both to organize the new markets and to mitigate their distributional effects. This linking of state and market quickly proved disorienting: "Whatever measures [the state] took impaired the self-regulation of the market, disorganized industrial life, and thus endangered society in yet another way. It was this dilemma which forced the development of the new market system into a definite groove and finally disrupted the social organization based on it,"[16] and it was this nexus of developments that oriented and challenged the new practitioners of social knowledge.

It was not capitalist industrialization or social unrest as such that commanded their attention, but a specific tension between two of the outstanding features of the period. On the one side, early industrial capitalism was marked by the emergence of independent labor markets (later supplemented by independent housing markets) lacking in the ameliorative traditions of Tory paternalism and the softening traditions of mutual responsibility or clientalism and by the concomitant development of a new social geography of work and home dictated by market forces. These features of proletarianization provided a crucible for new working-class identities, dispositions, and patterns of collective action.[17] On the other side, largely as a consequence of the working out of the implications of the American and French revolutions, the period was marked by the development of compelling conceptions of popular representation and citizenship. From the moment of these democratic revolutions, all members of civil society became actual or potential citizens. No longer could citizenship be restricted to those who, by holding property, demonstrated a stake in the existing commonwealth. Instead, the possibility of political (and military) participation was universalized, in the expectation that in a community of citizens people would act rationally in pursuit of individual, group, and common interests. Citizenship—perhaps more so at this time than at any moment since—possessed a radical, emancipatory edge.[18]

The consequence of the broadly simultaneous development of market rationality and market institutions for labor and a new ethic and practice of citizenship was this: precisely the same people who were workers and/or paupers in the new market regime also in fact either were citizens or potential citizens. It was in this novel circumstance that the "social problem" emerged. This emblematic term condensed the new tensions of markets and citizenship, and it put at the core of public life the question of whether, and to what extent, the political relations of citizens might modify the operation of markets, as well as the extent to which the rationale of the marketplace would dictate limits to citizenship. Prerevolutionary approaches to citizenship (whether Roman, Medieval, or Enlightenment) had not ignored the connection between citizenship and minimum levels of security, but they had dealt with it by excluding those without economic means from the community of citizens. No longer was this solution possible, at least not in more than the short run. As a result, as citizenship became more inclusive, states had no choice but to extend the scope of their policies aimed at organizing markets and mitigating their distributional inequities.

This moment of passage from the mercantile state to a state seeking to manage a liberal capitalist order with citizenship rights often is described as an age of laissez-faire. This depiction is misleading. In empirical terms, laissez-faire never actually existed, much because of the inherent impossibility of sustaining a market system entirely on its own terms in an age of citizenship. Even though it certainly is correct to see the early nineteenth century in the archetypical case of England as the moment of the achievement of a free labor market and the erosion of mercantile practices with the scaling down of tariffs and the freeing up of food trades, even at this heyday point when the state moved to deregulate commerce, laissez-faire was compromised by the remaining statutes of the mercantile era and by the beginning of the regulation of industry, initiated by the Factory Act of 1833 and extended by a host of legislative initiatives. "Throughout this period," Colin Holmes notes, "the trend was towards more rather than less central government intervention in economic and social matters."[19] In terms of political theory, moreover, laissez-faire never achieved more than a partial influence. Even in the hands of Adam Smith, the state was given a considerable role in the organization of capitalist markets, and there is clear evidence that laissez-faire as a doctrine seeking to leave self-seeking individuals and firms alone to pursue their interests was only one of many influences on policymaking.

If not an age of laissez-faire, the middle of the nineteenth century was a moment when the conjoining of large-scale economic and political developments led to the search for mutual and tolerable limits between the state and the post-mercantile economy, on the one side, and the state and civil society, on the other. This pursuit, by numerous actors both within and outside the state, was characterized by new sets of substantive and strategic transactions between the states of Europe and North America and their market economies and civil societies (now constituted not only by estates and groups but by individuals with rights). In forging these relationships, the organization of states and their institutions changed, as did forms and mechanisms of representation and the substance of economic and social policy. At the phenomenal level, the new relationships between these altered states and key others appeared as exchanges between the state and the marketplace and between the state and its citizenry, reflecting new circuits of interaction between three newly constituted sets of actors that had come into being.

We have seen how in the seventeenth and eighteenth centuries the post-feudal division between property and sovereignty had convened new forms of thinking about how to orient and guide a modern civilization divided into components of economy, polity, and civil society. In the nineteenth century, the transformations that produced an economy of markets and a polity of citizens and the struggles of groups and movements such as the Chartists, who responded to these changes and opportunities, provoked sharp alterations to the questions, methods, and organization of social knowledge. Subject matter, style, and institutions refocused and were remade. A modernist policy intelligentsia, nourished by Enlightenment conceptions of reason, considered citizenship, markets, and their intertwining with the confidence that they could find scientific solutions to ethical problems. Their methods specialized, and the professionals overtook the amateurs.

How did this happen? What were the characteristic features of this process? The restructuring of the patterns and rules of transaction linking states and markets within capitalist economies as well as those connecting states and citizens in civil society constituted the provinces of the new social knowledge. Rather than speak, as we commonly do, of these emergent ideas addressing problems of industrialization, modernization, or capitalism, a focus on these strategic domains of transaction invites more exact considerations of the loci of the problems, and the problems themselves, addressed by producers of knowledge: how should the state underwrite and confirm property rights, organize markets, and mitigate their distributional consequences; how should political and interest representation be organized and the relevant actors come to be defined? By focusing on the transactions between state and market and state and citizen, we can better understand how it was that these particular problem-sets helped stimulate the reorganization of institutions and ideas, and why it was that a distinctive repertoire of options became available to scholars and policy intellectuals as they crafted solutions to the problems they perceived under these new conditions.

Thinking about policy-relevant knowledge this way restores a place for intentionality without giving up considerations of enabling and pressuring structural conditions. It also helps us treat policy thinkers as actors concerned *about* specific realms of transaction and their constituent tensions within two sets of limits: those defined by the material situation on the ground and those imposed by the finited range of ideas and visions which possess an affinity for the challenges posed by the liberal duality of markets and citizenship.

In situations characterized by the crystallization of these new institutions, practitioners of social knowledge, perforce, had two very broad options: to accept or to repudiate these foundations of liberal social formations. Throughout the nineteenth and early twentieth centuries, deep reactionary currents of refusal and restoration, radical renunciations of the new moral economy, and forward-looking blueprints, the most important of which was a powerful Marxist critique and teleology, assertively rejected the new institutional and normative framework of liberalism. By contrast, the great majority of social analysts accommodated with varying degrees of enthusiasm to the new order and to its immanent power relations, and sought to solve problems within the boundaries of the liberal premise. Thus, the new social knowledge was inherently and inescapably liberal.

Within this framework, there existed a wide array of alternative conceptualizations, ways of organizing knowledge, and contestations about policies, from right to left (at both poles straddling the liberal/non-liberal divide); but these debates, no matter how hotly contested, remained circumscribed within a distinctive family of possibilities and they focused on a shared subject matter: the field of tension created by the simultaneous development of transactions between states and markets, especially as they concerned labor, and between states and citizens. The harsh realities of unequal and exploitative relations between economic actors helped create contentious class representations that intersected the radical impetus of citizenship to produce incendiary political possibilities, making both the modern state and modern capitalism precarious.

In these circumstances where inequalities of power and plenty undermined the naturalized status of the state and capitalism, the producers of social knowledge—as individual scholars and theorists, and in organized settings, such as universities, learned societies, political parties, organizations devoted to policy goals, and governmental bureaucracies—struggled with how to interpret and manage the new transactions linking state and market and state and citizen with very mixed and often confused motives: to preserve the social order and to reform it, and frequently both. These questions of "for what?" cannot be answered in ways that definitively resolve whether knowledge-holders were independent or subservient to dominant interests; at a self-conscious level, policy intellectuals have ranged from those positioned at the pole of radical criticism to those who wished to serve privilege without making independent assessments. What joined them together across this variety of structural and normative positions was their shared "about what" subject matter; this commonality defined the principal distinguishing characteristics of the new social knowledge that began to be elaborated in the middle decades of the nineteenth century.

Overall, this process of a shared agenda leading to an elaboration of policy-relevant social knowledge is best understood as a key element in the making of a revised liberalism, at home with the period's new separations and transactions yet deeply apprehensive about the stresses inherent in their development. Sometimes cast in a language of socialist transformation, sometimes in a conservative discourse, and sometimes in a vocabulary of individual rights, the center of gravity of the new social knowledge was located in the New Liberal attempt to find reference points and tools of administration for social policy which could integrate conceptions of individual and collective goods. The policy intellectuals who undertook this quest were not utopians. They saw no way to go back to a moment before citizenship and (labor) markets (indeed, in Britain, neither progressives nor conservatives in the late nineteenth century sought to return to the pre-1834 epoch, when social policy and economics were treated autonomously[20]), and no way forward to a post-liberal era within the ambit of normal politics. "New Liberal" social knowledge sought to secure a role for the state within this region of the possible, as Giovanna Procacci has put it, by finding a way to administer the "social problem." It did this both by freeing itself from non-interventionist liberal dogma that precluded a role for the state in organizing markets and in mitigating their distributional outcomes and by interpreting the tensions inherent in the relationship between liberalism and democracy. As a consequence, liberalism thickened, as it integrated the citizenship values of fairness and fraternity within its social philosophy and political economy.[21]

The rise of a social policy and social science intelligentsia concerned on an increasingly specialized basis with the new transactions of the nineteenth century has been distinguished from literary responses to the same social condition by Wolf Lepines. Both sets of intellectuals sought to make sense of experience, the one in a more hermeneutical mode, the other tilting toward models based on science and engineering. Reason contended with feeling; progress with the counter-Enlightenment. In France, the new sociology closely articulated with the Third Republic. The optimistic anti-clerical and republican program of the pupils of Comte and then of Durkheim sought to contend with the field of tension established by markets and citizenship while guarding against the predations of those who wished the Republic ill. In Britain, even those like the Webbs who sought to transform the country by replacing the institutions of capitalism stayed within the framework of objective scrutiny of existing patterns of transaction. There, New Liberalism conquered the field, displacing and reshaping virtually all its competitors; so too in the United States, within the framework of Progressivism. In Germany, the new social knowledge also partook of this character, but like so much else eventually suffered the fate of the country's precarious liberalism. Not surprisingly, in light of this fragility, German social science developed especially skittish and self-reflexive qualities.[22]

The broadly common development of a quest for knowledge about state-market and state-citizen relations in the major countries of the West proved both a discursive and an institutional matter. Scholars and intellectuals began to talk and write in innovative ways within increasingly intensive networks organized by new institutions. By late century, the people, the ideas, and the organizations of the knowledge community had begun to take on an enabling role in the policy process. Even in their more critical and collectivist aspects, such as Fabianism in Britain or institutionalist labor economics in the United States, knowledge professionals became policy intellectuals; in this sense, insiders. Although the twentieth-century welfare state hardly can be said to have been "caused" by these policy intellectuals, it owes its architecture to their assumptions, deliberations, and influence.

"New Liberal" Social Science and Policy Analysis

The place of pride in social analysis in the *ancien régime* had belonged to the moral sciences. Classical political economy had been elaborated within its embrace. Over the course of the nineteenth century, into the twentieth, this integrated social knowledge was replaced by professionalized, discipline-based attempts to grapple with the specific tensions inherent in the elaboration of markets and citizenship in liberal societies. At stake was the character of the extended responsibilities and jurisdiction of the state with respect both to markets and citizens. From the vantage point of the transactions between the states and markets, the central issue was how to shape the state's interventions to make markets function effectively and to make their distributional effects tolerable. From the perspective of transactions between states and citizens, at issue was the balance between freedom and domination. Together, these questions elaborated the themes of moral philosophy under radically revised conditions.[23]

This transformation in subject matter, style of work, and institutional organization was no simple linear development. At the risk of being far too schematic, we can distinguish two overlapping moments, each characterized by an important partition. In the first, spanning the 1860s through the second decade of the twentieth century, the knowledge community divided into specialists concerned with one or the other of the transactions of state-market and state-citizen. Integrated knowledge separated into distinctive zones for the study of economics, politics, and society, ultimately devolving into wholly separate professional disciplines, each with distinctive intellectual tendencies.[24] The founders of sociology in the last third of the nineteenth century and the beginning of the twentieth, a period of intense professionalization and crystallization of disciplines, considered market mechanisms inadequate to secure the social order, and in this way distinguished themselves from the economists, who, in turn, were coming, with the neoclassical marginalist revolution, to derive the main justification for markets from general equilibrium theory. Political science, too, found a distinctive voice, concerned mainly with constitutional matters of citizenship and the representation of interests. The second moment, from the 1890s through the 1920s, was characterized by a trend complementary to these new disciplinary divisions: a split between academic practitioners of the social sciences, located mainly in burgeoning institutions of higher education, whose policy concerns and impact were indirect, and scholars whose emphasis was placed far more directly on policy matters and public influence.

We can see this double process of division at work in the tugs and pulls of the development of an autonomous zone for the study of politics in nineteenth-century Britain; the type of social knowledge Stefan Collini and his collaborators designate as "that noble Science of Politics"—the complex way station between an eighteenth-century style that embedded politics within moral philosophy and the qualities of twentieth-century political science and policy studies. They show that at this moment of transition, the study of "things political," though still anchored in the moral sciences, began an attempt to be "objective, explanatory and useful." The dominion of this type of political studies already was more restricted than that of its predecessors in political philosophy, but it was much broader than the successor discipline of political science. During the middle decades of the nineteenth century, the study of politics continued to embrace "much of the territory now assigned to the semi-autonomous dominions of economics and sociology."[25] By looking at this distinctive moment for political studies, we can capture important aspects of how social analysts sought to make sense of the radically new situation on the ground at a time when there was yet little independent existence to social science disciplines and when university-based political science, economics, and sociology had yet to make an appearance in recognizably modern form.

Considering figures as diverse as Stewart, Malthus, Ricardo, the Philosophic Whigs, John Stuart Mill, and Bagehot, Collini and his colleagues find as common threads their attempts to maintain holistic portrayals of modern society while treating the specificity of the new transactions between its distinctive domains, and to do so by making the role of the state, in form and in policy, the centerpiece of their analyses. These pivotal thinkers were neither traditional political philosophers who deduced the character of the good society from first principles or moral ends, nor empirical social scientists who sought to comprehend the regularities governing the new transactions. Rather, based on an understanding of the centrality of the state to the new relations of market and citizenship, they refused to reduce the political to the social and economic. But neither were they comfortable with a separation between these domains. Instead, they focused on the ties that bound them to each other.

With politics at the center of their inquiries, the role of the state vis-à-vis markets and citizens was placed at the heart of their search for a "science of legislation." Political economy was not a separate part of this effort, but integral to it because the organization of markets appeared as one of the central political problems of the age. The meshing between political economy and theoretical and practical work on the role of the state—a joining for which John Stuart Mill may be considered the archetypical figure—had been presaged by the role Adam Smith saw for political economy as "a branch of science of the statesman or legislator," and had been concretized by such acts as the application by Ricardo to Mill's father, James Mill, for guidance about the "science of legislation."[26]

Though closely related, classical political economy that searched for capitalism's "laws of motion" and this new science of politics that sought to manage the tensions inherent in the new transactions between state, market, and citizen, became distinctive crafts. Writing as early as 1825, J. R. McCullough made this argument in his *Principles of Political Economy* by distinguishing broadly common economic imperatives across national boundaries from the political variations which distinguish one country from another:

> The science of Political Economy was long confounded with that of Politics; and that it is frequently impossible to treat those questions which strictly belong to the one without referring more or less to the principles and conclusions of the other. But, in their leading features, they are sufficiently distinct. The laws which regulate the production and distribution of wealth are the same in every country and stage of society.[27]

What is striking in this passage is McCulloch's belief that what varies in political affairs is not capitalism as such, understood at a rather high level of abstraction, but the rules governing its relations with the state and society.

When John Stuart Mill deductively worked out the consequences of people acting from the single imputed rational motive of a desire for the enhancement of wealth, he deliberately abstracted from the multiplicity of human motivations. As a result, his *Political Economy* was a very spare work that reads as a transitional period piece in its exclusion of specific policy recommendations and in its insistence that "the explanation of any actual sequence of events will always involved the findings of a combination of sciences."[28] Mill's project thus joined the ambition of discovering a coherent political economy to an acknowledgement of its limited practical significance:

> I confess that I regard the purely abstract speculations of political economy (beyond those elementary ones which are necessary for the correction of mischievous prejudices) as of very minor importance compared with the great prac-

> tical questions which the progress of democracy and the spread of Socialist opinions are pressing on, and for which both the governing and the governed classes are very far from being in a fit state of mental preparation. . . . There is therefore abundance of occupation for moral and political teachers such as we aspire to be.[29]

For Mill, the most important theorist of nineteenth-century liberalism, the reason to focus on political economy was to better be able to guide a "science" of politics and legislation with regard to the organization and regulation of the economy. Equally, but separately, he also focused on the new transactions linking the state and its citizens, not only in his famous considerations of liberty and representative government but in other works, such as the *Logic of the Moral Sciences,* where he mingles the vocabulary of citizens and states with that of individuals and societies.

Mill's discrete focus on each of the two new transaction sets found important resonance in his country's first significant social science institution, the Social Science Association, founded in 1857. Created to consider the problems of social economics and to promote legislative reforms in the House of Commons with regard to education, law, penal policy, public health, and the regulation of markets, the Association self-consciously viewed itself as a conduit between politicians and an expanding citizenry with political rights, and it came to play an important interstitial role in the Victorian state by proposing ways to manage the "social problem" attendant upon the simultaneous existence of labor markets and an expanded citizenry. The Association flourished as an intellectual and political center for three decades. Officially, it was nonpartisan, but there is no doubt it was a quintessentially liberal institution. The Association was guided by the conviction that the central matters of political life were constituted by the liberal institutions of markets and citizenship, and led by key members of the Liberal Party. In July 1868, just a few months before he became prime minister, Gladstone presided over an Association meeting on wage rates, labor relations, and labor markets that led to the formation of an Association Committee on Labour and Capital, which engaged in the mediation of labor disputes for a five-year period.

Like Germany's Verein für Sozialpolitik, the Association fused reform and social science in its attempt to provide expert knowledge on behalf of a project its members conceived of as an endeavor of social integration. Working before the development of separate social science disciplines and before the creation of an autonomous and politically ambitious labor movement, the Association succeeded in joining under liberal auspices a wide array of intellectuals as well as Liberal Members of Parliament, trade union and cooperative movement leaders, and other reformers in a quest to bring expertise to bear on the project of creating a new liberalism capable of surmounting the now manifest inadequacies of traditional political economy.[30]

As late as 1870, near the close of this transitional period, political science yet could be defined by John Seely as "political economy and history together." In the next fifty years, political science secured a disciplinary status divorced in large measure from both. It came to focus in a specialized way on constitutionalism, law, political parties, interest groups, voting, and other mechanisms of representation—that is, on the rules of state-citizen transactions. During the same period, political economics shed its adjective and its claim to be an aspect, in its science, of moral philosophy. Recast as a scholarly craft in the mathematical language of post-Jevons marginalism, it was not so much that economics no longer wished to concern itself with larger questions of human nature and social organization. Rather, the economists of the period sought to elaborate a science of markets on the basis of an elegant simplification about just these issues, but not for the sake of science alone. This new economics, for whom the key figure certainly was Alfred Marshall, was created in the service of the ethical goals of the period's New Liberalism. Under his remarkable influence, deductive work within economics replaced historical scholarship. This narrowing of focus was accompanied by a widening of theoretical ambition to create an economics as a timeless and institutionless body of knowledge. Only in the peripheralized field of economic history did time and place persist as legitimate foci of inquiry.[31] Yet, as Reba Soffer has stressed, at no time did Marshall lose sight of social obligation grounded in the progressive and rational liberal impulse. Introducing a distinction between explanation and improvement, he sought to found a science capable of pragmatically informing public life.[32]

Indeed, Marshall was an exceptionally important figure at two junction points: between classical political economy and disciplinary social science; and between the latter and the world of public policy. His *Principles of Economics,* published in 1890, explicitly sought to place pioneering analytical techniques at the service of human improvement. While Marshall's economics was neoclassical in the sense that all its aspects concerned the fluctuating equilibrium of supply and demand, this equilibrium depended for him on the subjective decisions of producers and consumers in pursuit of qualitative time-bound goals in pursuit of a better life. Thus, although he was at odds with radical liberals and socialists like J. A. Hobson and R. H. Tawney, who lacked a grounding in solid economics, Marshall tried to establish an empirically sound economics in the service of social concerns both through his activities (such as the Economics Club he founded in 1899 that brought together economists, businessmen, and proto-Fabians, and was a precursor of the Fabian Society) and especially through his work, which sought to make economics a science of welfare. "He did this," Soffer writes, "by developing flexible tools of economic analysis that served the rational and moral progress of human nature in society, and by setting the professional standards of social responsibility that would later characterize the economics of A. C. Pigou, John Maynard Keynes, and Joan Robinson." Although Marshall became more aloof from policy concerns in his later years, this, in her judgment, "does not vitiate the genuinely liberal impulse that made him the remarkable founder of an economics with social welfare and self-respect as its ends."[33]

Marshall, in fact, proved to be a transitional figure in at least one important sense he neither sought nor anticipated. Once his new mathematical tools became central to economics, the discipline developed in ways that elaborated technique at the expense of his value-laden preferences. The new Marshallian economics deepened its scientific capacities at the expense of its practical effects on policy issues of the day and on its ability to analyze, or even take an interest in, the rules of transaction governing the relations of state and market in particular historical settings. The increasing ambitions of marginalist economics in its own sphere, and its self-confident divorce from the traditional moorings of political economy in moral philosophy, historical studies, and political theory, soon had the somewhat paradoxical effect of distancing economics as a "science" from the problems in society its founders sought to understand and effect. Just at the moment when, in the late nineteenth and early twentieth centuries, the social tensions of markets and citizenship intensified under the impact of economic depressions, the radical transformations in industrial size and class structure entailed in the second industrial revolution, international rivalries for markets, a new geopolitics characterized by imperial ventures and, ultimately, by total war, the academic discipline of economics lost a good deal of its capacity to function as a practical policy science. In part this was a matter of a distancing from practical affairs, in part a flight to abstraction, in part a deliberate decision in favor of the ambitions of science at the expense of the ambitions of moral discourse.

Throughout most of the nineteenth century, the language of political economy had shaped debate about the role of the state (alongside both history and law, which also commanded a great deal of prestige). By the end of the century, classical political economy virtually had disappeared, and the gentlemen generalist historians and lawyers had become archaic figures. These "all-rounders" were steadily replaced, on the one side, by academic scholars in specialized social sciences and, on the other side, by a growing body of policy specialists who claimed knowledge that both drew upon and crossed over the boundaries that divided the social sciences. Labor experts, social workers, organizers of social surveys, public administration specialists, reformers concerned with social policy, and intellectuals within social movements and political parties—both inside and outside the administrative apparatuses of states—tried to come to grips with the intensification of the "social problem" inherent in interactions between states, citizens, and markets. These policy intellectuals were a novel and distinctive breed. Their main orientation was not to the social science disciplines as such; nor were they amateur seekers after a science of legislation in the manner of their mid-nineteenth century predecessors. Generalists continued to lead the civil service and go for careers in politics and journalism; but increasingly, the choices they had to make were defined for them by the specialist policy intellectuals.

In spite of its abstraction and distancing from practical affairs, economics—and economists—were not left without influence. To the contrary, the new scientific economics achieved something of an encompassing contextual role with regard to the development in this epoch of a new kind of policy-relevant social knowledge that coexisted with, and drew upon, university-based social science disciplines.[34] Economics set limits to common sense, by putting on a "scientific" basis the assumption that market outcomes are likely to be the most optimal, at least in the sense of the most efficient.[35] This presumption in favor of competitive markets derived its legitimacy from general equilibrium theory; its effect on policy was to shift responsibility for disproof to disbelievers, a turn that continues to prevail to the present day. The new social knowledge—even when produced by socialists—had to take care not to disturb market mechanisms more than necessary for specified, targeted, justifiable social purposes. The supercession of the market required the onus of demonstration, one that could be achieved only in dire economic circumstances and during wartime, and with a staying power that did not easily outlast the instigating emergency.

But if economics emerged secure in this role, policy analysis (unlike the policy studies of today grounded primarily in microeconomics) principally adopted the language of public administration and social engineering.[36] This language, nestled within the assumptions of Marshallian economics, facilitated a self-image for policy intellectuals much like that of the earlier liberals of the Social Science Association, which stressed the role of social knowledge in helping to transcend class conflict within a framework that accepted, at least implicitly, the divisions between state, economy, and civil society. The central concern of these policy intellectuals was how to build a state capable of dealing with the challenges of increasingly assertive working classes both as economic actors and as poorly integrated citizens. They sought to provide the state with institutional prescriptions, but also with instrumental tools such as labor statistics to contribute to the management of these tensions and demands. The focus of these efforts pivoted on what only later, in the 1940s, came to be called the welfare state—the cluster of policies and institutions concerned both with the mitigation of market distributions and with the substantive content of citizenship.

The May 1945 Hobhouse Memorial Lecture by economic historian H. L. Beales wonderfully captured this central tendency of the knowledge community. It was written at the high point of confident assertion for the New Liberalism. With the tools provided by Keynes and William Beveridge in hand, it now was in a position to guide social and economic policy for the postwar years in spite of the collapse of the Liberal Party as an electoral force of any consequence (the social liberalism of postwar Britain was legislated by the first majority socialist government in the West and codified by successor Conservative governments in the 1950s). Beales's subject was "The Making of Social Policy," which he understood in terms of the establishment of "the conditions of rational co-operation in creative citizenship." Unlike mercantilist interventions by the state with regard to markets and citizens, the new welfare state, he argued, is not "based on a rigid social stratification—it is becoming, or is, classless." Social policy thus has Janus-like facings: it is "a collective term for the public provisions through which we attack insecurity and correct the debilitating tendencies of our 'capitalist' inheritance," and "it has also made the positive declaration of civic minima" to preclude a return "to the primitive simplicities of economic liberalism." In Beales's optimistic reading, the welfare state joined the new social knowledge, solutions to social problems, and a classless professionalism in a successful institutional elaboration of the New Liberalism, and it provided the key instruments for mastering the charged transactions between state and market and state and citizen by its "policy of freedom through organization."[37] Within this matrix of people, organizations, and ideas, the socialist impulse in favor of greater distributive justice could be accommodated without the sacrifice of core liberal principles.

Liberal Knowledge and Social Power

Beales's lecture defined the normative and practical location of the new social knowledge. To one side lay the pre-liberal conservatism of a Bismarck, who had sought to make workers a new estate subservient to and dependent on the state; to the other lay the strong socialist assertion that only the transcendence of markets and the integration of the domains of state, market, and citizen could resolve the contradictions of modern capitalist societies. The new liberal social knowledge decisively rejected these alternatives. Based on what Michael Freeden has called "a mutual buttressing of science and ethics," liberals from T. H. Green to Keynes, and from L. T. Hobhouse and J. A. Hobson to Beveridge, modified the individualist and utilitarian bases of an earlier liberalism to make it speak to the tensions inherent in the new institutions, separations, transactions, and societal contradictions they observed and sought to master. Utilitarianism was made social. Individuals were treated as socially rooted. The welfare of the whole community was substituted for that of its parts. The state, the bête noire of an earlier liberalism, now was seen as the only available instrument for capitalism and mass politics in the service of social utility. ("We have come to recognize, with Aristotle, the moral function of the State," D. G. Ritchie wrote in 1891 in his *Principles of State Interference.*) The new liberalism retained from the old the ideas of rationality, human progress, and a concern with law, representation, and constraints on state power. But it did not endorse the most unfettered ideas about economic freedom. It was not the market it made the centerpiece of attention, but the relationship of the state and the market; and it was not the rights and status of individual citizens on which it focused, but the patterning of interactions between the state and its citizens.[38]

What came to be called New Liberalism developed in a complicated dialogue with socialist currents of politics and thought that produced not so much a convergence but a homology in which the new liberalism came to establish the basic terms of the relationship. In facing the "social question," liberals confronted the same issues of practical reform as socialists. Even though liberals differed from socialists about intellectual premises and long-term goals (there were innumerable public debates at the turn of the century in Britain between individualism and socialism), once liberals adopted the view that people are social beings and once they began to focus on how the state should regulate markets and mitigate market distributions in the name of citizenship values, their proposals for social reform and legislation came to resemble the blueprints of Fabians and Labourites very closely. Indeed, John Stuart Mill's posthumously published *Chapters on Socialism,* which appeared in 1879, had presaged this development in its call for attention to basic issues of distributive justice. Where liberals differed from socialists was in their wager that a social liberalism would prevent the emergence of a collectivist society, while socialists bet on just the reverse.

The socialists, from their side, by deciding to participate in normal democratic politics and to accept, at least for the short run, the liberal institutional premises of markets and citizenship based on a division of property and sovereignty, developed sets of ideas and proposals that differed very little from those of the liberals. Writing in 1910, Sidney Webb acknowledged this correspondence: " . . . much of what is claimed as the progress of socialism," he wrote, "might be equally well described as a merely empirical development from the principles of Charles John Canning, Robert Peel, Jeremy Bentham, and Gladstone."[39] Liberals and socialists borrowed generously from each other, but in a manner of unequal exchange; socialist ideas were made to fit within liberal ground rules, not the other way around. In this process, social democracy became a left-liberalism.

Fascism (and, to a lesser extent, communism) aside, what is striking is just how encompassing the new liberalism has proved to be, and how dominant the policies promoted by practitioners of liberal social knowledge had become by the end of the Second World War.[40] With fascism defeated and communism the new enemy, this expanded liberalism faced no serious competition in the normal politics of the Western democracies. This is not to say that consensus replaced conflict; rather, conflicts about the contours of domestic issues took the form of debates about this or that essentially social liberal alternative even in situations where some of the most important contestants for power presented more radical alternatives for the long haul.[41] From quite far left to quite far right, political competitors accommodated to liberal principles and institutions. Political contests became no less vigorous, but certainly less fundamental: not capitalism versus socialism or democracy versus totalitarianism (though this antinomy defined the discourse of competition between the Soviet and American blocs), but a politics about rules of transaction between spheres within capitalism and democracy. Coherent repertoires of positions about these questions, pivoting on the degree to which the state should be assertive in organizing markets and in utilizing social policy for distributional goals, and on how the institutions of political participation and the representation of interests should be organized distinguished left from right formulas about state-market and state-citizen transactions. Each position was given voice by its own identifiable policy intellectuals, but together they constituted a single, inherently liberal, knowledge community.

The benefits secured for liberal societies by the robust development of social knowledge by this kind of policy intelligentsia ought not to be gainsaid, especially in light of this century's cruel alternatives. But we should also be aware that by conceptualizing their "about what" problems at the level of economic and political market exchanges, most policy intellectuals have left unexamined a host of issues about class and state, inequality and power. By working at the level of transactions between states and markets and states and citizens and by focusing on the welfare state as the target and culmination of their efforts, they tacitly have pushed the macrostructures of capitalism and states into the background of their work. In so doing, they have underscored the great normative achievements of liberalism, but also have become complicit in the silences inherent in the liberal project.

Today, well after the heyday of the New Liberalism and soon after the collapse of anti-liberal communism, it is pressing to think once again about the title question of this chapter. Inescapably, those of us in the West who earn our keep in the social science and policy communities are stamped by the ways our predecessors defined the objects of their attention. We are marked, therefore, not only by their liberal virtues but also by their complacencies.

I have profited from comments by Richard Bensel, Ted Perlmutter, Uri Ram, Dietrich Rueschemeyer, Margaret Weir, and Aristide Zolberg, as well as the members of the Yale University Seminar in American Politics and Institutional Development, and the anonymous reviewers for Princeton University Press.

Notes To Chapter 1

1. I have found a recent paper by Donald Winch to be particularly instructive in thinking about influence and the causal status of social knowledge which would have to be assessed in relationship to such other factors of agency in the history of social and economic policy as class-based pressures and demands, the role of state officials, and the preferences of the clergy and others concerned with ethical and moral stances, to such structural determinants as shifts in the character of markets, the organization of the state, demographic changes, and the impact of modern warfare. In his contribution to the conference, "The State and Economic Knowledge," held at the Smithsonian Institution in September 1988, Winch reflected on the emergence of economic intelligence as a central feature of twentieth-century states, and on how to situate ideas and their production within a larger causal perspective:

> in seeking an alternative to mechanical and mono-causal analyses and conclusions, observers need not limit their scope to opaquely holistic notions of zeitgeist or to pure pragmatism, on the one hand, or circumstantial determinism, on the other. Nor do they need to employ functionalist interpretations of ideology which leave little scope for the free-spirited advocacy of change based on new knowledge of how society actually works or ought to work. Ideas do not have to be treated instrumentally. Ideas, theories, and professed principles are the only way people can confer meaning on action; they can be fruitfully yet straightforwardly treated as the reasons that make best sense of our actions and recommendations for action by others. In societies that regularly require reasons to be given for public actions; in societies that have inherited a rich vocabulary of principles that can be invoked when discussing public affairs; in societies that possess elaborate forums and procedures for examining the adequacy of the reasons supplied by public actors, the history of ideas in relation to practice requires no special commitment or prior act of faith. It becomes no more (or less) than an extension of the rules of everyday conduct to the study of past beliefs, actions and debates. Differences of opinion between historians are not, therefore, about whether ideas have played a large or negligible role in history, but about what kinds of ideas—elaborate, conventional, explicit or otherwise—have to be invoked to make sense of which past actions.

Donald Winch, "Economic Knowledge and Government in Britain: Some Historical and Comparative Reflections." In Mary O. Furner and Barry Supple, eds., *The State and Economic Knowledge: The American and British Experiences*. Cambridge: Cambridge University Press, 1990.

2. Dorothy Ross, "Socialism and American Liberalism: Academic Social Thought in the 1880's." *Perspectives in American History* XI (1977–1978), p. 79. For a fuller discussion, see her *The Origins of American Social Science*. Cambridge: Cambridge University Press, 1991. Ross argues it is a mistake to see this outcome as having been preordained. Various religious and classical crosscurrents in American political culture provided potential crossovers to socialism and bridges between socialism and

liberalism. During the moment of the late nineteenth century when a generation of scholars in American universities transformed liberal thought from classic laissez-faire to the new social liberalism of Progressivism, socialism appeared as a possible alternative. The divide between socialism and liberalism, we will see, is not always easy to discern; nevertheless, it is clear that Americans, far more than their British counterparts, emerged virtually exclusively on the liberal side of the line. Why so? Ross argues mainly in terms of the instrumental incentives and disincentives provided for the intellectuals, particularly the power of the business classes to deny employment to left-wingers within American universities. While I would not want to put aside these micro-pressures as not relevant, if I were to pursue an explanation, it likely would be along other institutionalist lines that would focus, as Schweber does in this volume, on why amateur social science outside universities was relatively more successful in Britain than the United States. In Britain, knowledge professionals in institutions like the Social Science Association and the Fabian Society developed close affiliations with programmatic political parties. By contrast, the failure of analogous American figures to be influential in the same way helped promote the more academic, university-oriented, bent of social science in the United States. There is a neat irony here. A great deal of historiographical effort has been expended on explaining the relative weakness of British sociology as compared to American. The attainments of sociology in the United States may be due to the relative political failures of its practitioners on the left; British scholarly weakness, by contrast, was the product of political success. For a suggestive comparative discussion, see Lawrence Goldman, "A Peculiarity of the English? The Social Science Association and the Absence of Sociology in Nineteenth Century Britain." *Past and Present* 114 (February 1987). On the relatively vigorous growth of American universities as a more important venue for the new social sciences than their British and other European equivalents, see Konrad H. Jarausch, "Higher Education and Social Change: Some Comparative Perspectives." In Jarausch, ed., *The Transformation of Higher Learning, 1860–1930: Expansion, Diversification, Social Opening, and Professionalization in England, Germany, Russia, and the United States*. Chicago: University of Chicago Press, 1983. The American essay in the volume is by Colin B. Burke, "The Expansion of American Higher Education." As in Britain, the American knowledge community developed a split between more academic, disciplinary, university-based social scientists and intellectuals who sought to make a direct difference to public policy. But in the United States, the policy-oriented producers of social knowledge did so within more technocratic, "value-neutral," and social science-based institutions like the National Bureau of Economic Research and the Brookings Institution than their British counterparts. For fine discussions, see Guy Alchon, *The Invisible Hand of Planning: Capitalism, Social Science, and the State in the 1920s*. Princeton: Princeton University Press, 1985; and William J. Barber, *From New Era to New Deal: Herbert Hoover, the Economists, and American Economic Policy, 1921–1933*. Cambridge: Cambridge University Press, 1985. A parallel comparison could be drawn between the role of intellectuals in British municipal socialism and American knowledge producers in Progressive municipal reform. A most useful and suggestive work is the comparative study by James T. Kloppenberg, *Uncertain Victory: Social Democracy and Progressivism in European and American Thought, 1870–1920*. New York: Oxford University Press, 1986, which can usefully be read in tandem with R. Jeffrey Lustig, *Corporate Liberalism: The Origins of Modern American Political Theory, 1890–1920*. Berkeley: University of California Press, 1982.

3. Leonard Krieger, "The Idea of the Welfare State in Europe and the United States." *Journal of the History of Ideas* 24 (October–December 1963), pp. 554–55. Krieger defines "the state as that kind of independent body politic constituted by the direct and reciprocal relations which subsist between the supreme—or sovereign—government and the governed in a regionally-sized—i.e., supra-local—territory." Starting from this perspective, he argues that from the start every modern state has been a welfare state combining utilitarian and edificatory functions. The term "welfare state," which we attach to late nineteenth-century and twentieth-century state activities aimed at securing minimum standards for all citizens, is from this perspective an aspect of this larger history of modern states.

In an essay that can be read as a complement to Krieger's treatment of this larger history, George Thomas and John Meyer emphasize the cultural dimensions in the emergence of a system and principles of sovereignty within which the various post-feudal states were embedded. Like Krieger, they stress that states and the bureaucratic form are not identical (the degree of bureaucratization proved a variable), and that the ensemble of institutions possessed by a state is only one of its characteristics. For them, the hallmark of modernity was the shift from a stateless and imperial culture to a culture of states in an international system with no single overarching sovereign. George M. Thomas and John M. Meyer, "The Expansion of the State." *Annual Review of Sociology* 10 (1984).

4. Daniel Bell, in a footnote in an essay on American exceptionalism, takes note (without providing a citation) of a paper by Quentin Skinner who argues that

> the word *State* came to be recognized when political philosophers [he singled out Hobbes] sought a term that would identify an emerging realm of power distinct from *res publica* or *civitas* [since those terms designated popular sovereignty] and from the literal power holders, such as the monarch, who insisted that fealty be sworn to them as persons, rather than to an institution. The *State,* thus, was an entity that double abstracted sovereignty from the rulers and the ruled and combined the rights alienated from both into the *persona ficta* of "the State."

Daniel Bell, "'American Exceptionalism' Revisited: The Role of Civil Society." *The Public Interest* 95 (Spring 1989). The paper Bell cited has since been published: Quentin Skinner, "The State." In Terence Ball, James Farr, and Russell L. Hanson, eds., *Political Innovation and Conceptual Change*. Cambridge: Cambridge University Press, 1989. Thomas and Meyer remark with respect to this process, "Political sovereignty shifted upward to the state; and private political rights and obligations, down into a society that retained direct normative linkages with the wider Church and culture." Thomas and Meyer, "The Expansion of the State," p. 468.

5. Henri Pirenne, "The Stages in the Social History of Capitalism." *American Historical Review* XIX (April 1914), p. 497. Likewise, in an analysis that considers cities as "containers and distribution points for capital," by contrast to states which are "containers and deployers of coercive means, especially armed force," Charles Tilly treats the spirited urbanization in Europe from roughly 1000 to 1350 as emblematic of the early appearance of capitalism. There were substantially more

states than there were cities with populations larger than 10,000 at the beginning of this era, reaching rough parity at the end, with a dramatic inversion of the early medieval ration by the nineteenth century as the number of cities grew while the number of states contracted. Charles Tilly, *Coercion, Capital, and European States, AD 990–1990*. Oxford: Basil Blackwell, 1990, Chap. 2. The best study of urbanization in Europe is Jan de Vries, *European Urbanization, 1500–1800*. Cambridge: Harvard University Press, 1984.

It is important to be cautious about the relationship of the development of towns after 1000 and the rise of capitalism. Towns were embedded within agrarian feudal social, political, and economic relations. As Paul Bairoch observes in a section of his work devoted to the city and economic development in Europe from 1000 to 1500, "the surge of urban growth" in early feudal Europe "received its fundamental impetus from economic progress, especially from progress in agriculture." Paul Bairoch, *Cities and Economic Development: From the Dawn of History to the Present*. Chicago: University of Chicago Press, 1988.

6. Douglass C. North and Barry R. Weingast, "Evolution of Institutions Governing Public Choice in England: The 17th Century." Unpublished paper, 1986. Douglass C. North, "Transaction Costs in History." *Journal of European Economic History* 14 (Winter 1985).

The separation of politic and economics within capitalism, as Ellen Wood stresses, is a secret of its stability because this division displaces key class-based issues from the sphere of politics and separates economistic conflicts from political struggles. From this vantage point, capitalism represents a privatization of political power at the very same moment the state assumes unprecedented public qualities and responsibilities. Within the framework of the separation of property and sovereignty, capitalists relinquished day-to-day control over laborers outside the workplace itself, thus increasing the autonomy of civil society. Ellen Meiksins Wood, "The Separation of the Economic and Political in Capitalism." *New Left Review* 127 (May–June 1981).

7. North, "Transaction Costs," p. 566.

8. Capitalism is unique in history in having not one but two centers of authority, one built around the "economic" prerogatives of the business system, the other around the "political" prerogatives of the governmental system. In all other societies, from primitive to socialist, a single source of authority—village council, king, priesthood, party—makes both the determinations of war, law, and public ceremony, which we recognize as political, and the decisions on what shall be produced and how it shall be distributed, which we call economic. . . . Under capitalism, [the] cloak is torn in two, and the realm of activities having to do with material life is removed from the reach of political authority.

Robert Heilbroner, "The Triumph of Capitalism." *The New Yorker* (January 23, 1989) p. 102.

9. Stephen D. Krasner, "Sovereignty: An Institutional Perspective." *Comparative Political Studies* 21 (April 1988), p. 86.

10. John G. Hall and John Ikenberry, "The State." Unpublished book manuscript, 1988, pp. 34, 35. If we understand representation, as Hannah Pitkin does, "as a standing for something absent," and as "authority, the right to make com-

mitments and incur consequences for another," both the concept and the institutions embodying it emerged in medieval Europe, but took a decisive step in the seventeenth century with the linkage of representation during the English Civil War "with agency and acting for others, and linking the institutions with democracy and matters of right." Hannah Fenichel Pitkin, "The Concept of Representation." In Pitkin, ed., *Representation*. New York: Atherton Press, 1969, pp. 4, 8, 10.

11. Like many others, I have been instructed in these regards by Albert Hirschman's wonderful essay, *The Passions and the Interests: Political Arguments for Capitalism before Its Triumph*. Princeton: Princeton University Press, 1977. Enormously useful is the encyclopedic, if iconoclastic, work by Joseph Schumpeter, *History of Economic Analysis*. New York: Oxford University Press, 1954.

12. For a rich discussion of these issues, see Margaret Levi, *Of Rule and Revenue*. Berkeley: University of California Press, 1988, especially Chaps. 2 and 8. On the role of intellectuals at such moments, see Zygmunt Bauman, "Love in Adversity: On the State and Intellectuals, and the State of the Intellectuals." *Thesis Eleven* 31 (March 1992).

13. Krieger, "The Idea of the Welfare State," p. 557; Perry Anderson, *Lineages of the Absolutist State*. London: New Left Books, 1974.

14. Krieger, "The Idea of the Welfare State," p. 557.

15. Karl Polanyi, *The Great Transformation: The Political and Economic Origins of Our Times*. Boston: Beacon Press, 1957. Drawing on Polanyi, Jean-Christophe Agnew has traced the key shift in the history and meaning of markets from specific place-locations where transactions occurred to a non-place-specific set of flows that are hard to see, feel, or touch. By becoming abstract they appear timeless and outside history, driven by a static grammar of motives. Jean Christophe Agnew, *Worlds Apart: The Market and the Theater in Anglo-American Thought, 1550–1750*. Cambridge: Cambridge University Press, 1986, especially Chap. 1.

16. Polanyi, "The Great Transformation," pp. 3–4.

17. This is the subject matter of Ira Katznelson and Aristide Zolberg, eds., *Working-Class Formation: Nineteenth-Century Patterns in Western Europe and the United States*. Princeton: Princeton University Press, 1986.

18. An excellent and provocative discussion of these issues may be found in Herman van Gunsteren, "Notes on a Theory of Citizenship." In Pierre Birnbaum, Jack Lively, and Geraint Parry, eds., *Democracy, Consensus, and Social Contract*. London and Beverly Hills: Sage Publications, 1985.

19. Colin Holmes, "Laissez-Faire in Theory and Practice: Britain, 1800–1875." *Journal of European Economic History* 5 (Winter 1976), p. 685.

20. On this point, I have profited from reading Jose Harris, "Economic Knowledge and British Social Policy." In Furner and Supple, eds., *The State and Economic Knowledge*. For a remarkably sensible discussion of the 1834 watershed, see Peter Mandler, "The Making of the New Poor Law Redivivus." *Past and Present* 117 (November 1987). Commenting on the two dominant historiographical readings of the New Poor Law—one seeing it in terms of the triumph of laissez-faire, the other as a resurgence of paternalism—Mandler views the law as shifting the burden with regard to poverty to the pauper while, simultaneously, enhancing the responsibilities of the governors of the system within the gentry, the class that emerged as

the dominant governing class. The New Poor Law, in this reading, thus encapsulated some of the main tensions in the new emergent relationships between the state and society and the state and economy.

21. Giovanna Procacci, "Sociology and its Poor." Unpublished manuscript, 1987; Wolfgang Fach and Giovanna Procacci, "The Thin Man: On Life and Love in Liberalism." Unpublished manuscript, 1987.

22. Wolf Lepines, *Between Literature and Science: The Rise of Sociology.* Cambridge: Cambridge University Press, 1988. For a discussion of the institutional organization, ideas, and status of liberalism in the German knowledge community, see Fritz K. Ringer, *The Decline of the German Mandarins: The German Academic Community, 1890–1933.* Cambridge, MA: Harvard University Press, 1969; Harry Liebersohn, *Fate and Utopia in German Sociology, 1870–1923.* Cambridge, MA: MIT Press, 1988; and Woodruff D. Smith, *Politics and the Sciences of Culture in Germany, 1840–1920.* New York: Oxford University Press, 1991.

23. For a discussion, see Thomas and Meyer, "The Expansion of the States," pp. 470–77, who see state-building in terms of a moral, secularized, cultural project. It is striking how little these terms of reference have changed in the twentieth century. I think W. G. Runciman is quite right to insist that with respect to questions of equality and liberty concerning the role of the state in capitalist democracies, academics, journalists, and political leaders are still acting within the set of ideological constraints and assumptions that are very much like those of the New Liberalism of the late nineteenth and early twentieth centuries, and that the terms of debate between Left and Right have altered very little in the interim. All the more reason to focus on the emergence of new kinds of social knowledge at that time. W. G. Runciman, "Diary." *London Review of Books* (4 August 1988).

24. Social knowledge about economics, politics, and civil society initially developed without institutionalized supports and legitimation. There was little independent existence or organization of the disciplines until the 1870s. In the last third of the century, the development of separate disciplines went hand in hand with the substantial growth of universities. The solidification of both the universities and the separate social sciences took place only after World War One. For a fine discussion of the American case in these terms, see Dorothy Ross, "The Development of the Social Sciences." In Alexandra Oleson and John Voss, eds., *The Organization of Knowledge in Modern America: 1860–1920.* Baltimore: Johns Hopkins University Press, 1979. A complementary essay is Edward Shils, "The Order of Learning in the United States: The Ascendancy of the University," also in Oleson and Voss.

25. The phrase taken for the title of this book is T. B. Macaulay's; Stefan Collini, Donald Winch, and John Burrow, *That Noble Science of Politics: A Study in Nineteenth-Century Intellectual History.* Cambridge: Cambridge University Press, 1983, p. 3.

26. Collini et al., *That Noble Science,* pp. 12, 69.

27. J. R. McCulloch, *Principles of Political Economy.* London: 1925, p. 38; cited in Collini, et al., *That Noble Science,* pp. 68–69.

28. Collini et al., *That Noble Science,* p. 137.

29. Letter from Mill to Karl Heinrich Rau, cited in ibid., p. 141. For a stimulating discussion of Mill and social knowledge, as well as a broader consideration of the changing role of intellectuals, universities, and professions, see Stefan Collini,

Public Moralists: Political Thought and Intellectual Life in Britain, 1850–1930. Oxford: Clarendon Press, 1991.

30. Lawrence Goldman, "The Social Science Association, 1857–1886: A Context for Mid-Victorian Liberalism." *The English Historical Review* CI (January 1986).

31. The school of historical economists resisted these changes, mounted a powerful critique against the new ahistorical scientific universalism, and sought to secure the primacy of political categories and modes of analysis for economic inquiries. Like Polanyi more than a half century later, a key figure like Marshall's student William Cunningham insisted that the deductive theorems of economics were most apt for a particular moment in the development of markets, and that economic analysis, to be meaningful, must be located within a historically specific cultural and political frame. In celebrated debates with Marshall and in the various editions of his *The Growth of English Industry and Commerce* from 1882 forward, Cunningham and like-minded colleagues thus rejected the universal aspirations of economic theory, arguing that much too high a price was paid in the contraction of focus for the broadened aspirations of this new science. Whether or not, as Soffer argues, Cunningham misrepresented Marshall as the formulator of absolute economic laws of behavior and causality, in the end, the force of his critique was deflected almost entirely into the field of economic history. Most histories of economic thought do not pay much attention to the historical economists because they were losers vis-à-vis neoclassical economics within both the academic and policy worlds. Their rearguard actions within the university and their claims to possess the true interpretation of the classical heritage of political economy failed, except in the respect of establishing an autonomous subfield within the discipline. Many of the historical economists by World War One had become rather cranky neo-mercantilists and, in some cases, quite conservative. See Collini et al., *That Noble Science,* Chap. IV: and G. Koot, *English Historical Economics, 1870–1926*. Cambridge: Cambridge University Press, 1988.

32. Here and in the discussion below, I draw on Reba N. Soffer, *Ethics and Society in England: The Revolution in the Social Sciences, 1870–1914*. Berkeley: University of California Press, 1978. A useful overview of disciplinary history is provided by John B. Parrish, "Rise of Economics as an Academic Discipline: The Formative Years to 1900." *The Southern Economic Journal* XXXIV (July 1967). For a suggestive overview linking the growth of economic knowledge from the sixteenth century forward to the well-being of the state, including military affairs, see Gordon H. McCormick, "Strategic Considerations in the Development of Economic Thought." In Gordon H. McCormick and Richard E. Bissell, eds., *Strategic Dimensions of Economic Behavior*. New York: Praeger, 1984. An excellent edited collection on the character of modern economics is Daniel Hausman, ed., *The Philosophy of Economics: An Anthology*. Cambridge: Cambridge University Press, 1984.

33. Soffer, *Ethics and Society,* pp. 70, 104, 108. Marshall's difference with those to his left within the broad embrace of the New Liberalism was his explicit acceptance of the notion that in the middle and long term, capitalist property rights, business hegemony, and liberal markets would continue to be the basis of the economic system.

If Marshall's technical innovations were aspects of a liberal project, the same could not be said for the development of modern statistics, a craft that was deeply grounded in eugenics, a relationship that affected its questions as well as its methods. For a discussion, see Donald A. MacKenzie, *Statistics in Britain, 1865–1930: The Social Construction of Scientific Knowledge*. Edinburgh: Edinburgh University Press, 1981.

34. This formulation to some extent exaggerates the departure of economics from the field of practical social reform. After all, individual economists—think of John Commons and Richard Ely as examples—continued to try to be influential and remained engaged as advisors to policymakers and reformers. Nonetheless, with the intensification of economics as an abstract, scientific discipline, this older style became much harder to sustain. A useful discussion can be found in Robert L. Church, "Economists as Experts: The Rise of an Academic Profession in the United States." In Lawrence Stone, ed., *The University in Society; volume 2: Europe, Scotland, and the United States from the 16th to the 20th Century.* Princeton: Princeton University Press, 1974. For an overview from the Progressive Era forward in the United States that also stresses the wish of economists to be influential in public policy, see Robert Nelson, "The Economics Profession and the Making of Public Policy." *Journal of Economic Literature* XXV (March 1987).

35. In her contribution to the Smithsonian conference, Jose Harris, who argues that the impact of economic knowledge on modern social policy has been more episodic, diffuse, and informal than most historians of policymaking have allowed, nonetheless sees clearly that the new economic knowledge was intrinsic to the new social policy knowledge by virtue of its ability to penetrate the thinking of policymakers as common sense. This layperson's economic literacy set limits to policythinking, and provided a framework of economic laws that were understood to be beyond question in the making of state policy. See Harris, "Economic Knowledge and British Social Policy." In Furner and Harris, eds., *The State and Economic Knowledge*.

36. In the United States, the gap between these kinds of discourse can be read on the pages of two landmark studies: *Recent Economic Changes in the United States,* published by the National Bureau of Economic Research in May 1929, which embodied state-of-the-art advances to analyze developments within American capitalism, and *Recent Social Trends in the United States,* which appeared in 1933 under the auspices of President Hoover's Research Committee on Social Trends, an enterprise that provided a Progressive grand application of social engineering to concrete social problems.

37. H. L. Beales, *The Making of Social Policy.* L. T. Hobhouse Memorial Lecture. London: Oxford University Press, 1946. The citations are from pp. 5, 7, 8, 9, 25. On the importance of Green and other key liberal figures such as Hobhouse and Hobson, see the discussion by Briggs, pp. 245–46. The impetus to reinvent liberalism to make it appropriate to the management of state-market and state-citizen linkages at a distinctive historical moment was also the project of Beveridge and Keynes in the 1930s and 1940s. Like earlier liberals, they sought to demarcate an appropriate sphere of state intervention disciplined by the goal of making freedom and social equity compatible in a regime characterized simultaneously by a democratic politics and a capitalist economy. See the fine discussion in Karel Williams,

Beveridge and Keynes: Defining Liberal Collectivism. London: Routledge & Kegan Paul, 1986.

38. D. G. Ritchie, *The Principles of State Interference.* London: 1891, cited in Michael Freeden, *The New Liberalism: An Ideology of Social Reform.* Oxford: Clarendon Press, 1978, p. 15. Freeden's book is the best treatment of the late nineteenth- and early twentieth-century transformation of British liberalism.

39. Sidney Webb, "Modern Social Movements." In *The Cambridge Modern History of the World, XII.* Cambridge: Cambridge University Press, 1910, p. 760; cited in Freeden, *The New Liberalism,* p. 49.

40. For a seminal comparative discussion in a Polanyian vein, see John Gerard Ruggie, "International Regimes, Transactions, and Change: Embedded Liberalism in the Postwar Economic Order." *International Organization* 36 (Spring 1982).

41. Both the new economics of democratic socialism that developed within the framework of the Labour Party in the 1930s, as well as the Thatcherite impulses of 1970s and 1980s conservatism, shared broadly in this framework by accepting the tripartite world of states, citizens, and markets, and the need to manage their relations without elision and without transcending the terms of the social liberalism of the early twentieth century. For a particularly illuminating discussion of the former, see Elizabeth Durbin, *New Jerusalems: The Labour Party and the Economics of Democratic Socialism.* London: Routledge & Kegan Paul, 1985.

2

Social Knowledge, Social Risk, and the Politics of Industrial Accidents in Germany and France

ANSON RABINBACH

Toward a History of Social Knowledge

The origin of modern Western European welfare states is closely linked to two novel ideas that gained enormous prestige during the last two decades of the nineteenth century. The first was an expansion of the concept of rights to include the obligations of society toward the individual to reduce or minimize risk and inequality. A corollary of this idea was that social responsibility can be grounded scientifically and demonstrated by statistical laws. It followed that if risks and responsibility were both social in nature, then certain legal conceptions which still defined risk and responsibility in terms of contracts, negligence, and individual liability were obsolete. In practice, this meant that the task of the state was to regulate and enhance social bonds with the aid of an increasing arsenal of laws, based on information gained through statistical surveys and empirical investigations. The appearance of public and private institutions entrusted with accumulating and disseminating potentially useful social knowledge was the direct outgrowth of these new ideas, as were new professions like social medicine and social hygiene, and new specializations (labor law, insurance law) which emerged in tandem with social reform legislation in the earliest phase of European state social policy.

The 1880s and 1890s thus generated a complex relationship between new forms of knowledge—sociological, legal, medical—and the political requirements of states. Yet, it is important to recognize that the state was not a single monolithic institution but a broad spectrum of agencies that often fulfilled different, and often contradictory, requirements: a guarantor of social control, regulator of markets, and guarantor of rights. It would thus be a gross oversimplification to see social knowledge as either simply fulfilling the imperatives of states for instrumental purposes, or as the primary engine of the reforms themselves. Knowledge did not merely serve to justify the implementation of reform, but the politics of reform also accelerated the demand for and production of knowledge. The complex dynamic of knowledge and politics in this period requires attention to both the internal development of the types of knowledges involved and the political imperatives of reform legislation.[1]

Much of the early reform legislation on the Continent was the product of an unstable coalition of conservative traditionalists, liberal reformers, and moderate socialists. To consider the first state social policies as the product of a homogenous ideology or class strategy is to disregard the complex mixture of motives behind their initial inception. For example, in the case of the famous German law of 1884 establishing a system of state accident and health insurance, the financial requirements of large and small industry and local governments, the political motives of the dominant political elites, and even the increasing claims of workers all contributed to the passage of the new law. It is certainly true, as Hans Ulrich-Wehler has argued, that the reform policy was viewed by the chancellor as an effort to apply the Bonapartist methods he had observed in France to the "taming" of the workers movement—in tandem with the anti-socialist laws.[2] But other, equally important motives played a considerable role in both its conceptualization and implementation. As Florian Tennstedt points out, at the outset, the short-term electoral gains which Bismarck hoped the reform proposals might achieve far outweighed the long-term strategic goal of defusing the working-class movement.[3] Immediate pressures on provincial and local governments faced with burgeoning responsibilities for the sick and aged (returning from industrial centers), and fears of industrialists overburdened by increasing legal claims, also played a role in the formation of a national policy.[4]

Finally, a combination of enlightened idealism and domestic realpolitik among the political elite also has to be acknowledged. Dietrich Rueschemeyer and Ronan Van Rossem stress the impact of the Verein für Sozialpoliitk in "transforming the public view of social and economic problems" and in making socially interventionist liberalism *salonfähig* in Germany.[5] As Bismarck's liberal minister of commerce, Itzenplitz, noted more than a decade before the passing of the 1884 reform:

> An interference of the existing state in the socialist movement is by no means to be equated with the triumph of socialist doctrine. Rather, from my point of view, the action of state power as it exists today appears to be the only means of halting the socialist movement in its path of error; to steer it in a more beneficial direction it is necessary to acknowledge that which is justified in the socialist demands and can be realized in the framework of the state and social order.[6]

Apart from these broad motivating factors and intellectual premises is the expanding role of knowledge and the availability of a new set of "scientific" arguments on behalf of reform policies. After 1890, European liberals, rejecting traditional laissez-faire economics and impatient with the enmity of labor and capital, frequently had recourse to a positivist calculus: that society is governed first and foremost by social laws, and that social ethics consists in fitting human behavior more closely to those generalizable laws.[7] Such reformers saw their own sophisticated methods and arguments as evidence of a higher and more scientific stage of social reflection, that of sociologized man. In France, liberal intellectuals, including the influential economists Charles Gide, Charles Rist, Paul Cauwès, and Raoul Jay, grouped around the *Revue d'economie politique,* founded in 1886, developed a set of arguments based on the interdependence of productivity, consumption, and social justice as a rationale for reform. Similarly, the Durkheimian Celestin Bouglé, argued for a solidarist view of society premised on advances in social knowledge.[8] Like Max and Alfred Weber, and the other German reformers of the Verein für Sozialpolitik in the same period, these French academic intellectuals believed that the cause of reform could best be served by the results of empirical social science. In 1904, Jay summed up their arguments in this way:

> a nation that permits the destruction or reduction of the mental or physical forces of the manual workers makes one of the worst calculations. Those physical and moral forces are a part of the national capital like the sun or machines. The industrialist who, in order to reduce the costs of production, permits his machines to deteriorate . . . would be considered a fool. . . . If we do not think the same of an industrialist who imposes an excessive labor on his workers or pays them an insufficient wage, that is because we know that he will never have to repair the damage caused by his criminal negligence. The damage is charged to the nation.[9]

Jay's eloquent statement, in a treatise devoted to promoting the legal protections of the working class, underscored the elective affinity that emerged by 1900 among social hygiene, economics, and reform: the labor of the worker was the "capital of the nation" that should not be misused or wastefully consumed.

Another crucial aspect of the impact of knowledge on the new reform legislation has been emphasized by François Ewald in his massive study of the debate on the accident law in France.[10] Ewald argues that the debates and legal precepts surrounding the reform legislation introduced an entirely new kind of legal framework, which redefined "risk" as the central social problem, and which made the maintenance of an acceptable level of personal and social risk the basis of social solidarity, giving rise to what he calls the actuarial or "Providential State." "Society" is thus constructed out of myriad efforts at the administrative and personal levels to remove, predict, and repair the damages of dysfunction. Public debate—another sphere of social knowledge—is thus restricted to the calculation of the limits of acceptable risk. Devoted to the perpetuation of social solidarity, regularity, and normality, a main purpose of the state is to juridically regulate risk—a task that also requires the production and consumption of vast amounts of social knowledge.

By investigating the problem of industrial accident reform in a comparative framework, I think it can be shown that new conceptions of risk, responsibility, and liability did in fact emerge from the new legislation of the 1880s and 1890s. Although this survey concentrates on developments in Germany and France, its emphasis is less on the differences between conceptions of insurance (public vs. private), or the class coalitions that brought reform into being, than on how in both countries the establishment of a new legal norm or ideals of "social risk" led to a displacement of conflict over accidents from the direct relations of employer and employee to the sphere of jurisprudence and, ultimately, to conflicts among statistical and medical experts. This chapter is an analysis of how industrial work became subject to a wide range of social knowledges as a consequence of reform, but also how political and social conflict could not be divorced from the conflicting claims of knowledge, which increasingly became a field of social contestation.

Industrial Death and Dismemberment

In the last quarter of the nineteenth century, industrial accidents were increasingly viewed as a problem of crisis proportions, a perception confirmed by the shocking statistics garnished to demonstrate the phenomenal rise in workplace tragedies.[11] In Germany, between 1885 and 1908, there were over two million industrial accidents, and in France, industrial deaths (not including mining or metallurgy) rose from 1,562 in 1900 to 2,138 in 1905.[12] Between 1865 and 1890, 1,928 miners were killed, and 2,645 injured in over 128 accidents.[13]

As reformers sought a reversal of government policies, which almost universally placed the burden of proof of negligence on the worker, proposals for a massive restructuring of the accident compensation laws were widely debated in both France and Germany. Workers' organizations also paid greater attention to the accident issue, encouraging victims to press claims, creating private funds and associations for mutual assistance, and sometimes even forcing plant owners into expensive litigation.

For the worker, a serious accident often meant the end of the capacity to earn a living, dependence on family or charity, and in some cases, loneliness and isolation from the social milieu.[14] Yet, at the same time, the dramatis personae of the industrial accident expanded to include attorneys, judges, lawmakers, government officials, medical experts, and the insurance specialists. New professions emerged in the accident crisis: the accident claims adjustor, the expert physician attached to the firm, and the technical safety expert. The perception of the industrial accident as an urgent matter of public social policy, and the need for relatively precise information about accidents, their causes, frequency, and social or occupational distribution, were inextricably linked. The accident and the knowledge of the accident, while distinct for the victim, became fused in the positivist *mentalité* of the second half of the nineteenth century and influenced the acts of legislators, doctors, judges, and politicians. Situated at the intersection of working-class politics, the law, and the new profession of social medicine or hygiene, the industrial accident became the crucible of a changing relationship between knowledge and political power.

Rather than focus on the social consequences of the accident for the individual worker, or even for a specific trade or locality, this chapter is concerned with the way that accidents altered knowledge or, more precisely, restructured knowledge along different social and political axes. The industrial accident is significant, not only because of its impact on the victim, but also because it was the crucial point at which social and political forces first confronted each other to determine responsibility for the personal costs of industrialization. The concept of occupational risk or, in the French usage, *risque professionnel,* provided for an entirely new set of rights and obligations in the workplace. With the first efforts to exert public control over the alarming accident rate, relations among labor, capital, the state, law, medicine, and scientific knowledge entered into a new constellation. Basic to this constellation were three questions, which, though simple in appearance, proved remarkably complex and resistant to solution: What is an accident? What is its cause? Who is ultimately responsible? Protracted political, legal, and medical struggles over these questions defined a quarter century of efforts to come to terms with the accident issue.

In Europe, the industrial accident became the example par excellence for the idea that by acquiring special juridical rights labor could compensate for its more substantive inequality in the workplace. For the first time, the accident issue raised the question, to what extent do the risks of industrial life transcend the private interests of capital and the formal requirements of law, and permit the state to intervene, not only to determine the conditions of work (hours, ages, sanitation), but to guarantee safety or security?

Until the mid-nineteenth century, European jurisprudence held that the firm's liability for an accident had to be proven by the victim or his (or her) family, which was financially prohibitive, even if it could be established. Like other forms of equality in the marketplace, however, the free labor contract secured legal equality while increasing the laborer's weaker economic and social position. If liability was permanently shifted to the firm or owner, as many reformers demanded after 1880, did this not, liberal jurists protested, eliminate all possible guilt or negligence on the part of the worker and destroy the free labor contract? Firm owners protested that capital should not be made to bear the full or even partial financial burden for what were simply the risks of modern life.[15] Indeed, if negligence was abolished and guilt presumed, would not the liberal ideal of equality before the law, or individualism itself, suffer irreparable damage?

Socialists, on the other hand, saw in these reform proposals a cynical attempt to undermine their own position: did not the willingness of state and industry to compensate the dead and the maimed demonstrate only callousness toward the living labor they so ruthlessly exploited?[16] Industrial accidents simply exemplified the normal relations between labor and capital, and a particularly shocking incident such as the terrible mining disaster, at Montceau-les-Mines in 1894, served as an example of how *responsabilité patronale* was really "*crime capitaliste*."[17]

Apart from these broad divisions produced by class perspective, a controversy emerged over the claim that it was the industrial scourge that was responsible for the rise in accidents. Why, for example, if risk was social, should the law only apply to industry and not to agriculture? Did the rise in statistics reflect an increase in real dangers, more accurate reporting or, as medical specialists claimed, was the law itself not the cause of an epidemic of worker fraud or "simulation"? These conflicts, perhaps even more than those based on divergent class position, brought the expertise of insurance companies (public and private), legal theorists, legislators, doctors, and scientists to a sphere previously regarded as the private terrain of conflict between employer and employee. By opening the factory to the scrutiny of these competing discourses, the workplace became the scene of empirical investigation, legal theorizing, statistical review, juridical decision, and medical supervision. The legal hermeneutics, medical quandaries, and statistical conundrums arising over the nature of the industrial accident created a situation in which scientists and doctors concerned with the deleterious effects of industrial work could exercise a hitherto unthinkable influence.

One particularly important consequence of these debates is the importance which the study of worker fatigue assumed in the attempt to demonstrate the social character of industrial accidents. Scientists and physiologists concerned with the industrial laborer began to focus on the distribution of accidents according to the workday and workweek. Though the science of fatigue had already become a significant academic enterprise by the 1890s, by 1900 it underwent a political transformation in relation to the debate on industrial accidents.[18] Emerging from the confines of the laboratory, knowledge could prove that an accident was neither a willful act on the part of the worker nor the result of a malevolent entrepreneur, but a statistical fact linked to the body's relationship to the work process. The industrial accident was the product of fatigue, a physiological response to the acceleration of the work tempo and the length of the working day. It followed that the state, armed with the irrefutable truths of science, and perched above rival interests, could ensure surveillance of the workplace, reduce accidents, and resolve some of the pressing dilemmas of industrial work and labor conflict.

Before the Law

Until the Europe-wide insurance legislation of the 1880s and 1890s (Germany, 1884; Austria-Hungary, 1887; Sweden, 1891; Norway, 1894; Denmark, 1898; France, 1898; Belgium, 1903; Italy, 1905; Switzerland, 1906), the burden of financial assistance to ill or disabled workers fell largely to the private aid societies (*freie Hilfskassen* or *sociétés de secours mutuels*) formed largely after 1848 as workers' self-help organizations.[19] Throughout Europe, workers' accident protection was a confused and overlapping network of weak local, national, and craft organizations, almost all of which were inadequate to the task of providing more than minimal assistance in few and extremely needy cases.

The German Imperial Employer's Liability Act (Reichshaftpflichtgesetz) of June 7, 1871 established the conditions for compensation of accidental death or injury directly caused by a deputy or representative of the firm during the course of his duties.[20] In the French and Belgian Napoleonic Code, as well as under German commercial law, employer liability could only be claimed in cases where negligence was proven by the worker, usually only after long and costly litigation.[21] In cases where employers were inadequately insured, failed to maintain premiums, or simply when owners or insurance companies refused to pay, a worker's claims became a dead letter.[22] Accident cases were the source of enormous resentment by workers deprived of compensation, while industrialists complained of heavy expenses incurred under the voluntary private insurance system.

The first broadly comprehensive system of obligatory "public-legal" accident, sickness, disability, and old age insurance was introduced by Bismarck in the German Reichstag in March 1881 and adopted in July 1884.[23] The German system was entirely state administered by the Imperial Insurance Office (Reichsversicherungsamt), a newly created body composed not only of civil servants, but of parliamentary (*Bundesrat*) deputies, employer's organizations, and worker's representatives.[24] The state assumed two-thirds of the cost, the employers one-third through the employer corporations (*Berufsgenossenschaften*).[25] At the outset the accident insurance covered only the most "dangerous" occupations, including mining, quarrying and, of course, hazardous industries like iron and steel. All German workers in industrial concerns were eventually insured and compensated to a maximum of two-thirds of their income in case of total disability and loss of earning capacity. Subsequent revisions extended the law to agriculture, maritime, and transport.[26]

In December 1887, Austria followed suit with a similar compulsory accident insurance on the German model. Other European countries proved far more reluctant to base their systems on the *Zwangsversicherung* of the Germans. An interesting case is Switzerland, which approved a compulsory system after lengthy parliamentary debate, but submitted it to a popular referendum in May 1900, where it was overwhelmingly rejected. Opponents of the law campaigned to identify accident insurance with German authoritarianism, and even distributed thousands of silk neckties with the inscription: "vote no on May 20th."[27] The Swiss referendum became a symbol for the lack of popular support for the German system and its paternalist and authoritarian connotations.[28] By the beginning of the twentieth century only Austria, Hungary, Norway, and Luxembourg had followed the German lead and adopted state-administered compulsory worker's insurance.[29]

France adopted a private insurance system on April 9, 1898, Belgium in 1903, and Italy in 1905.[30] Great Britain made private compulsory insurance part of the 1897 Workman's Compensation Act, which was expanded in 1906 and 1909.[31] The United States lagged far behind European developments; most states passed workmen's compensation acts between 1911 and 1948, but the power of free trade and the free labor contract inhibited any strict liability doctrine.[32]

Despite the limited success of state-sponsored insurance, the emergence of a Europe-wide system of accident compensation law amounted to a fundamental redistribution of social risk and responsibility. To a far greater extent than any prior labor legislation including the British factory acts of the 1840s, the legal basis of the relationship between labor and capital was transformed by insurance law. In this respect, the German law was pathbreaking in its articulation of the principle that industrial accidents are caused less by the design of the plant, or by the particular owner, than by the special conditions of industrial work.[33] Though some German industrialists pressed for a radical diminution of pension in cases of gross negligence (*grobes verschulden*), even this modification failed on the grounds that it reintroduced employee responsibility through the back door.[34] Worker negligence was limited only to illegal and purposeful actions covered by the criminal code, while management negligence—to the dismay of the worker's organizations—was entirely nullified.

By removing the entire question of negligence from the insurance law, German jurisprudence admitted the fundamental inequity of the free labor contract. The accident insurance legislation of the 1880s and 1890s was a tacit admission, as many contemporaries recognized, that the free labor contract could only be maintained by recognizing the fundamental *inequality* of the two parties involved. The principle that the state or society should guarantee protection to the weaker party against the vicissitudes of industrial labor was a frontal assault on the free labor contract as a normative and regulative principle.[35] The wage was no longer sufficient recompense to warrant the risk of death or injury. Accident laws were based on "an actuarial conception of social risk," in which the causes of the accident are attributed to the greater chance involved in the social nature of the work, based on the law of statistical averages, as opposed to personal fault.[36] The risks of industrial labor were thus compensated by what Jacques Donzelot has called the "juridical requalification" of the worker.[37] The substantive consideration of industrial risk overshadowed the formal principle of the equal relations of both parties and was ultimately justified by the idea of "the state as the guardian of the moral order."[38]

The Modernity of Risk

The German law profoundly influenced other European reforms by altering the balance of risk and responsibility. Ironically, the shift to employer responsibility was justified by the assertion that the nature of modern industry and not personal negligence exposed workers to greater risk, a claim that would not be sustained by accident statistics. Though initially applauded by French reformers who pointed to its extraordinary breadth (including sickness insurance), liberal opponents of the German law characterized it as a Prussian invention designed to impose the power of the state over civil society. The proposal introduced in the French Chamber of Deputies in 1882 was supported by an unstable coalition of government officials, professionals (especially from journalism and medicine), a small group of industrialists, conservatives, radicals, and a few Socialists. Though the Chamber of Deputies was more favorably disposed to the accident law than the conservative Senate (dominated by the traditional propertied groups [*propriétaire*], liberal opposition to state intervention in both houses obstructed its passage for more than a decade and a half.[39] In France, as Sanford Elwitt and Judith Stone have shown, the dedication of reformers to securing the social peace was resisted by the alliance of small producers and large industrialists, and by the strong republican tradition of property rights as opposed to state intervention.[40] As a radical departure from *liberté de travail,* the accident law was consistently opposed by those who warned, as did the noted entrepeneur and reformer, Emile Cheysson, that a breach of common law in favor of the workers might open the floodgates of socialism. Supporters of the law emphasized that the employer "owed the worker a guarantee of this right to subsist from the day on which an accident lowers his capacity to work."[41] But it was only after employers were won over by a narrow restriction of the law to large industry, by the promise of lower expenses, and by the guarantee of private insurance, that it finally passed on the eve of the April 1898 election.[42]

The French law removed the demand for proof of "the fault, the negligence or the imprudence of his *patron* or his representatives," and shifted responsibility to the owner of the firm, while eliminating all personal fault in determining compensation.[43] In the original proposal, "When a man rents his labor to another man, and is injured in the course of performing his duty the employer is responsible *en plein droit,* except if he proves that the accident was the result of a fault committed by the victim."[44] Clearly reformers intended that the law take into account changes in "social evolution," and that solidarity replace individual responsibility in the industrial sphere. According to the monarchist Albert de Mun, "*Patrons* and workers are considered as individuals with no relations in common, . . . as if the work contract was not a special kind of contract, whose conditions are necessarily subordinated to certain considerations of the social order, to certain duties, to certain reciprocal obligations."[45]

According to the doctrine of *risque professionnel,* which was introduced by Félix Faure on February 11, 1882, the *patron* was declared responsible in all cases where industry itself, or the *fatalité du milieu ambiant,* constituted a special hazard insofar as "work is responsible for the accidents that it causes."[46] Emile Cheysson provided the most precise definition of *risque professionnel* as "the risk assignable to an occupation which is ascertained independent of the fault of the workers or *patrons*."[47] However, since the doctrine of *risque professionnel* held employers responsible while simultaneously arguing for the social assumption of risk, there appeared to be a contradiction between risk and responsibility which, some advocates of the German model maintained, could only by removed by a state system.

The first version of the French law was restricted to large industrial establishments where workers were servants of hazardous *moteurs mécaniques*.[48] "Each invention which augments the productivity and perfectability of industrial work," noted one commentator, "makes it more complicated to use and control machines, and thus makes the situation for those who utilize them . . . more dangerous."[49] Mechanization constituted a social, as opposed to individual, risk.

Unlike the German law, the French law did not include health insurance, and at the outset of the debate, narrowly restricted the notion of social risk to large-scale industrial production. *Risque professionnel* also implied that a work-related accident was a quasi-public event, insofar as the public weal is enriched by labor: "The social risk of work must be distinguished from other risks, which are individual in nature," because "the worker who is injured on the field of honor of work merits a more generous insurance than the citizen who is the victim of an accident outside of work or of an illness."[50]

As in the German case, *risque professionnel* was predicated on a statistical conception of fault. "Insurance," noted Cheysson, "is the compensation for the effects of risk by the organized mutuality according to statistical laws, that is to say, according to the economic laws that govern the course of things."[51] In the spirit of Durkheim, the sociological regularity of the accident made its accidental character social. When this supreme conception came into conflict with the precepts of liberalism and freedom of contract, the ideas of free agency and will had to be modified:

> Demographic facts, social facts themselves, are subordinate to inflexible rigor of the average. . . . It is that permanence which becomes the basis of insurance and which confers on it the character of scientific truth. If the individual is relieved of danger and its caprices, the masses on the other hand obey the laws of certainty and fall under the grip of calculability.[52]

In 1898, *risque professionnel* prevailed and accidents were declared compensable, regardless of the cause if they resulted from the "industrial life of the victim," except, of course, if they were malevolently induced or self-inflicted. Although the concept of *faute lourde* or gross negligence was ultimately dropped, *force majeure* (acts of God), and the somewhat ambiguously phrased *faute inexcusable* were substituted when it became clear, as in the German case, that any consideration of personal negligence reintroduced the possibility of firms holding victims liable for accidents. On the other hand, the doctrine of employer responsibility found only a "faint echo" in the jurisprudence because it inequitably burdened the heads of firms with a responsibility for which there was no parallel responsibility on the part of the workers.[53] The law noted only that any *chef d'enterprise* was in principle responsible and had to maintain adequate insurance if he entered into a labor contract with the victim of an accident.[54]

Rejecting the German system, France adopted a noncompulsory insurance scheme based on private insurance companies (*assurance libre*), with state financing only in case of the failure of a firm or private insurance company to pay an indemnity. An accident was designated as "all bodily injuries caused by the action of a sudden and external cause," a definition that was modified to include the phrase "inherent in the work" the following year.[55] Occupational ailments, however, were defined as the "slow consequences of fatigue" (*insalubrités du métier*) and were not included. The law was applied to all industry, manufacturing, mining, building, public enterprises, and transportation, but did not include commercial or agricultural occupations.[56] As in Germany, the idea of social risk was considered to be a consequence of industrial modernity, recognizing that impersonal forces rather than individual wills were often the determinants of a person's destiny. With the advent of social insurance law, the positivist credo, which sees social laws as more decisive than individual passions and interests, morality and guilt, was embedded in a political context.

If France was relatively slow to adopt a work accidents law, this was in no small part the result of intense political conflict evoked by such novel principles. French liberals saw the various drafts of the law as threats to the very political conception on which the nation was founded.[57] "Socialism," they complained, "was being substituted for the labor contract by the introduction of *risque professionnel*."[58] The accident law was above all a subversion of freedom of contract, "a germ of destruction in our judiciary system" and a "German vice."[59] The presumption of employer responsibility amounted to "the creation of a new privileged [working] class," and conversely the creation of "a juridically inferior race," the entrepreneur. It was a return to the principle of aristocracy in the name of democracy, the reaffirmation of a special "privilege and exception" for workers in a jurisprudence only recently expunged of such notions.[60] Instead, the liberals proposed the doctrine of *responsabilité contractuelle*, based on the moral obligations of the free labor contract (which parallel the medieval idea of a master's responsibility for his servants) as an alternative to *risque professionnel*. Advocates of *responsabilité contractuelle* agreed that the burden of proof of negligence should be transferred to the *patron*, without, however, the accompanying transfer of a priori fault.[61]

For the French Patronat, unlike the more servile German industrialists of the Second Reich, the new law represented the irrepressible growth of state control over industry in the Third Republic. They responded by organizing L'Association des Industriels de France contre les Accidents du Travail (1883), devoted to resisting the new legislation. The association called upon entrepreneurs to establish private initiatives such as employee protection plans and plant safety programs, and proposed collectively assuming the premiums for the most dangerous occupations.[62] In the decade before the passage of the law, the French Patronat was remarkably imbued with a vigorous sense of Christian responsibility and a will to preserve its moral prestige, dramatically demonstrating a "note of nostalgia for the social relations of the ancien régime."[63]

The question that dominated the stormy debates in the Chamber of Deputies was why should the risks of mechanization supercede all other "normal" risks? Did this not place modern industry at a disadvantage, legislating a disincentive to progress by penalizing an employer simply for introducing "the most highly developed tools"?[64] Would an employer choose to adopt modern techniques if faced with higher insurance premiums? While a few radicals claimed that the elimination of employer negligence encouraged immorality by giving him a "a premium for the assassination of the worker," the most articulate opponents of the law argued that it would retard economic progress, depriving the worker of his means of livelihood.[65] One critic even suggested that the *risque professionnel* borne by the *patron* should be balanced by a *risque vital* borne by the worker, who would be required to provide a certificate of medical good health before entering the factory.[66]

Though far less effectively than their French counterparts, a few German liberals, like Lujo Brentano, campaigned against the Bismarck compulsory insurance law.[67] The state, Brentano maintained, should only protect those persons directly in need of protection in order to ensure the sanctity of the free labor contract.[68] A liberal order, he argued, could not tolerate an insurance law which only strengthened the hand of the entrepreneur (*Unternehmer*) at the expense of the worker's associations and the *freie Hilfskassen.*[69] The *Kathedersozialisten,* or "socialists of the chair," on the other hand, led by the economist Gustav Schmoller, supported the compulsory insurance program as "a pedagogical instrument" (*Erziehungsmittel*), which could educate the working classes in the potential benefits of the state. Schmoller appealed to the "crown and bureaucracy" as the only neutral elements in the social class struggle.[70] Most German industrialists, especially those in steel and iron, supported the chancellor, but a recalcitrant few saw the law as a wild concession to Bismarck's political ambitions and denounced the system as an "irresponsible waste of work, time and money."[71]

A central issue in both the French doctrine of *risque professionnel* and in the German Insurance Law was the distinction each drew (in the public debates as well as in the compensation provisions of the law) between the modernity of mechanized industry and traditional forms of work which did not involve a social risk. Martin Nadaud, a former worker who became the leading defender of the insurance idea in the French chamber, emphasized that *risque professionnel* did not apply to the manual trades, still covered by the civil code, in which "*le péril n'a pas augmenté.*"[72] For its opponents, however, the distinction between the "modern" plant and the old artisanal enterprise was entirely arbitrary and did not correspond to the *specific* risks involved in any particular form of work. The argument that *risque professionnel* was an imperative of modern industry and its unanticipated dangers was, in their view, historically and statistically false; modern industry with its equipment and organization was far less dangerous than the nonmechanized trades: carpentry, roofing, naval construction, wagon or cab driving, seagoing trades and, above all, mining. The connection between modernity and risk was subjected to its most scathing critique by Léon Say, the liberal economist and leader of the opposition, when he declared that "the great *risque professionnel* of humanity is that each human being is mortal and might lose his physical or mental faculties."[73]

Were work accidents a consequence of modernity? The statistical evidence largely bears out the contentions of the opponents of *risque professionnel.* In both France and Germany, nonindustrial accidents, especially in shipping and milling, were the most serious, while the "elementary dangers" of mining, quarrying, and maritime work outstripped the hazards of industry. Mechanized industry proved only moderately dangerous, accounting for roughly one-fourth of all accidents.[74] However, the modernity of risk was borne out insofar as accidents involving machinery rose more rapidly than others, though fatalities declined.[75] Overall, accidental death remained relatively stable over the first decade of the German law, while disabilities (both temporary and permanent) increased. The debates in Germany and France demonstrate that the notion of social risk prevailed, not because of any "objective" considerations, but because it was consistent with the view that modernity required a new principle of "fault" in order for social risk to triumph over liberal protestations that freedom of contract was being trampled on. If social risk was not truly a consequence of modernity, then the success of the German law as well as the doctrine of *risque professionnel* attest to the power of a perception of reality that far outweighed all arguments to the contrary.

What Is an Accident?

The French law passed in April 1898 underscored the definition of an accident as a sudden and unanticipated event, as opposed to a long-term illness, disability, or exposure ruinous to health. Most eloquent was Léon Bourgeois, president of the commission empowered to draft the French law, who defined an accident as "*un evénement soudain, violent*" as opposed to "*la maladie qui est, au contraire, un état continu et durable, né d'une cause également continue et durable.*"[76] His language, taken literally, meant that the "doors of the law" would remain forever closed even to the most deadly of toxic emissions: "If death comes in two hours, *monsieur le ministre,* it is not an illness!," his opponents cried out in the Chamber.[77] His supporters, however, ridiculed the idea that a job-related "accident" might occur over a long period of time, by pointing out that if that were true, the rampant alcoholism among waiters might as well be considered an industrial accident, since it occurred as part of normal intercourse with customers.[78] To be sure, the definition of an accident as a time-bound, sudden occurrence was problematic. In France, the moderate socialists supported the law in the Chamber, but faulted *risque professionnel* for its failure—in stark contrast to the German inclusion of sickness insurance—to provide a broader definition of accident which also included the effects of an occupational disease or disability. If special hazards of industrial life were indeed a social responsibility, then social liability could not be limited to accidents alone, but should be naturally extended to all occupational maladies.[79] The socialists thus threatened to open the Pandora's box of coverage for occupational diseases, which the advocates of *risque professionnel* wanted to avoid at all costs. Even in Germany, where the health insurance law paralleled the accident law, the relatively higher pensions paid to victims of accidents encouraged industrial hygienists to extend the notion of "accident" to include occupational diseases of a chronic nature.[80] The German expert, Georg von Mayr, analyzed the dilemma at the Milan Congress of Industrial Accidents in 1894: "An accident is a social occurrence, which under certain forms appears indubitably as such; but, it also takes other more ambiguous forms, wherein it approaches an occupational illness."[81]

The issue of what constituted an industrial accident was also controversial in Germany where mounting confusion over a decade of contradictory rulings by the Imperial Insurance Office called attention to the vagueness of the 1884 law. Exactly what might be included in a plant accident—what injuries, which external causes, or what time span could elapse between cause and injury—remained unspecified. For example, the German law specifically excluded all "types of plants which do not involve the risk of accident for the persons employed therein."[82] Although the German high court (oberster Gerichtshof) ruled that the accident had to be connected to the plant, "not only in time and place, but also causally," it did not set forth whether "only accidents connected to the special dangers of the plant in question are to be considered as plant accidents," or whether those "which simply occur as a consequence of the general danger that threatens all persons" employed in that plant should also be included.[83] Initially, the Imperial Insurance Office interpreted the law in the narrow sense (e.g., that accidents had to be causally connected to the risks associated with a particular kind of work in the plant), but by 1888 it was already shifting toward a broader interpretation that compensated victims of any accident occurring in the plant.[84] German legal experts like the noted jurist Heinrich Rosin challenged the Imperial Office on the grounds that only that aspect of the accident which was literally a social risk, for example, industrially caused, should be covered. Rosin distinguished between an accident "occurring in a plant" (*Unfall beim Betriebe*) and a "plant accident" (*Betriebsunfall*) requiring that a "special danger" (*besondere Gefahr*) exist, "caused by the particular dangers of a plant that go beyond the dangers of normal life."[85] For example, he disputed a Berlin decision on behalf of a woodcutter in a public park who was awarded a pension for a broken leg that occurred while walking from the canteen to the woodcutting area after midday break.[86] In another case, a worker was pensioned for an accident that took place while lounging in a dangerous area of the plant. Rosin contended that "neither the time nor the locality of the accident" was alone "decisive" for the "causal connection" of the accident, and the "special dangers" of the plant were not a direct cause in either case. If his distinction might appear "cold blooded," he added, the intent of the law was not simply to insure plants with a higher risk and exclude others, but rather to insure those workers "whose work exposed them to a special risk of accident."[87] However, for the *Kathedersozialisten,* Rosin's strict interpretation undermined the very principle of the law, since the elimination of negligence made it necessary for all accidents, without exception, to be covered by the insurance.

> The essential difference between accident care which rests on the basis of the [old] Employer Liability Act and one which is based on the [new] insurance principle, is precisely that the former can only take into account accidents which result from the special dangers of the plant, while in the latter case these limitations are removed.[88]

These protracted legal and juridical hermeneutics over the meaning of "accident" were an expression of the new political principle which both the German and French law introduced: the double linkage of risk of its social causes, on the one side, and to the modernity of those causes on the other. Despite the differences between state and private insurance, and the lack of health coverage in France, both insurance doctrines shifted the political center of gravity of the issue from one of individual guilt and responsibility, to the social character of risk, to time, and to circumstance. The modernity of risk was embodied in the notion of *risque professionnel* and in the "special danger" of industry as the criteria for compensation in Germany. The debates over what was an accident were directly linked to the juridical interpretation of social risk. However, by invoking the notion of "special danger" or *risque professionnel,* legal theorists also left themselves open to an even wider challenge: if it was the nature of work that produced the risk to be borne by society, as opposed to either the employer or employee, why should liability be restricted only to the most dangerous industries, and not to all industry, to particularly risky occupations, to agriculture, commerce, or transportation? To support their claims, all sides in this legal controversy appealed to the higher law of numbers. If it could be shown that accidents were linked either to specific types of industry or even to the nature and organization of work, then compensation could hardly be restricted to either the most dangerous trades or the modern industrial enterprise.

The Revelatory Power of Numbers

After the first decade of compulsory accident insurance in Germany and the adoption of similar laws elsewhere in Europe, the question of the relationship between mounting claims and allegations of employee fraud became the center of international debate. Did not the astonishing rise in claims which the German law elicited, and which the French law also brought about, demonstrate, as some experts claimed "the correlation between the institution of that insurance and the increase in the number of accidents," or even prove that insurance itself added to the risks of modern industry?[89] Did the new law encourage the reporting of minor or invented mishaps, and perhaps also provide an incentive to workers to "commit" an accident? Was the physician now placed in the position of judge in deciding the legitimacy of those claims? And finally, could not the assumption of risk by society ultimately destroy society's ability to bear the costs of the swelling army of maimed and disabled veterans of industry?

By 1896, the number of recorded accidents in Germany increased sixty percent, and compensations tripled between 1886 and 1896. In Austria, claims doubled in half that time.[90] Moreover, accidental death remained relatively stable over the first decade of the German law, while disabilities (both temporary and permanent) skyrocketed. Such figures reinforced the anxiety among insurance experts, politicians, and jurists that the startling rise in less serious accident claims resulted either from growing negligence and carelessness or, more malevolently, from the desire of some workers to escape the duties of work. Critics of the liability system often distinguished between "real accidents" and the growing number of "legal accidents."[91] The statistical deluge appeared to confirm the claim already put forth in the French parliamentary debates, that compulsory accident insurance was "an incentive for the inattention and the negligence of the worker."[92]

French and German experts also disagreed about whether or not a state-administered compulsory insurance scheme on the German model, or the private scheme favored by the French, encouraged greater or fewer accidents. French supporters of the private system pointed out that if the entrepreneur and not the state assumed the greatest burden for the premiums, it would induce him to undertake accident prevention in the interests of reducing costs and claims. In 1891, for example, the French monarchist and critic of the German system, Octave Keller, argued that the frequency of accidents in Germany could in part be attributed to the fact that there were fewer incentives for German entrepreneurs to take precautions against accidents, since the state assumed the greater part of the fiscal responsibility.[93] However, by 1891, German law explicitly required firms to enact accident prevention measures, and employers could be fined if found negligent by the state insurance system. The German system also seemed to encourage workers to press illegitimate claims since, as one expert noted, "when face to face with his *patron* a worker might feel some shame in taking advantage of the slightest pretext to claim a pension." But in the German or Austrian systems he is confronted with "that impersonal being, the State, which anyone might exploit without scruple."[94] Von Mayr, however, rejected the conclusion that the rising numbers were a direct result of rampant negligence on the part of the workers. Instead, he pointed out that the stringent system of reporting encouraged the frequent notation of accidents of secondary importance with only temporary disability. Above all, he argued, the real difficulty was dealing with firms that maximized profits by accelerating the rapidity of machine work. Such efforts led workers "to resist as much as possible the length of the work done with a feverish pace and to obtain a normal working day that is as short as possible."[95] During a heated debate in the Chamber of Deputies in 1900 the solidarist economist Raoul Jay noted that if lesser accidents with temporary or partial disabilities increased disproportionately to deaths, the mounting number of smaller claims could be explained only by lax attitudes of the corporations, tribunals, and doctors. If, however, fatalities increased at the same rate as the most serious injuries, then "neither employers were more negligent, nor were workers more imprudent." It was the nature of the work that was at fault.[96]

The rising accident statistics were also accompanied by a chorus of voices calling for an increase in state control over industry and for accident prevention schemes including worker education, stricter plant regulations, and the use of preventive equipment. Major international expositions of preventive techniques were held in Berlin (1889), Brussels (1897), Vienna (1900), and Frankfurt (1901), and industrialist associations for the prevention of accidents were founded throughout Europe.[97] By 1903, with the founding of the Deutsche Verein für Versicherungswissenschaft, an organization devoted solely to the study of insurance, specializing in workers' claims, with over six hundred members, we can speak of a "science" of accident insurance.[98] The Kongress über Unfallschutz und Unfallversicherung held in Vienna in 1913 was an international gathering of the crème of insurance specialists, among them the thirty-year-old Franz Kafka, whose professional writings had already distinguished him as one of the most promising young Czech experts.[99] Museums of "industrial hygiene" displaying safety devices for workers were set up in Zurich (1883), Vienna (1890), Amsterdam (1900), Munich (1900), and Berlin (1903).[100] The German Imperial Manufacturing Ordinance (Reichsgewerbeordnung) of June 1, 1891, stipulated that industrial firms were required to "organize their plants and its equipment so that the dangers for the life and health of the worker are eliminated as far as possible," and delinquent employers were subject to fines.[101] The largest German firms ostentatiously complied. The Berlin Allgemeine Elektrizitätsgesellschaft (AEG) set up a permanent display of photographs of dismembered limbs, with the skeleton of a severed hand prominently featured.[102]

The effect of these efforts to reduce accidents was, however, largely disappointing and often restricted to the largest firms. Smaller firms proved to be sorely lacking in even "an elementary understanding" of health and safety measures.[103] Some firm owners even refused to inform their workers of the insurance law for fear of rising absenteeism. The debate on the crisis of accident statistics grew with the expanding numbers. The direct conflict between accident victim and employer gave way to parliamentary debate; the new laws led to intensive juridical and jurisprudential duels, and the experience of a decade of rising claims and statistics led to interpretive battles over the numbers and the great controversy over the causes of accidents. Work was no longer the sphere of the simple relations between employer and employee, but the fulcrum of widely divergent moral, legal, and medical perceptions. By 1900, the charge of "fraud or simulation" in claims became the chief focus of the debate on the accidents. Medical experts on insurance fraud read in the accident claim charts the signs of a vast deception perpetrated on unprepared doctors and unsuspecting insurance administrators by the working class. In both Germany and France, elimination of individual risk did not obliterate the problem of fault, but removed it to a different plane, where abuse of the law became a new subject of medical and legal knowledge.

Fraud and Its Discontents

Almost immediately after the French insurance law was enacted, the statistics seemed to replicate the German experience. By 1900, an enormous increase of 36,000 accidents over the previous year, caused public alarm from legislators, industrialists, and physicians against "the epidemic of simulations," the "professionals of industrial accidents," and the fraudulent abuse of the law by those who took advantage of naive medical practitioners not trained in "*la médecine soupconneuse* [suspicious medicine]."[104]

German industrialists, doctors, and legal experts had already warned their French colleagues to expect an epidemic of accident fraud. Indeed, by 1891, the total costs of administration and claims in Germany had more than tripled. German employers' organizations complained bitterly of their "heavy sacrifices," charging that "workers wanted to make capital out of the smallest accidents while drawing out the period of cure."[105] Some leading medical specialists agreed with their assessment. According to Professor Fritz Stier-Somlo, a leading expert on medical ethics, fraud was rampant in all areas of social insurance, but was most pervasive in cases of industrial accidents. Medical fraud, he said, was already "a mass experience" (*Massenserscheinung*), and "pension addiction" (*Rentensucht*) a plague (*Volkskrankheit*). The problem had taken on such a "terrifying dimension" that in one small section of the city of Darmstadt, for example, a study of the construction industry revealed that 125,000 marks in fraudulent payments had been made in 1905 alone.[106] Some German physicians declared the new "pension-hysteria" to be so bad that it had to be "met head-on" by a new collaboration between medicine and the law.[107]

The issue of industrial accident fraud became a new point of intersection between work, medicine, and the law. For the first time it brought the doctor into an intimate relationship with aspects of the law, which had heretofore been the preserve of criminal cases involving negligence. The medical expert became the acknowledged "court of last resort between the adversarial parties: worker and industrialist, as well as the judge who pronounces his final judgement."[108] French and German medical specialists were in agreement that clinical observation revealed that workers often fraudulently manufactured or, at the very least, exaggerated their injuries. "Today, there is unanimity among civil doctors," remarked Dr. Hubert Coustan, author of several studies of the problem in military medicine, "who almost all admit to the abuse of idleness and the epidemic character of fraud."[109] Treatises on the simulation of accidental injury proliferated, and doctors were urged to work closely with insurance experts to curb the appetites of the workers.

Ambroise Tardieu's 1879 *Etude médico-légale sur les blessures,* the first full-scale, medical-legal textbook of occupational accidents, also included an extensive discussion of the "false or exaggerated allegations and frauds employed by plaintiffs in their appeals for claims of indemnity."[110] Citing the case of a miller, who sued for 60,000 francs plus 3,000 francs annual pension for "simple contusions of the legs and arms, and an incapacity for work which I evaluated at roughly three months," Tardieu emphasized that he had been struck by how "ridiculously elevated" such claims were. He remarked that he had often been called upon by the courts to give an impartial opinion of the physical damages resulting from an accident. His patients demonstrated many different and interesting types of simulation, such as attributing the effects of old accidents to new and less serious ones, and he warned that such cases tended to "degenerate into a veritable hypochondriachal mania."[111]

Tardieu's pioneering work was only the prototype of what soon became a standard medical discourse: the elaborate taxonomy of fraud, deceit, and exaggeration in industrial accident cases. A comprehensive work on the subject published in France in 1907 contained a bibliography of no less than 2,181 items.[112] Beginning in 1905, international medical congresses were held almost annually to discuss specific issues concerning the simulation of accidents. Most medical experts admitted that "the premeditated simulation of a serious injury" was extremely rare, but cautioned that "in the very large number of cases where there is some fraud by the insured, there is an insignificant accident, imaginary pain, or simply a refusal to work even if completely cured."[113] Alfred Bienfait, a doctor at Liége, conducted an important survey that concluded that "if simulation proper is unusual, the enormous exaggeration of a real mishap is frequent."[114] French workers' argot frequently referred to the voluntary absenteeism gained by the self-inflicted accident as "*faire le macadam*."[115] Though such cases of workers who inflicted real injuries on themselves to appear as the result of an accident were the least prevalent form of abuse, medical textbooks catalogued self-inflicted or phony injuries to assist doctors in identifying them. "Criminal and fraudulent abuses cannot be revealed except by the special knowledge of the doctor," noted one expert "astonished to see how great is the ingenuity of certain insured individuals in creating new lesions, more or less unknown to medicine."[116]

Henri Secrétan, the leading Swiss medical expert on accidents, recounted the story of a young man, who fell from a horse onto the soles of his feet, complaining of pain in his left leg. He became so expert in mimicking the effects of sciatic back injury that he received three months' pension. He walked badly and was once even found lying in the street, after which he claimed he could no longer even visit the doctor and was treated at home. Finally, it was decided to perform an operation on his sciatic nerve. At the moment the operation began, he was overcome by a *terreur panique,* threatened all present, and "galloped from the hospital."[117]

The complaint of nonxistent injuries, nervous ailments, paralysis, or muscular pains after an accident was common. Even more so was the exaggeration of minor injuries.[118] It was rare for workers to continue working after incurring even a minor injury that required a dressing, and the payment of lump sums for permanent minor injuries that were not especially debilitating, such as the loss of a toe or part of a finger, was considered a special incentive for abuse.[119] The effects of old illnesses or injuries were often presented as the product of a recent accident, and doctors were especially warned to examine all hernia cases with special attention to the possibility of *anciennes lésions*.[120] The French law in particular seemed to encourage this kind of abuse precisely because it entirely excluded occupational illness from compensation. Ailing workers, the experts charged, often provoked or simulated an accident in order to achieve their *juste dû* for uncompensated illnesses.[121] French Socialists countered such charges, however, by pointing out that the conditions of work often produced slower and less dramatic ailments that could only be denied compensation by the cold-blooded and narrow interpretation of the 1898 law and, more important, that employers often sacrificed safety measures in order to pay insurance premiums.[122]

In his comprehensive report to the Congrès International des Accidents du Travail in Rome in 1908, Charles Juillard graphically described what he called "the fecundity of the human spirit in imitation."[123] Where the indemnity was equal to or approximated the salary of the victim, the tendency to prolong the period of absence from work was "a constant preoccupation."[124] Juillard concluded that "provocation and simulation have reached the proportions of a plague."[125] French workers were also accused of using the half-day pay they received for convalescence "to satisfy their alcoholic passion, retarding the cure indefinitely."[126] Secrétan estimated that twenty of every hundred days paid by insurance companies could have been normal workdays. These figures, he emphasized, only referred to "absolutely abusive idleness" and not to minor injuries for which claims were paid, which would "raise the figure considerably."[127] Some doctors noted false claims as high as thirty or forty percent and, in a sensational report, a railway physician, Dr. Möller of Kirschseeon, Germany, declared that ninety percent of all claims brought to his attention were fraudulent.[128]

In France the question of medical confidentiality (*le secret médical*) was widely debated in the interest of making doctors more responsible for reporting fraudulent claims to the state authorities.[129] Doctors were encouraged to ignore their sympathies for "some poor devil whose claims were ill founded" and to remain firmly within the law, lest the abuses proliferate.[130] German doctors too were pressed "to combat the epidemic of simulations in all its forms," and "to build a dam against hysteria and simulation."[131] Despite such stern warnings, some physicians saw it as a *grande illusion* of the legislators and jurists to believe that medical experts could be the shock troops of the "struggle for the pension."[132]

Physicians, on the other hand, sometimes complained that service on the official employee health boards (*Krankenkasse*) forced them to act not only as therapists but as "expert medical judges of whether social services should be provided or not."[133] Often, they permitted claims to extend beyond the intent of the law. Because of the lack of health coverage, French doctors were sometimes motivated by the "desire to extend the notion of *risque professionnel* to injuries which are the indirect results of work."[134] Illnesses that result from extreme physical or mental fatigue were sometimes awarded compensation, since for the physician it was "preferable to limit the unemployment of an insured who does not show any objective injury, than to contest the unemployment of a worker whose inflammation absolutely prevents him from working for several weeks."[135]

Greater familiarity with the cases brought up for review led many medical specialists to reverse themselves and admit that the initial perception of fraud was exaggerated, and that the medical profession should not rush to judgment in the denunciation of the accident victim. Dr. Carl Thiem, one of the leading German authorities on illnesses related to accidents, noted in his oft-cited *Handbuch der Unfallerkrankungen* (1898) that "as a result of my most recent experiences I can no longer maintain my earlier view of ten percent simulation."[136] If exaggerations were common, "real simulations" or "deceit" were "uncommonly rare." He concluded that most diagnoses of fraud later proved mistaken, and with greater experience "the previously assumed percentage of simulated accidents stands in an inverse relationship to scientific knowledge." Often, Thiem added, a case worsened after the original medical report written by the employer corporation physician was made. Even when the victim produced a more favorable report from his or her own private physician, he advised doctors not to resort to a "Pfui" when confronted with such documents, except for the most egregious cases of doctors who sought to expand their fees and practices by providing such exaggerated reports. He also counseled physicians involved in cases with the Imperial Insurance Office to act as "technical assistants," and for those who wanted to act as judges "to study law and not medicine."[137]

In his speech to the International Congress of Social Insurance in Rome, Juillard distinguished five separate types of abuse including "tolerable or excusable abuse," "inevitable abuse," "avoidable abuse," and "criminal, punishable, and fraudulent abuse."[138] For example, "precautionary abuse" usually meant the prolonged care of an injury during convalescence and could hardly be condemned—the Germans, in fact, called such necessary extensions of compensation during the period following cure, *Schonungsrente*. "Inevitable abuse," was systemic; for example, it concluded the faking of an accident where a severe occupational ailment did not warrant compensation.[139] A German doctor even identified "honest simulation" as an abuse also created by the insurance system; for example, when an accident victim confronted with a medical expert who "systematically reduces the indemnity to which he is entitled," embellishes his symptoms.[140] In short, earlier predictions of rampant fraud, drawn largely from statistical arguments, were revised on the basis of greater familiarity with the injuries themselves.

Such modifications, however, hardly balanced the bellicosity of physicians, academics, and publicists who continued to warn that the "pestilence of fraud" was "a cancer on the organism of our entire working population" and stood in "a direct and causal relationship" to the accident insurance law.[141] In his widely read polemic, *Unerwünschte Folgen der deutschen Sozialpolitik,* published in 1913, the nationalist economist Ludwig Bernhard claimed that only the British economy profited from the fact that "the [German] working class has in part succumbed to the "pension addiction" that has crippled its energy and joy in work."[142] The ever-vigilant Coustan warned that the new law was "a clear menace to the laboring Frenchman," who, "upon entering the hospital or the bedchamber as a result of an occupational accident, dreams of only one thing—not of departing cured, but of departing with an income."[143]

Class Struggle for the Pension

After 1900, the physician took center stage in the "struggle for the pension," which the burgeoning insurance claims produced. In France the awarding of a pension depended on medical certification by an expert attached to the firm or, in Germany, to the Imperial Insurance Office, which could rarely be challenged by the victim. Especially in France, where there was no parallel health insurance system, the certification of a claim often meant the difference between a pension or none at all. Insurance medicine was a specialization produced by social policy legislation, leading to an almost instant enmity between medical experts and worker's representatives.

In Germany, the Socialists closely monitored the problem of insurance abuse, claiming that the almost exclusive focus on abuse and fraud only diverted attention from the failure of German industrialists to introduce effective accident prevention. From the outset, the Social Democrats counterpoised worker protection (*Arbeiterschutz*) to workers' insurance, emphasizing protective legislation, state surveillance, and safety devices as opposed to compensation.[144] In France the Conféderation Générale du Travail (C.G.T.) emphasized the need for more factory inspectors, a shorter work week, more rest days, and above all safety measures.[145] Victor Griffuelhes, secretary of the C.G.T., charged that French judges were being "counselled" on their responsibility to find cases in favor of the companies.[146] Socialists insisted that the accident issue was tied to dangerous working conditions, inadequate safety precautions, long hours, fatigue, and the intensification of work, all of which contributed to the burgeoning number of claims.[147]

Even before the 1884 law was adopted, German Social Democrats denounced the notorious passage in the "*Denkschrift*" (the memorandum drafted by the Bochum industrialist Louis Baare, which was the basis for Bismarck's Reichstag speech), which referred contemptuously to the hypothetical worker who "intentionally places himself in danger" in order to "live an enviable life as a pensioner," or of the "*lebensmüde*" worker who commits industrial suicide "in order to secure the future existence of his family."[148] Once the German law was passed, the Socialists charged that medical experts assigned to insurance cases through the employer corporations were partisan to the industrialists. Though initial statistics showed the most serious accidents to be declining, the reality, they protested, was that compensation was being systematically reduced. Physicians attached to the employer corporations were awarding only partial disability claims in more severe cases and overburdening accident victims by refusing to acknowledge less serious claims. The Social Democrats accused the professional association of company doctors (Institut der berufsgenossenschaftlichen Vertrauensärtze) of having only one purpose: "to send the worker back to work as soon as possible."[149]

The Socialists were extremely bitter about the overall trend of judgments by the Imperial Insurance Office which, by 1906, reflected a clear "shift to the disadvantage of the victims."[150] "The employer's charges of *exorbitant burdens,* and the complaints of certain doctors about *pension mania,* have apparently, at least partly served their purpose."[151] German workers' slang included the term *Rentenquetschen* (rent-squeeze) to describe the behavior of company physicians who "declare every small improvement to be a major one to justify a reduction of the pension."[152] Doctors were also reluctant to challenge the opinions of their colleagues and feared that if their own judgments were challenged, "the claims of the injured would expand beyond all bounds."[153]

Accident Neurasthenia

One major area of dispute was not, however, accidents in general, but an ambiguous form of accident claim in which psychological rather than physical effects of the accident prevented the worker from returning to the job.[154] Sudden accidents or near-misses which did not result in gross physical injury were those most likely to produce the symptoms of traumatic neurosis because, as Freud later explained, the anxiety that allowed the individual to "work through" the incident was often absent. Victims were haunted by dreams, whose purpose was to "master the stimulus [the accident shock] retrospectively by developing the anxiety whose omission was the cause of the traumatic neurosis."[155]

Labeled *Unfallneurasthenie, Unfallhysterie, Rentenneurose,* or *Unfallneurose,* these newly discovered disorders were the subject of enormous controversy in the medical and popular press, a sort of dress rehearsal for the notoriety that they would receive some years later as "war neuroses." With accident insurance, cases of this type swelled, and institutions reported numerous patients suffering from accident-related neurasthenia and hysteria. The Sanitorium der Landesversicherungsanstalt Beelitz, near Potsdam, for example, reported a rise from eighteen to forty percent in the number of patients suffering from worker's neurasthenia in the period from 1897 to 1903.[156] "If Bismarck had foreseen what an inflation of nervous weakness and nervous suffering, including complete mental breakdown, that social legislation would cause," said one doctor acquainted with these cases, "he would have certainly prevented its introduction."[157] The most common manner of handling such complaints was a prescription of the "healing power of work" and to return the "accident-hysteric" to the scene of the mishap as soon as possible.[158] The only way to to eliminate this contagion, another prominent doctor argued, was to absolutely refuse any compensation for traumatic neurosis, even if it meant that legitimate cases were deprived of a claim.[159]

For the moderate German Socialists, grouped around the *Sozialistische Monatshefte,* this attitude was another callous form of medical abuse: "a healthy nervous system soon overcomes a serious mental shock, but an already weak or sick one will show symptoms of illness much sooner, and these are what are classified under the concepts of accident-neurasthenia and hysteria."[160] What the press failed to report, they noted, was how many cases later proved that the doctor had been mistaken and that there was indeed "a serious mental disturbance resulting from the accident."[161] Often cited was the well-publicized case of a miner in Gelsenkirchen, who, after surviving a catastrophic cave-in, complained of severe headache and nervousness and was declared a fraud until he suffered a complete mental breakdown. Echoing the view of the New York psychologist George Beard, who had invented the term, the Socialists claimed that neurasthenia was the disorder of civilization, or "American Nervousness," as Beard called it. They argued that the "increase in complaints of simulation was closely related to the growth of nervous disorders, which unfortunately have found a wide basis among the working population." "This rise of nervous suffering is not a direct consequence of social legislation," as critics of the law had argued, "but an indirect consequence of the enormous economic development which Germany has undergone in the last century."[162] In 1897, the Imperial Insurance Office confirmed their arguments: the diagnosis of "traumatic neurosis" explains "a large number of apparent contradictions, that is, phenomenological combinations which contradict our logical, scientific preconceptions and experiences, but of which we know one thing, that they are not *consciously simulated.*"[163]

Accidents and the Triumph of Fatigue

The new role of social knowledge in the politics of the workplace provided a unique opportunity for a relatively unknown community of European physiologists and hygienists, who, since the early 1890s, had been assiduously investigating the phenomena of fatigue, energy, and efficiency in industrial work. Until the early 1900s advocates of the newly emerging European "science of work" (*Arbeitswissenschaft* or *Science du Travail*) had been confined to laboratory investigations of the impact of modern industrial tasks on worker's physiology and psychology.[164] Although new methods of measuring fatigue, most notably Angelo Mosso's *ergograph* (1884), could provide reliable data on the course of individual fatigue, few practical uses could be found for these new discoveries. The controversy over industrial accidents provided its advocates with new evidence and a new issue to demonstrate their shared conviction that fatigue was not only a scourge for the worker, but for the expenditure of energy in the nation as a whole. If fatigue could account for industrial accidents, their social character could be demonstrated.

Moreover, the science of work was becoming an international movement, assisted by the growing number of international organizations concerned with the accidents issue: The International Congress of Hygiene and Demography, the International Congress of Industrial Accidents, and the International Congresses of Social Insurance. These organizations did not merely facilitate exchanges of information, but afforded the social hygienists and physiologists advocating a scientific solution to the worker question a forum to demonstrate their approach to the accidents issue. In both Germany and France the mandatory reporting of accidents made a careful study of the time, day, and nature of the occurrence possible for the first time. Analysis of the distribution of accidents during the day and the week would, the industrial hygienists speculated, reveal a correlation between fatigue and the cause of most accidents: "The number of accidents would increase as the workers became more tired, and the distribution of those accidents according to the hours of the day in which they occur would furnish a means to evaluate the degree of fatigue of the workers who are victims."[165] If proven, this hypothesis would finally lay to rest the charges of deception and chicanery while irrefutably demonstrating the social character of the accident as a consequence of the nature of the modern work experience. Such evidence would establish the necessity for state intervention in the workplace, for more progressive legislation, and above all for a reduction of the length of the working day.

Armand Imbert, a Montpellier physician and reformer who attempted to demonstrate the utility of scientific expertise for solving the "worker question," denied that it was either worker's simulation and greed, or negligence and callousness by management that accounted for the vast majority of incidents. The complaints of rising worker abuses by the insurance companies, of excessive premiums by the *patrons,* of duplicity by medical experts, and of the denial of their claims by the workers, was not, he argued, "an inevitable consequence of the conflict of opposed interests."[166] It was a "profound error," he claimed, "to regard the workers and the insurance companies as natural enemies."[167] Imbert disputed the claims of the medical experts and insurance companies with the same statistics they cited to perpetrate the great fear of simulation and fraud. Exaggerated claims could also be attributed to the relationship between the indemnity and the availability of work, he noted: where there was little work, for example, among longshoremen, a half-day compensation might even amount to the equivalent of double the normal wage.[168] "A great number of accidents result directly from a state of physical or cerebral fatigue of the worker at the moment when he is victimized," he claimed, "and it is easy to provide multiple proofs of this assertion, which . . . would result in the possibility of greatly reducing the number of victims."[169]

In his observations of the dockworkers of Sète, Imbert concluded that the private insurance companies were wrong to believe that the disproportionate number of accidents, as opposed to other ports, indicated the likelihood of organized fraud and premeditation on the part of the workers. Rather, since the tonnage of merchandise handled at Sète was far greater than at other dockyards, fatigue was also more marked: "The larger number of accidents thus appears as a physiological consequence of the particularities of the work, independent of the struggle between the workers and the bosses."[170]

In order to graphically prove his point, Imbert (with the Inspecteur du travail of the département of Hérault, M. Mestre) undertook a series of detailed investigations of the 2,065 accident victims in that department in 1903.[171] The accidents generally climbed uniformly in the period before the midday break, repeating that pattern even more acutely during the afternoon, with the highest proportion of accidents falling in the last few hours of work. They concluded that "the influence of occupational fatigue, given our mode of organization of work, on the production of accidents" was undeniable.[172] The statistics revealed that "the number of accidents more than doubled in the course of each half-day," and conversely, showed the considerable impact of midday rest on the number of accidents occurring at the beginning of each afternoon. Fatigue, Imbert noted, "renders the worker less able to avoid an unexpected accident, because he is unable to respond with an effort as intense, or with movements as rapid, as in the normal state."[173]

Imbert predicted that a significant reduction in accidents would result from a half-hour rest pause during each half day in all industries. Society could not remain indifferent to the deterioration of the energy-producing organism, he declared:

> it is dangerous, moreover, in view of the complete development of that organism and its future efficiency to extract a usage that is too premature and too intensive; it is not indifferent, on the other hand, to how many hours of work are consumed, and whether those hours are consecutive or punctuated by one or many rest periods.[174]

Statistics collected from other departments, as well as in Germany, Belgium, and Sweden, confirmed the fatigue-accident correlation: "industrial accidents occur in a definite relationship to the hours of the day."[175] An 1897 German study of the distribution of accidents showed that there were twice as many plant accidents in the three hours before midday break than in the previous three hours, and that the most accidents occurred between 3 and 6 P.M.[176] What was previously thought to be the result of negligence or carelessness on the part of the worker, "in the great majority of cases now appears as the consequence of the onset of fatigue."[177]

In the German case, however, the fact that the number of accidents falling on Monday was greater than those falling on Saturday indicated that "besides work itself, the conduct of life is of decisive importance for safety and for the question of fatigue."[178] Delicately put, reports of disappearance of "*Blauer Montag*" (Saint Monday) were premature.[179] Even the Socialists, who rarely commented on the issue, began to complain of the high rate of drunkenness during working hours.[180] The French also noted the higher relative accident rate for Monday vis-à-vis the other weekdays. Imbert studied the accidents in Hérault in 1904 by days of the week, finding that though there was a higher accident frequency on Mondays, the figures were deceptive since "a good number of workers rest on Monday from the fatigue of Sunday, which diminishes, in a proportion that is impossible to determine with precision, the working population on the first day of the week, and increases the relative importance of the Monday accident rate."[181]

By 1900, many physicians with industrial experience agreed that the struggle against the effects of alcoholism on the workplace was an essential aspect of labor's well-being. Social hygienists trained in preventive medicine and sympathetic to the Socialists promoted the general spread of "hygienic culture," demanding the expansion of communal health services and educational programs. The German Association for Social Medicine, founded in 1905, put pressure on local authorities and fostered research into the social conditions of workers' health.[182]

The statistical data yielded an even more unexpected result. Against all predictions, as the hours of work decreased, the accident rate rose even more sharply. The German industrial hygienist, Emannuel Roth, admitted in his detailed report to the 1907 Congress of Hygiene and Demography, that the "progressive rise in general accidents stands in a certain causal relationship to the reduction of labor time, and to some extent represents its reverse side."[183] If the reduction of labor time produced greater fatigue and accidents as a result of the intensification of work, the exclusive emphasis of reformers like Imbert on a shorter workday or rest periods was misplaced. The shortening of the workday represented at best "the equivalent of the greater intensity of the activity."[184]

The accident question brought into focus what was already evident to both labor and capital: that the shortening of labor time created a new problem, the speed-up of the machinery to compensate for lost time.[185] As Roth pointed out, it was crucial that

> the intensity of work, the energy expended for a given work process within a specific period of time not exceed a certain amount. The energy expended does not depend simply on the absolute amount of work, but also on the distribution of the work over time. Thus, the true art of work is not to exceed the amount of energy which the organism can tolerate without permanent damage.[186]

It was becoming increasingly clear that the real issue was not simply wages and hours, but control over the speed and tempo of work, over time and motion.

> The question of fatigue of the working class could not simply be limited to the question of the hours of work, or even to the organization of work and the design of the workplace, from a more or less technical point of view, but to a large number of other questions of a social, economic, personal and psychological nature.[187]

Concern with fatigue, time and motion, and the quality of the work environment reflected deep social changes in the nature of the factory. "Chronic fatigue and exhaustion," noted one of the resolutions adopted in 1907 at the International Congress of Hygiene and Demography, [is] "observed in all factories where the intensity of labor is regulated by the machine."[188] The reduction of fatigue would greatly reduce the number of accidents, and science could thus provide the means to effect a profound change in the nature of work. In some occupations, for example, the amount of energy expended during a normal workday was so excessive that the fatigue accumulated did not permit the "elimination of wastes" during the hours of rest. At the onset of the next day, the worker was "impregnated with poisonous substances."[189]

But even such "more or less restrained" proposals were met with the resistance of all parties concerned. Imbert's sensational findings on the causes of industrial accidents, which were cited, for example, in the Socialist Minister of Commerce Alexandre Millerand's report to the President of the Republic and widely republished, did not remain uncontested. The industrialists' *Revue Industrielle* carried a biting rebuttal in its October 8, 1904, issue by Philippe Delahaye entitled "La prétendue fatigue des ouvriers envisagée comme cause des accidents du travail." Delahaye criticized Imbert and Mestre for "a priori" applying the explanation of fatigue "to the statistics," and denounced their suggestions for reform as "irreconcilable with the conditions of industrial work."[190] Imbert and Mestre responded in kind, noting that one does not have to affirm or deny a priori the existence of exhaustion, on that subject we can form an opinion by observation alone."[191] The trade unions also resisted efforts to reduce labor time so long as they were not matched by wage payments for the lost time.

By the end of the first decade of the century, experts on accident claims were convinced that the efficient deployment of the energies of society could not be realized in the atmosphere of class antagonism, and that the state should provide the necessary surveillance to ensure "a permanent medical supervision of all manufacturing enterprises."[192] The work of the body had to conform to the laws of energy rather than to the imperatives of politics. The economic advantages of such supervision were evident: by reducing accidents, "the deterioration of the sources of energy on which prosperity depends" could also be lessened.[193] Such radical prescriptions naturally provoked skepticism about the practicality of the science of labor. As Hector Depasse, a member of the Conseil superieur du travail and a liberal politician, remarked as early as 1895: "it is possible, to a certain extent, to supervise the employment of time, but how do you supervise the employment of energy?"[194] Nevertheless, the testimony of the accident experts was echoed in the French parliamentary debates on the length of the workday, particularly in the discussions of February 1912, when Catholic reformers as well as Marxian Socialists like Edouard Vaillant made use of Imbert's work to emphasize the "evident relation between the long day and the industrial accident."[195]

Certainly this expectation that the state would perform the task of ensuring a thorough rationalization of the workplace in the interests of both capital and labor was premature. In fact, though the state in both Germany and France expanded greatly its supervision of industry before World War I, it was not until after the war that anything approaching effective surveillance became widespread. The accident issue was in many respects a laboratory for the kinds of social experiments that later began the march toward a postwar socialization of the industrial sphere and the rise of the rationalization movement in both Germany and France.[196]

Despite the differences between state insurance in Germany and the private system adopted in France and elsewhere, the debates on the definition of the accident, on the causes of the burgeoning statistics, and on the extent of fraud and simulation were remarkably similar. The protracted debates on the causes and definition of industrial accidents, the question of the modernity of risk, the crisis of simulation and fraud, and the political debates which these issues engendered, reflected a new tendency to subject work to a wide range of knowledge: legal, medical, statistical, sociological, and technical. The abolition of negligence corresponded to a new conception of risk which no longer sought the blame for an accident in the weaknesses of individual character, but in the shared hazards of industrialization. The importance of legal experts, who debated the definition of an accident as linked to the time, circumstances, and nature of the work, and the appearance of medical experts who adjudicated claims attested to the new forms of professional knowledge that emerged as a consequence of new social legislation. The rise of positivism as a neutral social discourse—in the concept of social risk, in the medical mediation of disputes, in the analytics of statistical tables, and in the science of work—all represented a changed politics of knowledge.

Yet, as this chapter has tried to show, the politics of knowledge was hardly a terrain free of conflict. As liberals challenged the assault of the new legislation on the free labor contract, conservatives were skeptical of the linkage between modernity and risk, and socialists in both France and Germany disputed the narrow definition of an accident and challenged the partisanship of medical authorities in awarding claims. Professional experts also offered new techniques of accident prevention and new methods of ferreting out illegitimate claims. The study of fatigue as the primary cause of industrial accidents revealed the relationship between worker physiology and the rhythms and organization of work. In short, with the advent of social reform legislation, work became the object of a wide range of state-sanctioned interventions and analyses: health and safety regulation, frequent inspection, statistical surveys, legal decisions, and medical opinion. Though the scientific language of positivism was always evident, the claims of expertise were hardly immune to the political tensions that characterized the industrial arena. The subjection of work to knowledge did not eliminate social conflict, but it displaced the direct conflict of classes onto the plane of intellectual exchange, politicizing knowledge.

This project was supported by the German Marshall Fund of the United States.

Notes To Chapter 2

1. See the suggestive paper by Peter Wagner and Björn Wittrock, "Social Sciences and Societal Developments: The Missing Perspective." *Wissenschaftszentrum Berlin für Sozialforschung* Papers, pp. 87–94 and the introduction to this volume.

2. Hans-Ulrich Wehler, *The German Empire 1871–1918*. Kim Traynor, trans. Dover: Berg Publishers, 1985, p. 133.

3. Florian Tennstedt, *Vom Proleten zum Industriearbeiter: Arbeiterbewegung und Sozialpolitik in Deutschland 1800 bis 1914*. Cologne: Bund-Verlag, p. 291.

4. Ibid., p. 335.

5. See Dietrich Rueschemeyer and Ronan Van Rossem, "The Verein für Sozialpolitik and the Fabian Society: A Study in the Sociology of Policy-Relevant Knowledge," in this volume.

6. Cited in Tennstedt, *Vom Proleten zum Industriearbeiter,* p. 370.

7. See Theodor M. Porter, *The Rise of Statistical Thinking 1820–1900*. Princeton: Princeton University Press, 1986 and Ian Hacking, "How Should We Do the History of Statistics." *I&C: Power and Desire, Diagrams of the Social* (Spring 1981): 14–26.

8. Judith F. Stone, *The Search for Social Peace: Reform Legislation in France 1890–1914*. Albany: State University of New York, 1985, pp. 38, 39.

9. Raoul Jay, *La protection légale des travailleurs*. Paris: L. LaRose 1904, p. 129.

10. François Ewald, *L'Etat providence*. Paris: Grasset, 1986; Jacques Donzelot, *L'invention du social: Essai sur le déclin des passions politiques*. Paris: Fayard, 1984.

11. The great pioneer of the worker's survey and conservative reformer, Louis-René Villermé devoted a pioneering article to the mechanized accident in 1850, L.-R. Villermé, "Accidents occasionnés par les appareils mécaniques dans les ateliers industriels." *Annales d'Hygiene Publique et de Médecine Légale* 43 (1850): 261–89. Most early nineteenth-century hygienists, however, generally held to the traditionalist view (based on seventeenth-century medical treatises) that the work environment in specific trades—especially the long-term effects of toxic substances in the air, gaseous vapors, poor ventilation, inadequate light, and sundry unsanitary conditions—were ruinous to health and reduced longevity. See Arlette Farge, "Les artisans malades de leur travail." *Annales (Economies, Sociétés, Civilisations)* (September, October 1977): 993–1007; Bernard-Pierre Lécuyer, "Les maladies professionnells dans les 'Annales d'hygiène publique et de médecine légale' ou un première approche de l'usure au travail." *Le Mouvement social* (July, September, 1983): 45–60; Alain Cottereau, "Usure au travail, destins masculins et destins féminins dans les cultures ouvrières en France au XIXe siècle." *Le Mouvement social* (July, September 1983): 71–112.

12. Georg Zacher, "Unfallstatistik." In Johannes Conrad, Ludwig Elster, Wilhelm Lexis, Edgar Loening, eds., *Handwörterbuch der Staatswissenschaften,* 3rd ed. Jena: Gustav Fischer 1911, p. 56; H. Mamy, "Aperçu des succès obtenus par les mesures préventatives contre les accidents." *Bericht über den XIV. Internationalen Kongress für Hygiene und Demographie,* Berlin, 23–29 September 1907 (Berlin, 1908), IV(2): 663.

13. Véronique Brumeaux, La question des accidents du travail à la fin du XIXe siècle. *Mémoire de maîtrise*. Université Paris X-Nanterre, 1979, p. 73.

14. Labor historians have often overlooked this *terra peligrosa*. An exception is Dieter Groh, "Intensification of Work and Industrial Conflict in Germany 1896–1914." *Politics and Society* 8:4 (1978): 387.

15. Philippe Hesse, "Les accidents du travail et l'idee de responsabilité civile au XIXe siècle." *Histoire des Accidents du Travail* 6 (1979): 36. The position of German industrialists is discussed in Monika Breger, *Die Haltung der industriellen Unternehmer zur staatlichen Sozialpolitik in den Jahren 1878–1891*. Frankfurt am Main: Haag Herchen 1982), pp. 87, 88.

16. Paul Kampffmeyer. "Die Gewerkschaften und die Arbeiterschutz- und Arbeiterversicherungsgesetzgebung." Sozialistische Monatshefte 1:1 (January 1904): 35, 36.

17. Cited in Brumeaux, La question des accidents du travail, p. 109.

18. See Anson Rabinbach, *The Human Motor: Energy, Fatigue and The Origins of Modernity.* New York: Basic Books, 1990.

19. Georg Zacher, "Arbeiterversicherung in Deutschland. In Conrad et al., *Handwörterbuch,* p. 800; H. B. Oppenheim, *Die Hilfskassen und Versiche rungskassen der arbeitenden Klassen*. Berlin, 1875; Max Hirsch, *Die gegenseitigen Hilfskassen und die Gesetzgebung*. Stuttgart, 1876; Albert Schäffle, *Der korporative Hilfs-kassenzwang*. Tübingen, 1884. In France it was not until the 1830s that the legal status of the *sociétés de secours mutuels* was restored. Before 1848, more than 1,088 such associations were founded. G. Hubbard, *De l'organisation des sociétés de prévoyance ou de secours mutuels*. Paris, 1852, Georg Zacher, "Arbeiterversicherung (Frankreich)." In Conrad et al., *Handwörterbuch* pp. 820–39.

20. Zacher, "Arbeiterversicherung in Deutschland," pp. 797–801; William Harbutt Dawson. *Social Insurance in Germany 1883–1911, its History, Operation, Results*. London: T. Fisher Unwin 1912, pp. 8–11.

21. Dawson, *Social Insurance in Germany,* p. 9.

22. Zacher, "Arbeiterversicherung in Deutschland," p. 788.

23. For a close analysis of Bismarck's views on the law, see Walter Vogel, *Bismarck's Arbeiterversicherung: Ihre Entstehung im Kräftespiel der Zeit*. Braunschweig, 1951, especially chap. X. On Bismarck's social policy see Albin Gladen, *Geschichte der Sozialpolitik in Deutschland: Eine Analyse ihrer Bedingungen, Formen, Zielsetzungen und Auswirkungen*. Wiesbaden: Franz Steiner Verlag; Klaus Witte, *Bismarck's Sozialversicherungen und die Entwicklung eines marxistischen Reformverständnisses in der deutschen Sozialdemokratie*. Cologne: Paul Rugenstein Vlg., 1980; Vernon Lidtke, "German Social Democracy and German State Socialism 1876–1884." *International Review of Social History* 9 (1964): 202–25.

24. Zacher, "Unfallversicherung." In Conrad et al., *Handwörterbuch,* p. 49.

25. Though workers were required to contribute to the sickness insurance, they did not directly support accident insurance. However, workers indirectly contributed to the accident system since a substantial portion of the accident insurance fell under sickness insurance, for example, the first thirteen weeks of disability (*Karenzzeit*). In Germany, Austria, and Luxembourg workers contributed two-thirds, employers one-third to the sickness insurance system. In Hungary, Norway, Italy,

Finland, the Netherlands, and Luxembourg, workers were also not required to make any contribution to the accident insurance.

26. Zacher, "Arbeiterversicherung in Deutschland," p. 804.

27. Fanny Imle, "Das schweizerische Kranken- und Unfallversicherungsgesetz und sein Schicksal." *Sozialistische Monatshefte* 4 (1900): 410.

28. See, for example, the debates of the *Congrès International des Accidents du Travail et des Assurances Sociales,* 5th Congress, Paris, 25–30 June 1900, pp. 18–22 (hereafter cited as *C.I.A.T.A.S.*).

29. R. van der Borght, "Arbeiterversicherung (Allgemeines)." In Conrad et al., *Handwörterbuch,* p. 787; T. Bödiker, *Arbeiterversicherung in den europäischen Staaten.* Leipzig, 1895; Maurice Bellom, *Les lois d'assurance ouvrière à l'étranger.* Paris, G. Roustan 1892; and Georg Zacher, *Die Arbeiterversicherung im Auslande,* 5 vols. Berlin, 1898–1908.

30. Alfred Manes, "Arbeiterversicherung (Belgien)." In Conrad et al., *Handwörterbuch* p. 819; M. Magaldi, "Rapport sur la législation italienne des accidents du travail et son application." *C.I.A.T.A.S.,* p. 23.

31. F. L. Finninger, *The Workman's Compensation Act 1906-1909.* London: Stevens 1910, pp. 14–24.

32. Carl Gersuny, *Work Hazards and Industrial Conflict.* Hanover, NH: University of New Hampshire Press, 1981, pp. 98, 99.

33. R. van der Borght, "Arbeiterversicherung (Allgemeines)," p. 790.

34. Ibid.

35. Else Conrad, *Der Verein für Sozialpolitik und seine Wirksamkeit auf dem Gebiet der gewerblichen Arbeiterfrage.* Jena: Gustave Fischer 1906, p. 86.

36. Morton J. Horowitz, *The Transformation of American Law 1780-1860.* Cambridge, MA: Harvard University Press, 1977, p. 228.

37. Jacques Donzelot attributes this shift "from contract to status" to the deskilling of work. See Jacques Donzelot, "Pleasure in Work." *Ideology and Consciousness* 9 (Winter, 1981, 1982): 3–28; and *L'invention du social,* pp. 121–78.

38. The persistent efforts of the German government to introduce criminal prosecution for breach of contract—a measure directed against strikes—was also predicated on the overriding principle of the state as guardian of the social order. Conrad, *Der Verein für Sozialpolitik,* pp. 151–57; Alfred Böninger, *Die Bestrafung des Arbeitsvertragsbruchs.* Tübingen: Verlag der Lauppschen Buchhund-lung 1891.

39. Yvon Le Gall, *Histoire des Accidents du Travail.* Nantes: l'Université des Nantes, 1982, p. 23.

40. See Stone, *Search for Social Peace,* pp. 99–123; Sanford Elwitt, *The Making of the Third Republic: Class and Politics in France 1868-1884.* Baton Rouge: Louisiana State University Press, 1975.

41. Cited in Stone, *Search for Social Peace,* p. 106.

42. Ibid.

43. Albert Berger, *Modifications introduites dans la législation des Accidents du Travail,* 1902. Paris: J. B. Baillière et Fils, 1903, pp. 2, 8.

44. Le Gall, *Histoire des Accidents du Travail,* p. 35.

45. Ibid., pp. 15, 17.

46. Cited in Hesse, "Les accidents du travail," p. 34.

47. Ibid., p. 29.

48. Le Gall, *Histoire des Accidents du Travail,* p. 36.

49. Berger, *Modifications Introduites dans la législation des Accidents du Travail,* p. 4.

50. Henri Secrétan, *L'Assurance contre les accidents: observations chirurgicales et professionnelles,* 3d ed. Geneva, Libraire A. Eggiman & Cie. 1906, p. 110.

51. Emile Cheysson, "France, Les assurances ouvrières," *Congrès International des Accidents du Travail et des Assurances Sociales, Bulletin du Comité Permanent* (1893): 329 [hereafter cited as *C.I.A.T.A.S. Bulletin*].

52. Ibid.

53. Berger, *Modifications Introduites dans la législation des Accidents du Travail,* p. 7.

54. *C.I.A.T.A.S.*

55. Hubert Coustan, *De la simulation et de l'evaluation des infirmités dans les accidents du travail.* Montpelier, 1902, p. 14.

56. *C.I.A.T.A.S.* p. 95.

57. See Richard F. Kuisel, *Capitalism & The State in Modern France: Renovation & Economic Management in the Twentieth Century.* Cambridge: Cambridge University Press, 1981, pp. 8–26.

58. *C.I.A.T.A.S.* p. 19.

59. "Le projet de loi sur les accidents du travail au Comité international des accidents." *Revue pratique des droit industriel* (1893): 449; Le Gall, *Histoire des Accidents du Travail,* p. 11; Hesse, "Les accidents du travail, p. 55.

60. Hesse, "Les accidents du travail," pp. 12, 36; Le Gall, *Histoire des Accidents du Travail,* p. 7.

61. Berger, *Modifications Introduites dans la législation des Accidents du Travail,* p. 5; Hesse, "Les accidents du travail," p. 23.

62. Brumeaux, La question des accidents du travail, p. 81.

63. Ernst Gruner, *De la Responsabiité des accidents du travail d'un point de vue chrétien.* Nimes, 1891.

64. Le Gall, *Histoire des Accidents du Travail,* p. 37.

65. Hesse, "Les accidents du travail," p. 39.

66. Jules Jamin, *Critique médicale de la loi sur les accidents du travail* diss. Paris, 1902, p. 12.

67. Voge, *Bismarcks Arbeiterversicherung,* pp. 68–70; Lujo Brentano, *Die Arbeiter-versicherung gemäss der heutigen Wirtschaftordnung.* Leipzig: Duncker & Humblot 1879; *Der Arbeiter-versicherungszwang, seine Voraussetzungen und seine Folgen* Berlin: C. Habel 1881.

68. Conrad, *Verein für Sozialpolitik,* p. 86.

69. *Schriften des Vereins für Sozialpolitik,* Bd. XLVII, p. 258.

70. Gustav Schmoller, "Haftpflicht und Unfallversicherung." *Schmoller's Jahrbuch* (1881): 311. Also see Dieter Lindenlaub, *Richtungskämpfe im Verein für Sozialpolitik, Vierteljahrschrift für Sozial- und Wirtschaftsgeschichte, Beiheft* Nr. 52 Wiesbaden: Franz Steiner Verlag 1967, pp. 44–52.

71. *Stahl und Eisen: Zeitschrift der nordwestlichen Gruppe des Vereins deutscher Eisenhüttenleute* 7 (No. 8) (1887), p. 585.

72. Cited in Hesse, "Les accidents du travail," p. 5.

73. Cited in Le Gall, *Histoire des Accidents du Travail,* p. 45.

74. Zacher, "Unfallstatistik," p. 47.

75. Gruner, "Résultats Statistiques des six prémieres années," Franz Steiner Verlag p. 74.

76. "Extraits du procés-verbal officiel de la séance de la chambre des députés, du 28 octobre 1897." *C.I.A.T.A.S. Bulletin* (1897), p. 396.

77. *C.I.A.T.A.S. Bulletin* (1897), p. 396.

78. Cited in Coustan, *De la simulation,* p. 15.

79. Maurice Bellom, "La quatrième session du congrès international des accidents du travail et des assurances sociales." *C.I.A.T.A.S. Bulletin (1897),* p. 516.

80. Dietrich Milles, "From Worker's Diseases to Occupational Diseases: The Impact of Experts' Concepts on Workers' Attitudes." Paul Weindling ed., *The Social History of Occupational Health.* Dover, NH: Croon Helm, 1985, pp. 55–77.

81. Georg von Mayr, "L'assurance et la fréquence des accidents." *Congrès International des Accidents du Travail et des Assurances Sociales.* 1–6 October 1894 Milan: Reggiani 1894, p. 344.

82. Reichsunfallgesetz, § 1., Abs. 7.

83. Ludwig, Fuld, "Der Begriff des Betriebsunfalles im Sinne der deutschen Gesetzgebung." *Archive für soziale Gesetzgebung und soziale Statistik* (1888): 418.

84. The legislative draft of 1881 noted that the purpose of the law was to compensate either victims (or heirs) of accidents caused by "occupational work characterized by the danger of accident." Heinrich Rosin, "Der Begriff des Betriebsunfalls als Grundlage des Entschädigungsanspruchs nach den Reichsgesetzen über die Unfallversicherung." *Archiv für Öffentliches Recht* 3 (1888): 419.

85. Ibid., p. 320.

86. Reichsversicherungsamt, *Amtliche Nachrichten* III:355 (hereafter cited as R.V.A./A.N.).

87. Rosin, "Der Begriff des Betriebsunfalls," p. 330.

88. Fuld, "Der Begriff des Betriebsunfalles," p. 421; "Betriebsunfall." In Hrsg. Eugen Baumgartner, *Handwörterbuch des gesamten Versicherungswesens einschliesslich der sozialpolitischen Arbeiter-Versicherung.* Strassbourg: Verlag Karl J. Trübner, 1899, p. 721.

89. Georg von Mayr, "L'assurance et la fréquence des accidents." *C.I.A.T.A.S.* Milan, 1894, p. 340; also see Georg von Mayr, "Unfallversicherung und Sozialstatistik." *Archiv für soziale Gesetzgebung und Statistik* (1888): 203–45.

90. Ernst Gruner, "Résultats de dix années d'assurance obligatoire en Allemagne et de cinq annés en Autriche." *C.I.A.T.A.S. Bulletin* (1897): 338.

91. *C.I.A.T.A.S.,* p. 98.

92. von Mayr, "L'Assurance ét la fréquence des accidents.," p. 339.

93. *C.I.A.T.A.S.* Bern, 1891, p. 340.

94. Gruner, "Résultats de dix années d'assurance obligatoire," p. 347.

95. von Mayr, "L'assurance et la fréquence des accidents," p. 343.

96. *C.I.A.T.A.S.,* p. 79.

97. Emile Cheysson, "La prévention des accidents." *C.I.A.T.A.S. Bulletin* (1893): 303, 313. The Italian industrialist association also introduced broad measures of accident prevention; see P. Pontiggia, "Aperçu des succès obtenus en Italie par les mesures préventives contre les accidents du-travail." *Bericht über den XIV. Internationalen Kongress für Hygiene und Demographie,* Berlin, 23–29 September

1907. Berlin, 1908, IV(2): pp. 668–73; Mamy, "Aperçu des succès obtenus," pp. 661, 662.

98. "Rundschau," *Sozialistische Monatshefte. Internationale Revue des Sozialismus* IX, 2:7 (1903): 534.

99. Klaus Wagenbach, *Franz Kafka: Eine Biographie seiner Jugend 1883-1912.*, Berlin, Francke Verlag, 1958, pp. 144–49.

100. Konrad Hartmann, "Überblick über die Erfolge der Unfallverhütung in Deutschland." *Bericht über den XIV. Internationalen Kongress für Hygiene und Demographie,* Berlin, 23–29 September 1907. Berlin, 1908, IV(2): pp. 648–59.

101. Ibid., Several journals were devoted to accident prevention: *Concordia: Zeitschrift der Zentralstelle für Arbeiterwohlfahrtseinrichtungen; Gewerblich-Technische Ratgeber; Sozialtechnik.*

102. Henning Rögge, *Fabrikwelt um die Jahrhundertwende am Beispiel der AEG Maschinenfabrik in Berlin-Wedding.* Cologne: DuMont, 1983, pp. 133, 134.

103. Emannuel Roth, *Kompendium der Gewerbekrankheiten und Einführung in die Gewerbehygiene.* Berlin, 2nd ed., Schoertz 1909, p. 2.

104. "Rapport au Ministre du commerce." *Journal officiel* (22 December 1901); Hubert Coustan, *De la simulation,* p. 9.

105. "Bericht der am 13. Januar 1887 stattgefundenen General- Versammlung der Nordwestlichen Gruppe des Vereins deutscher Eisen- und Stahlindusutrieller." *Stahl und Eisen* 2 (February 1887): 125; Gruner, "Résultats Statistiques des six prémieres années," p. 68; also see Breger, *Die Haltung der industriellen Unternehmer,* pp. 87–89.

106. Fritz Stier-Somlo, "Ethik und Psycholgie im deutschen Sozialrecht." *Archiv für Rechts- und Wirtschaftsphilosophie* 1 (1907/1908): 232–47.

107. Ibid., p. 247.

108. Coustan, *De la simulation,* p. 13.

109. Ibid., p. 9.

110. Ambroise Tardeiu, *Étude médico-légale sur les blessures.* Paris: J. B. Baillière et Fils, 1879, p. 449. The standard military medical work is Duponchel, *Traité de médecine légale militaire.* Paris: Filix Alcan, 1890.

111. Tardieu, *Étude médico-légale sur les blessures,* p. 452.

112. René Sand, *La simulation et l'interpretation des accidents du travail.* Brussels: Maloine, 1907. For some other works of this genre see: R. Giraud, *Étude sur les blessures simulées dans l'industrie.* (Lille: Thèse, 1893; Jamin, *Critique médicale de la lois sur les accidents du travail*; P. Chavigny, *Diagnostic des Maladies Simulées dans les Accidents du travail.* Paris: J. B. Baillière et Fils, 1906.

113. Secrétan, *L'assurance contre les accidents,* p. 75.

114. Alfred Bienfait, "La recherche de la simulation chez les victimes des accidents du travail." *Congrès international médicale des accidents du travail à Liége,* 29 May 1905, *Rapports et Communications.* Brussels, 1905, question vi, p. 5.

115. Rene Michaud, *J'avais vingt ans.* Paris: Editions Syndicalistes, 1967, cited in Patrick Fridenson, "Genese de l'usine nouvelle." *Recherches* 32/33 (September 1978), p. 381.

116. J. Juillard, "Simulation et abus dans les assurances ouvrières au point du vue médicale," *C.I.A.T.A.S.* Rome, 1908, p. 812.

117. Secrétan, *L'assurance contre les accidents,* p. 78.

118. Bienfait, "La recherche de la simulation chez les victimes des accidents du travail," p. 5.; S. Baudry, *Étude médico-légale sur les traumatisme de l'oeill et de ses annexes*. Paris: J. B. Ballière et Fils, 1904, p. 54

119. Juillard, "Simulation et abus dans les assurances ouvrières au point du vue médicale," p. 801.

120. E. Patry, "De l'utilité de l'examen de tous les assurés au point de vue de la hernie." *Revue Suisse des accidents du travail* (1908): 193.

121. Juillard, "Simulation et abus dans les assurances ouvrières au point du vue médicale," p. 809.

122. Brumeaux, La question des accidents du travail, pp. 116, 117.

123. *C.I.A.T.A.S.*, p. 79.

124. Secrétan, *L'assurance contre les accidents, p. 7.*

125. Juillard, "Simulation et abus dans les assurances ourvrières au point du vue médicale," p. 813.

126. Georges Touchard, "Lenteur judiciaire." *Nouvelle Revue* (October 1903): 43.

127. Secrétan, *L'assurance contre les accidents,* p. 109.

128. P. Möller, "Die Simulation in der Unfallversicherung." *Kompass* (1909): 20, 40.

129. Paul Camille Brouardel, *La responsabilité médicale*. Paris: J. B. Baillière et Fils, 1898, pp. 72–88; and the debate at the Congrès International de médecine légale in Brussels, 4 August, 1894, reported in *Annales de hygiene et de médecine légale* 38 (1897): 379; Charles Valentino, "Critique du secret médical." *Revue Scientifique* 13:2 (24 September 1904): 390–94.

130. Secrétan, *L'assurance contre les accidents,* p. 77.

131. Stier-Somlo, "Ethik und Psychologie," p. 247.

132. Secrétan, *L'assurance contre les accidents,* p. 78.

133. Alfons Labisch, "Doctors, Workers and the Scientific Cosmology of the Industrial World: The Social Construction of 'Health' and the 'Homo-Hygienicus'." *Journal of Contemporary History* 20:4 (October 1985): 599–616; Uwe Frevert, "Professional Medicine and the Working Classes in Imperial Germany." *Journal of Contemporary History* 20:4 (October 1985): 637–58.

134. Secrétan, *L'assurance contre les accidents,* p. 107.

135. Ibid.

136. Dr. Carl Thiem, *Handbuch der Unfallerkrankungen auf Grund Artzlicher Erfahrungen*. Stuttgart: Verlag Ferdinand Enke 1898, p. 38.

137. Ibid., p. 39.

138. Juillard, "Simulation et abus dans les assurances ouvrières au point du vue médicale," p. 802.

139. Ibid., p. 805.

140. Paul von Bruns, "Die traumatischen Neurosen-Unfallneurosen." In Nothnagel, ed., *Spezielle Pathologie und Therapie,* Bd. XII, Teil 1. Vienna, 1901, p. 96.

141. Cited in Paul Kampffmeyer, "Tendenzwissenschaft gegen Sozialpolitik." *Sozialistische Monatshefte* 1:1 (January 1913): 11.

142. Ludwig Bernhard, *Unerwünschte Folgen der deutschen Sozialpolitik*. Berlin, 1913.

143. Coustan, *De la simulation,* p. 7.

144. Witte, *Bismarck's Sozialversicherungen;* for the distinction between *Arbeiterschutz* and *Arbeiterversicherung,* see Hertha Wolff, *Die Stellung der Sozialdemokratie zur deutschen Arbeiterversicherunggesetzgebung von ihren Entstehung an bis zur Reichsversicherungsordnung.* (Diss.) Freiburg, 1933.

145. Paul Louis, *L'ouvrier devant l'état.* Paris, 1904, p. 283; M. Pierrot, *Le travail et surmenage.* Paris, 1911, pp. 27–29. For a detailed study of the eight-hour-day movement, see Gary Cross, "The Quest for Leisure: Reassessing the Eight-Hour-Day in France." *Journal of Social History* 18:2 (Winter 1984): 195–206.

146. Victor Griffuelhes and Louis Niels, *Les objecifs de nos Luttes de classes.* Paris: La Publication Sociale, 1909, p. 19.

147. Witte, *Bismarcks Sozialversicherungen,* pp. 114–19; also Paul Kampffmeyer, "Die Gewerkschaften und die Arbeiterschutz- und Arbeiterversicherunggesetzgebung." *Sozialistische Monatshefte* 1:1 (January 1904): 35, 36.

148. Anon. "Bismarcks soziales Programm." *Der Sozialdemokrat* 41/42 (17 October 1880).

149. Rudolf Wissell, "Täuschung und Übertreibung auf dem Gebiet der Unfallversicherung." *Sozialistische Monatshefte* 1:10 (June 1909): 635.

150. Julius Frässdorf, "Die Rechtsprechung in der Unfallversicherung." *Sozialistische Monatshefte* 2:9 (September 1906), p. 786.

151. Ibid. Also see Johannes Heiden, "Die Rechtsprechung in der Arbeiterversicherung." *Sozialistische Monatshefte* 2:9 (September 1909): 1115–23.

152. Frässdorf, "Die Rechtsprechung," p. 787.

153. Robert Schmidt, "Der Streit um die Rente." *Sozialistische Monatshefte* 1:5 (June 1909): 422; Frässdorf, "Die Rechtsprechung," p. 787.

154. Robert Schmidt, "Simulation im Streit um die Unfallrente." *Sozialistische Monatshefte* 2:14 (1908): 878, 879.

155. Sigmund Freud, *Beyond the Pleasure Principle.* James Strachey, trans. *The Standard Edition of the Complete Psychological Works of Sigmund Freud,* Vol. XVIII (London, 1955), p. 32. Also see Otto Lipmann, *Unfallursachen und Unfallbekämpfung* Veröffentlichungen aus dem Gebiete der Medizinalverwaltung, Band 20, Heft, 3, Arbeitswissenschaftliche Monographien aus dem Institut für angewandte Psychologie in Berlin (Berlin, 1925).

156. P. Leubischer and W. Bibrowicz, "Die Neurasthenie in Arbeiterkreisen." *Deutsche medizinische Wochenschrift* 21 (May 25, 1905): 820–24; M. Schönhals, *Über die Ursachen der Neurasthenie und Hysterie bei Arbeitern.* Berlin, 1906. A survey of the neurasthenia diagnosis among workers indicates that, in contrast to the hysteria diagnosis, neurasthenic symptoms were more equally distributed along age and gender lines.

157. Dr. Franz Schröter, "Über die Simulation bei den Versicherungsanstalten." *Ärtzliche Zentralanzeiger* (April/May 1909): 13.

158. Schmidt, "Streit um die Rente," p. 425.

159. Dr. Sachs, *Die Unfallneurose, ihre Entstehung, Beurteilung und Verhütung.* Breslau, 1908, p. 17.

160. Schmidt, "Streit um die Rente," p. 422.

161. Wissell, "Täschung und Übertreibung," p. 630.

162. Ibid., p. 633.

163. R.V.A./A.N. (1897), p. 474.

164. Rabinbach, *The Human Motor,* Chaps. 7, 8; and "The European Science of Work: The Economy of the Body at the End of the Nineteenth Century." In Steven Kaplan and Cynthia Koepp, eds., *Work in France.* Ithaca: Cornell University Press, 1986, pp. 475–513.

165. A. Imbert and M. Mestre, "Statistique d'accidents du travail." *Revue Scientifique* 13:11 (September 24, 1904): 386.

166. Armand Imbert, "Les accidents du travail et les compagnies d'assurances." *Revue Scientifique* 1:23 (4 June 1904): 711.

167. Ibid., p. 718.

168. Ibid., p. 712.

169. Ibid.

170. Armand Imbert, "Le surmenage par suite du travail professionnel." *Bericht über den XIV. Internationalen Kongress für Hygiene und Demographie,* Berlin, 23–29 September 1907. Berlin, 1908, IV: 1, p. 644.

171. Armand Imbert and M. Mestre, "Statistique d'accidents du travail," pp. 385–90.

172. Ibid., p. 386.

173. Imbert, "Les Accidents du travail," p. 715.

174. Imbert and Mestre, "Statistique d'accidents du travail," p. 385; Imbert cited statistics from nine additional departments in the area around Toulouse which show strikingly similar general characteristics. Imbert and Mestre, "Statistique d'accidents du travail," p. 387.

175. Emannuel Roth, "Ermüdung durch Berufsarbeit." *Bericht über den XIV. Internationalen Kongress für Hygiene und Demographie,* Berlin, 23–29 September 1907. Berlin, 1908, IV:1, p. 618; H. Bille-Top, "Die Verteilung der Unglücksfälle der Arbeiter auf die Wochentage nach Tagesstunden." *Zentralblatt für allgemeine Gesundheitspflege* Jg. 27 (1908): 197; Hugo Münsterberg, *Grundzüge der Psychotechnik.* Leipzig: Verlag von Johann Ambrosius Barth, 1914, p. 394.

176. Roth, *Kompendium,* pp. 14, 15.

177. Ibid., p. 15.

178. Roth, "Ermüdung durch Berufsarbeit," p. 606.

179. On the fate of *blauer montag,* and *saint lundi* in the late nineteenth century, see Josef Ehmer, "Rote Fahnen—Blauer Montag: Soziale Bedingungen von Aktions-und Organisationsformen der frühen Wiener Arbeiterbewegung." In Detlev Puls, ed., *Wahrnehmungsformen und Protestverhalten: Studien zur Lage der Unterschichten im 18. und 19. Jahrhundert.* (Frankfurt am Main: Suhrkamp 1979, pp. 143–174; Douglas A. Reid, "Der Kampf gegen den 'Blauen Montag'1766 bis 1876," in ibid., pp. 265–95; Susanna Barrows, "After the Commune: Alcoholism, Temperance and Literature in the Early Third Republic." *Consciousness and Class Experience in Nineteenth Century Europe,* John Merriman, ed., New York, 1979, pp. 205–18; Jeffrey Kaplow, "La fin de la Saint-Lundi, étude sur le Paris ouvrier au XIXe siècle." *Temps Libre* 2 (1981): 107–18.

180. Edmund Fischer, "Trinken und Arbeiten." *Sozialistische Monatshefte* 1:5 (May 1908): 360–67.

181. Armand Imbert and M. Mestre, "Nouvelles statistiques d'accidents du travail." *Revue Scientifique* 4:17 (October 21, 1905): 525.

182. Frevert, "Professional Medicine and the Working Classes in Imperial Germany," p. 643.

183. Roth, "Ermüdung durch Berufsarbeit," p. 619.

184. Roth, *Kompendium,* p. 13.

185. Fridenson, "France-Etats Unis," p. 382.

186. Roth, *Kompendium,* p. 12.

187. Zaccharia Treves, "Le surmenage par suite du travail professionnel." *Bericht über den XIV. Internationalen Kongress für Hygiene und Demographie,* Berlin, 23–29 September 1907. Berlin, 1908, IV:1, p. 626.

188. Armand Imbert, "Le surmenage par suite du travail professionnel au XIVe congrès international d'hygiène et de démographie Berlin, 1907." *L'Année Psychologique* (1908): 243.

189. Imbert and Mestre, "Nouvelles statistiques d'accidents du travail, p. 522.

190. Philippe Delahaye, "La prétendue fatigue des ouvriers envisagée comme cause des accidents du travail." *Revue Industrielle* (8 October 1904): 408.

191. Imbert and Mestre, "Nouvelles statistiques d'accidents du travail," p. 520, and A. Imbert and M. Mestre, "A propos de l'influence de la fatigue professionnelle sur la production des accidents du travail." *Revue Industrielle* (5 November 1905): 449.

192. Imbert, "Le surmenage par suite du travail professionnel au XIVe congrès international d'hygìene et de démographie." Berlin, 1907, p. 232.

193. Imbert, "Les Accidents du travail," p. 717.

194. Hector Depasse, *Du travail et de ses conditions (Chambres et Conseils du travail*). Paris: J. B. Baillière et Fils, 1895, pp. 52, 53.

195. Séance du 22. Fév. 1912, Journal Officiel du 23, fév, p. 416. Cited in Jean Desplanque, *Le problème de la réduction de la durée du travail devant le parlement français.* Paris: Libraire Arthur Rousseau, 1918, p. 179.

196. See Charles Maier, *Recasting Bourgeois Europe: Stabilization in France, Germany, and Italy in the Decade After World War I.* Princeton: Princeton University Press, 1975, pp. 544, 567, passim.

3

Social Science and the Building of the Early Welfare State

TOWARD A COMPARISON OF STATIST AND NON-STATIST WESTERN SOCIETIES

BJÖRN WITTROCK AND PETER WAGNER

MANY ASPECTS of the linkage between social knowledge and the origins of social policies can be analyzed in the context of a double institutional transformation—that of political institutions, which is usually termed the emergence of the welfare state, and that of scientific institutions, which can be labeled the "rise of the research-oriented university."[1] Late nineteenth- and early twentieth-century North American and West European societies were deeply affected by a conjunction of these two long-term processes. This conjunction was clearly not coincidental, as shall be argued in more detail below, but different sets of rules, as they were embodied in the respective institutions, came to bear on the actions of individuals involved in these processes.

The achievement of early social-policymaking implied a major transformation of the modern Western states. It went along with marked changes in discourses on society, changes which have often been portrayed as the very emergence of modern social science in its professionalized and disciplinary forms. It would be no gross overstatement to argue that the foundations of both the system of political institutions and its welfare policies and the system of scientific institutions and its rules for social science discourse, as they exist to the present day, were laid in this period in the late nineteenth and early twentieth centuries. Each of these two transformations, that is, in the relations between state institutions and society and in the academically legitimated discourses on society, had a major impact on the other. Taking this hypothesis and the questions that follow from it seriously involves taking issue with many of the views on social science developments which were long the predominant ones.

Institutions and Discourses: Beyond Functional Reductionism and Non-Agential Internalism

The social sciences have often been seen as little but a mirror of social and political processes. Many observers hold that, as Daniel Lerner wrote three decades ago, "the roots of social science lie in its responsiveness to the needs of modern society for empirical, quantitative, policy-relevant information about itself."[2] In recent years, similar statements have been echoed time and again in both academic and public discourse: "The key social science disciplines were conceived as intellectual responses to the 'social question' of the nineteenth and twentieth centuries."[3] Such statements acknowledge, albeit on a highly general level, the social nature of all social knowledge. However, they are largely unable to account for cognitive structures which are transmitted in intellectual traditions or embodied in the rules of scientific institutions. Thus, they tend to systematically neglect the ways in which such structures constrain and enable new ways of understanding, and dealing with, societal transformations such as industrialization and urbanization. Indeed, the very phrasing of the "social question" was the first step to a new cognitive framework for the analysis of deep-seated transformations of society. Against the intellectual shortcut inherent in most such functional accounts, Michel Foucault—ambiguous though his position may be in some respects—stated clearly that, while it is without doubt important to look at the French Revolution, and at the changes which its consequences entailed for societal balances, it is equally important to understand that the appearance of sociological thinking, the very possibility to make humans and society the object of scientific thought, has also to be regarded as "an event internal to the order of knowledge."[4]

Once one takes issue with a functional reduction of knowledge to the needs of societal and systemic interests in the study of intellectual developments, however, it has been notoriously difficult to avoid the opposite tendency to conceive of discourses as ordered entirely by their own inner logic and dynamics. Two major analytical positions may be discerned that share this view but that have highly different implications. The first one is discourse analysis of the Foucaultian type, an archeology of discourse formations, their origins, rise, and fall, which focuses on the changing elements and structures of the discourse and only indirectly alludes to particular societal and institutional contexts and to the effects of human agency in those contexts. At least in this respect, Foucault has been rightly criticized even by sympathetic readers: "Although nondiscursive influences in the form of social and institutional practices constantly intrude into Foucault's analysis he must locate the productive power revealed by discursive practices in the regularity of those same practices. The result is the strange notion of regularities which regulate themselves."[5] Foucault's response to criticisms of this sort was to link the notions of discourse and power, thus trying to complement his analysis of systems of thought with a political theory of modern society. This linkage, however, was conceived in a rather conflationary way, which opened his conceptualization to the reverse reproach. Thus it could, and sometimes was, seen as a sophisticated version of an implicit functionalist reasoning with concomitant risks of reducing discourse practices to mere reflections of an all-pervasive and permeating system of functionally necessary power relationships.[6]

Another—and much more prevalent—analytic tradition links an internalistic history writing to what might be termed a "whiggish" self-understanding of the development of disciplinary social discourse.[7] In this perspective, contemporary forms of disciplinary discourse appear as epitomes of intellectual advances. Earlier contributions are invoked so as to help constitute a tradition leading up to this particular form of knowledge and self-reflection. Not seldom the result is a serious misrepresentation of the actual variation of alternative discourses existing at any point in history in a given setting. Discourses are then depicted as evolving along their own self-defined paths and exclusively according to internally constituted systems of rules.

An interesting and highly articulate example of this type of analysis is Edward Shils's cross-national account of the early development of the social sciences in terms of "an ecological process as well as a process of institutionalization." His perspective is far from any simple view of the emergence and evolution of the social sciences as a linear process of enlightenment and an internally driven progress of reason. One of Shils's key categories is the notion of intellectual traditions, which, as the foundations of knowledge evolution, he sees as having a spatial extension as well as a cognitive component. The evolution of these traditions is not merely an intellectual process but a process in which institutionalization provides constraining and enabling rules and "affects the direction of the spatial movement of ideas" just as it is a mechanism of the "elaboration, promotion, or suffocation of ideas."[8] However, once full academic institutionalization is achieved—in Shils's view, this occurred in rudimentary form in turn-of-the-century United States—the basic requirements for an autonomous intellectual development are met. The stage is then set for orderly discourse and growth of knowledge in the social sciences. "External" influences continue to play a role and may be reflected in the substantive focus of social science research. However, such influences no longer lead to fundamental redefinitions of the "consolidated central tradition," nor do they imply systematic intellectual redirections, such as processes of "epistemic drift" toward subordination to bureaucratic worldviews in the modern interventionist state.[9]

Shils's analysis, thus, stops exactly at that point of social science developments on which this volume focuses. To him the development of the academically established social sciences is, if not unproblematic, then largely a given condition and sociologically, therefore, not very interesting. To the contributors to this volume, in contrast, the debates and struggles around the institutionalization of the social sciences, or at least certain aspects of the contemporary discourses on society, were highly interwoven with the political conflicts about early social policies. Social-knowledge production and social-policymaking were similarly uneven processes and, as such, require careful comparative investigations. Such investigations of discourse transformations may shed light on the conceptual conditioning of political struggles, and studies of political-institutional changes may similarly elucidate ways in which the structuration of discourse has been socially conditioned.

In such a perspective, this chapter looks at the structuration of the social sciences, in the period of their academic institutionalization and disciplinary demarcation in the context of the formulation of early social policies. Such policies were formulated against the backdrop of new social knowledge elaborated and propagated, often from positions of intellectual and social authority. The forms in which social science approaches emerged were in turn related to the specific distribution of positions of authority—intellectual and political—in different societies. Within the wide range of linkages between social scientists and social-policy makers, one major distinction may be made between statist and non-statist societies, the former being mostly the Continental European ones, and prime examples of the latter being the United States and the United Kingdom. The effects of this divide will be explored throughout. The final section of this chapter will then focus on the consequences of such an analysis for a comparative-historical sociology of entire social formations.

The Discursive Constitution of Social Policies and the Structuration of the Social Sciences

All societies under analysis in this volume saw themselves as in some fundamental way faced with "the social question" in the latter part of the nineteenth century. Immense intellectual efforts were devoted to exploring ways of solving that question, efforts which in many cases came to translate into the constitution of new types of policies such as accident, old age, or sickness insurance.

The policy innovations related to solutions for the social question involved a major societal reorientation. Thus the protagonists of poverty relief, in the one case, and for workers' accident insurance, in the other, were perfectly well aware of the fact that the creation of new collective institutions might involve a major step in a fundamental reorganization of society. A basic form of argument of the proponents of innovation was that society itself had changed and needed institutional adaptation. Industrialization had changed the nature of work and of wealth; what was required were new concepts of risk and of poverty. In Rabinbach's words, "the idea of social risk was a phenomenon of modernity, a recognition that impersonal forces rather than individual wills were often the determinants of destiny." Such a discourse, to be found in the words of many contemporary actors, entailed a decisive break with a traditional individualist liberal idea of society.[10]

In a traditional liberal perspective, "the social question" should not have emerged in the first place. More or less automatic adaptation of individual wills and preferences would have precluded persistent imbalances of this sort. Such a belief, however, had lost most of its plausibility when poverty and hardship spread, when the increase in the wealth of the nation appeared to be delayed for too long for too many, when uncertainty prevailed after many people had moved out of the social contexts they were socialized into, and when they had already begun to resort to collective action. Reform movements during the latter half of the nineteenth century tried to reestablish a degree of solidity and certainty in the social fabric by way of collective action rather than individual adaptation.

Intellectuals in the late nineteenth and early twentieth century were generally well aware of the shortcomings of liberal theory, in politics as well as in economic matters. In intellectual terms, classical sociologists had started from liberal assumptions, had recognized that societal developments had superseded classical liberalism, but insisted that revisions had to be made that preserved a basic continuity of that political tradition.[11] They faced a societal constellation that seemed to call for a major political realignment and sought to grasp this situation in broad conceptual terms and to outline a possible vision that might serve as guideline in a process of restructuring. Unable to stick to the idea of a quasi-automatic regulation of social conflicts but similarly unwilling to move away completely from the tenets of classical liberalism, they devoted their analytical efforts to the search for those phenomena which might provide for a sustainable development of society.[12] Theories of "organic solidarity" and the relationships between religion and morality as in Durkheim, of forms of legitimate domination and "charisma" in Weber, of the political class and the "circulation of elites" in Vilfredo Pareto were all examples of such attempts at reconceiving somehow orderly relations between extended social practices, uprooted social identities, and polities in need of adaptation.

However, this apparent parallelism in attention to problems cross-nationally must not conceal the fact that both solutions sought and, indeed, the precise nature of the problems perceived, were premised on significantly different discourses and institutional constellations. In fact, the proposals for reorganization showed great variety. In a first step, this variety may be traced to different ways of transcending the limitations of a traditional liberal conception of society.

For France, this change can be closely related to the traumatic experience of the failed revolution of 1848. Before that, republicans often argued that any hesitation to transfer sovereign power from the king to the people was nothing but a delay which would exacerbate social conflicts around the issue of the legitimacy of the central power. However, when the National Assembly of 1848 immediately came into conflict with its own electorate over the latter's social interests, a conflict which in the course of three years led to the end of the republic, then it became evident that the mere form of a democratic polity was no solution to the issue of societal organization. In a broad sense, it may be argued that this insight formed the basis for all subsequent formulations of the "social question" in the French context. In the words of Jacques Donzelot, "the social question appears first of all as the identification of a deficiency in social reality with regard to the political imaginary of the Republic."[13]

In contrast to Italy and Germany, in France the republican political imaginary was undisturbed by any allegedly unsolved national question. In the former two countries, however, political intellectuals fused their ideas about an enlightened state with the need to ground it on a culturally and linguistically homogeneous people. Again, 1848 was a crucial year, a year in which the national-liberal revolts failed. In the wake of this defeat, the "political professors" of the *Vormärz* gradually accustomed themselves to the idea that the realization of political liberties somehow could be postponed, if the ruling elites were only ready to push ahead with nation-building. At the same time, forceful new social movements were on the horizon also in these countries. In Germany, Lorenz von Stein wrote about French socialist and communist movements to alert his compatriots, and Robert von Mohl tried to describe a liberal state from the experience of the regulating state of absolutism and with a view to the need for social intervention in the future. In Italy, the intellectuals of the *Risorgimento* increasingly recognized that national unity, should it come, would find the elites unprepared. Some of them strongly advocated empirical and statistical inquiries to know the heterogeneous parts of the new state better. Statistics was proclaimed the science of democracy in the new nation-state, a science that would consider every citizen as an entity with equal status.

All foresight notwithstanding, the process of nation-building in the decade between 1861 and 1871 changed the terms of political debate and the orientations of social scientists markedly in both Germany and Italy. Ultimately, the idea of social betterment through social knowledge had found the appropriate addressee, the nation-state.[14] The identification of social science and national problems was most pronounced in Germany. The Verein für Sozialpolitik (Association for Social Policy), the most important German social science organization until far into the twentieth century and a model for many others, was founded in 1872/73 immediately after the inauguration of the Reich. Its founders left no doubt about the intimate linkage between the two events: "Now that the national task is about to be accomplished, it is our foremost duty to contribute to solving the social question."[15]

Common to all these social science approaches was that they were directly defined with a view to social and political objectives. Many of their proponents were located in academia, but this was not yet a distinguishing criterion of great relevance. The Fabian Society in England and also the Association for Social Policy were explicitly open for nonacademics—often reform-minded individuals in Britain and state bureaucrats in Germany. Public debate and state administration were as important as addresses of the research as fellow academics. Little attention was given to the cognitive link to the other sciences. Frédéric LePlay, who propounded a program of empirical research on the living conditions of families in rural and industrial areas, called his work *science sociale,* an encompassing denomination that never caught hold in French academia. The German *historische Nationalökonomie* (historical national economics) comprised historical and economic as well as legal and social studies. For all these reasons, it seems appropriate to label this kind of social science *ameliorative,* that is, reform- and problem-oriented, in contradistinction to predominantly academic and disciplinary social science.

The specific ways in which the liberal conception of society was rephrased differed between countries not least according to the prior strength of the liberal tradition itself. In the German debates in the Association for Social Policy, the dominant group around Gustav Schmoller adhered basically to a conception of the state as a being with a superior mission standing above class struggles and other particular conflicts in society. Its task, to be pursued through a strong bureaucracy in a monarchic system, was to secure a harmonious development of society, to intervene everywhere conflicts could mount to endanger the well-being of the nation. Seeing themselves called to contribute to the accomplishment of the new state's task, the founders of the Association stressed the healthy continuity of Prussian stateness which, in their view, was the most important asset Germany could draw on when facing the turmoils of industrialization and organized class dispute. They themselves stood, apart from some minority positions, in the tradition of state-centered thinking, from Hegel onward, which saw the state as the embodiment of some higher reason. With all their empirical orientation, they would, therefore, not subject state institutions to social science analysis; the peculiar lack of a political science movement in Germany during this period—as compared with France and Italy, for instance—can be understood in this context.[16]

While there was something of a brief era of liberalism in German states in the mid-nineteenth century, liberal ideas never achieved full societal hegemony in Germany, and liberal institutions flourished only momentarily and only on parts of the territory of the later nation-state. In terms of academic discourse, classical political economy—"Smithianism" or "Manchesterism" as it was called somewhat disdainfully by many scholars—never asserted itself strongly, and in the tradition of the state sciences (*Staatswissenschaften*), it rather remained an interlude. The work of Robert von Mohl, one of the southwestern liberals, has rightly been characterized as transitory:

> Mohl's policy science as a work of transition looks Janus-faced to two eras. On the one side, there is the old police state, . . . much governing, regulating from above, busy and concerned for everything, but without clear objectives and without understanding the bourgeoisie's striving for autonomy; on the other side, the social movements of the second half of the nineteenth century announce their appearance from afar, movements which will pose giant tasks to public administration.[17]

French society, in contrast, was shaped by a relatively successful bourgeoisie striving for autonomy, and her state tradition, while extremely strong, was of a different nature than the German one. The continuity of this tradition was important for the struggles on social policy. It gave the proponents an opportunity not to argue for a complete break with earlier principles, but for a rephrasing of a century-old concern in French politics. "Governments of the Third Republic thought they had the means fully to apply in a methodical way the principles stated in 1789, and they eventually laid down the bases for the modern institutional set of social services in contemporary society."[18] Among these principles, of course, were both freedom, on the one side, and solidarity, on the other. While, as Anson Rabinbach points out (in this volume), under these circumstances it could never be successfully argued that some superior institution could violate freedom of contracts and the equality principle in labor contracts and shift burdens of responsibility for accidents one-sidedly to the employers, as German insurance laws did, it proved possible to propose substantive state intervention in another way, namely through the solidarity principle. Much of the republican debates in the 1880s and 1890s were based on solidarism, a political theory which became something of an official social philosophy of the Third Republic.

Solidarism introduced the idea of society as a sort of a priori collective into political theory and endowed society with rights and obligations which co-existed with and were related to individual rights. Human beings did not enter into relations with others as isolated individuals, but as already social beings; thus, social rights could be formulated alongside individual rights. The theory of solidarity and the political slogans of solidarism had close links to Durkheimian sociology and its grounding of a theory of society in "social facts." The hegemony of the political philosophy of solidarism can hardly be understood if unrelated to the academic discourses. Nor can the successful entry of Durkheimian sociology into academic institutions be analyzed without reference to the political project of building the republic.

In contrast to both France and Germany, intellectuals in the United States have tended to be reluctant to posit state and society as collective entities over or beside individuals. Even if the case for individualist liberalism as the predominant politico-intellectual tradition throughout American history is overstated, the American counterpart to such thought, civic republicanism, is still comparatively much more liberal and individualist than the variants of nationalism, socialism, and organicist social theories that have shaped European debates over the past one and a half centuries.[19] In this context, the continued reluctance to embark on European-style welfare policies in the United States can be related to the lack of a politically feasible intellectual synthesis between "collectivist" and "individualist" positions.[20]

This intellectual specificity of the situation in the United States is mirrored by an institutional feature that has shaped the specific professional strategies of those academic entrepreneurs who advocated social reform.[21] These advocates of reform were opposed to the politics of patronage and corruption, but also distrustful of increasing the power of the state. Instead, they tended to advocate the complementary strategies of reform and competence, a type of "profession-based" social policy. For their colleagues in high-prestige, state-run institutions in Europe, most pronouncedly so in the case of Germany, it came quite natural in intellectual, institutional, and social terms to see the state as the key social policy institution. The American social reformers, however, were not only doubtful about the "rightness" of state intervention in terms of liberal political theory, they had also no reason to connect a reputation-seeking strategy fully to the state. Their authority was to be based on knowledge claims inherent in the existence of strong autonomous professions rather than on the intellectual and social status of representatives of the university as a key institution in the process of nation-building.

Social-policy measures can be interpreted as a way of institutionalizing responsibility of a collective for the fate of its member individuals. They have to determine issues such as the form of being responsive, the occasion of exerting responsibility, membership of the collective (eligibility), and the extension of the collective itself. While all these issues were at stake in the construction of social policies around the turn of the nineteenth century, it is the latter one that made this international wave of policy innovation appear specific, namely as the nationalization of social responsibility. "Social policies" existed in great varieties at the local level before, designed and administered by communes and cities. However, the changes in forms of production and related increase of migration made these practices appear untenable and, often, unjust.

The construction of national social policies should then be seen as an extension of the idea of community. According to the strong current of nationalist thought in Europe during the nineteenth century, it could relatively easily be argued that the nation was the relevant, responsibility-bearing community and the state its collective actor, the head and hand, as it were, in the design and implementation of social policies. In Europe, the nation-state was regarded as the "natural" container of rules and resources extending over, and mastering, a defined territory. This, however, was much less the case in the United States, where no strong central locations of authority existed. If the widening of social responsibility was the issue, professions were then designed as a non-statist way to extend validity claims for knowledge over time and space. The specific professional form of the academic institutionalization of social science in the United States was the result of such considerations and was very far from being seen as a universal model at that time.

Early European social scientists, in contrast, can be described as a professoriate at high prestige, state-controlled academic institutions, as "a closed corporation legitimated by tradition and class position whose authority and power was fully established. . . . Already privileged and influential in the highest circles of government and finance and, in Germany and France, key figures in the state monopoly on education, the professoriate had no wish to alter its ways."[22] These different linkages between institutional positions and intellectual developments should then be more closely examined, and this forms the focus of the following section.

Intellectual and Institutional Transformations Interlinked: Universities and State Structures

The second half of the nineteenth century was the period when the research-oriented university emerged as the key institution uniting the tasks of advanced scientific research, elite training for all core professions of society, and general "liberal" education. Its organizational structure had a decisive impact on the social organization of knowledge in this phase. At the same time, the institutional structures of the nation-states were either formed in the process of territorial consolidation as in Italy and Germany, for instance, or reshaped as a consequence of the strains put on society by immigration and urbanization in the United States, or with the advent of a republic that was born out of deep political crisis as in France. In their cognitive orientations, in their social organizations, and in the way they came to help discursively underpin the search for solutions to "the social question," early social science knowledge and the incipient projects of a science of society were shaped by this conjunction of two major restructurings occurring during the latter half of the nineteenth century.

Broad changes in the role of universities across Europe in the late nineteenth century provided the preconditions for continuous forms of scientific activity. They also created the conditions not only for systematic inquiry on a sustained basis but for the reproduction of such forms of inquiry via the teaching and training of new generations of scholars. In general, systematic social inquiry dates back in Europe to the absolutist period when the monarchic rulers tried to organize the gathering of information on the state of the country, its population, and economic resources. The eighteenth century saw the simultaneous growth of a wide array of state and policy sciences and of inquiries into the *problematique* of that encompassing field of philosophical, economic, and political analysis which went under the overarching label of "the moral sciences." However, during the first half of the nineteenth century, many of these forms of knowledge either lapsed into oblivion or disrepute (Marx's harsh words about "the miserable cameral sciences" being but one expression of such sentiments) or else were being transformed beyond recognition. It is only with the nineteenth century and the rise of the research-oriented university that the precursor projects of modern social science took form as intellectual activities with delimited boundaries and efforts to establish a codification of standards and norms to guide these activities.[23]

This process was not only related to the organizational linkage of research and teaching in the reformed European and American university but premised on it. In practical terms, this linkage entailed that a category of university teachers and professors—rather than, say, amateur scientists or general social reformers—ensured both the production of new knowledge and the standardization and codification of the knowledge stock and its subsequent diffusion in the teaching of new students. "Only professors could decide what was correct (minimum standards) and promising (optimum norms) scientific work and who was thus suitable to be joined into the ranks of the teachers at the university."[24] By the same process, activities at the university came increasingly to be distinguished from "amateur" activities. Scientific knowledge came, maybe for the first time, to be recognized by its institutional locus of production—and this in an institution which had, at best, played a marginal and more normally an adversary role in almost all major intellectual innovations in Europe since the Reformation. However, in late nineteenth-century Europe, "it was less possible than before for the outsider to maintain a standpoint in scientific questions without just being dismissed as 'amateur' by the real scientists, and it became more and more difficult for the outsider to go straight into the university as a teacher in scientific matters."[25]

While the natural scientists were more rapid and more successful in achieving this distinction, setting up standards and norms, much of the social scientists' arguments in their debates of the late nineteenth and early twentieth century can be understood in similar terms. Such a shift in primary orientation, toward academic and away from political criteria, transformed the cognitive structures of social science around the turn of the twentieth century. Durkheim saw the *science sociale* as amateurish and devoted a lot of his energy to carefully defining the relation of his sociology to the already established disciplines of philosophy, psychology, and economics. In the United States, the American Social Science Association (ASSA) witnessed the creation of a number of associations, all branching off with the intent to set a certain intellectual approach on a truly scientific footing and to overcome the eclectic dilettantism of the mother organization. Thus were founded the American Economics Association (AEA) in 1885, the American Historical Association (AHA) in 1884, the American Political Science Association (APSA, actually branching off from AHA) in 1903, and the American Sociological Society (ASS, today ASA) in 1905.[26] In Germany, some of the founding members of the German Society for Sociology (1911), most notably Max Weber, who had started the dispute over value-neutrality a few years before, saw this endeavor as an attempt to overcome the political contamination in much of the Association's work and secure a place for neutral, scientific research and debate.

Demarcations against amateur activities and against other scientific approaches were all part of the strategic actions of the proponents of different scientific projects in their effort to secure both scientific-intellectual legitimacy for their programs and to safeguard an institutional position within the research-oriented university. Once such a position was held, the organizational structure of the university provided conditions for the reproduction of an approach in the form of a scientific discipline.

This university restructuring coincided with the restructuring of states. Social scientists and other scholars or would-be scholars contributed critically both to the shaping of the institutional structure of modern nation-states, to the constitution and construction of national identities, and to efforts at solving major social problems. In so doing, their attempts at formulating and demarcating various intellectual projects were sometimes successful in the sense that these projects could receive a more favored position in institutional terms by way of their societal-political prominence or legitimacy. This process could work directly, as for instance in the case of Anders Kjaer's pioneering work in sampling statistics within the framework of the Norwegian central statistical office, but more often indirectly, as for instance in the case of Durkeimian sociology in France or, though to a much lesser extent, Weberian sociology in Germany. However, this also meant that these projects inevitably tended to be to some extent permeated, not to say contaminated, by a focus on key policy issues of the time. Thus, far from being captured by external actors, discursive programs trying to establish their autonomous position in institutional terms could often only do so by entering into some kind of discourse alliance with a major societal grouping to which they might have a sufficient discursive affinity to be an interesting and useful partner in a dialogue on state and society. Only seemingly paradoxically, thus, it was through their active involvement in these matters that some social scientists were able to promote a move of their discourses away from the immediate reach of the polity.

For Italian sociology, for instance, Giorgio Sola explains: "It is, in fact, national unification, the realization of an independent and united state, the basic process which for Italian sociology has the same role and assumes the same function which for other European sociologies . . . have been fulfilled by the emergence and affirmation of industrial society."[27] A closer look reveals that indeed much the same could be said for the activities of the Association for Social Policy in early German social science and that, in modified terms, the same largely holds true for the changing political structure of the French nation-state with Durkheimian sociology as the "republican ideology" of the secular and democratic Third Republic, which had to assert itself against the resistance of the old aristocratic and Catholic elites.[28]

Thus, the emergence of the social sciences and the cognitive orientations which they would acquire were closely related to the political structures of the societies in which they developed. To be related to political structures implied both being furthered by political interests in social science discourse about society and in social analysis, and in being limited by the specific nature of those interests and by the types of *problematiques* which major elites tended to be preoccupied with—or to neglect, as several derailed and defunct sociological and political science projects in, for instance, the Austrian and the Italian cases amply testify to.

Making universities institutions which simultaneously advanced scientific knowledge and taught this knowledge to practitioners as well as to the following generation of scholars "meant that schools of thought could insure their continued existence after the death or the retirement of their leaders, and so intellectual traditions became organized and embodied in control over resources."[29] Thus, the conditions for continuous reproduction of cognitive orientations were created, at the same time as, of course, structural limits for future cognitive changes were introduced.

Intellectual approaches that were successfully established in this formative period would set institutionally controlled cognitive boundaries for future scientific programs in the same field. A consequence of

> locating much scientific research in university career structures was the "departmentalization" of scientific fields. . . . University departments and research institutes became the institutional location for . . . research resources and the "national" units of intellectual production and coordination. Particular scientific ideals, goals, and standards thus became entrenched in departments as separate "disciplines," and problems or issues which did not fit into such units received little attention. . . . Disciplinary elites, or "establishments," thus become highly influential groups in the direction of scientific research and allocation of awards, both material and nonmaterial.[30]

This process took place in all the countries under consideration here, but to greatly varying extents and in rather different forms. As we see also in Libby Schweber's analysis (in this volume), it was most pronounced in the United States and, probably, least so in the United Kingdom. In the United States, modern universities, significantly extending beyond the activities and ambitions of traditional liberal arts colleges as well as of land grant colleges, were only really being built up in the last two decades of the nineteenth century. Even as late as the late 1920s, a leading American university reformer of the day, Abraham Flexner, soon to found and direct the Princeton Institute for Advanced Study, could complain that American universities were in imminent danger of succumbing to the short-term pressures of markets and users and of losing whatever German-style academic research credibility they had painfully been able to acquire in the preceding decades.[31]

American universities, by virtue both of the fact that they came, in varying ways, to incorporate different domestic and European traditions of higher education and of the fact that they could not expect to routinely establish their own authority in terms of the outflow of authority of a strong state—or take its continued financial support for granted—came to exhibit rather wider terms for their institutional structures and intellectual traditions. Furthermore, in what seems to have been a constructive misunderstanding of the German university model, American institutions were built along a department system and not on the basis of institutes hierarchically directed by the individual chairholder. While the latter system left more room for individual idiosyncrasies, the former enhanced a more organized building of fields of knowledge. The United States became the country where the disciplinary partition of the social sciences became first and most solidly established.

At the other extreme, English universities largely remained wed to the tradition of a nonprofessional and non-research-oriented—and most of all not too specialized—type of liberal education which had characterized them throughout the latter part of the nineteenth century, not least in the field of the humanities broadly conceived.[32] Especially at Oxford and Cambridge, this tradition and its intellectual ideals were clearly related to the role of these universities as loci of elite education with strong informal links to the acting political and administrative elites. Fields such as economics and, not political science but rather, government or politics in many ways developed parallel to their counterparts in the American and European context, although here, as well, the specificities of the higher education institutions and the particular nature of their informal links to government came to exert a powerful influence both on their intellectual development and on the nature of their, largely indirect and limited, impact on policy processes.[33]

Policy and Discourse: Two Paths of State Development

On the basis of such observations, a basic distinction between an Anglo-American and a European path of development can be made, a distinction which rests to a large extent on the different structures of the state. The importance of state structures for the shaping of society can hardly be overestimated in the case of continental Europe. Whether one looks at coalition-building and interest formation, at the workings of higher education institutions, or at the cognitive contents of academic discourses on society, the specificity of continental Europe and its characteristics as "state-centered societies" become clearly visible. Three decades ago, H. Stuart Hughes, in his study of societal discourses around the turn of the century, stressed that "the countries on the Western and Central European Continent shared institutions—and an intellectual heritage in philosophy, law and in the structure of higher education—that presented their leading thinkers with a similar set of problems."[34] And in his account of political restoration after the First World War, Charles S. Maier emphasized in similar terms for France, Italy, and Germany that "despite major differences, the three nations all had traditions of sharp ideological dispute and fragmentation, concepts of liberalism and labels for distinction that set them apart from Britain and the United States."[35]

Far from being a universal model of societal organization, the development of the modern state has its roots specifically in the history of continental European societies.[36] The reference case for state developments is France with its history of early centralization and political consolidation on a rather stable territorial basis within clear boundaries, a development which, in fact, had a structuring impact on the political strategies of elites in neighboring European societies. The essential features of the modernization of the French state in the postrevolutionary period have been aptly captured by Douglas Ashford:

> In hardly more than a decade, France acquired a supreme legal advisory body, the Council of State; a number of highly trained administrative bodies or grands corps, each with their designated duties, privileges and rules; a rigidly hierarchical educational structure . . . ; and a carefully designed territorial structure. Napoleon, distrustful of the common law, also set in motion the systematic codification of the rules and procedures governing every aspect of French Life. . . . Democracy languished while a modern institutional and administrative structure was superimposed on the society.[37]

The existence of such state structures before those "modernizing" processes took shape which political sociologists have long directed their main attention to—democratization and industrialization—makes for the crucial difference between continental European and Anglo-American societies. Ashford describes the formalization of rules—public law—and of central institutions—public bureaucracy—which specify and codify the relation of political authority to societal actors, and which are underpinned by institutions for socialization and rule enforcement which reach deep into societal structures. In comparative terms, such a concept translates as follows: "In Prussia and in some of the other large German states the rationalization of rule left the rationalization of economic production far behind while in England the reverse was the case."[38] State structures, thus, shaped the emergence of those defining characteristics of modern society and gave continental European societies specificities that can only be explained by reference to those rules and institutions.

Such a characterization of the state carries important implications. It describes the state not—merely and grandiosely—as a unitary entity detached from and clearly opposed to civil society, as much of nineteenth-century European social thought would like to have it. In contrast, it sees the state analytically as a set of interrelated rules and institutions, which reach deeply into society and shape the relations between elements of civil society itself. It is in this sense that we have argued elsewhere for a need to analyze the state in constellational and relational, instead of unitary and directional, terms.[39] The adequacy of a state analysis then hinges on its ability to grasp the constellation of rules and institutions in a specific historical setting and the relation of these rules and institutions to societal actors.

In such terms, the specificities of continental European developments as compared to English and American ones need to be characterized. The differences, for instance, between the rising research-oriented university in late nineteenth-century United States, such as Johns Hopkins, Clark, and the University of Chicago, and the state-run German universities, for which it was a constitutive task to provide training for administrators in a well-developed bureaucracy and whose staff was closely aligned with the nation's elites, reside basically in these institutions' different relations to the state and different ways through which they might have an impact on, or are themselves shaped by, state developments. This is similarly true, for that matter, for "private" associations such as the Fabian Society in England, on the one hand, and the Association for Social Policy in Germany, on the other.[40]

After the broader distinction between statist and non-statist societies is established, it becomes easier to historically situate the divergences in state development between the two major Anglo-Saxon countries analyzed in this volume (Great Britain and the United States) and their impact on the processes of policy formation in the late nineteenth and early twentieth centuries. Thus, in both countries, broad movements of social reformers emerged, which advocated social policies on the basis of research findings.[41] Policy differences between them, however, were clearly linked to the different degrees of accessibility of state structures for a particular type of actors, namely social scientists. In the British case of an informally linked "elite culture of rational reform," which the two major universities were part of, this access was relatively unproblematic. In American society, on the other hand, undergoing a process of rapid societal change, old elites were about to be pushed back, and a more formal reorganization of universities as well as a disciplinary professionalization of the discourse on society was one way of ascertaining the establishment of scientific authority in the intellectual field and some degree of closure in terms of advisory legitimacy in the broader societal one. Although there were "progressive coalitions" (Schweber) in both countries, they were of a clearly distinct nature. Insofar as they were successful, they were working, in the British case, through the informal networks of the elites.[42] In the American case, the avenues to policy impact were premised on the new formalization of rules in the scientific institutions, that is, the establishment of social science disciplines, and in the relations between universities and political institutions, that is, on the attempts to link political credibility to scientific authority.

This analysis discerns typical aspects of the respective state structures in the two countries. Thus, in the British case, the "relative statelessness," to use Nettl's problematic term as a shorthand,[43] stems from a gradual, century-long development of rather nonformalized state institutions bound together by an elite culture which is reproduced and, as a comparatively open one, modified in the academic institutions. The British pattern of largely noncodified, localized rule systems reflected the well-entrenched position of a landed aristocracy and commercial and industrial elites, hostile to efforts at formalized, central control and rule. The "statelessness" of the United States, in contrast, dates back to the community orientation and aversion against centralization of the early democratic federation. In this latter context, there is a strong tendency for major policy changes to proceed through the formal establishment of institutions and codification of rules.[44] The social policy innovations forming the focus for this volume are one major example of these features; the New Deal and the reform legislation of the 1960s are two others. Most changes in Britain, in contrast, have involved a process of largely informal adaptations.

Conclusions

The comparative-historical approach, as advocated in this volume and in this chapter, reveals profound differences between countries in the range of political and societal institutions and their relations to each other, differences which appear to account for dissimilarities or even divergences of broad policy developments. These dissimilarities cannot be dispelled by limiting their relevance purely to their temporal positioning, for example, by analyzing them in terms of "delays," or "lags," or some similar concept that might be easily encompassed within a framework of a universal modernization theory. Rather, there are deep-seated institutional and intellectual differences which tend to set the stage for substantially different outcomes in terms of policy and social structure. That is one major reason for the need for an explicitly stated "constellational" or "conjunctional" approach in the study of states and political institutions, an approach that focuses on the specific institutional structures in a given historical situation and takes differences in such historical constellations of institutions as a starting point for an explanation of deviations in developments between countries.

Allowing a focus on spatiotemporal specificities that provide the precise conditions under which social actors are able to give meaning to their existence in the world and to formulate strategies for action, in our view, is a necessary turn away from a view on history as the actorless evolution of abstract, universal processes. To realize the full potential of such a conceptual reorientation, it is essential to consider institutional structures not merely as constraints on human action, but as sets of historically established rules of action and as "containers" of resources and rules, which actors can draw upon and which enable them to pursue their courses of action. The notion of "coalitions of social reform" or "progressive coalitions" between actors differently located in societal institutions, as reiterated in several of the contributions to this volume, is indicative of a conceptualization of this type which starts out from the actions of human beings as they draw on, and are limited by, the institutional structures in which they are situated and which they reproduce—as well as change—through their own actions.[45]

At the same time, however, it is essential to stress that societal institutions develop as interrelated sets of phenomena in a world-historical context. Nation-states, for instance, develop—and possibly increasingly so—in interrelation to and, partly, interdependent with each other. During the nineteenth century, Franco-German relations provide a good case in point for the relevance of such interdependencies for the formation of courses of action as well as for the reconstruction of institutions. Thus, the Prussian university reforms early in the century, as well as administrative reforms—in fields such as taxation, municipal administration, and recruitment of civil servants and military officers—in the same period, were undertaken as a response to the Napoleonic Wars in an attempt to rebuild state power and to lay the foundation for a revival of national strength. Similarly, France experienced a so-called "German crisis of French thinking" after the Franco-Prussian War of 1870/71. The creation of the Ecole Libre des Sciences Politiques, the educational reforms that led to the reshaping of universities in 1896, and even some aspects of early Durkheimian sociological thinking were clearly shaped by this crisis and, in part, by "German models." Such diffusion of institutional models and migration of intellectual traditions never leads to a direct transfer but to a rearrangement in the specific societal setting. But it shows the interlinkage between societies and their joint location in one world history, a fact which simultaneously enables comparability by the existence of joint reference points and limits it, because it also points to the uniqueness of a historical event.

Such an approach, therefore, allows for efforts at situating social formations in a context of world history without subordinating their specificities to stages in a developmental path. Our brief overview has highlighted differences between continental European and Anglo-American states, and inside the two groups. It has also tried to show how these divergences were related to two key transformations that deeply affected each other in most countries under study in the late nineteenth century, namely the rise of research-oriented universities and reform or constitution of nation-states. It is against the backdrop of these two institutional transformations that the social policies of the early welfare states take form, shaped not by abstract rule systems but by human beings interpreting and negotiating images of the social order and probing the reach and force of new policy practices in an age when societal interactions tended to become both less transparent and more extended in spatial and temporal terms. The early welfare state entailed efforts to make some of these societal effects more sustainable and to achieve a degree of reembedding in conditions of greater uncertainty and disruption.

Thus in this period parallel, but certainly not identical, efforts occur in a range of countries to link new forms of knowledge to new discourses on social policy and reform legislation. A clear focus on institutionally situated human agents permits a recognition of such parallels but rules out any interpretation that collapses human action into a sequence of inevitable steps in the unfolding of a process of alleged historical necessity.

Notes To Chapter 3

1. Björn Wittrock, "Dinosaurs or Dolphins? Rise and Resurgence of the Research-Oriented University," In Björn Wittrock and Aant Elzinga, eds., *The University Research System. Public Policies for the Home of Scientists* Stockholm: Almqvist and Wiksell, 1985, pp. 13–37. See also the contributions to Sheldon Rothblatt and Björn Wittrock, eds., *The European and American University Since 1800: Historical and Sociological Essays*. Cambridge: Cambridge University Press, 1993.

2. Daniel Lerner, "Social Science: Whence and Whither," In Daniel Lerner, ed., *The Human Meaning of the Social Sciences*. Cleveland: Meridian Books, 1959, p. 19.

3. "Social Sciences in Disarray," *Times Higher Education Supplement* 678 (November 1, 1985).

4. Michel Foucault, *L'ordre du discours*. Paris: Gallimard, 1971, p. 424.

5. Hubert L. Dreyfus and Paul Rabinow, *Michel Foucault: Beyond Structuralism and Hermeneutics*. Chicago: University of Chicago Press, 1982, p. 84; see also Axel Honneth, *Kritik der Macht*. Frankfurt/M: Suhrkamp, 1985, p. 169.

6. Jürgen Habermas, *Der philosophische Diskurs der Moderne*. Frankfurt/M: Suhrkamp, 1985, pp. 317, 320; see also Leslie A. Pal, "Knowledge, Power and Policy: Reflections on Foucault," In Stephen Brooks and Alain G. Gagnon, eds., *Social Science, Policy, and the State*. New York: Praeger, 1990, pp. 139–58.

7. On the term, see Herbert Butterfield, *The Whig Interpretation of History*. London: G. Bell, 1931; but also Stefan Collini, Donald Winch, and John Burrow, *That Noble Science of Politics*. Cambridge: Cambridge University Press, 1983.

8. Edward T. Shils, "Tradition, Ecology and Institution in the History of Sociology." *Daedalus* 99 (1970): p. 782.

9. Shils, "Tradition," p. 799; the notion of "epistemic drift" is Aant Elzinga's, see "Research, bureaucracy, and the drift of epistemic criteria," In Wittrock and Elzinga, *University Research System,* pp. 191–220.

10. On the changing meaning of poverty and risk in the late nineteenth century, see also François Ewald, *L'Etat-providence*. Paris: Grasset, 1986; and Adalbert Evers and Helga Nowotny, *Über den Umgang mit Unsicherheit*. Frankfurt/M: Suhrkamp, 1987.

11. Steven Seidman, *Liberalism and the Origins of European Social Theory*. Oxford: Blackwell, 1983, p. 278.

12. Pietro Rossi, "La sociologia nella seconda meta del'ottocento: dall'impiego di schemi storico-evolutivi alla formulazione di modelli analitici." *Il pensiero politico* 15, 1 (1982): p. 199.

13. Jacques Donzelot, *L'invention du social. Essay sur le déclin des pas politiques*. Paris: Fayard, 1984, p. 33.

14. On this concept see also Zygmunt Bauman, *Legislators and Interpreter on Modernity, Post-Modernity and Intellectuals*. Cambridge: Polity, 1987.

15. Gustav Schöneberg, one of the initiators, on the occasion of the foundation, quoted after Ursula Schäfer, *Nationalökonomie und Sozialstatistik als Gesellschaftswissenschaften*. Vienna: Böhlau, 1971, p. 286.

16. Peter Wagner, "The Discourse on Politics among the Social Sciences. Political Science in Turn-of-the-Century Europe." In Sakari Hänninen and Kari Pa-

lonen, eds., *Texts, Contexts, Concepts: Studies on Politics and Power in Language*. Helsinki: The Finnish Political Science Association, 1990, pp. 262–81.

17. Hans Maier, *Die ältere deutsche Staats- und Verwaltungslehre*. Munich: Piper, 1966, p. 232.

18. Giovanna Procacci, "Facing Poverty: American and French Philanthropy Between Science and Reform." Contribution to the conference on *Social Knowledge and the Origins of Social Policies*, New York, May 1989.

19. Louis Hartz, *The Liberal Tradition in America*. New York: Harcourt, Brace, and World, 1955; and J.G.A. Pocock, *The Machiavellian Moment*. Princeton: Princeton University Press, 1975, are the two basic references to the debate on American politico-intellectual history. Even the recent debate on communitarianism, apparently a turn to less individualistic reasoning, is held in surprisingly liberal terms, from a European perspective.

20. Procacci, "Facing Poverty."

21. As, for instance, portrayed by Libby Schweber, in this volume.

22. Peter T. Manicas, *A History and Philosophy of the Social Sciences*. Oxford: Blackwell, 1987, p. 209; see also Manicas, "The Social Science Disciplines: The American Model." In Peter Wagner, Björn Wittrock, and Richard Whitley, eds., *Discourses on Society: The Shaping of the Social Science Disciplines*. Dordrecht: Kluwer, 1991, pp. 45–71; as well as Dorothy Ross, *The Origins of American Social Science*. Cambridge: Cambridge University Press, 1991.

23. Björn Wittrock, "The Modern University: The Three Transformations." In Rothblatt and Wittrock, *The European and American University Since 1800*, pp. 303–62. On the following, see in more detail Peter Wagner, *Sozialwissenschaften und Staat. Frankreich, Italien, Deutschland, 1870–1980*. Frankfurt/M: Campus, 1990.

24. Rolf Torstendahl, "Transformations of Professional Education in the Nineteenth Century." In Rothblatt and Wittrock, *The European and American University, Since 1800*, p. 139.

25. Rothblatt and Wittrock, *The European and American University Since 1800*, p. 122.

26. Among a great number of analyses, we note some of the most recent ones: Manicas, "The Social Science Disciplines"; and John G. Gunnell, "In Search of the State: Political Science as an Emerging Discipline in the United States." Both in Wagner, Wittrock, and Whitley, *Discourses*, pp. 45–71 and 123–61, resp.; Ross, *The Origins*.

27. Giorgio Sola, "Sviluppi e scenari della sociologia italiana: 1861–1890." In Filippo Barbano and Giorgio Sola, *Sociologia e scienze sociali in Italia, 1860–1890*. Milan: Angeli, 1985, p. 85.

28. George Weisz, "L'idéologie republicaine et les sciences sociales." *Revue française de sociologie* 20, 1 (1979): pp. 83–112.

29. Richard Whitley, "The Structure and Context of Economics as a Scientific Field." *Research in the History of Economic Thought and Methodology* 4 (1987): p. 184.

30. Ibid., p. 185; see also Norbert Elias et al., eds., *Scientific Establishments and Hierarchies*. Dordrecht: Kluwer, 1982; an incisive account of the structuring impact of discursive boundaries remains Foucault, *L'ordre*.

31. Abraham Flexner, *Universities: American, English, German*. New York: Ox-

ford University Press, 1930; for an excellent overview, see Roger Geiger, *To Advance Knowledge: The Growth of American Research Universities 1900–1940*. New York: Oxford University Press, 1986.

32. See Wittrock, "Rise," Sheldon Rothblatt, "The Limbs of Osiris: Liberal Education in the English-Speaking World," and also Sven-Eric Liedman, "In Search of Isis: General Education in Germany and Sweden." Both in Rothblatt and Wittrock, *The European and American University Since 1800,* pp. 19–73 and 74–106, resp.

33. For these two fields see, for example, Keith Tribe, "Political Economy to Economics via Commerce: The Evolution of British Academic Economics 1860–1920"; and Malcolm Vout, "Oxford and the Emergence of Political Science in England 1945–1960." Both in Wagner, Wittrock, and Whitley, *Discourses,* pp. 273–302 and 163–91, resp. See also Margaret Weir and Theda Skocpol, "State Structures and the Possibilities for 'Keynesian Responses' to the Great Depression in Sweden, Britain, and the United States." In Peter B. Evans, Dietrich Rueschemeyer, and Theda Skocpol, eds., *Bringing the State Back In*. Cambridge: Cambridge University Press, pp. 107–63; and Joseph A. Pechman, ed., *The Role of the Economist in Government*. New York: New York University Press, 1989.

34. H. Stuart Hughes, *Consciousness and Society: The Reorientation of European Social Thought, 1890–1920*. New York: Knopf, 1958, pp. 13–14.

35. Charles S. Maier, *Recasting Bourgeois Europe: Stabilization in France, Germany, and Italy in the decade after World War I*. Princeton: Princeton University Press, 1975, p. 5.

36. Charles Tilly, ed., *The Formation of National States in Western Europe*. Princeton: Princeton University Press, 1975; Gianfranco Poggi, *The Development of the Modern State*. Stanford: Stanford University Press, 1978.

37. Douglas Ashford, *Policy and Politics in France*. Philadelphia: Temple University Press, 1982, p. 13.

38. Dietrich Rueschemeyer and Ronan Van Rossem, in this volume.

39. Björn Wittrock and Peter Wagner, "Social Sciences and State Developments." In Brooks and Gagnon, *Social Science,* pp. 113–37.

40. See Reuschemeyer and Van Rossem, in this volume.

41. See, for example, Schweber, in this volume; Martin Bulmer, "Mobilizing Social Knowledge for Social Welfare: Intermediary Institutions in the Political Systems of the United States and Great Britain, 1900–1940," contribution to the conference on *Social Knowledge and the Origins of Social Policies,* New York, May 1989; and Bulmer, "National Contexts for the Development of Social-Policy Research: British and American Research on Poverty and Social Welfare Compared." In Peter Wagner, Carol H. Weiss, Björn Wittrock, and Hellmut Wollmann, eds., *Social Sciences and Modern States. National Experiences and Theoretical Crossroads*. Cambridge: Cambridge University Press, 1991, pp. 148–67.

42. See also Cyril S. Smith, "Networks of Influence: The Social Sciences in the United Kingdom since the War." Wagner, Weiss, Wittrock, and Wollmann, *Social Sciences,* pp. 131–47, for a similar view on British social science in the early post–World War Two period.

43. J. P. Nettl, "The State as a Conceptual Variable." *World Politics,* 20, 4 (1968): p. 562.

44. Stephen Skowronek's characterization of the early American state highlights those very aspects of the American experience (*Building a New American State: The Expansion of Administrative Capacities 1870–1920*. New York: Cambridge University Press, 1982).

45. For our own formulation in terms of "discourse structuration" and "discourse coalitions," see Björn Wittrock, Peter Wagner, and Hellmut Wollmann, "Social Science and the Modern State: Policy Knowledge and Political Institutions in Western Europe and the United States." In Wagner, Weiss, Wittrock, and Wollmann, *Social Sciences,* pp. 28–85; and Wagner and Wittrock, "Epistemic Drift or Discourse Structuration? Transformations in the Societal Position of the Social Sciences." In Thorsten Nybom and Ulf P. Lundgren, eds., *Professionalisation and the Role of Intellectuals in Welfare Society.* London: Jessica Kingsley (forthcoming).

Part II

REFORMIST SOCIAL SCIENTISTS AND PUBLIC POLICYMAKING

4

The Verein für Sozialpolitik and the Fabian Society

A STUDY IN THE SOCIOLOGY OF POLICY-RELEVANT KNOWLEDGE

DIETRICH RUESCHEMEYER
AND RONAN VAN ROSSEM

THE German Verein für Sozialpolitik and the English Fabian Society played critical roles in the initiation of modern social policies in Germany and Britain. Their political influence was based on knowledge claims and the authority of expertise. At the same time, their activities, and the conflicts they generated, had a lasting impact on the development of social science in the two countries. Studying them should therefore offer fascinating insights into the interconnections between policy formation and the creation of social knowledge.

Both groups faced similar issues of knowledge and politics in different historical situations. Both dealt with the impact of capitalist industrialization on their societies. Both undertook to shift the hegemonic culture of their country so that it acknowledged the *soziale Frage*—the enormous social problems engendered by capitalist industrialization—as the central challenge of the new industrial social order. And both sought to mobilize the state for the attainment of their goals. Both, finally, attained significant intellectual and political influence. However, the bodies of knowledge they created and utilized, the strategies they used to deploy this knowledge, and the specific policy goals they pursued were quite different. In fact, the very character of the two groups differed profoundly.

Comparing the projects of the Fabians and the "socialists of the chair" (as the professorial leaders of the Verein were called by their opponents) puts a sharp focus on the interplay between information and analysis, on the one hand, and the norms, values, and policy goals advanced by knowledge-bearing groups, on the other. Any development and transmission of knowledge is likely also to carry a certain amount of "ideological" baggage, ranging from broad value orientations to policy recommendations, from new definitions of policy-relevant situations to even the creation of a new public language with its own key words and "persuasive definitions." This flow of ideological matter may be nearly fused with the supply of information and analysis or it may be quite clearly separated from it. We will argue that this issue is closely related to the contrasting patterns of social and cultural authority of these two knowledge-bearing groups as well as to the different prevailing modes of political discourse, conflict, and domination.

These differences also shaped the political and intellectual paths taken by the two groups in the course of their existence. The initial cohesion and broad authority of the Verein as well as the internal tensions and conflicts it experienced later cannot be understood without the context of a politically exclusive *Kulturstaat* in which the Verein took its place. This context first engendered particular assumptions of intellectual objectivity, trustworthiness, and authority based on social and political position as well as scholarly work. When with advancing democratization of state and society this constellation changed, the fusion of intellectual and moral-political authority began to dissolve. The political project of the Verein effectively came to an end in the last decade before World War I. These changes had a profound impact on the development of the social sciences in Germany. The famous *Werturteilsdebatte,* the debate about the place of value judgments in social inquiry in which Max Weber took an influential part, was a direct outgrowth of these developments. It led to the founding of the German Sociological Society, and it put Germany sociology on a new nonpolitical, academic trajectory.

By contrast, the Fabian Society has to be understood in the context of a democratizing liberal oligarchy. The relative openness of the British political system and the particular place that intellectuals had in state and society gave the Fabian project a very different character from that of the Verein. This also helps account for the fact that the Fabian political project did not end because of internal and external conflicts forcing a separation of cognitive and political agendas; rather, the Fabian political goals became incorporated within the Labour Party after the First World War, while the generation of social knowledge retained both political relevance and its empirical orientation.

This chapter will focus primarily on the Verein für Sozialpolitik. The Fabian Society will serve as a comparative foil allowing us to see more clearly the distinctive features of the Verein and to highlight a number of analytic issues. We begin with a descriptive overview of the two groups. This is followed by a comparative sketch of some of the background conditions in which they arose and operated. We then turn to the conflicts and tensions that marked especially the history of the Verein. And we conclude with reflections on comparative and analytic issues.

The Verein für Sozialpolitik

In 1864–65, the prominent conservative-liberal journal *Preussische Jahrbücher* published a series of articles on the *Arbeiterfrage* by Gustav Schmoller. The problems of the industrial working class, he argued, were a challenge for state policy; they would not be solved by the interplay of self-interest mediated by the market. Public policy could not rely on the optimistic predictions of social harmony underlying classic economic theory. Similar challenges to the "Manchester liberalism" then dominant in German politics, state administrations, and the press were advanced by others at the same time. Ernst Engel, the director of the Prussian Statistical Bureau, had pushed for research on working-class problems in Prussia/Germany and in England; Lujo Brentano followed the lead and published his work on English "worker guilds" in 1871 and 1872; and Adolf Wagner, up to then an adherent of classic economic doctrines, delivered in 1871 a passionate appeal to a Protestant audience in the Berlin Garnisonskirche for an active public policy tackling the social problems created by capitalist development.

It was these critics of unfettered capitalist development and of a "naturalistic" conception of economics that viewed state intervention in the political economy as inherently futile, who founded the Verein für Sozialpolitik. At the first meeting in 1872, Schmoller articulated the position and goals of the Verein. Its founders were concerned, he said, about the "deep cleavage that cuts through our society, the conflict that pits entrepreneur against worker, the owning against the propertyless classes, the possible danger of a . . . social revolution." The economy did not, in their view, follow unalterable laws nor did the market aggregate all interests in an ultimately harmonious way as claimed by orthodox liberal economists. A strong state was necessary to avoid destructive class conflict and "alternating class rule." And Prussia/Germany had excellent historical preconditions for an active role of the state. The founders of the Verein "see in the two hundred year old struggle, which the Prussian civil service and the Prussian monarchy victoriously fought for equality before the law, for the elimination of all privileges and special entitlements of the higher classes, for the emancipation and amelioration of the lower classes, the best heritage of our German state institutions that we must never desert."[1]

The position of the Verein was one of conservative social reform. It was negatively defined by its rejection of both unrestrained capitalist development and unmitigated class struggle. Positively, the Verein had a vision of social justice and aimed for the social and political integration of the working class. But at the same time, it did not push for an extension of democracy with equal voting rights at all levels of government, and it fought socialism. In fact, it offered its reform proposals as the most promising strategy against the socialist movement and mounting revolutionary pressures. A socially oriented monarchic state, not yet effectively restrained by democratic institutions, was to be fused with a capitalist economy, and it was in this capitalist monarchy that social justice and a stable social order were to be realized. After the "external" foundation of Imperial Germany under Prussian leadership, a reformist restructuring of society was to lay the internal foundations for a powerful and harmonious nation-state.

On closer inspection, the new association encompassed, of course, a spectrum of quite divergent opinions. Lindenlaub[2] distinguishes a "conservative" faction, which relied with particular confidence on state intervention and was most radically represented by Adolf Wagner's "state socialism," from a "liberal" wing, represented most prominently and consistently by Lujo Brentano. Brentano saw the collective organization of workers as the most important instrument for dealing with the social problems of capitalism. This difference—the state or autonomous organizations as the major tools of social reform—was related to a more fundamental ideological divergence. The conservative view focused on distributive justice between classes, the collectives that make up the body politic; it put less emphasis on the rights of individuals, and it accepted social inequality as natural. Brentano and Karl Bücher built their arguments instead on individualist and—in ultimate principle—egalitarian foundations. However, these liberals shared with the conservatives the fundamental conviction that state action was critical for their goals. "Ever since the state exists," write Brentano, commenting on the Wagner's position, "there has not been a moment when it did not influence the shape of economic life; without state action we simply could not exist."[3] In turn, the conservatives, too, saw an essential role for cooperatives and unions.

The specific positions taken by the different groupings and leading figures changed over time and in reaction to political developments. Yet it is fair to say that from the foundation of Imperial Germany in 1871 until the beginning of the First World War in 1914, the moderate conservative position represented by Gustav Schmoller prevailed in the Verein, and the liberals were a minority which remained attached to the association not least because of the personal friendship between Schmoller and Brentano.

The Verein was dominated intellectually and politically by professors. But its membership was more complex. Chambers of commerce and industry, other official and voluntary associations, towns, and university institutes belonged to the Verein as well as individuals—civil servants, industrialists, members of the free professions, journalists, farmers and, of course, professors. The latter constituted about one-sixth of the membership and one-quarter of the participants at meetings; yet they dominated the permanent committee which prepared meetings and publications with a two-thirds majority.[4]

It was decided early to make membership in the Verein as inclusive as possible. Entrepreneurs and agrarian estate owners were invited to join as well as "moderate Social Democrats." Social Democrats, however, refused to become members or even speak at the meetings of the Verein until 1893,[5] and they never played a significant role.

The professors were mostly political economists. Law professors and historians were rare (V. Gierke, Hans Delbrück); but in the roster of *Staatswissenschaftler*, of economists and political scientists, there were many whose names are still familiar in their disciplines. The central figures of the founding generation were Wagner, Brentano, and Schmoller. And the protagonists of the next generation are even better known today—Werner Sombart, Tönnies, and the brothers Max and Alfred Weber.

The politicians and administrators who belonged to the Verein also included some quite important men: von Berlepsch was Prussian trade minister, von Miquel was Prussian minister of finance, von Rottenburg was a close associate of Bismarck in the chancellor's office and, after Bismarck's resignation, undersecretary of the Imperial Office of the Interior. In addition to a number of city mayors, there were also a few parliamentary politicians, including Franz Hitze of the Catholic Center Party and Friedrich Naumann who founded the National-Social Association, a short-lived quasi-party.

How did the Verein and its members make their opinions heard? There were first the general meetings. The topics to be discussed at these meetings, though always based on thorough preparatory studies, were carefully chosen in relation to political events and developments. On occasion, the timing of a meeting was changed for maximum impact; thus, in 1879, the meeting on the hotly debated issue of trade protectionism was scheduled so that the Verein's discussion would occur before the parliamentary debate. From the beginning, the Verein made it a practice to publish the papers and research monographs prepared for the meetings. Between 1872 and 1914, the Verein published 134 volumes of historical and statistical research.

Individual members made their opinions known by publishing in various newspapers and periodicals.[6] A number of them also had direct personal access to important administrators and politicians. In Berlin such contacts were formalized in the elitist Staatswissenschaftliche Gesellschaft. Founded in 1883 by Gustav Schmoller, it consisted of thirty-six members, half of whom were high-ranking politicians and administrators, while a third were professors; most also belonged to the Verein für Sozialpolitik.[7]

By and large, members of the Verein and especially the professional core of the Verein shunned direct involvement in party and parliamentary politics. Their aim, however, was clearly a political one—"*Stimmung zu machen,*" as Schmoller put it, to influence public opinion, for social reform.

Of greatest direct importance for their influence was the teaching of the professorial members of the Verein. Their students became mostly civil servants. But their influence was not confined to the professional instruction of university students. It was quite common that townspeople also attended regular lectures if a professor had a reputation for speaking appealingly about important matters. Brentano had such an appeal: "When he lectured each afternoon at four, the University of Munich's largest lecture hall was filled to capacity with students and townspeople."[8] Later, in the 1890s when university extension efforts became generally more widespread, the Verein organized special summer courses for audiences interested in problems of social policy. One such course in Berlin in 1895 attracted 791 participants; more than a dozen leading economists of the Verein spoke.[9]

A number of associations were more or less closely linked to the Verein für Sozialpolitik and enlarged its impact. Social science student associations were an outgrowth of the teaching of people like Schmoller, Sombart, Brentano, and others. Other associations outside the university had a broader influence. The left wing of the Catholic Center Party and various other Catholic organizations came under the influence of Franz Hitze and, less directly, Lujo Brentano.[10] Other organizations—especially those in the milieu of Protestant reform-oriented educated circles, the "home turf" of the leading members—were much more closely interconnected with the Verein.[11] In 1901, members of the Verein founded the Gessellschaft für soziale Reform as a political association that would be able, better than the Verein, to get involved in public "agitation." The Gesellschaft für soziale Reform had numerous local branches throughout the country, and by 1910 there were among its affiliated organizations non-socialist unions representing 1,600,000 members; but it never succeeded in penetrating the whole working class as was originally intended.[12]

What was the impact of the Verein für Sozialpolitik? Even a summary answer must differentiate between different forms of influence, and even then there is some disagreement among different studies as well as observers at the time.

Sheehan comes to the conclusion that "its direct influence on German politics was negligible." Lindenlaub concurs when it comes to specific policy measures: "The influence of the Verein für Sozialpolitik can only be described in generalities and is seldom amenable to concrete proof." And: "A concrete influence on administrative policy measures and legislation can be established with the available evidence nearly without exception only for individual members of the Verein." Vom Bruch, on the other hand, lists a number of quite specific instances of direct policy influence.[13]

But we must not put the question too narrowly and focus only on specific interventions and proposals of the Verein as such and on their direct and unequivocal effects. In a broader sense, the political impact of the Verein seems to have been considerable. Brentano wrote in his obituary for Schmoller: "It is true that he could say that it was in a sense his ideas that triumphed in the work of Bismarck in economic and social policy." And Schmoller boasted in a letter to Brentano in 1912:

> Today the Verein für Sozialpolitik dominates intellectually the people who govern. And that is the essential thing. How often have you said yourself that the whole Catholic social policy community copies . . . our writings. The decisive people in the Imperial Office of the Interior were during the last ten years Caspar and Wiedenfeld; they take our position completely. And the ministers Bülow, Posadowsky, Bethmann, Delbrück basically do the same; they just cannot announce it as openly as we do, because they would too much irritate agrarians and feudalists as well as the barons of coal and iron.[14]

Even if the authors and the occasion of these assessments suggest some caution, there is little doubt that core members of the Verein—above all Schmoller—had a considerable personal influence on important managers of the state apparatus and that the Verein gave them not only a platform but prestigious scholarly support. That the political impact of the Verein—and not only the personal influence of individuals—was considered significant by contemporaries who were not members is indicated by the bitter attacks to which it was exposed, first from orthodox economic liberals in economics and politics, then from the industrial entrepreneurs and their association, and intermittently also from the government. We will return to these conflicts.

The Verein—or perhaps more precisely, the intellectual and scholarly movement of which the Verein was the organizational center, as Schmoller put it at the twenty-fifth anniversary meeting in 1897—achieved its greatest impact, however, not by influencing policy measures directly but by transforming the public view of social and economic problems and of the role and the responsibility of the state. Sheehan comes close to agreeing with this judgment when he concludes: ". . . the Verein did play a central role in the academic and intellectual life of imperial Germany."[15]

The first arena in which the new orientations won out were the academic disciplines of the Verein's professorial members. The policy views of classical economics had been of some importance in German universities before the 1870s and they were dominant among politicians and in the state administration.[16] During the 1870s, however, they lost most of their influence to the political economists of the "younger historical school" and their allies in social reform. While the roots of historical and national orientations in German economics reach back to earlier generations, it was in the Verein für Sozialpolitik that earlier calls for an economic and social responsibility of the monarchic state found a coherent organizational crystallization. The association that represented the views of economic liberalism and laissez-faire, the Kongress der deutschen Volkswirte, was dissolved in 1885.[17]

Winning out in academic controversy does not constitute a change in the hegemonic political culture. Yet the members of the Verein did succeed in carrying their views beyond the university. They had a profound impact on the outlook of the professional classes. Friedrich Meinecke, an eminent historian but also a paradigmatic representative of the educated circles of late Imperial Germany, aptly summarizes the influence of the scholars organized in the Verein für Sozialpolitik: "In the first instance they had an effect as advisors of the rulers and educators of the civil service, and their influence on the wider circles of the educated came about only slowly, then however in no small measure."[18]

The Fabian Society

Thomas Davidson, a Scottish ethical anarchist, inspired a circle of intellectuals interested in social reform that gathered in 1882 in London. They read economic and socialist literature and discussed the future of their society and of the socialist movement.

> They wanted to do for their time what Bentham had done for liberalism at the beginning of the century. Sidney Webb became the thinker, George B. Shaw the fighter of the group, which in 1884 separated itself from Davidson and called itself the Fabians; they intended to proceed like Fabius Cunctator—first wisely hesitating, then acting decisively when the time was ripe.[19]

Like the Verein für Sozialpolitik, the Fabian Society rejected class struggle and revolutionary Marxism. Socialism could be reached through education and persuasion. George Bernard Shaw, a forceful spokesman for the Society, argued that the struggle for socialism was not a battle between workers and bourgeoisie, but one that crosscut the classes.[20] The ultimate goal of the Fabians was a thorough transformation and modernization of the social order—the establishment of a social-democratic society. Full democracy and socialism were closely intertwined. As Shaw put it: "The object of the Fabian Society is to persuade the English people to make their political constitution thoroughly democratic and so to socialize their industries as to make the livelihood of the people entirely independent of private capitalism."[21]

These goals were to be achieved not through revolution but by constitutional means. Sidney Webb held that socialism would be attained through the slow collectivization of British society, and the rise of social-democracy would be the result of a natural evolution. Thus, one could confidently reject "the violence of radical Marxism." It was against the existing communist and socialist groups that both Webb and Shaw agitated. Shaw put it colorfully in his preface to the 1908 edition of *Fabian Essays in Socialism,* envisioning an

> evolution of Socialism from the Red spectre on the barricade, with community of wives (all petroleuses), and Compulsory Atheism, to the Fabian Society and the Christian Social Union, constitutional, respectable, even official, eminent, and titled. . . .[22]

This reformism and pragmatism of the Fabians did not fail to arouse the anger of more radical socialists and Marxists. F. Engels, in a letter to A. Sorge, calls the Fabians

> a well-meaning gang of educated bourgeois who have refuted Marx with the rotten economics-made-simple of Jevons, which is so simple that one can make anything out of it, even socialism. Their main purpose is to convert the bourgeois middle class to socialism and thus to introduce the thing peacefully and constitutionally.[23]

Shaw puts the last point without Engels's irony: The Fabians seek "to make it as easy and matter-of-course for the ordinary respectable Englishman to be a Socialist as to be a Liberal or a Conservative."[24]

The main program points of the Fabians emerge from their leaflets and tracts:

1. Extension of democracy and the improvement of the machinery of democratic government.
2. Extension of government powers to improve community welfare (especially the welfare of the working class).
3. Positive government action to promote equality.[25]

Their publications give a detailed picture of the direction in which they want society to move. Besides a broader participation of the whole population in the political system, they want to expand and modernize the activities of the state. Within this context, they develop ideas for a comprehensive social security system. Their proposals often outlined an array of very concrete measures (earning them the label of a "gas and water socialism") but, in spite of some reserve toward philosophical speculation and ideology, they also formulated some overarching conceptions of a "democratic collectivism." Especially in the thought of Sidney Webb, this vision of socialism took on a statist and technocratic character, which even after World War II was the subject of critical debate in the Labour Party.[26]

Despite the numerous detailed and practical plans for social reform, Fabian socialism retained strong utopian features. It did not just aim for radical change in society but, in the first place, for a new kind of human being. This becomes clearest in some of the literary writings of Fabians like G. B. Shaw and H. G. Wells. But Sidney Webb as well makes remarks in this direction, as for example in a letter to Beatrice Potter-Web of December 12, 1891:

> what we want is to teach "collectivism" to the whole People. That will involve more than an intellectual conversion; it will need a growth of certain moral qualities in the whole nation, not only in the working class.[27]

For the Fabians, socialism was not merely an economic and political system, but above all a moral state.

The Fabians firmly held the belief that social ills were due to ignorance —ignorance on the part of the working class as well as ignorance on the part of the upper classes and of the state. Critical for a solution were, therefore, education and information.[28] This is expressed in their motto "Educate, Agitate, Organize," of which especially the first two elements were emphasized.

Who were the Fabians? Their project grew out of the unease and indignation of middle-class intellectuals with the living conditions of the working class and out of their fear of a revolutionary uprising of the working class. Only one of the initial members was a (retired) working man. Beatrice Webb described herself and her companions as belonging to "the B's of the World—bourgeois, bureaucratic and benevolent."[29]

The uncertain social position of these intellectuals influenced their views. Hobsbawm argues that "(t)he middle-class socialism of the Fabians reflects the unwillingness, or the inability, of the people for whom they spoke, to find a firm place in the middle- and upper-class structure of late Victorian Britain."[30] Their ambiguous and uncertain position enabled these intellectuals to become intermediaries between capital and labor. But at the same time, their values and attitudes were still very much of the middle class. As Mannheim put it, ". . . nothing could be more wrong than to . . . maintain that the class and status ties of the individual disappear completely by virtue of . . . 'belonging to the intelligentsia.'"[31]

Gustav Schmoller presents us with a very flattering picture of the Fabians when he describes them at the eve of the First World War as: "a select circle of influential writers, speakers, scholars, top civil servants, members of parliament and of local authorities."[32] Shaw's early description of their beginnings is a lot less flattering than Schmoller's:

> It was a silly business. They had one elderly retired workman. They had two physical researchers: Edward Pease and Frank Podmore, for whom I [G. B.

> Shaw] slept in a haunted house in Chapman. There were anarchists, led by Mrs. Wilson, who would not hear of anything Parliamentary. There were young ladies on the look-out for husbands, who left when they succeeded. There were atheists and Anglo-Catholics. There was Bland's very attractive wife Edith Nesbit, who wrote verses in The Weekly Dispatch for half a guinea a week and upset all the meetings by making scenes and pretending to faint. She became famous as a writer of fairy tales. Bland was in financial straits, militarist and very censorious, though he was living with two women besides his wife.[33]

And then there was Shaw himself, an unsuccessful journalist supported by his mother and descending from decayed nobility, while his friend Sidney Webb, raised in a lower-middle-class family, used to work as a clerk in the Colonial Office while studying for an external law degree.[34]

Many of the Fabians had little formal schooling, but their autodidactic learning was often of high quality. Beatrice Potter, for instance, had never had any formal training in the social sciences. But she was introduced to social science and politicians through the social environment in which she grew up. She met Herbert Spencer, Joseph Chamberlain, and eventually joined Charles Booth in his research on poverty in London.

Quite soon, however, especially after the publication of the very successful *Fabian Essays in Socialism* (1889), the Fabian Society not only gained in popularity, but in membership and prestige as well. In 1891, membership of the London Fabian Society for the first time exceeded three hundred. It stayed under a thousand until 1906, when the number of members skyrocketed until it reached almost 2,400 in 1913.

Meanwhile, from the early 1890s on, local or provincial societies arose rapidly. While the London Fabians succeeded in attracting mostly intellectuals and people with influence as is evident from Schmoller's description quoted above, the provincial societies were more composed of working-class people and were also more closely linked to the efforts to organize the British working class. Many of them were only short-lived as they merged, in 1893–94, into the Independent Labour Party, a merger that was neither approved nor liked by the London Fabian Society, which itself refused to enter the ILP.[35]

Many of the London Fabians were actually glad to see the provincial followers go, since the local societies, with their larger proportion of working-class members, did not fit well with the intellectual orientations of the middle-class London Fabian Society.[36] While they tried to emancipate the working classes through education and integration in the existing political economy, the other side of their activities was a politics of ideas aimed at a strategically located elite. As Sidney Webb put it in a letter to Pease of October 24, 1886: "Nothing in England is done without the consent of a small intellectual yet highly practical class in London not 2000 in number. We alone could get at this class. . . ."[37] (in Mackenzie 1978, 101; and Wittig 1982, 333).

The members of the London Fabian Society differed strikingly from intellectuals in the Verein für Sozialpolitik. Virtually all members of the Verein had a university education, and the central figures were professors. Of the leading Fabians only a few had such an education, and none was connected to a university. If the members of the Verein can be described as established elite professionals, the leading Fabians were mostly "men of letters"—people with a general education, often of their own design, who had no publicly recognized professional expertise but dared to express an opinion on the most diverse topics. If the London Fabians approximated Alfred Weber's and Karl Mannheim's "free-floating intellectual," the professors and political administrators of the Verein were intellectuals firmly attached to and grounded in institutions at the core of Germany's political economy.

Sidney and Beatrice Webb sought to establish social research as a new field of expertise, and they were passionate advocates of expert authority and administrative rationality. It was on their research that the Fabians rested their claim to offer specific and reliable knowledge. Beatrice Potter-Webb was already involved in social research before she joined the Fabians. In 1883, she started working for the Charity Organization Society, and later collaborated with Charles Booth in his extensive study of the nature and extent of poverty in London. By the end of the 1880s, she had a reputation as an expert on social problems. The early empirical research documenting the character of social problems was later supplemented by historical research on the evolution of institutions. The Webbs frequently gave respected testimony before governmental and parliamentary committees of inquiry. The founding of the London School of Economics and Political Science (LSE), under the influence of the Webbs, was an attempt to construct an institutional base for objective research that could further the cause of Fabian socialism. In a letter to the Hutchinson Trustees (February 1895), Sidney Webb argued that the LSE was needed because

> it seems to me clear that we should make it our main object to promote education—not mere propaganda in the parties or controversies of the hour, but solid work in economic and political principles.
>
> The greatest needs of the collectivist movement in England appear to me
>
> (a) An increase in the number of educated and able lecturers and writers, as apart from propagandist speakers;
>
> (b) The further investigation of problems of municipal and national administration from a collectivist standpoint. This implies original research, and the training of additional persons competent to do such work;

> (c) The diffusion of economic and political knowledge of a real kind—as apart from collectivist shibboleths, and the cant and claptrap of political campaigning.[38]

There were deep differences of opinion in the London Fabian Society. Especially in the beginning, the Fabian Society comprised a strange mix of ideologies, ranging from liberalism to anarchism. As time passed, the "extremes" on both sides disappeared, and only the social-democratic center was left. This heterogeneity makes it difficult to speak of a consistent Fabian ideology, particularly in the first decades of their existence. In the *Fabian Essays,* we find little consensus among the different authors even on fundamental issues that go beyond the common ground indicated earlier.

The thought of the Fabians was influenced by a complex set of intellectual figures and philosophical currents, among them John Stuart Mill, Auguste Comte, Herbert Spencer, the economists Jevons, Wallace, and Ricardo, positivism, and Marxism.

> Fabianism derived from two mainstreams of thought. The first was the English Liberal tradition, transmitted through the late writings of John Stuart Mill. . . . The other mainstream was the Socialist one, especially its most powerful current, Marxism.[39]

But as argued earlier, the Fabians were much less radical than contemporary Marxist movements. Wittig stresses the evangelical background and the crisis of belief many members had in common. Faced with growing tensions and problems arising from capitalist development of the economy, a social order resisting change, and an oligarchic political system that slowly expanded the suffrage, this ". . . group of young men and women . . . felt the need to create an organization to help reconstruct society on more morally accepted lines." "The suffering of industrial workers was the root of the Society's foundation."[40]

The Fabians were familiar with some aspects of the work of the Verein, especially with those of the older generation within the Verein für Sozialpolitik such as Brentano and Schmoller.[41] Unlike the German reformers of the Verein, the Fabians believed in progress. They saw their enterprise as built on tendencies inherent in historical evolution. Thus Sidney Webb argues against reservations of Alfred Marshall in a letter: "Your difficulty appears to be in realizing adequately that the course of social evolution is making us all Socialists against our will."[42] Like many of the contemporary philosophers, the Fabians adhered to a rationalistic view of the world, and saw humans as basically rational. This contrasts with socially moved writers like Thomas Carlyle and Dickens, who were anti-rationalists and saw humans as basically emotional and held, like the Verein, a more pessimistic view of the future.[43]

In contrast to the German "socialists of the chair," the Fabians wholeheartedly embraced the process of democratization as part of the overall social evolution. Yet they were elitist at the same time.[44] It is the intellectual elites that have to govern the masses and lead them to socialism. The emphasis on the education of the masses allowed the Fabians to combine their elitist and democratic ideas.

Yet the Fabians resolutely acted within the context of democracy. Thus, in contrast to the Verein, the Society opted for a party-oriented strategy. While the Verein für Sozialpolitik largely refrained from overt politics and instead tried to influence the state apparatus and educated opinion, the Fabians deliberately entered the political arena, even though one can detect in their politics, too, traces of a tension between intellectual authority claims and party politics, and especially, Sidney Webb's ideas had a strong technocratic streak.[45]

The tactic used by the early Fabian Society was the "permeation" of the Liberal Party.[46] Only when this tactic failed, and the Fabians either left the Liberal Party disappointed or were kicked out, did they reluctantly turn toward the project with which their name now is most closely associated—the formation of a labor party. But throughout their history, they were deeply involved in democratic party politics.

In the long run and on the national level, the permeation tactic proved to be unsuccessful. In retrospect, it seems rather that it was the Liberals who used the Fabians for their purpose, namely for attracting the working-class vote. We can wonder who was playing the ". . . tricks with the Liberal thimbles and the Fabian peas."[47] It was only when the Gladstone government, after the 1892 Liberal election success, refused to implement the Newcastle Programme, which had been influenced by the Fabians,[48] that in their leaflet "To your tents, O Israel!" the Fabians broke with the Liberal Party and became—in theory—more devoted to the founding of a separate working-class party.

Yet the relations between the Fabians and other socialist groups and organizations, including the Social Democratic Federation (SDF) and the Independent Labour Party (ILP), remained tense. The Fabians only reluctantly sent delegates to the first congress of the ILP in 1893, and these representatives—among them Shaw—found it difficult to have their credentials confirmed. In 1900, at the founding of the Labour Representation Committee (LRC), which was later to become the Labour Party, the Fabian Society officially kept aloof, although several Fabians individually were involved in the event and the organization of the LRC resembled fairly well a plan proposed in 1894 by Shaw (and the Fabian Society) in a *A Plan of Campaign for Labour*.[49] This envisioned an organization based upon the trade unions rather than on individual membership. Gradually, the leading Fabians seem to have accepted the new organization, and by the end of the First World War the Fabian Society was integrated into the Labour Party.

The Fabians were quite successful in spreading new ideas through their publications. The publication that made the Fabians known to a wider public, the *Fabian Essays in Socialism* (1889), had its first printing of 1,000 copies sold in less than a month and, by March 1897, 33,000 copies were sold. Before the 1892 local elections the Fabians distributed about 700,000 leaflets of Webb's *London Programme*.[50] Schmoller reports that between 1907 and 1912 they annually distributed between 96,000 and 251,000 publications and leaflets.[51] In addition, numerous articles of several Fabians were published in newspapers and magazines.

Another way in which the Fabians tried to spread their ideas was by giving lectures, usually before audiences of Radicals and/or working men. In the year ending in March 1888, the Fabians claimed to have given 324 lectures, while in the year ending March 1892, this number had climbed to 3,339.[52] In later years the lecturing activities of the Fabians decreased substantially.

Equally important as these educational and agitational activities were the personal contacts of the Fabians with politicians of the emerging socialist movement and of the long established Liberal and Conservative parties, but especially with the Radical faction of the London Liberals. National politics was still dominated by a relatively small political elite that was concentrated in London. It was on this group that the Fabians focused using their permeation strategy. Because of their literary and social status, the London Fabians moved in circles where they had access to leading politicians whom they sought to convince of their ideas. Individual ties between Fabians and Liberals were important for the diffusion of the Fabian ideas of social reform. The Webbs in particular remained, even in the first decade of the twentieth century, close to the Liberals. It was only with the Webbs' campaign for the Minority Report that they started to estrange from their Liberal friends. But even then, in 1910, the Liberal leaders asked Sidney Webb for advice on social reforms.[53]

The Fabian strategy fitted quite well into the prevailing practices of nineteenth-century British politics. Extra-parliamentary agitation, combined with voter mobilization, mass meetings and demonstrations, petitioning, propaganda, and the lobbying of members of parliament, ministers, and bureaucrats were well-established strategies in the politics of nineteenth-century Britain. Several other pressure groups had used similar methods, such as the Anti-Corn Law League, the Liberation Society, the National Education League, and the U.K. Alliance.[54]

How do we ultimately assess the impact of the Fabians on British political history and social policy? This question is difficult to answer with any precision, more difficult perhaps than in the case of the Verein für Sozialpolitik. Many of the Fabian ideas were an expression of more general currents of thought. Thus it is hard to attribute any realization clearly and unambiguously to the Fabians. Yet once broad margins of error are granted, there is little doubt that their work did have an impact. They and their allies documented empirically the existence and the extent of social problems, they advanced proposals for working-class political strategy, and above all, they advocated socialist ideas and welfare state measures as part of the vision of a fully modernized society.

Schmoller assesses their role in the social movements of their time as follows: "Surely the unification of the union representatives and the socialists would not have succeeded if the Fabians had not made a great effort of enlightenment from the 1880s till today [1914]." Other authors see this differently and consider the actual influence of the Fabian Society on the transformation of the socialist movement in Britain as minimal.[55] And the skeptical interpretation can point to the fact that, indeed, the London Fabians were quite reluctant to join a united socialist movement.

It is our judgment that the Fabian Society had a greater impact on actual social policy through the diffusion of ideas about the modern welfare state than as catalysts for working-class political organization. That the social reforms they proclaimed were not implemented by a socialist government but by the Liberal government after the 1906 elections in an attempt to stop the rising power and size of the Labour Party, cannot be taken as proof of the failure of the Fabians, but it makes it difficult to estimate with any precision the real part played by the Fabians in the beginning of the welfare state in Britain.

Their main impact was perhaps in the realm of ideas. Wittig concludes: "Even if one views with skepticism the optimistic proclamations of success, which the Fabians themselves spread about their impact, it is no exaggeration to claim that the history of the influence of the Fabians as an intellectual grouping is without parallel in twentieth-century England." The Fabians were carriers of new ideas and attitudes, and they were able to formulate and communicate them in a way that was acceptable to segments of the working class as well as to old and new political elites.

Are the two groups and their agenda comparable at all? We think so and we deem the comparison instructive. We found our judgment on the parallels between the two groups confirmed by Gustav Schmoller, who casually stretched one of our conclusions. He wrote in a survey of the social movement in England from 1770 to 1912:

> In spite of all differences, one could compare the Fabian Society with the German Verein für Sozialpolitik, which pursues since 1872 similar goals, though it has a more academic character and leaves the practical agitation to the Gesellschaft für soziale Reform whose leadership is largely identical with that of the

> Verein. It is just that the German association—corresponding to the civil service character of the German state—seeks more to influence government and the corps of civil servants, the Fabian Society—corresponding to the free constitutional life of England—public opinion.[56]

The Fabians were less academic, but they were no less active in the creation and diffusion of knowledge. Both groups very much pursued political goals as well as broader ideological aims, but both focused their work on the development of specific empirical information and specific policy proposals. The characterization of the Fabian Society as a "social science information service" for many of those interested in social reform[57] would not be widely off the mark when applied to the Verein, although the publications of the Verein's professors had a more academic character and lacked the literary sparkle that George Bernard Shaw lent to some of the Fabian tracts.

Even though after the publication of the *Fabian Essays* the Fabian Society had become a "national institution" of sorts,[58] it did not have as central a place among the different groups discussing social reform as the Verein für Sozialpolitik acquired in the network of German reform groups. Both on the left and in the liberal center of English political discourse, there were groups and associations that were in no way dependent on, socially subordinate to, or less influential than the Fabian Society. In Germany, the socialist left was—officially and de facto—sectioned off from the established discourse, while in the latter the Verein had a central, if not exclusively dominant, place. This does not invalidate a comparison but it must be kept in mind when we draw our conclusions.[59]

Contrasts in State and Society

The contrasts and similarities between the Verein für Sozialpolitik and the Fabian Society must be seen against the historical background of their societies. Especially relevant are the course of capitalist transformation, the structure of the state, and the role of the educated classes. Here, of course, we can give only a rough sketch of some aspects of these contrasting historical backgrounds and take a brief look at the social and political constellations in which the two associations originated.

Different Historical Backgrounds

The major contrasts between the political economies of England and Prussia/Germany in the eighteenth and nineteenth centuries are well known—

so much so that simplistic stereotypes suggest themselves all too easily. A first and most significant fact is that the capitalist transformation began in England well before it took hold in Germany. England thus attained previously unimagined prosperity much earlier than Germany.

This advance in economic development gave Britain a preeminent position in Europe. In the words of a contemporary, Max Sering: "It was the splendor and the power of economic and social life pulsing in Britain that have until the present spread in Germany English views of life and political ideas no less successfully than the works of classical economics earlier."[60]

As in later developing countries, attitudes toward the lead country were shot through with ambivalence. The political economists who founded the Verein für Sozialpolitik stood in a long tradition that developed counterpositions against the dominance of classical English economics. Virulent anti-Western sentiments, however, developed in Germany only toward the very end of the nineteenth century and were not characteristic of most of the "socialists of the chair"—divided as they were over the moral and political validity of English developments as a model for Germany.

A second major contrast between English and German historical development, again one commonly acknowledged, is that political unification under Prussian leadership came late, while England had achieved a rough form of unity already with the Norman conquest. The previous fragmentation of political authority in the German-speaking territories shaped the outlook of the educated classes, especially in the smaller territories, encouraging interest and participation in ideological debates that far transcended their provincially limited opportunities for action and practical experience.[61]

The political fragmentation of the German territories must be seen together with the bureaucratic rationalization of rule in the larger German states. Rule of "governors by profession," as John Stuart Mill called bureaucracy,[62] turned the Prussian state apparatus into an efficient and rather autonomous administrative machine. In Prussia and in some of the other large German states, the rationalization of rule left the rationalization of economic production far behind, while in England the reverse was the case.

By continental standards, the state bureaucracy even of Victorian England was small; but both the tasks and the size of public administration grew rapidly throughout the nineteenth century. It was in the second half of the nineteenth century that the civil service, previously staffed primarily through patronage, became more efficient and more effective as well as more bureaucratized.[63] And the penetration of civil society by the British state increased as well. By the 1880s governmental checks on economic liberalism in the form of social legislation were already well established.

With the expansion of state action, expert knowledge became a crucial asset. Rational, effective, and efficient decision making requires sufficient and accurate information. In Germany, the state relied on the state apparatus itself for such information and on experts in one of the state-controlled universities. Britain, lacking a similar bureaucracy and university system, made more use of outside expertise. Throughout the nineteenth century, new forms of information gathering were introduced and old ones were expanded and perfected. The number of select committees and royal commissions grew rapidly after 1830.[64]

The dominance of the Prussian/German state machineries over civil society did not simply rest on this advantage in rationalization. During the nineteenth century, it increasingly came to be based on a broad repression of organized activity in civil society—first in the Restoration period after the Napoleonic Wars, then in the wake of the revolutionary years of 1830–31, and again after the attempt at revolution in 1848–49. Well into the experience of the members of the Verein für Sozialpolitik, women and youths were not allowed to join political associations or participate in their activities. Professional associations, unions, and political parties were subject to selective control, depending on the perception of threat.[65]

The history of English politics constitutes, already well before the nineteenth century, the paradigmatic case of a fairly open contest about public policy among restricted elites, of an "oligarchic liberalization" of politics. From the 1860s onward, this system slowly opened to working-class interests as well.

Similar patterns of accepting opposition from outside the state apparatus were far less developed in Prussia. There was considerable discussion *within* the bureaucracy, but public contestation and the right to political opposition were not firmly established at all, when Bismarck introduced universal and equal male suffrage for the new German empire, while retaining a three-class voting system in Prussia, the political center of the empire. Throughout the life span of Imperial Germany, government responsibility to elected representatives was not constitutionally secured, and constitutional issues were not subject to judicial review.[66]

These broad, historically determined contrasts in economic development, state organization, and political process set the context for the place of the educated in state and society. The educated classes are of special interest here. It is not only that both associations arose from these groups; the educated also constituted their most important immediate audience. Without resonance in this audience, the voice of the Fabians and of the "socialists of the chair" would not have carried far in their countries. Yet here, too, we can offer only a few broad strokes to indicate how a fuller portrayal of the character of the educated classes in Germany and Britain might be drawn.[67]

That relatively backward Germany became, during the nineteenth century, the leader in science and scholarship represents a puzzle. Its solution is found in a new involvement of the state in the social and economic establishment of science. While in England and France scientific activities derived their strongest support from broader intellectual movements, in Germany they were promoted, funded and—if need be—protected within a backward society by states that saw the uses of scientific research for their political and economic projects as well as for their long-term vision of social and economic development; in the language of modernization theory, this was a classic case of "partial modernization" induced by rather autonomous state action.[68]

This first full institutionalization of science was grafted onto universities that had been transformed from their medieval foundations to become state-run training schools for the higher civil servants of the growing bureaucracies and for professional groups that in Prussia/Germany developed in close relation to, and under the control of, the state. The universities, too, were dependent on and controlled by the state. *Reichsfeinde*—enemies of the political establishment—were barred from teaching positions, and although officially the universities were places of research where science and politics were ideally separated, state-defined "national causes" were held up as guides for the work of academics. Academic freedom was limited. In the words of Max Weber: "The 'freedom of science' exists in Germany within the limits of ecclesiastical and political acceptability. Outside these limits there is none."[69]

By contrast, the English universities retained their inherited medieval insulation and autonomy much longer. During the nineteenth century, they did not become state institutions in funding or purpose. As they broadened their mission beyond the education of clergy and teachers, they became institutions of liberal learning, not training schools for professional specialists. The professions retained considerable autonomy and often controlled their own institutions of training.[70]

If in Germany the paradigmatic educated person was a civil servant—an administrator, a judge, a teacher in the state-run high schools, or a minister—his English counterparts were autonomous professionals (more autonomous from state control than their German colleagues were even in the private practice of law or medicine) and men of letters, not infrequently independently wealthy and often with quite idiosyncratic paths of intellectual formation.[71]

The authority of the knowledge-bearing strata was rooted both in Germany and in Britain in their education and presumed expertise. But for the German civil servant this authority was fused with the authority of the state he represented. In England, if there was any social reinforcement, it came from autonomous professional bodies such as the Inns of Court or the medical colleges that strengthened the authority of the learned individual. Most English intellectuals, however, derived their moral authority and influence not as much from their education, but rather from their position in society. Many of them came from wealthy and noble families or were members of the clergy.

The state-supported establishment of advanced scholarship in a backward society is the background for the peculiar role the professoriate was to acquire in the unified nation-state of Imperial Germany. It became a major partner in the national power structure, side by side and institutionally integrated with state administration, the army, and the business elite. The new Germany was to be a great power whose future depended on *Wirtschaft und Wissenschaft,* on economy and science. In this conception, *Wissenschaft* referred not only to the most obviously useful natural science, but also to law, history, economics (which significantly was called *Nationalökonomie*), and even theology. Many tensions and conflicts among disciplines and institutional spheres notwithstanding, the new power was to be at once a technologically and economically potent actor in the international scene and a Kulturstaat. The social sciences—history, law, and later political economics—were deeply involved in the creation and in the subsequent inner consolidation of the new empire. Neither the character of advanced scholarship in Imperial Germany nor the realpolitik of its foundation and consolidation can be understood in isolation from each other.[72]

The position of the intellectuals in Britain was remarkably different from the situation in Germany. Professionals in the modern sense did not emerge in Britain before the end of the nineteenth century. Before that, intellectual life in Britain was characterized by an informality and independence of the state that was unimaginable in Germany. Hickox argues that several factors shaped the idiosyncratic development of the British intelligentsia. First, unlike Germany, Britain never developed a "middle class of educators" linked to the central bureaucracy. Second, the British intelligentsia was well incorporated into the dominant social and political elites. Third, the role of intellectual in Britain was also closely linked to that of gentleman. And fourth, the British intellectuals were closer to the centers of powers and had access through traditional institutions.[73] It is especially the absence of a dependence on the state that sets the British intelligentsia apart from the German. The relatively open political system and intellectual tolerance within the elite, combined with the perceived economic and political lead of Britain over the rest of the world, created an environment in which different options for social reform could be advanced within a framework of evolutionary optimism.

> The new [English] social scientists were social reformers who expected progress to occur, in the final analysis, when individuals were able to behave rationally

and responsibly. Unlike the alienated, disillusioned Europeans, the English were encouraged in their optimistic expectations by consistent personal, family, and educational experiences.[74]

Historical Constellations at the Two Associations' Origins

The more immediate historical constellations in which the Fabian Society and the Verein für Sozialpolitik were created and in which they defined their agenda were shaped in England by the experience of the Chartist movement, and later by successive extensions of suffrage and new forms of party politics with mass appeal. In Germany, the situation was defined by political unification and the successful economic "takeoff" preceding it.

The Chartist movement had declined rapidly by the middle of the century. It is commonly regarded as a failure. Yet even if its failures stand out, the experience of Chartism had significant consequences. In 1890, Brentano countered the argument that comparisons with England were irrelevant for German social policy because the German working class was so much more radical than the English, by giving vivid descriptions of Chartist radicalism and violence. The Chartist movement engendered fear in the bourgeoisie, but also reactions of concern. Not only Marx and Engels learned from Chartism; the work of Dickens was also written under its impact, and Brentano describes the slow but complete turnaround in the attitudes of the educated classes toward the workers movement. Carlyle, John Stuart Mill, Kingsley, and Disraeli were all strongly influenced in their views. What survived politically after the breakup of Chartism was a middle-class radicalism that was both liberal and individualistic and that blamed the conduct of the ruling class for popular distress.[75]

For the working class, the Charter movement brought gains in protective legislation for women and children and the ten-hour day, but not suffrage and other major goals. "Perhaps the most important gain in the Chartist period, [however] was in the sphere of independent working class organizations with limited aims."[76] It was these autonomous working-class organizations that inspired Brentano's vision of a liberal future of industrial society.

The general adherence to a laissez-faire ideology did not prevent the English state from developing early forms of social policy and intervening occasionally in economic and social issues, for instance through the poor laws, factory regulation for the protection of workers, and the Corn Law. While public social welfare remained largely a matter of local administration, there developed in the second half of the nineteenth century a pattern of state intervention in factories, workshops, and mines.[77] Although the level of this intervention was moderate and the enforcement insufficient, it established a precedent for later, more thorough state regulation.

If the Charter movement was forcibly put down and failed to win suffrage for workers, the issue of suffrage did not disappear. In 1867, the Liberals expanded the franchise to include the upper strata of the working class. Tripling the number of voters, this move established a strong link between organized workers and liberalism. From then on, an ever more inclusive democratic polity was a generally accepted prospect.

The extension of suffrage required new methods of voter recruitment. The patronage system that had functioned well in previous times was no longer adequate. Organized political parties gained in importance. Both Liberals and Conservatives began to compete for the working-class vote—Gladstone with a vision of one middle-class nation, Disraeli with a program that would maintain the class structure as well as the leadership of the landed aristocracy but unite the country through social reform. New forms of association, of journalism, of lecturing responded to the new class-transcending forms of political participation. It was this situation that gave groups like the Fabians—capable of broad political appeal as well as of intelligent elite argument—a chance of political influence that did not exist before.

Dorothy Thompson points to an important corollary of the slow process of including the working class into the electorate that began in 1867 and was completed at the end of the First World War:

> The power of the non-parliamentary elements of government, the civil service, the judiciary, and the various advisory organizations, grew in the same period, and these were accessible only to those who had been educated within a system from which working people were totally excluded.[78]

This change had its counterpart in civil society where the professions expanded significantly and rose to new levels of importance and affluence. Both of these developments formed the background for the more elitist and, later, technocratic orientations among the Fabians.

Political unification of the German territories—long the goal of liberal politics in which professors, students, and professionals played a prominent role—came in 1871, but it came in the wake of wars and after a constitutional conflict in which the Prussian chancellor prevailed over his liberal opponents. Bismarck introduced in the new empire universal male suffrage, but the Imperial parliament had limited control over state policy, and the largest member state, Prussia, retained its three-class voting system.

The new empire faced major problems of internal consolidation, above all the political integration of an increasingly politicized working class.

The working class represented an alien world ignored or viewed with hostility by the educated classes. Faced with working-class demands, these groups "either withdrew into the comfortable security of the way of life available to the middle class (*Mittelstand*) or they indulged in dark and emotional prophecies about the coming decline of culture into materialism and revolution."[79]

In 1864, Ferdinand Lassalle had founded in Leipzig the Allgemeiner deutscher Arbeiterverein. This association, which put great faith in the role of the state and favored Bismarck's project of political unification under Prussian leadership, soon lost out to its rival, the Verband deutscher Arbeitervereine, led by August Bebel and Wilhelm Liebknecht, which in 1869 transformed itself into the Social Democratic Workers Party. If the Socialists' Eisenach Program of 1869 was still a mixture of Lassallean and Marxist ideas, the latter won out in the Gotha Program of 1875, even though Marx and Engels still found much to criticize. The Paris Commune of 1871, welcomed by Bebel in a speech in parliament as a symbol of the hopes of the European proletariat, dramatically increased the fears of class conflict and revolution in the political elite of the new empire.

Bismarck opted for a policy that combined political repression with an active social policy by the state. He came early to a position remarkably close to that of the "socialist professors"; but he did not make his views public, and he favored a degree of repression unacceptable even to the conservative wing of the Verein.[80] The repression, even after the anti-Socialist legislation of 1878, was moderate perhaps by the standards of our century, yet it was harsh enough to reinforce class and status divisions. In unintended ways, it also fostered sentiments of class solidarity in many workers that replaced narrower occupational and local identifications.

If Bismarck's position expressed the pragmatism of a conservative state manager, the position of the "socialists of the chair" had deep roots in the development of economics in Germany. While for the first two-thirds of the nineteenth century English classical economics was very influential in public administration and, though perhaps to a lesser extent, in the universities, Adam Müller had early in the century developed a romantic counterposition to the ideas of the Scottish enlightenment, and Friedrich List argued against free trade and for the protection of infant industries. Both took a critical stance toward the ideas spreading from the capitalist lead country, England, and emphasized a historical and national perspective for the study of economics. This perspective gained a foothold in the universities with the "older historical school" of Hildebrand, Roscher, and Knies. Their heirs, commonly labeled the "younger historical school," were the founders of the Verein für Sozialpolitik. They responded intellectually to political developments in England and France and were influenced by Comte, John Stuart Mill, Lorenz von Stein (whose work in 1842 opened a window on socialism and communism in France), as well as Marx. Sheehan concludes an excellent thumbnail sketch of this intellectual line of descent by placing the group in the political and intellectual context of their own time:

> It is hardly surprising that these young economists sought an alternative to classical liberalism in the ideas of Müller, List, and Knies. The historical tradition's concern for empirical reality and its national orientation seemed far better equipped to solve the problems of German society than laissez-faire liberalism. Equally important, this tradition was much more in harmony with the spirit of the years of the *Reichsgründung* and with the entire temper of German intellectual life in the second half of the nineteenth century, which was increasingly permeated by historically and nationally directed disciplines.[81]

It is important to understand these intellectual roots of the "socialists of the chair" and to realize that their mode of thought accorded well with that prevailing in other disciplines, above all jurisprudence and history. It is equally important, however, to keep in mind that their political project —of active intervention of the state in the new social and economic conditions created by capitalist development—was by no means similarly appealing to their colleagues in other fields of the academy or to the political representatives of their class. Historians and jurists had been the foremost academic spokesmen of liberal and national aspirations that came to a conclusion with the *Reichsgründung,* the creation of a unified Germany, in 1871. They remained staunchly liberal in their economic views, regardless of whether their political positions were closer to the liberal or the conservative end of the spectrum that defined bourgeois political opinion.

These, then, are some of the quite different social structural, political, and intellectual conditions in which the Fabians and the "socialists of the chair" undertook their projects. Before we come to some comparative and analytic conclusions, we must once more return to the history of the Verein für Sozialpolitik and examine some critical turning points and its eventual demise as a political force.

From Spearheading Social Change to Academic Discussion: the Politics of Scholarly Social Reform

The first attacks on the "socialists of the chair" came from laissez-faire liberals. They feared that the new movement would encourage a political coalition between socialists and conservatives. Given Bismarck's position of *raison d'etat* and Lassalle's state-oriented socialism, this fear was not a completely fanciful apprehension. The attacks did nothing to change the course of the Verein. Rather, they served mostly to increase the Verein's visibility as well as its sense of mission and unity despite widely divergent views among its members.

The most important internal tension in the early life of the Verein—aside from the ideological contrast between more state-oriented "conservatives" and more union-oriented "liberals"—was that between professors and entrepreneurs. From the very beginning of the Verein's activities, the Saar industrialist von Stumm as well as a number of other entrepreneurs and their retainers were active participants in the association. The initial common bond between them and the Verein derived from the paternalist "company welfare" orientations of these entrepreneurs.

The self-conception of the intellectuals who formed the core of the Verein insisted that their political goals were independent of capital and labor. Free of material self-interest, they had a particular opportunity, and therefore a special responsibility, to fight for the common good. This view of their own role was virtually identical with the idealist vision of the state as standing above the contending interests of society and mediating between them. Replicating Hegel's conception of the civil service as the social incarnation of universal interests, it linked the professors' view of themselves to the ethos prevailing among higher civil servants more generally.[82]

Even if in retrospect it is hard to view these claims as anything but ideological delusions, they were powerful cultural constructions and real in their effects. Such an insistence on a position above class interests was bound to create tensions in the transactions with industrial entrepreneurs, no matter how much common class position and common concerns made it possible to bridge the gap that separated *Bildung und Besitz* (culture and property), the standard formula of the time for the two major components of the dominant classes.

Among the specific points at issue between the two sides during the 1870s was the question of full freedom of association for workers but also the question of protective tariffs and other issues of primary concern to the businessmen. Matters came to a head at the meeting of 1879 which dealt with protective tariffs and ended with a vote for them. The meeting had been packed with business participants favoring the tariffs.

After that meeting, it was decided to drop formal votes. Meetings would now be concluded with a summary speech of the president. From this point on, entrepreneurial participation in the Verein declined significantly. Even though the professorial members were themselves divided over the issue of protective tariffs, many in the intellectual core group felt they had been used to advance business interests.

But equally important for the future of the Verein were other, broader political changes. The protective tariff legislation of 1879 signaled a comprehensive political restructuring of the new empire. Bismarck at this point made a far-reaching break with the National Liberals and with liberalism, rejecting political pressure for greater parliamentarization of government policy. Yet the political restructuring of the empire was more than a shift in the party coalition on which the government relied. Government bureaucracies were subjected to a thorough purge of liberal civil servants. And in 1878, several years of administrative harassment of socialist organizations were crowned by formal anti-Socialist legislation.

How did the Verein react to these changes? It retreated, abandoning its overtly political role as a "spearhead of *Sozialpolitik.*" In spite of the fact that the 1880s saw the major social policy projects of the Bismarck era realized—health, accident, and old age insurance programs that were financed by contributions from workers, employers, and the state—the Verein moved in its public discussions away from social policy issues and dealt primarily with questions of agrarian policy. The circular to the members announcing the end of formal voting on resolutions declared also: "The Verein will give up its agitational orientation and devote itself exclusively to a many-sided and thorough discussion of the relevant issues."[83]

The retreat was not complete, however. Nor was it lasting. While the Verein itself became less political in character, the old agenda was pursued through more restricted channels as for instance in the Berliner Staatswissenschaftliche Gesellschaft: "In the confidential atmosphere of this elite circle it was possible even in the late Bismarck years, when the Verein retreated from currently contested issues, to deal with sensitive areas such as worker protection in the factories, social insurance as well as specific aspects of labor law, the development of which was in its very beginnings."[84]

Bismarck's rejection of liberalism appealed to some of the members of the Verein, including its central figure, Gustav Schmoller. However, the anti-Socialist legislation kept Schmoller and the Verein from going beyond evasive acquiescence to full support of Bismarck's policies. "Bismarck became hostile toward the working class, and the Verein took its distance from the chancellor."[85] The social reform orientations of the Verein were far stronger than its commitment to liberal political positions.

This period of dormancy of social policy concerns in the Verein came to an end in 1890, when the new emperor, William II, dismissed Bismarck and promised a "new course" of social policy initiatives. The Verein supported the new course with enthusiasm. The 1890 meeting discussed strikes and the development of labor contracts and matched Brentano against Bück, the secretary general of the Centralverband deutscher Industrieller, which opposed the new course. This confrontation symbolized the conflicts to come. If in the 1870s the Verein fought a battle about theoretical principles with liberal orthodoxy in economics, now, as Schmoller put it later at the meeting in 1909, it entered a period of "fights with real and tough interests." Now von Stumm and other industrialists began a bitter battle against the "demagogic socialism" of the Verein.

This opposition from business interests alone was not sufficient to muffle the Verein's voice or even to make its work difficult. "It turned out that the industrialists, whose goal it was since 1890 to remove the scholars from politics, were by themselves not a factor that represented a real danger to the university teachers associated in the Verein."[86] Lujo Brentano compared the effect of von Stumm's attack on the Verein to that of the anti-Socialist legislation on the Social Democrats; it strengthened it. Yet when it became clear that neither the repressive legislation nor the social security measures adopted in the 1880s nor the prospect of the "new course" could stop the advance of Social Democratic voting gains, the government also turned more hostile toward the Verein, while several friendly government leaders including von Berlepsch resigned. The Verein was again seriously embattled.

This time, the reaction of the Verein was not retreat but continued struggle. The height of struggle brought it more vigorous unity as well as support from broader intellectual circles, who saw academic freedom and the role of the professoriate in the power structure of Imperial Germany at stake. In 1895, when von Stumm launched a violent attack on Adolf Wagner, Wagner found himself not only supported by Max Weber, a young member of the Verein with a political position quite different from Wagner's, but also by the historian Heinrich von Treitschke, a long-time enemy of the "socialists of the chair" who now protested passionately against "such a millionaire coming along and proclaiming before the whole nation untruths about German professors." Hans Delbrück commented in the *Preussische Jahrbücher:* "Property and Culture, up to now jointly dominant in Germany, begin to part ways."[87]

This was also the period when the Verein for the first time established contact with the socialist movement, though relations remained distant.[88] Generally, the Social Democrats stayed away from bourgeois organizations and remained critical of the Verein's work. Franz Mehring attacked the dream "that the proletarian class struggle would be more and more understood by the bourgeois intelligentsia and thereby take on milder forms"; in reality, he argued, people like Schmoller and Delbrück remained partisan apologists of bourgeois interests.[89] Rosa Luxemburg contemptuously criticized the research of the Verein. It had mounted masses of detailed knowledge against classical economics and Marxism, dissolving all large issues, and hiding rather than revealing the real laws of movement of bourgeois society: ". . . in the one hundred and three volumes of the Verein für Sozialpolitik," she wrote in 1903, "[the real issues of] social science rest in a deep grave under an enormous sand pile of social knowledge."[90]

The period of "retrograde revisions of social policy" in government action, as Schmoller called the 1890s, came to an end at the close of the century. The liberal parties, the National Liberal Party and the Freisinnige Vereinigung, now also opened themselves for certain social policy initiatives. Yet as political attacks and political struggle had unified the Verein, the greater openness for social policy discussion in bourgeois parties and in educated circles—partly the result of the Verein's success—did not bring smooth sailing for the association. Paradoxically, this apparently more favorable situation was the beginning of the end of the political project of the Verein. The decade and a half before the Great War was a period of dramatic internal conflicts in the association. It prepared the final turn toward mere academic discussion that was characteristic of the Verein in the 1920s and 1930s as well as in the period after World War II.

The younger generation—of Werner Sombart, Ferdinand Tönnies, Max and Alfred Weber, Friedrich Naumann—adopted a perspective that might well be called "neo-Marxist" as it focused on the long-term development of capitalism. They looked at economic developments as a historical process that made the moral sentiments and the sense of justice that had inspired the older generation virtually irrelevant. People like Schmoller insisted on an ethically inspired policy orientation and argued, not without some justification, that the conceptions of the younger generation about long-term historical change set empirical reality aside in favor of metaphysical speculation.

In 1905, Naumann and Schmoller clashed over these issues—specifically over the inevitability of economic concentration and the realism of a policy favoring small business. They clashed in such a way as to put the very existence of the Verein in question. Brentano, whose ideas accorded best with the outlook of the new generation, mediated in the aftermath of the meeting. The unity of the Verein was saved, but the differences remained. They came again to the fore, though in different form, in the famous debate on value judgments.

A concern of various member publications since 1880, the question of value judgments became a central issue in 1909. At the meeting in Vienna of that year, a paper by the economist Eugen von Philippovich on the concept of productivity encountered vocal opposition from many, including Max Weber. Productivity, the opponents argued, could not be defined in purely economic terms and at the same time be viewed as an objective, indisputable value.

Externally perceived as a professorial quibble about iotas and other fine points, the discussion on value judgments touched the very heart of the Verein's agenda. The issue was not whether the Verein should or should not take moral or political positions; virtually all members were in favor of that. The central question was whether scientific authority could be used to support these positions. Related issues were whether value judgments could be settled in a scholarly way, whether value positions had any implications for social explanation, whether unanimity on values made value judgments "objective," and—an especially explosive point of contention—whether a given intellectual argument (usually that of one's opponent) contained value judgments in a hidden way, presented in purely cognitive and therefore scholarly garb. These questions directly put into doubt the claim to an authority that fused intellectual, social, and political elements. It was on the basis of such an authority that the professorial social reformers had advanced their intellectual and political project.

These questions were a symptom of an increasing divergence of opinion within the Verein and, in turn, they added to this divergence a methodological-philosophical dimension. They also derived from a renewed strength of classical, or now neoclassical, views among economists, represented intellectually most strongly by the Vienna school of economics. Economists outside the Verein used similar methodological arguments for attacking the Verein and its social policy goals, even though they themselves presented economic models with clear political implications as value-free social science.

In the first decade of the twentieth century, it became evident that in important respects the Verein's project of academic social reform was failing. This is not to retreat from the judgment that these scholars had transformed public opinion among the educated on the *soziale Frage* and on the need for social reform. What was failing was their conception of an integration of the working class into a monarchical nation-state—their fight against the socialist movement, their struggle for a monarchic state mediating between capital and labor, the thrust of the conservative majority in the Verein to avoid full democratization by substituting social policy measures.

In spite of both repression and significant social policy measures, Schmoller had to acknowledge that the Social Democratic Party had become a "political and economic power of the first rank and one with republican-revolutionary tendencies." In the national elections of 1903, the Social Democratic Party had won three million votes, nearly a million more than in 1898. With just under a third of the vote, it was now the strongest party. And yet it was still seen by the right and the political core of the dynastic state as "the internal enemy," against whom it was even legitimate to consider a rollback of the limited forms of democratic participation that existed. The conflict between capital and working class was deeper than ever, with the state openly taking a less than neutral position.[91]

In this situation, which put the reform conception of the Verein radically into question, the association moved away from its initial political project and turned finally into a mere forum for academic discussion. This time—in contrast to the late 1870s when things took a superficially similar turn—the move away from politics was not imposed from the outside and only overtly accepted from within; it was rather the result of internal intellectual developments that responded to broader historical change.

The common intellectual and moral foundation on which their project of scholarly politics was built in the 1870s had been eroded. There was now too much diversity among the most active members to sustain this common ground. They ranged in their positions vis-à-vis capital and labor from socialism to a modified liberalism, in their views of the state from democratic and pluralist positions to an acceptance of the autocratic status quo, in their conceptions of historical development from determinist models of capitalist development to much more contingent views of the future and the past, in their methodological conceptions from historical empiricism to a (renewed) deductive model building. And these differences did not develop in isolation from political and economic change; they clearly reflected the development of class relations, the continued alliance of state, junkerdom, and bourgeoisie, the spectacular growth of Social Democracy, the organizational mobilization of many different segments of German society and the corresponding demands for fuller democratization, and the changing role of Germany as an international power.

It is in this context of increasing pluralism that we must understand the contending views of the status of moral and political judgments in the *Werturteilsdebatte*. Max Weber's sharp separation of *Wissenschaft* from morality and politics and his insistence on an ascetic abstinence from value pronouncements within social science sought to insulate both social science and the academy from the political and ideological conflicts that were now evident also within this community of scholars. His position stood in sharp contrast to various—by now plainly contradictory—claims to scholarly authority in matters of ethical and political judgment, be it the implicit moral claims of orthodox liberal economics or the explicit claim to speak for social justice that had been the original common ground of the Verein für Sozialpolitik. Rejecting this original position—the claim that scholars in social science had a special opportunity as well as responsibility for impartial, informed and, in this sense, "objective" ethical and political judgments—was in one sense an obvious move: it only drew the logical conclusion from the fact of deep internal dissension. Yet it also served to undermine the authority of the Verein as a corporate political voice in the wider field of political opinion.

The Fabian Society was attacked from without and experienced much conflict within. We will not detail these fights here beyond the glimpses caught earlier. But while the Fabians' relations to other groups and to parties shifted and while they had intense disagreements about political strategy among themselves, these developments never altered fundamentally the basis of their influence nor did they affect their views on the role of social knowledge.

For the Fabians, therefore, epistemological issues and the relation between knowledge and political action never became a problem. For them knowledge was an instrument for political action, but it had to be solid knowledge. Even if guided in its questions by their "collectivist" position, scientific inquiry had to be separated from moral and political judgment as well as from agitation and propaganda. Their confidence that "objective" knowledge would further their political cause was grounded in the broad moral consensus that underlaid the liberal policy discourse and in their belief in a progress that was inscribed into the basic movement of history.

The *Werturteilsdebatte* led to the creation of the German Sociological Society, which was devoted to the study of social phenomena removed from moral and political contests. Three years earlier, in 1906, the Sociological Society in London was founded. It is instructive to note that on this occasion Beatrice Webb formulated a position on the relation of value judgments to research that quite exactly resembled that of Max Weber.[92] However, this position had long been taken for granted. Neither the Fabians nor the other English social researchers at the time had ever claimed to possess a specific political-moral authority based on scholarly expertise. Nor were they now interested in the development of social science for its own sake and for sheer intellectual reasons. Their basic orientation remained pragmatic. Research and the gathering of data had to be politically relevant and not merely aid theory development. Science should be an objective body of knowledge, available for instrumental use in policy proposals and political persuasion.

The Authority of Knowledge: Comparative Reflections

In conclusion, we will review the bases of the Verein's particular authority comparing it to the Fabians. Looking into the complex foundations of the authority—intellectual and political—of these knowledge-bearing groups throws a revealing light on central problems of the sociology of policy-relevant knowledge. For the material at hand, it identifies what we consider the crucial differences between the Fabians and the professorial German Verein. And it helps us to explain the very different trajectories of the development of social science in the two countries.

German university professors enjoyed an extraordinarily high status in society. Their elevated position gave them credibility and influence especially in closely related status groups—among other higher civil servants and among the educated strata generally, in the *Bildungsbürgertum*. In this first aspect of the groups' authority the Fabians differ, but they differ only in the particulars. Though more varied in their status and located in a status system very different in its particulars, they, too, achieved an elite position in society that gave them access to political and cultural opinion leaders.

The second basis of authority is also shared by both the Society and the Verein. Both operated in a time of increased social tensions and conflicts. In both countries, class conflict posed a threat to elites and their views of national unity and purpose. These conflicts and tensions created a certain openness for ideas on how to respond politically to the capitalist transformation of economy and social order.

The differences are, however, striking and obvious when we turn to the way in which the knowledge claims of the two groups were made and how they were received. The German professors stood at the apex of a system of specialized knowledge occupations that was to a large extent integrated with the bureaucratic apparatus of the state. They not only constituted the elite of this system in terms of prestige. Rather, their work decided about continuity and innovative change for the entire system of specialized professional work. And it was constitutive of the professional authority of all practitioners.

In England, we find, first of all, a very different structure of professional authority—not at all closely integrated with the state apparatus, largely independent from the universities, supported by separate guild-like organizations, and perhaps less reliant on certification in comparison to individually judged competence. Equally important, the Fabians were not recruited from the old established professions (excepting some children of ministers) nor did they themselves work in these occupations. Even though they sought to promote expertise and professional judgment in government and politics, they themselves were either men and women of letters or they were pioneers in transforming social research from an amateur activity on a large scale into an institutionalized professional pursuit. The London School of Economics was an outgrowth, not the basis, of their initiative.

Political discourse in late nineteenth-century British society and within the British state was much more open to opinion and expertise developed outside the state than was the case in Germany. Furthermore, the English royal commissions not only brought expert knowledge to the legislative bodies, but also made it available to the public, since these hearings were open to the public and reported in the press.

German university scholarship—*Wissenschaft* in that broad conception which goes far beyond "science"—was part of the established power structure in Prussia/Germany. Together with the top ranks of the Protestant church, state administration, army, and business, the professoriate formed the core of an exclusionary system, exclusionary not in the sense that it was completely self-recruited, which it was not, but in the sense that is was only paternalistically responsive to the interests and views even of the middle classes, not to mention workers, craftsmen, and peasants. If these were taken into account, they did not enter consideration directly but only as conceived by the established elites.

The authority of the political economists of the Verein, therefore, derived not only from respect for knowledge and learning, but from a combination of this intellectual status with the authority of higher civil servants and the regard for people who share, at least symbolically, in the apex of national power. Within that system, these scholars claimed—and were granted by established opinion—the authority of a special expertise in economic and social affairs. Such expertise on what were essentially political issues was the more accepted as valid the less a democratic ethos of citizenship and generalized civic responsibility had penetrated a civil society fragmented by class and status lines.

The Fabians had access to, and became part of, a political elite that was less sharply bounded institutionally, more hospitable to controversy, and in the process of opening up to the electoral participation of the working class. This elite was hardly more egalitarian in any rigorous sense; yet it was more diffusely defined and more fluid, and it had developed a culture of political contest in which the informed arguments of generalists could make a difference.

The German professors of the Verein claimed a position of disinterestedness that was grounded in their distance from capital and working class alike. Invoking the similar claim of the enlightened absolutist state, they found here the basis of an "objectivity" that was both social and intellectual in character and that allowed them to press advice on the state that was considered by many as informed as well as impartial. Given the inherently contestable nature of their "knowledge," this claim to impartiality was essential to their project of advancing a comprehensive *Sozialpolitik*—however dubious to the critical observer at the time or later. Attacks from "interested parties" served first to buttress the claim of disinterestedness. However, when the divergences of opinion within the Verein—mirroring the growing pluralization of German politics—increased beyond a certain point,[93] social and political impartiality was revealed as a social construction whose basis in the constellation of interest and power was crumbling. It was probably inevitable that in this situation the *Werturteilsdebatte* severed political value judgments from judgments of fact and theoretical generalization.

The Fabians never made similar claims for a particular authority covering cognitive as well as moral-political issues. They appealed to moral-political values on which the positions in their society or in the wider policy discourse never became as polarized and fragmented as in Germany. At the same time, they insisted on factual information and analysis that was to be as independent of their politics as possible. Their belief in a progress that was inherent in the central tendencies of history—a background belief shared by many—gave them a different and less challenged basis for integrating political goals with historical and contemporary knowledge and reasoned anticipations of the future. For the Fabians, "objective" facts served as instruments for their political struggle, and they were quite open about this pragmatic attitude toward scientific knowledge.

Both the Verein and the Society emphasized empirical description in preparation of their proposals. Empirical documentation of actual conditions was often sufficient—in conjunction with unstated and unquestioned conceptions about social justice—to create an urgent moral appeal. The Verein decided early to shun discussion of political and economic principles and to focus instead on detailed research in preparation for the agenda of each meeting. This reinforced its reputation of scholarly expertise, and it put theoretical and metatheoretical disagreements into the background. Aside from grand formulations about democratic collectivism, the Fabians also concentrated on specific analyses and practical proposals because they found this to be the fare most in demand in the political process. For both groups, then, empirical evidence served as a tool for the identification of social problems and for the justification of specific policy proposals. And both found that empirical knowledge claims buttressed their generalized authority.

Both the Verein für Sozialpolitik and the Fabian Society accepted major facets of the political, social, and economic status quo, and this also was a condition of their influence. Such compliance with dominant opinion in matters considered fundamental in turn opened the chance to shape opinion on matters of social policy. Substantively, accepting the fundamentals of the status quo entailed, of course, very different things in the two cases, and this difference shaped the character of the two groups, their strategies, and their history.

In contrast to the revolutionary ideologies of more radical socialist and other leftist groups, the strategy of the Fabian Society was a constitutional one, oriented toward gradual and peaceful social reform. Accepting the rules of the British political system and working within that system—a liberal oligarchy in the process of opening itself to wider political participation—made the Fabians much less threatening, and therefore more acceptable to the dominant elites. Operating within the system—from the permeation strategy to giving testimony before innumerable committees, from broad agitation to elite persuasion—also gave them more access to these elites, especially to members of parliament. Their social and intellectual status facilitated moving in these circles. This and their use of the political institutions provided the opportunity to spread their ideas within the political class.

Operating in an expanding liberal political system also opened the chance of contributing to far-reaching shifts in the electoral balance of political power. Together with other movements, the Fabian Society helped organize large parts of the working class.

The common ground of the Verein, at least until the turn of the century, included acceptance of a much less open political and economic structure. Most members of the Verein gave the "national interest," as represented and defined by the state and its elites, the highest value priority. Most, especially the conservative majority, accepted the nondemocratic political status quo (including the Prussian three-class system of suffrage and the absence of parliamentary responsibility of government policy in the Reich). And most, of course, embraced the fundamentals of the capitalist economic order. The envisioned integration of the working class through *Sozialpolitik* was an integration on the terms of the existing power structure and a substitute for full democratization. Part of this consensus survived beyond the turn of the century, but in other parts (especially in regard to the political status quo) it began to unravel among the younger generation. This development and the resurgence of neoclassical economics, which put the dominance of the old positions of the "socialists of the chair" in question, were the underlying issues that gave the debate on value judgments between 1909 and 1914 its particularly unsettling character.

The fusion of social and political authority on which the professorial reformers of the Verein based their project failed as more and more diverse forces entered the actual policy discourse in late Imperial Germany. It had grown out of a peculiar historical conjunction when the new German empire was founded, characterized by an incompletely democratized monarchy, by a peculiar concatenation of heterogeneous elites, of feudal, capitalist, administrative, and academic groups, by rapid industrial development, and by a thorough capitalist transformation of the old social order. It failed when this constellation passed, when political discourse within and without the Verein became more diverse, and when the initial vision of the "socialists of the chair" was manifestly incompatible with emerging political conflicts and realities. Out of this failure came new conceptions of social science, more or less radically set apart from political issues. In England, the pragmatic subordination of social science to a policy discourse that did not experience similarly radical discontinuities and transformations was combined with an equally pragmatic respect for empirical knowledge, and this combination continued for another two or three generations.

We owe thanks to a large number of colleagues. The chapter benefited from discussions at two workshops of the Committee on States and Social Structures of the Social Science Research Council, New York. It was revised when Dietrich Rueschemeyer was a fellow at the Wissenschaftskolleg, Berlin. In Berlin, it was discussed in the Kolleg's seminar on Culture and Science, led by Tim Lenoir, and at the Institute for Economic and Social History of the Free University of Berlin. We acknowledge gratefully the comments of Reinhard Bendix, Peter Evans, Gerald Feldman, Wolfram Fischer, Jon Harwood, Hartmut Kaelble, Ira Katznelson, Tim Lenoir, Anson Rabinbach, Klaus Tenfelde, Heinrich Volkmann, Norton Wise, and Björn Wittrock.

Notes to Chapter 4

1. For both quotes, see Franz Böse, *Geschichte des Vereins für Sozialpolitik 1872–1932*. Berlin: Duncker & Humblot, 1939, p. 6.

2. Dieter Lindenlaub, *Richtungskämpfe im Verein für Sozialpolitik. Wissenschaft und Sozialpolitik im Kaiserreich vornehmlich vom Beginn des "Neuen Kurses" bis zum Ausbruch des Ersten Weltkrieges (1890–1914)*. Wiesbaden: F. Steiner, 1967 (Supplements 52 and 53 to the *Vierteljahresschrift für Sozial- und Wirtschaftsgeschichte*).

3. Lujo Brentano, "Adolf Wagner über Agrarstaat und Industriestaat (I)," *Die Hilfe* 7 (23), (June 9, 1901): p. 3.

4. See Lindenlaub, *Richtungskämpfe,* p. 6, and Irmela Gorges, *Sozialforschung in Deutschland 1872–1914: Gesellschaftliche Einflüsse auf Themen- und Methodenwahl des Vereins für Sozialpolitik*. Königstein: Athenäum/Hain, 1980; 2nd ed., 1986.

5. Gerhard Albrecht, "Verein für Sozialpolitik," *Handwörterbuch der Sozialwissenschaften* 11(1961): pp. 10–16, at p. 13.

6. For their self-conscious strategy of publicity and the wide range of options among journals and newspapers, see the letters of A. Wagner published in Lothar Machtan, "Adolph Wagner und die Gründung des Vereins für Sozialpolitik." *Zeitschrift für Sozialreform* 34(9) (September 1988): pp. 510–23.

7. See Rüdiger vom Bruch, "Die Staatswissenschaftliche Gesellschaft 1883–1919, I: Staatswissenschaft, Bildung und Bürokratie im späten 19. Jahrhundert." In *100 Jahre Staatswissenschaftliche Gesellschaft. Festschrift*. Berlin, 1983; and idem, "Bürgerliche Sozialreform im deutschen Kaiserreich." In Rüdiger vom Bruch, ed., *'Weder Kommunismus noch Kapitalismus': Bürgerliche Sozialreform in Deutschland vom Vormärz bis zur Ära Adenauer. Munich: C. H. Beck, 1985.*

> Such circles, more than the large organizations of social reform, reflected that specific milieu of communication based on educated cultivation and government service which influenced a part of the educated classes and must be seen as a decisive segment of the political culture of Imperial Germany. It found in the Prussian and Imperial capital, which was at once a political, intellectual, publishing, industrial and administrative center, a unique concentration. . . . Even though there were deep differences of opinion on concrete questions about the need for social reform, such contacts without a doubt enhanced on the one side the conviction that the major political-administrative figures were capable of reform and in turn reinforced among the latter the appreciation of scientific competence in the further development of policies shaping society (Gesellschafts- und Ordnungspolitik). Vom Bruch, "Bürgerliche Sozialreform," p. 85.

8. James J. Sheehan, *The Career of Lujo Brentano: A Study of Liberalism and Social Reform in Imperial Germany.* Chicago: University of Chicago Press, 1966, p. 5.

9. Lindenlaub, *Richtungskämpfe,* p. 30. Brentano organized in Munich, against considerable bureaucratic resistance, university extension courses that he had come to admire in England; see Lujo Brentano, *Die Stellung der Gebildeten zur sozialen Frage*. Berlin: Verlag der Akademischen Blätter, n.d. (1890).

10. See Emil Ritter, *Die katholisch-soziale Bewegung Deutschlands im neunzehnten*

Jahrhundert und der Volksverein. Cologne: J. P. Bachem, 1954, and Sheehan, *The Career of Lujo Brentano,* p. 116.

11. Lindenlaub reports that in 1906 the action committee of the Evangelisch-Sozialer Kongress included A. Wagner, L. Bernhard, H. Delbrück, E. Francke, O. v. Gierke, F. Naumann, and the wife of G. Schmoller—all closely associated with the Verein (*Richtungskämpfe,* pp. 29–30, n. 66).

12. See Ursula Ratz, *Sozialreform und Arbeiterschaft: Die "Gesellschaft für soziale Reform" und die sozialdemokratische Arbeiterbewegung von der Jahrhundertwende bis zum Ausbruch des Ersten Weltkrieges*. Berlin: Colloquium Verlag, 1980, p. 230. It may be a mistake, as Klaus Tenfelde argued in a private communication, to view the relationship between the Verein and the Gesellschaft with Schmoller as a simple division of labor. Ratz documents that the goals of the Gesellschaft were more activist and less reserved toward the Social Democrats. See also Lindenlaub, *Richtungskämpfe,* pp. 29–30, 187–90; and vom Bruch, "Bürgerliche Sozialreform," pp. 130–52.

13. Sheehan, *The Career of Lujo Brentano,* p. 72; Lindenlaub, *Richtungskämpfe,* pp. 29, 35; vom Bruch, "Bürgerliche Sozialreform."

14. Both citations are from the Brentano papers, quoted in Lindenlaub, *Richtungskämpfe,* pp. 144, 149.

15. Sheehan, *The Career of Lujo Brentano,* p. 72.

16. See for instance Max Sering, "Die soziale Frage in England und Deutschland." *Schmollers Jahrbuch für Gesetzgebung, Verwaltung und Volkswirtschaft im Deutschen Reich* N.F. 14 (1890): pp. 343–91, at p. 374.

17. On this association, see Volker Hentschel, *Die deutschen Freihändler und der volkswirtschaftliche Kongress 1858 bis* 1885. Stuttgart: Klett, 1975.

18. Friedrich Meinecke, "Drei Generationen deutscher Gelehrtenpolitik: Friedrich Theodor Vischer—Gustav Schmoller—Max Weber," *Historische Zeitschrift* 125 (1922): 248–83; reprinted in Werke, vol. 9, Stuttgart: K. F. Köhler, 1979, pp. 476–505, at p. 489. Gerhard Ritter offers a similar assessment: "The publications of the *Kathedersozialisten,* together with their influence on the bureaucracy at ministerial level (still to be investigated by detailed research), signficantly contributed to creating a favourable climate for social reform among Germany's political and bureaucratic elites. . . ." See his *Social Welfare in Germany and Britain: Origins and Development*. Leamington Spa and New York: Berg, 1983, p. 28.

19. Gustav Schmoller, "Die soziale Bewegung Englands von 1770–1912 im Lichte der Marxistischen Klassenkampflehre." *Schmollers Jahrbuch für Gesetzgebung, Verwaltung und Volkswirtschaft im Deutschen Reich* N. F. 38 (1914): pp. 1–42, at p. 33.

20. A. M. McBriar, *Fabian Socialism and English Politics* 1884–1918, Cambridge: Cambridge University Press, 1962, pp. 66–7.

21. G. B. Shaw, *Report on Fabian Policy,* Fabian Tract No. 70. London: Fabian Society, 1896, p. 3.

22. G. B. Shaw, "Preface to the 1908 reprint." In G. B. Shaw, ed., *Fabian Essays in Socialism.* London: George Allen & Unwin, 1950, pp. xxix–xxxviii, at p. xxxv. For Webb's position, see Sidney Webb, *The Workers' Political Programme,* Fabian Tract No. 11. London: Fabian Society, 1890.

23. F. Engels, "Brief von Engels an Friedrich Adolph Sorge, 8. Februar 1890." In *Karl Marx—Friedrich Engels Werke,* vol. 37. Berlin: Dietz Verlag, 1967, pp. 352–55, at pp. 354–55. The text is worth being quoted in the original: ". . . die Fabians, eine wohlmeinende Bande von jebildeten Bürgern, die Marx widerlegt haben mit der faulen Vulgärökonomie von Jevons, die so vulgär ist, dass man alles draus machen kann, selbst Sozialismus. Ihr Hauptzweck ist . . . den Bürger zum Sozialismus zu bekehren und so die Sache peacefully und constitutionally einzuführen."

24. Shaw, "Preface," p. xxxiii.

25. McBriar, *Fabian Socialism,* p. 25.

26. See Peter Wittig, *Der englische Weg zum Sozialismus.* Berlin: Duncker & Humblot, 1982, pp. 46–54, 347–49.

27. N. Mackenzie, ed., *The Letters of Sidney and Beatrice Webb.* Vol. I. *Apprenticeships 1873–1892.* Cambridge: Cambridge University Press, 1978, p. 356.

28. A. Wright, "A Century of Fabianism 1884–1984." *History Today* 34 (May 1984): pp. 50–52.

29. S. Hynes, *The Edwardian Turn of Mind.* Princeton, NJ: Princeton University Press, 1968, p. 90.

30. E. J. Hobsbawm, *Labouring Men. Studies in the History of Labour.* New York: Basic Books, 1964, p. 268.

31. Karl Mannheim, *Ideology and Utopia.* San Diego: Harcourt Brace Jovanovich, 1985, p. 155.

32. Schmoller, "Die soziale Bewegung," p. 34.

33. G. B. Shaw and M. Cole, "Early days." In M. Cole, ed., *The Webbs and Their Work.* London: Frederick Muller, 1949, pp. 3–14, at p. 7.

34. See W. Wolfe, *From Radicalism to Socialism. Men and Ideas in the Formation of the Fabian Socialist Doctrines 1881–1889.* New Haven: Yale University Press, 1975; P. Pugh, *Educate, Agitate, Organize. 100 Years of Fabian Socialism.* London: Methuen, 1984, pp. 6ff.; and L. Radice, *Beatrice and Sidney Webb. Fabian Socialists.* New York: St. Martin's Press, 1984, p. 48.

35. McBriar, *Fabian Socialism,* pp. 165ff.

36. E. R. Pease, *The History of the Fabian Society.* New York: Barnes & Noble, 1963, p. 103. In 1900, only four local societies remained, numbering a total of 153 members, together with four university societies that, combined, had 87 members and associates, leading to a grand total of 240 members and associates for the local societies. But just like the London society, these provincial and university societies saw a revival from 1906 on, and this lasted until the beginning of the First World War.

McBriar (*Fabian Socialism,* p. 167) estimates that in 1913 the provincial societies had about 970 members, while the university societies had 477 members and probably accounted for almost all of the 323 associates. The figures given by Schmoller ("Die soziale Bewegung," p. 34) for the membership of all the societies in 1911–12 seem to correspond to those McBriar (*Fabian Socialism,* p. 165ff.) gives for the London society alone.

37. Mackenzie, *The Letters,* vol. 1, p. 101. See also Wittig, *Der englische Weg,* p. 333.

38. Mackenzie, Norman, *The Letters of Sidney and Beatrice Webb.* Volume II. *Partnership 1892–1912.* Cambridge: Cambridge University Press, 1987, p. 29.

39. McBriar, *Fabian Socialism,* pp. 7–8. For the complex patterns of influence, see also Wittig, *Der englische Weg;* McBriar, *Fabian Socialism,* passim; and Radice, *Beatrice and Sidney Webb.*

40. Pugh, *Educate, Agitate, Organize,* pp. 1, 6. See also Wittig, *Der englishe Weg,* and S. Pierson, *British Socialists. The Journey from Fantasy to Politics.* Cambridge, MA: Harvard University Press, 1979, p. 30.

41. There is no evidence they were also familiar with the younger members of the Verein such as Tönnies or Max Weber, certainly not in the period discussed here. Brentano and the Webbs knew each other relatively well. Beatrice Potter had met him in September 1890 at the meetings of the economics section of the British Association and she found him "attractive and sympathetic" (N. and J. Mackenzie, eds., *The Diary of Beatrice Webb.* Volume One. *1873–1892. Glitter Around and Darkness Within.* Cambridge, MA: The Belknap Press of Harvard University Press, 1982, p. 340). Later, in 1893, Brentano would translate Beatrice Potter's book on the cooperative movement into German. The Webbs in turn reviewed the English editions of Brentano's studies on the origins of guilds and trade unions and on working hours and wages. Sidney Webb also sent several students to work and study with Brentano.

42. Wittig, *Der englische Weg,* p. 335.

43. See R. N. Soffer, *Ethics and Society in England. The Revolution in the Social Sciences, 1870–1914.* Berkeley: University of California Press, 1978, p. 168; and W. Oddie, *Dickens and Carlyle. The Question of Influence.* London: The Centenary Press, 1972.

44. Soffer, *Ethics and Society,* pp. 222–23.

45. In the judgment of Wittig (*Der englische Weg,* p. 344), they neglected political loyalty and the building of trust in the expectation that rational reform models of independent intellectuals should have their own, overriding appeal.

46. See R. Moore, *The Emergence of the Labour Party 1880–1924.* London: Haddor & Stoughton, 1978, p. 57; McBirar, *Fabian Socialism;* H. Pelling, *The Origins of the Labour Party 1880–1900.* Oxford: Clarendon Press, 1965; Pease, *The History;* Pugh, *Educate, Agitate, Organize.*

47. G. B. Shaw, *The Fabian Society: Its Early History.* Fabian Tract No. 41. London: Fabian Society, 1899, p. 19. The permeation tactic was of course criticized by the more radical labor movement. Friedrich Engels's comment is characteristic: They "preached and practiced attachment to the Liberals, and what was to be expected happened: The Liberals assigned them four seats impossible to win, and the Fabian candidates failed gloriously." F. Engels, "Brief von Engels an Karl Kautsky, 4. September 1892." In *Karl Marx—Friedrich Engels Werke,* vol. 38. Berlin, Dietz Verlag, 1968, pp. 446–48, at p. 446.

48. See Pugh, *Educate, Agitate, Organize,* p. 25; Pease, *The History,* pp. 111–12; and Shaw, *The Fabian Society,* p. 19.

49. G. B. Shaw, *A Plan of Campaign for Labour.* Fabian Tract No. 49. London: Fabian Society, 1894.

50. Pugh, *Educate, Agitate, Organize,* p. 32.

51. Schmoller, "Die soziale Bewegung," p. 34.

52. The figures on the number of lectures are, however, not very accurate as the registration of lectures was poor (McBriar, *Fabian Socialism,* pp. 176ff.).

53. Pierson, *British Socialists,* pp. 315ff.

54. See D. A. Hamer, *The Politics of Electoral Pressure. A Study in the History of Victorian Reform Agitations*. Hassocks: Harvester Press, 1977.

55. See McBriar, *Fabian Socialism;* Pelling, *The Origins;* Moore, *The Emergence.* The quote is from Schmoller, "Die soziale Bewegung," p. 32.

56. Schmoller, "Die soziale Bewegung," p. 35.

57. Wittig, *Der englische Weg,* p. 336.

58. Ibid., p. 332.

59. Lawrence Goldman has compared the Verein to the English and the American social science associations; see his "A Peculiarity of the British? The Social Science Association and the Absence of Sociology in Nineteenth Century Britain." *Past and Present* 114 (February 1987): pp. 133–71. This, too, is an instructive comparison, focusing on the different sorts of "social science" that emerge from the success or failure of different political projects undertaken by social knowledge elites. The Social Science Association is indeed very important for an understanding of the overall patterns of interrelationship between social knowledge and policy formation in nineteenth-century Britain. Founded in 1857, it became an influential "outdoor Parliament." The Verein was never that central to the overall political process.

In our view, Goldman misjudges the Verein and its history in two respects: he sees it turning away from a political mission already in the early 1880s, and he views it as a fundamentally liberal organization. On this basis, he constructs a parallel to the American Social Science Association. Both were "self-confessed institutional political failures: . . . the Verein, preempted by Bismarck's statism, could have no role in a political system constructed in opposition to a liberal pluralism. In both cases the resort to the academy was an admission of impotence, a second-best option" (pp. 167–68). We will offer a different analysis below.

60. Sering, "Die soziale Frage," p. 374.

61. See Reinhard Bendix, *Nation-Building and Citizenship.* Berkeley: University of California Press, 1964.

62. John Stuart Mill, *Consideration on Representative Government.* London: Parker, Son, and Bourn, 1861, pp. 40–41.

63. See G. H. Fry, *Statesmen in Disguise. The Changing Role of the Administrative Class of the British Home Civil Service, 1853–1966.* London: Macmillan, 1969; also K. Thomas, "The United Kingdom." In R. Grew, ed., *Crisis of Political Development in Europe and the United States.* Princeton, NJ: Princeton University Press, 1978, pp. 41–97, at p. 81.

The majority of the bureaucrats in nineteenth-century Britain were employed either in the finance department or, like Sidney Webb, in the Colonial Office. The colonial expansion of Britain has been one of the major impulses for the growth of government bureaucracy in Britain.

64. See D. Macdonagh, *Early Victorian Government, 1830–1870.* New York: Holmes & Meier, 1977, p. 6.

65. It is once again John Stuart Mill who expresses this aspect of bureaucratic rule—and at the same time gives voice to the quite different English conditions and ideas—when he speaks with eloquent understatement of "the inexpediency of concentrating in a dominant bureaucracy . . . all the power of organized action, existing in the community, a practice which . . . is the main cause of the inferior capacity for political life which has hitherto characterised the over-governed countries of the continent, whether with or without the forms of representative government." John Stuart Mill, *Principles of Political Economy.* Boston: C. C. Little and J. Brown, 1848, vol. II, p. 538.

66. Gerhard Dilcher, "Das Gesellschaftsbild der Rechtswissenschaft und die soziale Frage." In Klaus Vondung, ed., *Das Wilhelminische Bildungsbürgertum. Zur Sozialgeschichte seiner Ideen.* Göttingen: Vandenhoeck & Ruprecht, 1976, pp. 53–66.

67. The educated classes and, more broadly, the middle classes in the nineteenth century have been the subject of major comparative research efforts in Germany. See J. Kocka, ed., *Bürger und Bürgerlichkeit im 19. Jahrhundert.* Göttingen: Vandenhoeck & Ruprecht, 1987; J. Kocka, ed., *Bürgertum im europäischen Vergleich.* 3 vols. München: Deutscher Taschenbuch Verlag, 1988; W. Conze and J. Kocka, eds., *Bildungsbürgertum im 19. Jahrhundert.* Vol. I. *Bildungssystem und Professionalisierung im internationalen Vergleich.* Stuttgart: Klett-Cotta, 1985; R. Koselleck, ed., *Bildungsbürgertum im 19. Jahrhundert.* Vol. II. *Bildungsgüter und Bildungswissen.* Stuttgart: Klett-Cotta, 1990; M. R. Lepsius, ed., *Bildungsbürgertum im 19. Jahrhundert.* Vol. III. *Lebensführung und ständische Vergesellschaftung.* Stuttgart: Klett-Cotta, 1992; J. Kocka, ed., *Bildungsbürgertum im 19. Jahrhundert.* Vol. IV. *Politischer Einfluss und gesellschaftliche Formation.* Stuttgart: Klett-Cotta, 1989.

68. See Joseph Ben-David, *The Scientist's Role in Society.* Englewood Cliffs, NJ: Prentice-Hall, 1971; see also Dietrich Rueschemeyer, "Die Entwicklung der Wissenschaft im Modernisierungsprozess." *Geschichte und Gesellschaft* 2 (1976): 501–13. For the relation between state-run universities and the professions, discussed below, see idem, "Professionalisierung: Theoretische Probleme für die vergleichende Geschichtsforschung." *Geschichte und Gesellschaft* 6 (1980): 311–25.

69. Cited in Charles E. McClelland, *State, Society, and University in Germany, 1700–1914.* Cambridge: Cambridge University Press, 1980, p. 315.

70. J. S. Mill captured the spirit of the British universities pretty well when he argued in 1867 that "the proper function of an University in national education is tolerably well understood. At least, there is a tolerably general agreement about what an University is not. It is not a place of professional education. Universities are not intended to teach the knowledge required to fit men for some special mode of gaining their livelihood. Their object is not to make skillful lawyers, or physicians, or engineers, but capable and cultivated human beings. . . . Men are men before they are lawyers, or physicians, or merchants, or manufacturers; and if you make them capable and sensible men, they will make themselves capable and sensible lawyers or physicians." John Stuart Mill, "Inaugural address at St. Andrew's." In F. A. Cavenagh, ed., *James and John Stuart Mill on Education.* Cambridge: Cambridge University Press, 1931, pp. 133–41.

71. Examples are the education of Herbert Spencer (see J.D.Y. Peel, *Herbert*

Spencer. Evolution of a Sociologist. New York: Basic Books, 1971); Charles Booth (Harold W. Pfautz, "Charles Booth: Sociologist of the City." In H. W. Pfautz, ed., *Charles Booth On the City: Physical Pattern and Social Structure* (Introduction). Chicago: the University of Chicago Press, 1967; Sidney Webb and Beatrice Potter-Webb (see Radice, *Beatrice and Sidney Webb*), and George Bernard Shaw.

72. See Pierangelo Schiera, "Deutsche Wissenschaft und Realpolitik. 1848–1914." In *Wissenschaftkolleg—Institute of Advanced Study Berlin—Jahrbuch 1982/83.* Berlin: Siedler, 1983, pp. 293–307.

73. M. S. Hickox, "Has There Been a British Intelligentsia?" *British Journal of Sociology* 37 (2) (1986): 260–68. See also C. Levy, "Introduction: Historical and theoretical themes." In C. Levy, ed., *Socialism and the Intelligentsia 1880–1914.* London: Routledge & Kegan Paul, 1987, pp. 1–34; and Soffer, *Ethics and Society.*

74. Soffer, *Ethics and Society,* p. 2.

75. Wolfe, *From Radicalism to Socialism,* p. 7. For Brentano's comments, see *Die Stellung der Gebildeten,* pp. 4, 7.

76. Thompson, *The Chartists: Popular Politics in the Industrial Revolution.* New York: Pantheon Books, 1984, pp. 336–37.

77. See P.W.J. Bartrip, "State Intervention in Mid-Nineteenth Century Britain: Fact or Fiction?" *Journal of British Studies* 23 (1) (1983): pp. 63–83. On the large role of local authorities, see J. R. Hay, *The Origins of the Liberal Welfare Reforms 1906–1914.* London: Macmillan, 1975, p. 40; and S. Checkland, *British Public Policy, 1776–1939. An Economic, Social and Political Perspective.* Cambridge: Cambridge University Press, 1983, pp. 155–56. On the control of the central state, see Checkland, pp. 196ff.

78. Thompson, The Chartists, p. 335.

79. Meinecke, "Drei Generationen," p. 488. Meinecke himself reveals his own views of an earlier class harmony and his feelings about class conflict when he exclaims about the early 1860s: "Where are they gone, these days, when the nation, though politically and denominationally divided, was not yet infused with the hatred of class conflict, the days preceding its rise, but also the days preceding its class division. . . ?" (p. 482).

80. Already in 1871, he noted in his papers: "Ignoring the socialist demands is futile. The state has to discuss them—the limited work day, wages, the problems of housing." Walter Bussman, *Das Zeitalter Bismarcks. Handbuch der deutschen Geschichte, III, 3.* Konstanz: Akademische Verlagsanstalt, 1957, p. 179. These comments must not be misunderstood. When, on the occasion of the parliamentary discussion on anti-Socialist legislation in 1878, he looked back at Bebel's support for the Paris Commune, Bismarck revealed again his fierce anti-Socialist position: "From that moment on, I was full convinced of the danger threatening us . . . the Commune's proclamation to the people was like a shaft of light which brought the point home and from then on I recognised an enemy in social democratic elements, against whom the state and society find themselves in a position of self-defense." Quoted by Ritter, *Social Welfare,* p. 24, n. 22.

81. Sheehan, *The Career of Lujo Brentano,* p. 52.

82. Thus Brentano described in 1872 the "socialists of the chair" as a group between the classes: ". . . by their social position oriented toward the interests of

the whole, they have on the one hand pressed demands against capital in the interest of the workers, and on the other rejected demands of workers in the interest of capital." (Lujo Brentano, "Der Ausgangspunkt und die dauernde Grundlage der sog. Kathedersozialisten." *Hamburger Korrespondent,* [November 1872], Brentano papers. Cited by Lindenlaub, *Richtungskämpfe,* p. 26.) Schmoller stated it similarly nearly thirty years later: "We do not fight for our income, we do not fight for our wealth, we do not fight for our personal economic interests. . . . We can see things in a non-partisan way; we are less wedded to certain formulae of party doctrine, which we face around us." (Lindenlaub, *Richtungskämpfe,* pp. 26–27.)

The positive definition of the interest of the whole shows the close connection between the established professoriate and Imperial Realpolitik— "the maintenance and further development of our national culture and our national position of power is, it seems, the special calling of those educated people (*Gebildete*) who are not personally involved with their interests on one of the two sides"—capital and labor (Brentano, *Die Stellung der Gebildeten,* p. 3).

83. Albrecht, "Verein für Sozialpolitik," p. 13.

84. Vom Bruch, "Bürgerliche Sozialreform," p. 85.

85. Lindenlaub, *Richtungskämpfe,* pp. 183–84.

86. Ibid., p. 52.

87. Ibid., p. 59.

88. In 1893, two Social Democrats participated for the first time in the meetings, criticizing the principles and the implementation of the Verein's research projects and especially Max Weber's paper on the agrarian workers in East Germany (Albrecht, "Verein für Sozialpolitik," p. 13). Emil Döblin, a Social Democrat representing the union of printers, was for a few years after that a member of the executive committee.

89. Anon. (Franz Mehring), "Eine Illusion," *Die Neue Zeit* 22, 2(50) (September 10, 1904): 737–40, at p. 739.

90. Lindenlaub, *Richtungskämpfe,* p. 284.

91. See Anon., "Eine Illusion," p. 737, who cites Schmoller's *Grundriss der allgemeinen Volkswirtschaftslehre.* See also Klaus Saul, *Staat, Industrie, Arbeiterbewegung. Zur Innen- und Sozialpolitik des Wilhelminischen Deutschland 1903–1914.* Düsseldorf: Bertelsmann Universitätsverlag, 1974.

92. Though it did not similarly separate social from natural science. See Wittig, *Der englische Weg,* pp. 111–15.

93. For long periods of time the Verein could claim to represent the dominant academic opinion on a wide range of issues. If there was never full consensus within the association, differences in opinion were held within limits, with the liberal wing and later the younger generation pushing for new ideas and initiatives and the conservative majority holding back. It was the fact that this majority-minority configuration was upset in the 1905 meeting that turned the Naumann-Schmoller clash into a deep crisis of the association.

Internal discussion and conflicts never really threatened the existence or the credibility of the Fabians. Even the conflict with H. G. Wells at the beginning of the twentieth century was more about organizational and practical issues than about ideology. Both the loose structure of the society and the reputation of the Fabians as free intellectuals gave them the capacity of dealing with disagreement in their own ranks. In general, the differences were of small magnitude, and when some larger problems arose this ended generally with the departure of the dissenters, as was the case not only with H. G. Wells but also with most of the Anarchists and Liberals long before.

5

Progressive Reformers, Unemployment, and the Transformation of Social Inquiry in Britain and the United States, 1880s–1920s

LIBBY SCHWEBER

PHILIP ABRAMS in *The Origins of British Sociology* suggests that the "failure" of British sociology can be ascribed to the availability of other institutional opportunities, most notably in the policy arena.[1] Thus, while British scholars had the intellectual insights to construct a theoretically informed empirical science of society (sociology), they lacked the institutional resources to do so. Leaving aside the somewhat essentialist notion of sociology, Abrams's thesis highlights the intimate relation between the history of nineteenth-century social science and social reform. It also suggests the interest of a British-American comparison; what Abrams presents as an ideal image of what could or should have happened to social inquiry in Britain can be identified as a reasonable description of the professionalization of the social sciences in the United States.

A comparison of the development of policy-oriented social inquiry (nineteenth-century social science) in Britain and the United States between 1880 and 1920 presents a number of puzzling contrasts. In the second half of the nineteenth century, researchers in the two countries worked from similar types of organizations with a similar vision of social science.[2] In terms of the history of social science as an academic discipline, social science "succeeded" in the United States and "failed" in Britain.[3] By the 1920s amateur social science in the United States had been replaced by numerous professional university-based disciplines. In England, the parallel endeavor retained its organizationally diffuse character. Empirical inquiry was largely divorced from social theorizing and neither were incorporated into the university structure.[4]

In terms of the original reform goals of the social science movement, however, British scientist-reformers registered a striking success while Americans failed miserably in initiating legislative change. The British National Insurance Act of 1911 largely conformed to the blueprint laid out by individual social scientists. In the United States, not one state legislature passed any type of social insurance legislation prior to the 1930s; the only social reform measures to be introduced during this period were programs for mothers' pensions and workmen's compensation. Not only, as Abrams argues, did knowledge experts have more opportunities in government in England, they were also more successful in achieving legislative reform.

But the story is not so simple; there are signs that social science *cum* social reform persisted in both Britain and the United States. In Britain, social surveys, mass observation studies, the Sociological Society, and academic departments of eugenics and social anthropology all did something which involved the "scientific" pursuit of knowledge about society, and all asserted the immediate policy relevance of their inquiries. In the United States, the incorporation of social science into the universities and its institutionalization into separate departments involved a reformulation, rather than an abandonment, of reform goals.[5] Beneath—or rather with the help of—the rhetoric of objectivity and value neutrality, academics actively attempted to gain access to the formal policy process.

In terms of the social sciences, the problem thus is not to explain why social science "failed" in Britain and succeeded in the United States, but why the specialization of social science assumed different forms in the two countries and how or whether differences in the history of social reform help to account for those variations. For the most part, histories of academic social sciences ignore this aspect, focusing instead on higher education, class and status groups, and epistemological requisites for the development of "true science."[6] Those works which do explore the relation between these two institutional developments tend to emphasize the similarity of the process (across Western Europe) and the positive nature of the correlation.[7] The expansion of the state and the professionalization of the social sciences are seen to be mutually constitutive processes.

The contrast between the British and American trajectories described above points to the need for a more nuanced understanding of the relationship between the development of the social sciences and the state. What particular arrangements, under what particular set of conditions, furthered which aspects of the development of the social sciences? Which aspects of the knowledge and practices that make up the social sciences affected which aspects of the policy process? What mechanisms facilitated these mutual patterns of development? And finally, what factors account for different patterns of mutual development?

The intent of this chapter is to contribute to that broader agenda by taking one of many possible points of entry, that of unemployment insurance, to consider one aspect of the problem, that of the specialization of the social sciences. By following William Beveridge and Hubert Llewellyn Smith in England and William Leiserson and John Commons in the United States in their campaigns for the legislation of unemployment insurance, I wish to explore the institutional conditions that help account for differences in the way nineteenth-century social sciences made the transition from a single social science to many social sciences. While there were clearly many other individuals involved in social reform projects, in different positions, I suggest that the institutional opportunities and constraints which this comparison highlights were characteristic of the milieu in which social science developed and, thus, are a fruitful point of entry into one aspect of the complex relations between social science and social policy.

The analysis is divided into two sections. The first part examines attempts by social scientists in Britain and the United States to introduce a new concept of unemployment as a social (rather than moral) problem and to achieve the legislation of unemployment insurance. In Britain, I look at the way in which Beveridge and Llewellyn Smith's positions in the Labour Department of the Board of Trade allowed them to promote and write the unemployment section of 1911 National Insurance legislation. In the United States, I examine the first and the most successful attempts to legislate unemployment insurance—that made by the American Association for Labor Legislation in Massachusetts between 1915 and 1916 (the first significant attempt to realize such a program) and that by Commons and Leiserson in Wisconsin in 1920 and 1923 (the most "successful" unsuccessful attempt in the United States prior to the 1930s). A comparison of these two national experiences highlights differences in the modes of political participation between British and American progressive social reformers. They also point to differences in the location of the policy process and social science in the two countries.

The second part begins from this identification of contrasting institutional forms. By adding an analysis of the transformations in higher education to that of state bureaucratization and political democratization as developed by Shefter and extended by Skocpol and Orloff, we account for differences in the ways in which social scientists participated in the policy process.[8]

Patterns of Political Participation: Social Scientists and the Campaign for Unemployment Insurance in Britain

Two figures, Sir Hubert Llewellyn Smith (1864–1945) and William Beveridge (1879–1963), were central in the formulation and passage of national legislation concerning unemployment between 1905 and 1911. Both men belonged to the "empirical school" of settlement reformers.[9] They approached social reform as a problem of "constructive administration" informed by social statistics and free from abstract theorizing. Although separated in age by fifteen years, they shared similar educational and career experiences.

While at Oxford, Llewellyn Smith was an active member of the "Inner Ring," presided over by Arthur Achland and the University Settlement Movement. Following his graduation in 1887 he worked at a number of settlement houses, including Toynbee Hall. In addition, he participated in various social inquiries, among them Booth's study of East London and investigations at the British Sociological Association, the Royal Statistical and Economic Societies, and the Dennison Club. He also continued his work with the university extension movement and other public lecturing engagements.[10]

By 1890, Llewellyn Smith had acquired a reputation as an expert economist and statistician. Through this work he established extensive contacts with Liberal, especially progressive, and Labour politicians as well as with other reformers, such as the Webbs, and leading figures in the social science movement. Between 1888 and 1892 Llewellyn Smith was also active in support of trade unionism. In 1893 Llewellyn Smith was appointed labor commissioner to the Board of Trade.

William Beveridge's career followed a similar path.[11] While at Toynbee Hall Beveridge participated in a newly formed study group on the issue of unemployment. The group's goal was the formulation of a "really sensible, non-philanthropic way of dealing with the problem."[12] These activities were paralleled by increasing involvement in journalism and with the university extension movement. In 1903, Beveridge took a job as editor of social policy articles for *The Morning Post,* an influential conservative daily. By 1905 he had acquired a name as one of the leading experts on unemployment, a reputation which was acknowledged by his appointment to the Central Unemployed Body, established to oversee the administration of the Unemployed Workmen's Act of 1905, as well as by an invitation to testify before the Royal Commission for the Poor Law in 1907. In 1908 Beveridge was introduced by the Webbs to Churchill. Following Churchill's appointment as president of the Board of Trade, Beveridge was asked to become a full-time member of the ministry for work on labor exchanges.

Llewellyn Smith and Beveridge's early careers illustrate the place of social science in the network of clubs, associations, and public activity linking Oxford Liberals with London's political elite and the access to politics which that informal culture provided. Both men were appointed to the Board of Trade on the basis of their expertise, acquired outside of the civil service, and personal introductions to key politicians.[13]

Unemployment: The Formulation of a Social Problem

Unemployment first appeared on the public agenda as a political issue in the late 1880s. A series of riots over unemployment, culminating in the

Trafalgar Square riot, precipitated the first official recognition of the problem. On March 15, 1886, Joseph Chamberlain, then head of the local government board, issued a circular encouraging local authorities to undertake public works in relief of unemployment. While the Chamberlain circular had little short-run effect, in the long run it contributed to the expectation among workers, radicals, and local Poor Law administrators that the national government could and should take responsibility for the problem.[14]

The economic depression of 1892 to 1895 and pressure from radical factions within Parliament and outside revived the demand for government action. In 1895 and 1896 the Liberal and Conservative governments, respectively, established the first national inquiries into the causes of unemployment and possible solutions. Their findings, however, were eclipsed by the Boer War and subsequent economic recovery. Between 1896 and 1903 unemployment virtually disappeared from the political agenda.

As the above discussion suggests, unemployment entered the public arena as an offshoot of a broader concern with the causes and scope of poverty and the breakdown of Poor Law administration. The spate of poverty studies which received extensive press attention in the late nineteenth century introduced a sense of the permanence of poverty and unemployment.[15] The notion that poverty was endemic to capitalist production and "progress" evoked three types of response among intellectuals. For some conservatives it pointed to the inevitability of the condition; poverty figured as an unfortunate price of economic growth and, therefore, was not a subject for economic theorizing. At the other extreme, radicals and socialists called for state interference in the distribution of goods. A third, more moderate, explanation, from within the "progressive" camp, was that provided by the empirical school as developed by William Beveridge.[16]

Building on the work of Charles Booth, Beveridge distinguished between those types of poverty and unemployment which were unfortunate yet necessary concomitants of progress and those whose elimination would not interfere with the basic production process. Whereas the former were inevitable, the latter could be eliminated by state intervention to the advantage not only of individual workers but of the economy and society as a whole.[17]

Beveridge identified the main cause of unnecessary unemployment in "specific imperfections of adjustment" between the demand for labor and supply of labor. Three principal economic factors accounted for this maladjustment: changes in industrial structure; seasonal and cyclical fluctuations in the level of economic activity; and the creation of reserves of labor.[18] This latter practice consisted of the existence of large groups of temporarily unemployed, who were hired, indiscriminately, to meet short-term needs for labor. The lack of coordination resulted in the creation of multiple labor markets while the practice of indiscriminate hiring worked against the selection of the best qualified worker.

In a discussion of policy recommendations, Beveridge stated that the solution to the problem of unemployment must consist in "smoothing industrial transitions, in diminishing the extent of the reserves or their interval of idleness and in seeing that men of the reserve are properly maintained both in action and out of it." The problem, he stated, "is essentially one of business organization."[19] Practically, Beveridge called for the creation of a national system of labor exchanges, which would collect information and on that basis facilitate the coordination of the market. For that unemployment which was the result of unavoidable fluctuations, he proposed a system of insurance, and for those individuals genuinely unable to work he proposed a separate system of relief.

Between 1903 and 1908 pressure on the Liberal Party to develop a national policy on unemployment was exerted by a number of groups including a growing proportion of social radicals within the party and organized labor.[20] In August 1905, under considerable pressure from local administrators, the Conservative Government passed the Unemployed Workmen's Act. The act called for the establishment of a central body and nationwide network of distress committees charged with coordinating existing local-level public and private provisions. From the perspective of progressive reformers within the Board of Trade, the act was significant in a number of respects. It instituted a national system of administration, provided reformers with extensive data on the scope of unemployment and, subsequently, through its obvious inadequacy, established the need for a national-level policy.[21]

Unemployment: The Policy Process

Despite these developments and increasing pressure, the Liberal Party continued to evade the call for an official policy stand. This reluctance pointed to the divisiveness of the issue. In contrast to other social legislation, social insurance involved unprecedented government intervention in the economy.[22] Social reform did not appear on the political platform in 1906 and was not a significant factor in the party's electoral victory.[23] By 1908, however, the situation had changed enough to make unemployment legislation politically attractive and feasible. The unemployment crisis of 1908–9, the renewal of Unionist agitation for tariff reform, presented as a solution to unemployment, and a series of by-election losses encouraged the party to look to working-class votes and social reform.

The replacement of Campbell-Bannerman by Herbert Asquith as prime minister and consequent changes in cabinet appointments provided progressives entry into party leadership which they had previously lacked. The prime minister, newly appointed Chancellor of the Exchequer Lloyd George, and president of the Board of Trade, Winston Churchill, were all strong supporters of the social radicals' proposals for reform. Churchill, in particular, was a strong supporter of Beveridge's program for a national system of labor exchanges. In 1909 a national system of labor exchanges was legislated, and in 1911 Parliament approved the National Insurance Bill, introducing a national program of unemployment and health insurance.

While a multiplicity of political factors explain the fact and timing of the legislation, the rapidity and relative ease (in comparison to health insurance) with which they were passed and the content of the legislation were the work of progressives within the party leadership and the administration. In contrast to earlier social legislation, the specifics of unemployment policy never figured as an issue for party politics or cabinet debate. Rather, they were primarily worked out by Llewellyn Smith and Beveridge at the Labour Department of the Board of Trade in collaboration with Winston Churchill.

The successful passage of unemployment legislation is generally ascribed to the personality of Churchill and other progressive politicians. Davidson and Lowe contest this thesis; in its place they argue for the importance of certain administrative conditions, most notably the semiautonomous position and highly developed statistical capacities of the Labour Department at the Board of Trade.[24] The basis for the Board of Trade's involvement with social legislation lay in the association of labor legislation with social statistics.[25] In 1893, the Treasury approved the formation of a Labour Department. The original mandate was for the establishment of a purely statistical department and for the regular publication of a *Labour Gazette;* it was on the basis of its statistical expertise that the new department was located in the Board of Trade, rather than in the Home Office. Under the directorship of Llewellyn Smith, the department developed into a major center for policy innovation. Davidson and Lowe identify a number of factors that contributed to this development, among them special recruitment procedures which brought outside specialists into the department, and special access to policymaking.[26] In addition, the reluctance of Liberal Party leadership to address issues of social reform at the cabinet level and a relaxation of Treasury control allowed for autonomous action on the part of Labour officials.[27]

Early in the fall of 1908, well before unemployment became a leading political issue, Llewellyn Smith initiated a series of investigations into the causes, effects, and possible remedies for unemployment. He and Beveridge, together, assembled a strong case for a system of national labor exchanges. In addition, the Labour Department entered into extensive negotiations with the Treasury, employers, and workers.[28] Armed with scientific and political backing, Churchill had relatively little problem convincing Asquith and the rest of the cabinet as to the desirability of the program.

In 1909 the Labour Exchange Bill passed. The Board of Trade was awarded full responsibility for the implementation of the program. This decision was consistent with Beveridge's view of labor exchanges as an aspect of labor information. Unemployment insurance, the second half of the Board of Trade's program for unemployment, was more controversial. Once again, Llewellyn Smith and Beveridge devoted considerable efforts to design a bill that was both "scientific" and politically feasible, and once again they drew heavily on investigations conducted by the bureau in previous years. In contrast to health insurance, unemployment insurance passed the House with a minimum of discussion and controversy.[29]

The role of the Labour Department in general and of Llewellyn Smith and Beveridge in particular in the formulation, legislation, and implementation of the Labour Exchanges Act and Unemployment Insurance attest to the successful realization of the British progressive model of the role of the intellectual in government. While their legislative achievements were significant, their administrative accomplishments were short lived. Beveridge and Llewellyn Smith both achieved their positions of influence in the policy process on the basis of a combination of expertise and social connections, acquired through participation in a quasi-political culture of social science and social reform.[30] Their political participation drew on a model of expert authority which differed significantly from that which was being institutionalized in both academe and the civil service. In place of a model of professional academic or bureaucrat, their careers exemplify the (temporary) incorporation of the clerisy ideal (see below) into the formal political arena.

The success of this model, however, depended upon a very particular conjunction of circumstances which supported the unusual autonomy of the Labour Department in the Board of Trade. After World War I, these conditions disappeared. Central coordination of government departments under the Treasury, standardization of recruitment procedures, and the creation of a separate Labour Bureau effectively eliminated the opportunities for the kind of political initiative practiced by the Labour Department of the Board of Trade.

Patterns of Political Participation: Social Scientists and Unemployment Insurance in the United States

Two men, John R. Commons and William Leiserson, were especially influential in the early formulation of the problem of unemployment for American audiences and its treatment. While it is difficult to generalize across American states, the history of their involvement with the issue illustrates the channels of political influence available to progressive social scientists.[31] John R. Commons (1862–1945) was typical of the second generation of midwestern, religiously inspired social scientists. He graduated from Oberlin College in 1888 and entered Johns Hopkins that year to pursue graduate work in economics with Richard T. Ely. In 1890 he left Hopkins, without having completed a degree, for an instructorship in economics at Wesleyan University. He was active in the social science movement and spoke out on the issues of free trade, currency and tariff reform, the single tax, and labor organization. In 1893 he helped to found the Institute of Christian Sociology.

Commons's early academic career was marked by a series of short-term appointments at Oberlin, Indiana University, and Syracuse University.[32] His political activities, however, brought him the censure of other economists and, in 1899, when his chair in sociology was abolished, Commons accepted the hint and left teaching. According to Furner, his quiet withdrawal was critical for his subsequent readmittance back into the academic community.[33]

Between 1899 and 1900 Commons worked at a research bureau in New York City, which compiled a weekly index of wholesale prices for the Democratic National Campaign Committee, prepared a report on immigration for the U.S. Industrial Commission, and served as assistant to Ralph M. Easley, secretary of the National Civic Federation. In 1904, at Ely's invitation, Commons returned to academic life, to an appointment in the Department of Political Economy at the University of Wisconsin, where he remained until 1932.

Among the new universities, public service goals were especially strong at the midwestern universities and Wisconsin, under the Progressive governor Robert M. LaFollette, was particularly receptive to university-state links.[34] During his years at Wisconsin, Commons drafted Wisconsin's civil service law (1905), its public utility law (1907), and its workmen's compensation act (1911). He also created the Wisconsin Industrial Commission and served as a member on the board between 1911 and 1913.

Like Commons, Leiserson's personal and educational background stands in sharp contrast to the patrician background of British progressives and earlier American reformers. In contrast to most social scientists and reformers, Leiserson was himself an immigrant. The Leiserson family moved to the United States in 1890 from Ravel, Estonia, and settled on the Lower East Side in New York. At the age of fourteen he left school to work in a shirtwaist factory. In 1904, having prepared for the New York Regents at night school, he went west to Wisconsin to study economics with Professor John R. Commons.

In 1907, Leiserson worked with Commons as a staff member on the Pittsburgh Social Survey, a study comparable in impact to the poverty studies of Charles Booth and Seebohm Rowntree in England. From Wisconsin, Leiserson returned to New York for doctoral work at Columbia. Between 1909 and 1911, he both completed a dissertation on employment in the state of New York and served as special investigator for the New York State Legislature's Commission on Unemployment and Workmen's Compensation.[35] His report for the New York State Commission represented one of the first official recognitions of the permanence of unemployment.

In large part, Leiserson's dissertation involved a direct application of Beveridge's analysis of the causes of unemployment and possible remedies to American conditions. Like Beveridge, Leiserson insisted on the permanency of the problem and on the cost, not only to the individual but to the economic and moral progress of the nation. He also shared Beveridge's approach to the problem as that of the organization of the labor market. Thus, Leiserson writes:

> While we cannot do away with the intermittent demands for labor, we can so organize the method of hiring unskilled laborers, as to shift them quickly from one place to another, and so enable them to have continuous work, although for different employers. (p. 50)

Shortly after completing his dissertation, Leiserson was offered an opportunity to implement his proposal. In 1911 Commons asked Leiserson to serve under him in Wisconsin as deputy industrial commissioner in charge of employment bureaus, apprenticeship, and the mediation of industrial disputes. While in Wisconsin, Leiserson also helped to found the National Association of Public and Private Employment Agencies, designed to facilitate the establishment of public employment offices throughout the country.[36]

Leiserson's work in Wisconsin brought him national recognition as a labor market specialist; it also brought him a university appointment. In 1915, Leiserson accepted a professorship in economics and political science at Toledo University in Ohio. His subsequent career was marked by continual movement between academe and public service in the areas of employment and industrial arbitration. During the 1930s, Leiserson designed a model of unemployment legislation for the Ohio legislature which provided a national alternative to the preventative emphasis contained in Commons's Wisconsin plan.

For our purposes Commons's and Leiserson's careers illustrate the kind of unofficial links that were established by the movement of individuals between certain universities, voluntary reform organizations, and temporary governmental appointments. Whereas for Beveridge and Llewellyn Smith, education at Oxford provided an initial entry into an elite culture of rational reform and, through that, access to party and government policy formulation, for Commons and Leiserson the university functioned as a permanent professional base from which they asserted claims to expertise, established political connections, and made temporary forays into the world of policy research and influence. Thus, whereas Commons participated in the political arena as an academic, Beveridge saw himself as a public servant.[37]

Unemployment: The Formulation of a Problem

As in Britain, unemployment entered the political agenda in the context of cyclical depression and industrial strife. But whereas in Britain political and administrative conditions and concerns contributed to keep the issue in the public (and political) eye and to maintain initial provisions, in the United States economic recovery led to the reversal of political gains. As noted above, our analysis focuses on two separate policy initiatives, one in Massachusetts, 1915 to 1916, and the other in Wisconsin in 1920 and 1923. While clearly not representative, these campaigns can be taken as illustrative of the nature and limits to social scientists' participation in the political arena (as social scientists rather than as government officials).

In both Britain and the United States, the last decades of the century were marked by growing recognition of the inadequacy of existing provisions for poverty. Whereas in Britain the rubric of the new Poor Law and an extensive network of loosely centralized agencies led to increased systematization and growing pressure for national coordination (of local government activities), in the United States social and political developments directed concern over unemployment into a variety of extragovernmental initiatives. As part of the growing movement by the middle class, and especially middle-class professionals, to carve out an extragovernmental forum for political activism, local citizens organized the establishment of permanent charitable agencies, the hiring of professional full-time workers, and more systematic relief methods.[38]

In contrast to this general trend, some social scientists looked to European experiments with social legislation and called for similar programs in the United States. As in Britain, acceptance of such proposals depended both on recognition of the permanence of unemployment and faith in the capacity of government to transcend partisan and other special interests to act in the interests of the common good. Neither idea was easily transplanted. The two types of arena—voluntary reform associations, most notably the American Association for Labor Legislation, and newly created nonpartisan administrative offices, most notably industrial commissions—provided the organizational base for this campaign.

In 1906, a number of social scientists founded the American Association for Labor Legislation (AALL) to coordinate state-level activity. In subsequent years, the organization provided a national base and information center for the activities of social progressives throughout the country. The explicit purpose of the association was to sponsor social investigation into the condition of labor and to propose model legislation for the improvement of adverse conditions.[39] As such, it embodied a model of the role of the expert in government similar to that espoused by Llewellyn Smith—the primary difference being that Llewellyn Smith worked from a strong department within government while the AALL was very much outside.

The British National Insurance Act of 1911 provided a catalyst for American progressives to adopt the issue. John B. Andrews, secretary of the AALL, introduced it in the program for the annual convention in December 1911. The decision at that meeting to establish an American section of the International Association on Unemployment effectively committed the association to a political campaign.[40] The AALL's activities included investigation into existing European programs and a political strategy of selective publicity and support for state-level legislative campaigns. In addition to lectures before civic and social work groups and journal articles, the association held two national-level conferences in February and December 1914.

The result of the association's investigations was a document entitled "A Practical Program for the Prevention of Unemployment," which served as a guideline for unemployment reform activity throughout the country. The document called for the creation of efficient employment offices, advanced planning of public works, unemployment insurance, and the regularization of employment by individual employers.[41] Over 22,000 copies were distributed to libraries, social work organizations, state departments of labor, leading corporations, labor unions and, interested individuals.[42]

Unemployment: The Policy Process in Massachusetts, 1915–1916

The most important attempt by the AALL to secure unemployment insurance legislation was in Massachusetts. Another economic downturn created the conditions for the introduction of legislation concerning unemployment. In 1915, a group of Massachusetts-based reformers established the Massachusetts Committee on Unemployment. They were aided in their efforts to formulate a bill for presentation in the state legislation by the social insurance committee of the AALL, as well as by two eminent Boston attorneys. The proposed law was presented as "following the general principles of the English Unemployment Insurance Act" and differed only in its greater emphasis on prevention provisions.

Extensive campaigning won the Committee on Unemployment the endorsements of the Massachusetts Republican Party, the Massachusetts State Federation of Labor, the New England Typographical Union, and several progressive employers. With this backing, progressive reformers introduced the first unemployment insurance bill in the United States. However, opposition by employers, especially over the issue of compulsory insurance, blocked the bill in committee. The Joint Rules Committee failed to return a favorable report.[43] A return of economic prosperity in 1916 lost progressives the political and business support which they had previously amassed.

For the purposes of this chapter, the history of the legislation is significant in that it illustrates the mode of political participation available to social progressives. In the absence of an autonomous state bureaucracy and an institutionalized commitment to state intervention, social scientists' and reformers' primary mode of access to government was through gubernatorial investigatory commissions set up in times of crisis on an *ad hoc* basis. While such commissions were granted investigatory authority, they lacked administrative authority of any kind. Actual legislation depended on the persuasive power of reformers. And while a national organization like the AALL provided help in the formulation and conduct of reform campaigns and, as in the case of workmen's compensation, helped to facilitate a certain degree of coordination between states which was critical for the adoption of that legislation, it could not provide the political backing necessary to push legislation past the myriad of objecting interest groups actively campaigning to defeat the legislation. In effect, the model was similar to that of British amateur social scientists, minus the type of social and political environment which rendered that model effective. It differed from the American amateur model in its rejection of popular outreach.

This situation, in turn, underscores the weight that reformers such as Commons placed on administrative innovation for the achievement of social legislation. The industrial commission, or rather the administrative form of government of which it was an example, constituted social progressives' contribution to political reform. Commons presented the commission as the institutional core for the creation of a new fourth branch of government, administration. Practically, the concept referred to the empowerment of investigatory agencies with the authority to specify regulations (legislate) and to administer labor legislation (adjudicate). In association with industrial commission, Commons called for the establishment of a series of advisory committees composed of representatives of industry, organized labor, and other associations directly involved in that specific problem area. Such committees participated not only in initial investigations, but also in the recruitment of employees to the industrial commission and in the framing of legislation.[44] Another crucial aspect of the industrial commission idea was the appointment of nonpartisan experts. In this way the industrial commission provided a professional alternative to the much more limited advisory role of the amateur social scientists on governmental commissions of inquiry.

Unemployment: The Policy Process in Wisconsin, 1920

One of the legacies of the successful legislation of workmen's compensation laws, just prior to the introduction of unemployment insurance on the agenda of the AALL, was the establishment of industrial commissions. By 1920, thirty-five of the forty-two states with compensation laws had established such agencies.[45] However, not all afforded academics and social scientists with the type of access which the Wisconsin Industrial Commission provided. A succession of Progressive governors in Wisconsin and the unique relationship between the university and the state provided Commons an opportunity to implement his vision of the relation between science and politics. For a short period, the Wisconsin Industrial Commission and the Legislative Reference Library, established to advise legislators on policy formulation, provided social scientists, located outside of government, direct access to the policy process. These administrative links were significant in facilitating the progressives' campaign for unemployment insurance.

During the early twenties, progressives introduced preventive unemployment legislation in a number of states. Only in Wisconsin, however, did such a bill seem to have even a possibility of success.[46] The timing of the 1921 campaign was largely due to the initiative of organized labor, while the content of the bill was the work of progressive academics. In 1920, union leaders collaborated with Commons to design the Huber Bill, which was presented to the senate in February 1921. The primary features of the bill were an insurance fund based on employers' contributions and the creation, by employers, of a mutual insurance company that would classify industries and adjust rates according to firms' individual employment histories.

Both Commons and his students and union leaders campaigned the public in an effort to rally support for the upcoming legislation. Despite the nature of the alliance, Commons directed his appeals at business interest and farmers. Consultations with these groups and conservative senators also led Commons to introduce a number of modifications into the bill. Ultimately, however, the conservatives won, and the bill was defeated 16 to 13.

A second attempt in 1923 followed similar lines—this time with organized opposition from the Wisconsin Manufacturers Association (WMA). Again, the progressives' campaign drew on extensive research and selective publicity. Campaign literature was designed for specific audiences, in particular, farmers. In addition, reformers recruited supportive businessmen to counter the image created by the WMA. Once again, the bill was defeated by only a few votes.[47]

As in Britain, the existence of a politically influential administrative agency, with highly developed statistical capacities, devoted to labor legislation, was crucial for progressive participation in politics and for their achievements. In this sense the Wisconsin Industrial Commission, and other similar national and state-level organizations, can be seen as American counterparts to the Labour Department of the Board of Trade in England.[48] In both countries, these agencies provided individual progressive reformers access to the policy process on the basis of their intellectual achievements and problem-area expertise. They did so, however, in very different political contexts with different associated possibilities and constraints.

Amenta et al., in a comparison of the history of unemployment insurance legislation in five American states, point to a number of features of the Wisconsin political context which explain its legislative history. In contrast to other states, popular partisan politics in Wisconsin was unusually free from patronage. This, coupled with the domination of a progressive Republican Party, produced an unusually programmatic style of politics in which issues, rather than special interests, and compromise and cooperation, rather than competition, guided everyday political activity.[49]

These broader political conditions are crucial to explain the relative strength of academics and of the Industrial Commission in the policy process. Popular patronage politics or an alignment of parties with conflicting interests would have precluded the authorization of such a body and paralyzed its work. Similarly, the existence of such an administrative apparatus helps to explain the relative success of social progressives in that state over the issue of unemployment insurance. As Amenta et al. note, by 1921 when the Huber Bill was first proposed, the Wisconsin Industrial Commission had already developed long-standing capacities for policy investigation, legislative maneuvering, and interest-group bargaining.[50] In the 1920s, the fragmented character of the American policy process and the strength of opposing interests led to the defeat of the Huber Bill. In 1930, however, these same political and administrative factors served Wisconsin and unemployment well. Wisconsin was the first state to introduce unemployment insurance. While the timing was due to political factors, the content of the bill was expressly the work of the Wisconsin Industrial Commission.[51]

In summary, social researchers in Britain and the United States brought a similar view of the role of their knowledge and of the "causes, conditions, and cures" of unemployment to the policy process. In both countries, these positions placed them firmly with a progressive coalition. In Britain this movement worked through the Liberal Party and achieved political influence through the ascendance of that party to government. In the United States, the nature of American partisan politics and absence of a developed state administrative apparatus placed social progressives outside of the formal political process. State-building was a central item on their political agenda. But to the extent that partisan politics was suspect in the eyes of many reformers, so too was any form of state expansion or intervention. Social progressives in the United States not only lacked a strong administrative base within government, they also lacked allies within the progressive movement as a whole.

An examination of the campaign for unemployment insurance in the United States illustrates the overall weakness of the social progressives' political base, while a comparison on the Massachusetts campaign of 1915–16 and the Wisconsin campaign of 1921 highlights the importance of university-community and university-state relations for the exercise of political influence by social scientists. In effect, the new university in the United States served a function similar to that played by the British elite culture of rational reform. And while the tight links between the University of Wisconsin and the state were an exception, political recognition of the authority of professional expertise was not. To the extent that government bureaucracies were established during this period and to the extent that expertise was called for, it was academics rather than New England upper-class amateurs who were granted those positions. More to the point, it was as academics and through the university and university connections that social scientists gained influential positions in both a more popular, new middle-class culture of rational reform and in government.

Political Democratization, State Bureaucratization, and the Democratization of Higher Education

The above analysis highlights differences in the opportunities and constraints that confronted progressive-minded social scientists concerned with problems of unemployment in Britain and the United States. Both sets of men addressed the problem through a project of administrative action (vs. philanthropy), research, and legislation. In both cases, they called for and worked through the creation of new types of administrative offices. They differed, however, in the channels of political influence which they used to promote their plan and in their effectiveness. Beveridge and Llewellyn Smith used their membership in an elite culture of social science to gain access to newly created administrative positions, in their case the Labour Department of the Board of Trade. Commons's and Leiserson's access to similar, albeit less influential, organs (notably, the Wisconsin Industrial Commission) passed through the university. While these were not the only channels by which experts entered government, they do seem to be characteristic of those who also retained a foothold in social science; as such it addresses our concern with the comparative study of the institutionalization of the social sciences during this period.

This contrast between amateur and academic culture and the relative influence of new administrative forms suggests the need to explore more systematically the conditions which produced these variations, most notably the articulation between the processes of state bureaucratization and the institutional transformations of social science. This is especially so given the similarity between British and American forms in the period prior to 1880. In the mid-nineteenth century both countries were characterized by a similar configuration of politically marginal universities and cultures of social science, weak bureaucracies, and patronage-style partisan politics. By the 1920s institutional conditions in both countries had been transformed, but along different lines. An analysis of these institutional transformations and the patterns they produced helps to explain the seeming trade-off between academic social science and social legislation, which the comparison of Beveridge's and Commons's projects for unemployment legislation illustrates.

Our analysis of the political environment in which social scientists asserted claims to political influence between 1880 and 1920 builds on the model of political transformation developed by Shefter and extended by Orloff and Skocpol. In contrast to many comparative studies which focus on differences in formal structures, these works examine variations in the conduct of party politics and state bureaucracies.[52] Thus Orloff and Skocpol explain variations in social legislation by differences in the conjunction of the extension of suffrage, the shift from popular patronage to programmatic politics, and the expansion of the state's administrative capacity. The particular state of these processes at the point when social legislation was introduced explains differences in policy outcomes. The analysis herein adds a fourth component to this model, namely the transformation of higher education (which was roughly coincident with state bureaucratization), to consider the effect of this context on social scientists' participation in the policy process, and thereby on the development of the social sciences.

As noted above, in both Britain and various American states, bureaucratization and the transformation of higher education occurred at roughly the same time. In Britain, these developments were introduced prior to the extension of the franchise (in 1867 to artisans, 1918 for all males, and in 1929 to women) and provided an organizational base for the separation of the policy process from the vicissitudes of grass-roots party politics—as well as from the "threat" of working-class control. Social legislation was introduced, debated, legislated, and implemented with the help of a relatively strong national and local-level bureaucracy. In the United States, in contrast, state bureaucratization and the transformation of higher education followed political enfranchisement (of white males during the 1820s and 1830s) and occurred simultaneously with the introduction of social legislation.

In both countries, the political influence of social inquiry was linked to the abandonment (or restriction) of popular patronage politics and the emergence of spheres of bureaucratic autonomy. And in both countries these developments, along with initial campaigns for social legislation, were the work of similar progressive coalitions, which included among their ranks social scientists. Differences in the pattern of institutional transformation, however, affected who made policy, how they made it, who practiced social science, where they practiced it, and how they influenced policy.

Institutional Transformation in Britain: Roots of the Clerisy Ideal

The 1860s witnessed the emergence of a progressive coalition in Britain led largely by northern-based, nonconformist, professional, middle-class activists (Shefter's "rationalizing bourgeoisie") in alliance with more established social political elites.[53] One of the issues which united them was university reform, in particular, the admission of nonconformists and a revitalization of the clerisy ideal. The clerisy ideal has been described as an "aristocratic model of professional growth." According to this model, the role of the university lay in the education of an intellectual clerisy which, through their participation in society, would direct the nation toward a more moral, harmonious state.[54] The main practitioners of the social sciences during the mid-nineteenth century came from this social group.

Institutionally, the success of this progressive movement can be seen in the establishment of a two-tiered system of higher education. In effect the higher tier preserved the hegemony of traditional institutions and groups, expanded to include new elites, while the second tier responded to the demands of an expanding industrial economy and new occupations. The

1850s had witnessed the removal of religious restrictions on entry into Oxford and Cambridge (at the dictates of Parliament). In the spirit of the clerisy ideal, an extensive system of fellowships was introduced to support students after graduation, either in the pursuit of training in the traditional professions or in their initial forays into the intellectual and political life of the capital.[55] It was this model of liberal education for public service which Beveridge and Llewellyn Smith followed.

The clerisy ideal was further buttressed by the linkage of civil service qualifications to the elite universities. An order of council in 1870 legislated the establishment of a two-tiered system of civil service examinations, linking the higher tier with the liberal curriculum taught at the elite universities, and laying the basis for the establishment of a professional state apparatus independent of partisan politics.[56] While regulations concerning recruitment by examination were introduced relatively quickly, it was not until 1920 that government departments were actually unified under the Treasury. As noted above, Beveridge and Llewellyn Smith benefited from their entry into political life prior to the consolidation of the hold of the civil service on upper-level administrative positions.

The National Association for the Promotion of the Social Sciences: Politics Outside of Politics

In terms of the political scene, progressive agitation figured at a time of unusually low levels of electoral participation and consequently of party competition. In this context, extraparliamentary forums became a crucial arena for political debate and decision making. The history of the National Association for the Promotion of the Social Sciences (NAPSS) illustrates the type of opportunities which the conjunction of these developments provided for the practice of a reform-oriented social science. While Beveridge and Llewellyn Smith worked directly through government, their access to those positions depended upon the types of networks which were consolidated in this and other similar forums.

The NAPSS was founded in 1857. The goals of the association, in the words of its founder Lord Brougham, were "to aid legislation, by preparing measures, by explaining them, by recommending them to the community, or, it may be, by stimulating the legislature to adopt them."[57] Between 1857 and the demise of the association in 1884, the NAPSS did just that. Almost every law and amendment passed during those years was either initiated or reformulated with advice from the association. Contemporary newspapers described it as an "outdoor Parliament," an "unofficial parliament," and "a parliament out of session."[58]

The political effectiveness of the NAPSS can, in large part, be explained by its social composition and central role in elite social life. Its membership included leading politicians (one-third of its governing board of 250 members were members of Parliament, of them three-quarters were from the Liberal Party), intellectuals, and civil servants. Both the opening of the elite universities to new social groups and the political influence of an organization such as the NAPSS attest to the incorporation of the nineteenth-century tradition of amateur social science into a newly expanded but highly integrated social, political, and intellectual elite class. Thus cultural incorporation helps to explain the absence of a professionalizing drive among "social scientists" (relative to the United States).[59] By dint of this new cultural location, reform-minded social researchers gained a kind of informal access to politicians, public opinion, and the policy process, which rendered efforts at formal professionalization or institutional change unnecessary.

Political Transformation and Progressive Reformers: The New Liberalism

The extension of the franchise in 1867 and associated reforms in the system of county and borough representation led to an increase in the level of electoral competition, a tightening of party discipline, and the introduction of a new style of politics. The election of 1880 was accompanied by the first national-level campaign with clear-cut programmatic differences between the candidates and parties.[60] The political environment in the 1880s was also characterized by the initial implementation of civil service reform and a general professionalization of politics. Under Gladstone and new forms of programmatic politics, membership in Parliament was (temporarily) transformed from an activity of gentlemen into a full-time occupation, and the composition of the House of Commons changed accordingly; there was a decline in the proportion of landowners and a parallel increase in representatives from industrial and commercial backgrounds.[61] Similarly, the basis of high-level administrative appointments changed. Whereas during the 1870s almost all appointments to the Treasury had been handed out as partisan rewards, by the 1880s two-thirds of new appointments were granted as promotions to civil servants within the Treasury.[62] In the short run, the revival of electoral competition and partisan politics limited the opportunities available to social scientists, at least as an extra-party organized movement and, according to Goldman, explain the demise of the NAPSS. While many academic liberals abandoned the party in 1886 in favor of a more conservative unionist position, the precedent of intellectual and academic participation in the formulation of the party's program persisted. Electoral defeat, Gladstone's retirement in 1894 and the consequent vacuum in party leadership, the abandonment of more conservative supporters (and patrons), and the threat of an increasingly organized, politically assertive, working-class constituency persuaded Liberal Party leaders of the need for ideological reformulation.[63] This openness provided social scientist/reformers with an opportunity for political influence.

During the 1890s academics and publicists reworked the guiding philosophy of the party. The "New Liberalism" as this reformulation came to be called was informed by a concern with social problems and a call for state intervention in the name of the public and individual good.[64] Beveridge's analysis of unemployment and his call for state intervention in order to insure the proper workings of the market illustrate the type of policies which this ideological balancing produced. Between 1894 and the return of the Liberal Party to government in 1906, this progressive coalition achieved a dominant position within the Liberal Party.[65] An indication of this transformation is the turnover in Liberal members of Parliament. Of the 401 Liberals returned to the Commons in 1906, 205 had never sat in the house before.[66] Under the cabinets of Sir Henry Campbell-Bannerman (1905–8) and Herbert Asquith (1908–28), the progressive faction of the party gained direct entry into government.[67]

From the perspective of this chapter, the crucial points to note include the persistence and strengthening of a nonprofessionalized elite culture of social science, the emergence of a progressive coalition for social legislation *after* the emergence of a relatively well-developed state bureaucracy, and the concomitant location of policy in a relatively strong cabinet that was similarly insulated from the demands of special-interest groups or patronage politics. In this context, the success of campaigns for social legislation and the assertion of the authority of expertise depended upon access to the party in government and, more specifically to influential ministers and ministerial departments. Beveridge and Llewellyn Smith owed their positions in the Labour Department and their legislative success first to the social networks which they had created through their participation in a world of settlement reform, the university extension movement, journalism, and numerous highly visible official and unofficial social inquiries (which gave them access to people like Churchill) and, second, to the rise of that culture under the title of "New Liberalism" to a dominant position in the Liberal Party and the succession of the Liberal Party to government in 1906.

Institutional Transformation in the United States

In contrast to Britain, the electoral franchise in the United States was extended to white males in the early nineteenth century, *prior to* the emergence of progressive coalitions for either bureaucratic autonomy or social legislation. During the second half of the century the legacy of the Civil War, rapid urbanization and industrialization, and large new waves of immigration contributed to the further diversification and division of the popular vote. Both sets of developments fueled the dominant system of popular patronage and contributed to an intensification of electoral competition. Building on extensive social dislocation, party politics served to challenge rather than buttress the authority of traditional ruling elites. In place of an autonomous state apparatus monopolized by an elite ruling class, politics in the United States were dominated by urban machines, party bosses, and the courts.

This mode of politics, in turn, influenced the nature of social policy and the effectiveness of mid-nineteenth-century forms of social science/social reform. Social policy was the product of patronage-based distributional politics in which political parties exchanged services for votes on a local and individual level. Neither political elites, entrenched in the patronage system, nor their mass base constituencies were available as partners for reform projects. In terms of social science, patronage politics placed both patrician social reformers and their voluntary institutions on the margins of the policy process. In the absence of broader social networks, their institutions and programs had little impact on the course of events. The success of social progressives thus depended upon their ability to bypass nineteenth-century political and knowledge arrangements and establish not only alternate channels of influence, but alternate institutional structures as well.

New England Mugwumps: The Failure of the Clerisy Ideal

An examination of the American equivalent of the British social science movement confirms the importance of particular kinds of social networks for the success of the nineteenth-century model of social science as social reform. American mugwumps provide a counterpart to English progressives of the 1860s on a number of grounds. Members of the Anglo-Protestant, New England elite, mugwumps differed from their contemporaries in their educational achievements, their orientation to British radical and liberal thought and reform, and their latitudinarian rather than evangelical, religious views and associated moralism.[68] Like the English, they supported civil service reform and social legislation.[69] Educationally, they provided the student body for the elite universities (Harvard, Princeton, Yale). Occupationally, they filled the traditional "status" professions (medicine, law, theology). They also constituted the social base for nineteenth-century amateur social science. Thus, the similarities of the mugwumps with the English progressives lies in their social position, a sharing of ideas and institutions,[70] and in a similar elitist orientation to reform. But whereas the English forged links with newly empowered dissenter and working-class groups, the Americans remained an isolated minority on the political scene.

Initially, mugwump reformers identified with the Republican Party. However, both their vision of a meritocratic (elitist) professional civil service and their mode of political participation were directly at odds with the dominant style of popular patronage politics. A decision in 1884 by mugwump reformers to support the Democratic presidential candidate brought them the criticism of both parties and severely limited their potential for political influence.[71] While they did secure the passage of the Pendleton Act, introducing a professional civil service in 1883, the provision did little to further the standing of the traditional professional upper classes in politics or to weaken the hold of the spoils system. This lack of political effectiveness is further borne out by the parallel failure of the American Social Science Association (ASSA) to gain entry to the policy process.

The American Social Science Association: A Case of Political Ineffectiveness

Like the NAPSS, the ASSA was founded for the promotion of inquiry into social problems with the aim of furthering legislative reform. And like the NAPSS, the ASSA aimed to influence policy through public education and political lobbying. Both organizations were founded on the assumption that knowledge of "social facts" would produce a consensus over the need for social legislation and the type of legislation needed, thereby automatically producing social reform. But whereas in Britain the integration of intellectual and political elites in the NAPSS and extreme weakness of partisan politics at the time supported this vision of the relation of social science and social reform, in the United States there were no comparable arrangements.

The political ineffectiveness of the ASSA relative to the NAPSS can be attributed to differences in the social base of the organization and in the nature of politics. Socially, the ASSA was peopled by members of the traditional professions, humanitarian reformers, and a few paternalist businessmen[72]—in other words, groups which were increasingly marginal to the political, economic, and social life of the country. According to Goldman, "the ASSA consistently failed to interest and involve the local and national political elites in the United States, and without their patronage, their 'power and influence'—an outstanding feature of the history of the SSA [NAPSS] in Britain—substantive reform via the statute-book was impossible."[73] Politically, the failure of the ASSA in particular and of the New England gentry more generally to realize their vision of rational reform can be ascribed both to the tightness of the broader political environment and to the absence of partners for a progressive coalition.

Political Transformation and Progressive Reformers: Politics Outside of Politics

In the early years of the twentieth century, both these political conditions were reversed. Following 1900, both electoral participation and party loyalty declined.[74] In addition, sectional realignment in the 1890s introduced a certain political stability which contrasted sharply with the fierce competition of earlier decades. On the national level, the Republican Party remained in control of the federal government until 1911;[75] at the state level, the Republicans dominated the North while Democrats achieved a majority in the South. While this situation did not eliminate patronage-oriented party organizations or distributional styles of policymaking, it did create openings for new forms of political influence.[76]

The emergence of the twentieth-century Progressive movement (or movements) involved a shift in the social base of agitation for political and social reform; it also presaged the introduction of a new form of politics onto the American scene. Rodgers locates twentieth-century progressivism in the cluster of extraparty pressure groups which filled the vacuum created by a breakdown in partisan politics.[77] These ranged from settlement houses and other social service organizations to manufacturers organizations, civic leagues, trade and professional associations, to organizations for municipal reform and social legislation. It was precisely these types of organization which marked the careers of both Commons and Leiserson.

Socially, these voluntary organizations provided a focus for the consolidation of a new type of progressive coalition linking new professional, business, and intellectual elites. It was this same group that supported the emergence of the new university and the professionalization of social science. Politically, these various organizations represented an alternate style of political participation to that of patronage-based politics, one in which organization and access to resources rather than mass support were the measure of political influence.[78] Ideologically, their work contributed to a particularly American form of New Liberalism, which balanced market forces and state intervention.[79]

For our purposes, one of the primary effects of the American situation of early democratization and the persistence of popular patronage politics followed by a loosening of electoral competition was the marriage of political and social reform. The term "social progressivism" has been used to refer to that group of progressive reformers which carried this call for social legislation and administrative reform.[80] More than any other strain, it was this particular submovement that attracted social scientists and other experts eager to realize the findings of "scientific" analysis of social problems in social legislation. Like other progressive groups at the time, social progressives attempted to influence the policy process from their position outside of the formal political arena. As illustrated by both the Massachusetts and Wisconsin campaigns for unemployment insurance, political influence depended upon the ability of reformers to put together (temporary) coalitions with other special interest groups around specific pieces of legislation.

Educational Transformation: The Professional Connection

As the cases of John Commons and William Leiserson suggest, American social progressives in the first decade of the twentieth century were of a very different background than either their mugwump predecessors in the ASSA or the British social scientists. Instead of being amateurs, they were full-time social scientists; and instead of being members of a traditional elite, they were part of an increasingly influential professional middle class. The existence of this new type of social scientist was largely the result of transformations in the system of higher education which occurred between 1880 and 1920.

Whereas the transformation of higher education in Britain had strengthened the political and social influence of traditional elites and elite institutions, the introduction of the modern university in the United States undermined them. The institutional origins of the new university lie in the initiative of a small group of entrepreneurial university presidents and a vision of higher education which combined teaching, research, and public service in a novel form.[81] Part of their success depended upon the integration of this new model of education into the occupational consolidation of new social elites.

The modern American university differed from the reformed British elite institution both in its internal organization and in its model for public outreach. Whereas in Britain the commitment to liberal arts or teaching retained an adherence to the classical curriculum, the modern American university was characterized by the replacement of the classical curriculum by an elective system and the introduction of graduate programs. These developments supported the appearance of academic departments, complete with faculty hierarchies, and a parallel administrative organization headed by a powerful university president. In terms of university faculty, the emergence of the American university was marked by an increase in the status and salaries associated with teaching. Between 1870 and 1900, the number of faculty members in the United States increased by three hundred percent.[82]

Internal innovation was accompanied by new modes of public legitimation and outreach. University presidents justified their institutions in terms of the mutual interests of individual career, scholarship, and the national welfare. At the center of this rationale was a deliberate separation of intellectual pursuit from advocacy. John Gilman, president of Johns Hopkins University, rejected a proposed merger of his university with the American Social Science Association on the grounds the "the Association and the University had divergent functions—agitation on the one hand and investigation on the other."[83] According to Haskell, Gilman's decision involved a recognition that among the two tasks, only the latter, that of investigation, could be professionalized.

Whether Haskell is correct on this score or not, his comment points to the convergence of middle-class professionalization and the emergence of the modern university. In contrast with the relatively well-established position of the traditional professions in Britain, professions in the United States, like the colleges, suffered a considerable loss of prestige during the nineteenth century. A collapse in state licensing systems early in the century and the breakdown of an effective apprenticeship system left the professions powerless in the face of challenge and internally divided. A number of scholars explain the success of both the modern university and late nineteenth-century professions by an alliance between certain factions of professionals with university reformers.[84] Academic professionalization, in this context, was a forerunner of a more general model of professional control.

While the transformation of the universities is often presented as the successful assertion of Protestant Anglo-Saxon cultural authority over an immigrant nation and while the new colleges continued to educate students from the upper and upper-middle classes, from the perspective of science (and social science) the shift involved the empowerment of a new type of intellectual.[85] Participants in the new universities were drawn from different social subgroups in the population. The contrast is aptly described by George Santayana as that of "polite America," by which he referred to the traditional aristocracy of the Eastern seaboard, and a second "crude but vital America," self-made men, descended from those without conspicuous social position.[86] This difference in social background was especially pronounced among social scientists. Many of the new generation of professionalizing social scientists came from rural or small towns, many were from the Midwest, and many were the sons of preachers and had been raised in an evangelical tradition which differed profoundly from the high church background of the founders of the American Social Science Association.[87]

This said, it is important not to ignore the association of the modern university, as an institution, with a particular type of local social elite. The rise of universities and a new type of scientist was paralleled by the relocation of rational reform from its position among an increasingly marginal group of gentlemen intellectuals to the settlement houses and voluntary associations of new civic leaders. In the first decades of the century, progressive reform groups turned to academic scientific knowledge as a source of legitimation while individual departments benefited from the philanthropic contributions which this association brought. For the individual social scientist, work in the public sector was an important factor in career advancement within the university.[88]

This link provided the context for the reformulation of the goal of public service or utility. In place of the broad public outreach encouraged by nineteenth-century amateur social science, professional public service was directed at the provision of expertise for policymakers and those aspiring to influence the policy process. But whereas in Britain changes in higher education furthered the incorporation of carriers of social science into a tightly integrated, multifunctional national elite, in the United States the emergence of the new university contributed to the creation of a second, politically marginal, locus for the practice of social science. In contrast with England, the carriers of social science in the United States were peripheral to the policy process. Rational reform and the application of social science to the policy process depended upon a circumvention of dominant political elites and channels of decision making. The importance of the new university, in this context, was the provision of an alternate institutional base from which professional social scientists in alliance with other types of aspiring elites asserted claims to political and social authority.

Contrasting Patterns of Institutional Transformation

Thus, whereas in Britain state bureaucratization preceded the extension of the franchise and issues of political reform were resolved and implemented prior to progressive calls for social legislation, in the United States the situation was reversed. The extension of the franchise prior to state bureaucratization and the socially disruptive effects of rapid urbanization, industrialization, and mass immigration strengthened the location of policy in highly competitive patronage-based parties and the courts. In the 1900s the transformation of higher education in conjunction with the consolidation of a new type of professional, urban social elite created the conditions for the emergence of a progressive coalition committed to both political and social reform.

As in Britain, initial access to the policy process by social scientists and by reformers in general depended upon a loosening of electoral competition. The breakdown of party politics following the turn of the century provided progressive reformers with new opportunities for entry into politics; the persistence of popular patronage politics and absence of an autonomous state bureaucracy rendered existing political elites and the formal political arena unavailable as partners for a progressive coalition or as a locus for political assertion. Instead, progressive reformers in the twentieth century worked from outside, combining efforts to create new, more acceptable forums for policy formulation and implementation with campaigns for social legislation.

In terms of social scientists, the success of British progressive reformers in realizing their goals for social legislation through the medium of the Liberal Party and government departments provided social scientists with the opportunity to realize their political goals. In the United States, in contrast, political parties were unavailable and unacceptable for the assertion of scientific authority in the political arena. This situation both blocked the development of amateur social science and predicated political influence on a process of state building. From the perspective of the political arena, the struggle between amateur and professionals over access to social science depended upon their ability to carve out new channels of access to the political process.

Differences in the timing of institutional transformation led to differences in the location of the policy process and of social sciences. In Britain, policy was located in government, and social sciences persisted as an amateur activity in extra-university, extragovernmental, "intermediate" organizations such as the NAPSS. With the consolidation of programmatic politics, individual social scientists gained access to positions within government ministries. However, as the case of unemployment insurance shows, this access depended upon the transitional nature of the movement toward centralized bureaucratic control, which allowed for the direct appointment of "experts" outside the civil service to positions of political influence.

In the United States, in contrast, policy was located in the formal political process while the social sciences were institutionalized in university departments. In this context, the political influence of "expertise" depended upon membership in delicately negotiated alliances between progressive reformers, other significant lobby groups, and key politicians. The direct participation of university-based social scientists in those coalitions was circumscribed by the public image which university presidents promoted of their institutions as both promoters of the public good and carriers of "objective" science. As the case of unemployment insurance illustrates, this situation encouraged limited participation in the public arena and in private and administrative commissions, as academic experts, on temporary leave from academic duty.

Conclusion

The above comparison of social scientists' attempts to promote unemployment insurance highlights two distinct modes of political participation. Beveridge and Llewellyn Smith relied heavily on informal channels of influence; personal connections with influential politicians allowed them to circumvent newly erected regulations for recruitment into the civil service and provided access to influential positions within governmental ministries. In contrast, Commons and Leiserson worked through progressive coalitions that tried to persuade other interest groups (organized labor, business, farmers) to join them in their lobbying of state legislatures. Thus, on a very simple level, the case study points to differences in the channels which social scientists used to influence social policy and variations in their success.

The second part explored differences in the institutional settings which encouraged these differences in strategy. In Britain, policy was formulated in the corridors of government and within the leadership of the governing party; in the United States, it was shaped in the public arena, at the intersection of political lobbying, party politics, and administrative politics. In Britain social science was located in amateur cultural institutions while in the United States it was a recognized academic profession. A brief historical survey of developments since the mid-nineteenth century suggests that these contrasts resulted from a divergence in the patterns of organizational development. Whereas in the mid-nineteenth century both countries were characterized by a popular patronage-style politics, the absence of state bureaucracies, and systems of higher education that were marginal to political and social life, by the turn of the century they had acquired the distinctive profiles described above.

In terms of the broader problematic, that of the mutual development of social science and social policy, the above analysis suggests a number of directions for further research. The British case points in the direction of a "fit" between "amateur" social science and a centralized policy process, removed from the vicissitudes of party politics. But it also points to limits to that relationship. It seems that the relation between centralized decision making and the social sciences varied with the level of state bureaucratization. In Britain, the success of the amateur model (at least from the perspective of its commitment to policy influence) depended in part on the transitional stage of civil service reform, which provided openings for the appointment of outside "experts" who had not risen through the ranks of the civil service.

At first gland, the analysis also seems to confirm Abrams's claim that the success of amateur social science in Britain worked against the "successful" development of the social sciences. But here it is important to not equate a particular path of organizational development (i.e., the American model of professionalization through the establishment of academic departments and professional societies) with the conditions for "success." As noted above, a variety of institutions in Britain continued to sustain a relatively vibrant tradition of social inquiry. Moreover, while sociology was only weakly institutionalized (in the LSE), other social sciences, most notably anthropology and economics, were firmly established. From this perspective, a more interesting set of questions would explore the effect of these differences in the organizational locus of both social science and social policy on differences in the range of social scientific projects which were institutionalized and the type of knowledge they produced.

As for the American case, at first glance the lack of political effectiveness would seem to challenge theses concerning the importance of state expansion for the professionalization of the social sciences. But this would be to attach too much weight to legislative outcomes as the only index of a mutual relationship. While the close ties between John Commons's group and the University of Wisconsin, on the one hand, and the state industrial commission, on the other, were the exception rather than the rule, they exemplify a model of the academic as public servant which existed in weaker forms across the country and which brought universities much needed funding and recognition. The location of the policy process in the midst of partisan politics in the United States suggests not that the social sciences and state followed autonomous trajectories but rather that the connections between the two may lie outside of the formal policy process.

Notes to Chapter 5

1. Philip Abrams, *The Origins of British Sociology.* Chicago, University of Chicago Press, 1968.

2. Lawrence Goldman makes a similar claim for the heuristic value of a comparison between social science organizations in England and the United States (he includes Germany), arguing that they "were organized in almost identical fashion, shared similar aims and outlooks, spoke a common language and yet diverged in historically significant ways in the course of their development. . . ." Lawrence Goldman, "A Peculiarity of the English? The Social Science Association and the Absence of Sociology in Nineteenth-Century Britain." *Past and Present* 114 (1987): p. 151.

3. This argument is first made by Philip Abrams in *The Origins of British Sociology.* It is further developed in Stephen Cole, "Continuity and Institutionalization in Science: A Case Study of Failure." In Anthony Oberschall, ed., *The Establishment of Empirical Sociology.* Evanston, New York, Harper & Row, 1972 and Reba Soffer, "Why Do Disciplines Fail? The Strange Case of British Sociology." *English Historical Review* 7 (1982): pp. 767–802. Goldman (1987) challenges this position, arguing for the need to evaluate "success" in terms of the goals of the social science movement at the time.

4. The main organizational forum for the pursuit of what was formerly the nineteenth-century amateur tradition was the Sociological Society, founded in 1903. As Abrams notes, the society failed to attract influential figures and most of its members were committed to other professions in Abrams, *The Origins,* p. 104. The one academic position in sociology was at the newly founded London School of Economics where the organizational division between a department of sociology and social administration institutionalized the intellectual division between empirical research and theoretical work.

5. Robert L. Church makes a similar point in his analysis of the institutionalization of economics. See Robert L. Church, "Economists as Experts: The Rise of an Academic Profession in America 1870–1917." In Lawrence Stone, ed., *The University in Society.* Princeton, Princeton University Press, 1974.

6. For examples of this approach as applied to the American case, see Oberschall, "The Institutionalization"; Alexandra Olesen and John Voss, "Introduction." In Alexandra Olesen and John Voss, eds., *The Organization of Knowledge in Modern America 1860–1920.* Baltimore, Johns Hopkins Press, 1979, pp. vii–xxiii; and Dorothy Ross, "The Development of the Social Sciences." In *The Organization,* pp. 106–38.

7. See Michel Foucault, *Discipline and Punish.* Random House, New York, 1979; Philip Corrigan and Derek Sayer, *The Great Arch.* Oxford, B. Blackwell, 1985; and Dietrich Rueschemeyer, *Power and the Division of Labor.* Cambridge, Polity Press, 1986.

8. Martin Shefter, "Party and Patronage: Germany, England and Italy." *Politics and Society* 7 (1977): pp. 403–51; Theda Skocpol and John Ikenberry, "The Political Formation of the American Welfare State in Historical and Comparative Perspective." *Comparative Social Research* 6 (1983): pp. 87–146.

9. José Harris, *Unemployment and Politics: A study in English Social Policy.* Oxford, Clarendon Press, 1972, p. 189.

10. Roger Davidson, "Llewellyn Smith, the Labour Department and Government Growth 1886–1909." In *Studies in the Growth of Nineteenth Century Government,* Gillian Sutherland, ed. London, Rowan & Littlefield, 1972, pp. 239–40.

11. The general outlines of Beveridge's biography are taken from José Harris, *William Beveridge, a Biography.* Oxford, Clarendon Press, 1977.

12. Ibid., p. 109.

13. For a discussion of the more general lessons to be drawn from Beveridge's career about the functioning of the British administration, see José Harris, "William Beveridge in Whitehall: Maverick or Mandarin?" In Roy MacLeod, ed., *Government and Expertise.* Cambridge, Cambridge University Press, 1988; pp. 224–41.

14. For a discussion of the Chamberlain circular and the events surrounding it, see Bentley B. Gilbert, *The Evolution of National Insurance in Great Britain.* London, Michael Joseph, 1966, chap. 1; Harris, *Unemployment and Politics,* chap. 2; and H. V. Emy, *Liberals, Radicals and Social Politics,* 1892–1914. Cambridge, Cambridge University Press, 1973, pp. 30–37.

15. On changing conceptions of unemployment, see Krishan Kumar, "Unemployment as a Problem in the Development of Industrial Societies: the English Experience." *The Sociological Review* 32 (1984) (2): pp. 185–223.

16. Harris, *Unemployment and Politics,* p. 115.

17. For a contemporary review of theories of unemployment in Britain and the United States, see Frederick Mills, "Theories of Unemployment." Ph.D. Dissertation. University of Chicago, 1917.

18. William Beveridge, *Unemployment: A Problem of Industry.* London, Longman's Green and Co., 1909, chaps. 3–6.

19. Beveridge, *Unemployment,* p. 193.

20. Harris, *Unemployment and Politics,* pp. 212–15.

21. Ibid., pp. 208–10.

22. Emy, *Liberals,* p. 166.

23. Harris, *Unemployment and Politics,* p. 233.

24. R. Davidson and R. Lowe, "Bureaucracy and Innovation in British Welfare Policy, 1870–1945." In W. J. Momonsen, ed., *The Emergence of the Welfare State in Britain and Germany.* London, Croom Helm 1981, pp. 263–95.

25. Harris notes that Davidson later modified her argument concerning the importance of statistics for the implementation of social policy. See José Harris, "Economic Knowledge and British Social Policy." In Mary O. Furner and Barry Supple, eds., *The State and Economic Knowledge: The American and British Experiences.* Cambridge, Cambridge University Press, 1990, p. 388, n. 23. The two positions by Davidson are developed in his "Llewellyn Smith" and *Whitehall and the Labour Problem in Late-Victorian and Edwardian Britain.* London, 1985. The argument would seem to revolve around whether labor statistics were actually used to formulate and administer policy, or merely to illustrate and legitimate it once formulated. In either case, our point concerning Beveridge and Llewellyn Smith's use of social scientific knowledge (in the form of empirical data and social models and theories) and their reputation as "experts" remains valid.

26. Davidson and Lowe, "Bureaucracy and Innovation," pp. 265–69.

27. Ibid., p. 275.

28. Accounts of these developments can be found in Davidson, "Llewellyn Smith," p. 255 and Harris, *Unemployment and Politics,* p. 153.

29. Harris, *Unemployment and Politics,* pp. 329–23.

30. Harris makes a similar point when she argues that those individuals with specialized economic knowledge who did participate in the policy process did so on the basis of their philanthropic experience or expertise rather than academic credentials. See Harris, "Economic Knowledge."

31. By focusing on unemployment insurance and these two individuals, we necessarily obscure other histories, most notably the role of knowledge experts in official government offices such as Caroll Wright at the Bureau of Labor Statistics. But whereas Commons and Leiserson gained access to the policy arena through their involvement in the social science movement and participated as academics, Wright was a politician turned administrator who participated in the world of social scientists on the basis of his position as chief of the Bureau of Labor Statistics. Thus, Wright's expertise does not teach us about the participation of social scientists as such in policy, nor about the impact of that mode of participation on the development of the social sciences.

For a discussion of the problems of how to treat state variations in a discussion of national variations in social policy, see Edwin Amenta, Elisabeth Clemens, Jefren Olsen, Sunita Parikh, and Theda Skocpol, "The Political Origins of Unemployment Insurance in Five American States." *Studies in American Political Development* 2 (1987): pp. 137–82.

32. "Commons, John Rogers." In *Dictionary of American Biography,* supplement 3. New York, 1973, pp. 176–80.

33. Mary Furner, *From Advocacy to Objectivity.* Lexington, University Press of Kentucky, 1975, p. 203.

34. See Jurgen Herbst, "Diversification in American Higher Education." In Konrad H. Jarausch, ed., *The Transformation of Higher Learning 1860–1930.* Chicago, University of Chicago Press, 1983.

35. For a biography of William Leiserson, see Michael J. Eisner, *William Morris Leiserson.* Madison, University of Wisconsin Press, 1967.

36. Ibid., pp. 31–35.

37. The Midwestern American university both constrained and encouraged academics' participation in the public sphere. Within certain limits university presidents encouraged and rewarded involvement by individual faculty in public affairs. Links were forged on both national and local levels. On the other hand, ideological assertions basing the value of scientific knowledge on its objectivity, and the vulnerable position of the new universities, led university presidents to censure controversial political activity. These limits were firmly established in a series of academic freedom cases in the course of the 1890s. This point is developed in Furner, *From Advocacy,* chap. 8, and Ross, "The Development." They were also evidenced in limits that universities imposed on the length of leaves which individual faculty could take for public service.

38. Daniel Nelson, *Unemployment Insurance: The American Experience, 1915–1935.* Madison, University of Wisconsin Press, 1969, p. 3.

39. On the AALL, see Irwin Yellowitz, *Labor and the Progressive Movement in New York State, 1897–1916*. Ithaca, Cornell University Press, p. 342, and Roy Lubove, "Economic Security and Social Conflict in America: The Early Twentieth Century, parts I and II." *Journal of Social History* 13 (1967/68): p. 335.

40. Nelson, *Unemployment Insurance,* p. 14.

41. Ibid., p. 16.

42. Yellowitz, *Labor and the Progressive Movement,* p. 352.

43. Nelson, *Unemployment Insurance,* p. 18.

44. John Commons, "Constructive Investigation and the Industrial Commission of Wisconsin," *The Survey* 29 (January 4, 1913): pp. 443–45.

45. Skocpol and Ikenberry, "The Political Formation," p. 108.

46. Nelson, *Unemployment Insurance,* p. 104.

47. Ibid., pp. 107–16.

48. The United States was among the earliest Western countries to set up bureaus of labor statistics. The first such bureau was established in 1869 in Massachusetts. While these bureaus were engaged in ongoing data collection and were often headed by individuals committed to programs of social reform, their concern to remain free from party politics and a particularly Baconian model of science (as the observation and collection of facts), which left interpretation to others, limited their potential as organizational bases for social progressives. Moreover, according to Leiby, by the late nineteenth century they had increasingly turned from monographic studies of particular problems (aimed at policy recommendations) to administration and routine, continuing investigations. See James Leiby, *Carroll Wright and Labor Reform: The Origin of Labor Statistics*. Cambridge, 1960, p. 89.

49. Edwin Amenta et al., "The Political Origins of Unemployment Insurance in Five American States," pp. 52–57.

50. Ibid., p. 57.

51. Ibid., p. 56.

52. Comparisons of British and American politics generally focus on the difference between the British parliamentary system, characterized by strong party discipline and the de facto supremacy of the executive, and the American federalist presidential system, characterized by a strict separation of powers between executive, legislature, and judiciary, and diffusion of authority between local, state, and federal levels of government. In terms of the policy process, the British system locates policy initiatives and formulation in the cabinet and ministerial departments, outside of the public eye, while the American system allows for multiple loci of policy initiative with multiple checks. See Martin Bulmer, *Social Science Research and Government*. Cambridge, Cambridge University Press, 1987, pp. 27–31. Far more than in Britain, policy in the United States depends upon persuasion of multiple groups, all of whom can effectively block the realization of policy initiatives. This point is developed in C. L. Mowat, "Social Legislation in Britain and the United States in the Early Twentieth Century." *Historical Studies* 7 (1969): pp. 81–96, and in Skocpol and Ikenberry, "The Political Formation."

While the formal structure underlying these differences was in place well before the 1880s, it was only during the period under examination that these implications for the locus of the policy process were realized. In Britain, the extension of the franchise and reform of the representation system, reform of the civil service, and the introduction of programmatic partisan politics all contributed to the emergence of a unified national government capable of initiating and implementing social legislation. The period between 1880 and World War I must be treated as a transitional period in which the effects of these developments were only beginning to work themselves out. In the case of unemployment insurance, it was as much the vacuums in political authority created by transformations in political practice, as these new structures, which facilitated the entry of social scientists into government (see below).

In the United States the possibility of national-level policy depended on extensive state building that only began to appear during the Progressive Era. Throughout the period under examination, social policy was largely confined to the state level (the one primary exception being civil service pensions; see Skocpol and Ikenberry, "The Political Formation.") At the same time, extensive communication and economic links between states led to a sort of informal coordination. The adoption of social legislation in one state usually depended upon and precipitated similar moves in other states.

The effect of these transitional arrangements on the outcome of specific campaigns recommends a study of the effect of political practices as well as formal structures on the policy process.

53. Shefter, "Party and Patronage," p. 435.

54. On the clerisy ideal, see Magali Sarfatti Larson, *The Rise of Professionalism: A Sociological Analysis*. Berkeley, University of California Press, 1977, chap. 7, and Sheldon Rothblatt, "The Diversification of Higher Education in England." In Jarausch, *The Transformation of Higher Learning*, pp. 131–48.

55. In the second half of the century, journalism in London was almost completely dominated by (nonconformist) Oxbridge graduates. See John Roach, "Liberalism and the Victorian Intelligentsia." *Cambridge Historical Journal* 13(1) (1957): pp. 58–81.

56. See Emmeline W. Cohen, *The Growth of the British Civil Service*. London, Allen & Unwin Ltd., 1941, and Christopher Kent, *Brains and Numbers: Elitism, Comtism and Democracy in Mid-Victorian England*. Toronto, 1978.

57. Lawrence Goldman, "The Social Science Association." *English Historical Review* (January 1986): pp. 95–134.

58. Goldman, "A Peculiarity of the English?" p. 137.

59. This argument refers solely to the professionalization, or rather absence of professionalization, of the practice of social sciences. In contrast, the leadership and membership of the NAPSS underwent a clear process of professionalization, passing from an association of wealthy philanthropists to one dominated by doctors, lawyers, and new professionals such as social workers and medical officers of health. See Eileen Yeo, "Social Science and Social Change." D. Phil. thesis, University of Sussex, 1972.

60. See Martin Pugh, *The Making of Modern British Politics, 1867–1939*. New York, St. Martin's Press, 1982, p. 5.

61. Ibid., p. 20.

62. Shefter, "Party and Patronage," p. 440.

63. See Pugh, *The Making of Modern British Politics,* and David Powell, "The New Liberalism and the Rise of Labour, 1886–1906." *The Historical Journal* 29 (1986) (2): pp. 369–93.

64. On the "New Liberalism," see P. F. Clarke, "The Progressive Movement in England." *Transactions of the Royal Historical Society* 5(24) (1974): pp. 159–81; Michael Freeden, *The New Liberalism: An Ideology of Social Reform.* Oxford, Clarendon Press, 1978; Stefan Collini, *Liberalism and Sociology: L. T. Hobhouse and Political Argument in England, 1880–1914.* Cambridge, Cambridge University Press, 1979.

65. The term "progressive" was introduced into the British political vocabulary around 1890 to refer to this group of social reformers. More recently, the term has been (re)introduced in the context of debates among historians concerning the origins of social legislation. Drawing on Clarke and Emy, we use the term to refer to the set of ideas and reform activities which informed the introduction of social legislation and the political agenda of the Liberal Party between 1906 and World War I. See Emy, *Liberals,* and Clarke, "The Progressive Movement." In contrast to theories that ascribe social legislation to demands from organized labor and the Labour Party, this view locates the origins of the welfare state in the initiative of a radical segment within the Liberal Party. See Pugh, *The Making of Modern British Politics,* pp. 136–37. From the perspective of this chapter, the term is particularly fortunate in that it serves to highlight the parallels between New Liberalism, and the broader ideology and constituency sympathetic to the movement, and social progressivism in the United States during the same period.

66. Pugh, *The Making of Modern British Politics,* p. 118.

67. Gilbert, *The Evolution of National Insurance,* p. 68.

68. On American mugwumps, see Geoffrey Blodgett, "The Mugwump Reputation, 1870 to the Present." *The Journal of American History* 66 (1980): pp. 667–87.

69. Other issues that united American mugwumps included antislavery, tariff reform, sound money, antimonopoly, and anti-imperialism. See Ari Hoogenboom, *Outlawing the Spoils: A history of the Civil Service Reform Movement, 1865–1883.* Urbana, IL, University of Illinois Press, 1968.

70. While the adoption of British forms by social reformers in the United States is often recognized, as evidenced by the inclusion of reviews of British and Continental developments in most inquiries into social policy by the AALL and other organizations at the time and by the spread of the settlement movement across the ocean, the reverse direction is less frequently identified. In terms of the topic of this chapter, Davidson notes that the Labour Bureau of the Board of Trade, founded in 1886, was directly modeled on the Massachusetts Bureau of Statistics (1972, p. 84).

71. Blodgett, "The Mugwump Reputation," pp. 867–87.

72. Thomas L. Haskell, *The Emergence of Professional Social Science: The American Social Science Association and the Nineteenth Century Crisis of Authority.* Urbana, IL, University of Illinois, 1977, p. 109.

73. Goldman, "The Social Science Association," p. 156.

74. For discussions of the changing nature of American politics, see Walter Dean

Burnham, *Critical Elections and the Mainsprings of American Politics*. New York, W. W. Norton, 1970, chap. 4; Martin Schiesl, *The Politics of Efficiency: Municipal Administration and Reform in America, 1880–1920*. Berkeley, University of California Press, 1977; Richard L. McCormick, "The Party Period and Public Policy: An Exploratory Hypothesis." *The Journal of American History* 66 (2) (1979): pp. 279–96; Richard L. McCormick, "The Discovery that Business Corrupts Politics: A Reappraisal of the Origins of Progressivism." *American Historical Review* 86 (1981): pp. 247–74; and Stephen Skowronek, *Building a New American State: The Expansion of National Administrative Capacities, 1877–1920*. Cambridge, Cambridge University Press, 1982.

75. Skowronek, *Building a New American State,* p. 167.

76. McCormick, "The Party Period," p. 259.

77. Daniel Rodgers, "In Search of Progressivism." *Reviews in American History* (1982), p. 116.

78. Rodgers argues that in the "newly fluid, issue-focused political contexts of the progressive era the better organized players—the professional lobbies, the well-disciplined interest groups and, above all, the corporations—had a massive political advantage." See Rodgers, "In Search of Progressivism," p. 121.

79. Furner identifies two distinct forms of American New Liberalism: a corporate liberalism—which recognized the separate, but compatible, interests of organically related social groups—and a more democratic, more statist collectivism. According to Furner the institutional possibility of this ideologically more varied response to the challenges that economic unrest posed to laissez-faire economics lay in the variety of different types of public agencies involved in social inquiry. See Mary O. Furner, "Knowing Capitalism: public Investigation and the Labor Question in the Long Progressive Era." In Mary O. Furner and Barry Supple, eds., *The State and Economic Knowledge: the American and British Experiences,* Cambridge, 1990.

80. This definition is suggested by Yellowitz, *Labor and the Progressive Movement.*

81. Key institutions for the development of this alternate model were Johns Hopkins (1876), Clark University (1887), and the University of Chicago (1892), while both Princeton and Harvard adopted features of this new model fairly soon after its introduction.

82. Burton J. Bledstein, *The Culture of Professionalism: The Middle Class and the Development of Higher Education in America*. New York, Norton, 1976.

83. See Haskell, *The Emergence of Professional Social Science,* p. 160.

84. On the alliance between professionals and university reformers, see Bledstein, *The Culture of Professionalism;* Randall Collins, *The Credential Society: A Historical Sociology of Education and Stratification*. New York, Academy Press, 1979; and Donald Light, "The Development of Professional Schools in America." In Jarausch, *The Transformation of Higher Learning.*

85. On cultural authority over the immigrant nation, see Collins, *The Credential Society;* on education of upper classes, see Burke (1983). Colin B. Burke, "The Expansion of American Higher Education." In The Transformation of Higher Learning (see n. 34).

86. Quoted in Veysey, 1965, p. 265.

87. On the assertion of Protestant Anglo-Saxon cultural authority, see Collins, *The Credential Society.* For a similar analysis of the social background of the first generation of professionalizing natural scientists, see George Daniels, "The Process of Professionalization in American Science: The Emergent Period, 1820–60." *ISIS* 58 (1967): pp. 151–66.

88. See Steven J. Diner, *A City and Its Universities: Public Policy in Chicago, 1892–1919.* Chapel Hill, University of North Carolina Press, 1980, pp. 17–33.

6

Social Knowledge and the Generation of Child Welfare Policy in the United States and Canada

JOHN R. SUTTON

MODERN states, following precedents set in the West, typically assume a number of responsibilities for the successful upbringing of children, often going so far as to institutionalize those responsibilities in their formal constitutions. This marks a sharp departure from traditional societies and patriarchal regimes, where the line between public and private spheres was drawn so as to leave authority over children in the hands of family and community. Most generally, mass schooling has supplemented family authority across societies as the dominant mode of "normal" childhood socialization.[1] In addition, and of more concern to this chapter, states claim the authority to protect children who are disadvantaged by poverty, disability, or family failure through programs of child welfare and family assistance. Children are, in short, the centerpiece of modern welfare states. In welfare regimes, the official supervision of childhood is seen as an effective method of assuring the improvement of human capital, the production of moral citizens, and the continuity of the nation itself.

This chapter is concerned with the development of a national policy competence in the area of child welfare in the United States and Canada. I choose this focus for two reasons: first, these two countries are widely seen as deviant cases in terms of the global trend toward the nationalization of child welfare, indeed of the development of comprehensive welfare systems more generally; and second, despite their many similarities, they chose paths of policy development that diverged in interesting ways. Standard textbook accounts say that the United States had no national child welfare policy until the passage of the Social Security Act, and the creation of the Aid to Dependent Children program, in 1935. A closer look suggests that Americans addressed the problems of children early and aggressively, but through institutional channels that deliberately carried no connotations of entitlement to social benefits. Specifically, the early introduction of mass schooling and the construction of a specialized juvenile justice system operated as functional equivalents of a comprehensive child welfare policy.[2] Research on the Canadian case is still sparse, but it is already clear that Canadians not only borrowed exemplary reforms from the United States, they also adapted those reforms to an entrenched set of indigenous institutions. Explicit comparisons of the child welfare policies of the United States and Canada are even rarer; one purpose of this chapter is to begin such a line of inquiry.

By use of the term "national policy competence," I mean three things. I am concerned, first, with the establishment of policymaking agencies as part of the national state; second, with the amount and type of policy-relevant information that those agencies utilized; and third, with the ability of those agencies to translate information into successful policy initiatives. More specifically and substantively, I will focus on the origin and development of the U.S. Children's Bureau (USCB), which was created in 1912, and the Canadian Council on Child Welfare (CCCW), created in 1920. The starting point for the analysis is their similarities: both agencies were created as a response to demands by progressive reform groups for a national commitment to the problems of dependent children; both were chartered by their respective federal governments with sole responsibility to gather and disseminate information on child welfare, and to generate policy initiatives; and both were in some sense "precocious" developments, stalking-horses for a broader set of policies that would emerge only in the wake of the Great Depression and World War II. But, of course, it is the differences between the two agencies that are most revealing. As I will describe in more detail below, the USCB and the CCCW differed in terms of their structures, their political agendas, and their approaches to social research, and they had divergent influences on the evolution of U.S. and Canadian child welfare policies well into the 1930s.

One theme that runs throughout this analysis is that choices about relevant social knowledge are fateful both for the definition of social problems and for the development of official policies. In the first section of this chapter, I describe two models of social knowledge that were prominent in varying degrees in U.S. and Canadian child-welfare reform movements. My point is to contrast the two models, suggest their political implications, and show how they were incorporated into movements that were antecedent to the USCB and CCCW. This discussion provides a prologue to the second section, where I present descriptive natural histories of the two agencies. This analysis will show that in this particular area of child welfare, American developments were unusually advanced relative to Canada: not only was the American agency created well before its Canadian counterpart, but also, despite its many weaknesses, it represented a more thorough and successful national commitment to child welfare. The third section of the chapter attempts to account for this unexpected difference. The analysis suggests that the different policy paths taken by the two countries are due to, first, the interactions of social and professional movements with political institutions and, second, the relative sequencing of institution-building and political development in the two countries. In shorter and more substantive terms, I argue that policies were influenced by the divergent models of social knowledge promoted by contending nongovernmental interest groups.

Ideology and Social Knowledge

As different interest groups promote different ideologies and policies, they may also advocate different forms of social knowledge. In this sense, ideology includes not only statements about the way the world is, but also about how we should come to know the world—in other words, about legitimate strategies of inquiry. It is now commonplace to recognize, following Weber, that the transition to modernity in Western societies involved the rejection of "nonrational" modes of apprehending the world through oracles, prophecy, or tradition in favor of the "rational" secular methodologies defined by science. It is less well recognized that in fully modernized societies, disputes may persist over competing and equally "scientific" methods, especially when the object of inquiry is the social world. In Anglo-American societies in the early twentieth century, major social policy debates contained within them a fundamental epistemological conflict about appropriate means for defining and studying dependency. On each side of this debate were arrayed a coalition of what Foucault has called "the disciplines"—networks of aspiring experts with a professional and political stake in their common mode of knowledge production.

On one side is the case method, which has its roots in a medical model of individual pathology, and farther back perhaps also in a Calvinist model of individual sin and redemption.[3] Knowledge production under the case method is a problem of diagnosis—that is, of reconstructing an individual biography in terms of a known, or suspected, etiological schema. It is the dominant cognitive style of the modern helping professions, and whatever specific scientific discourse is used, the discovered biography retains an unmistakable element of moral struggle. On the other side is what we might call, speaking generically, the survey method. Here the unit of analysis is shifted upward, to the collective level; it is mainly the domain of sociologists, demographers, and economists. The survey method bears roughly the same relation to the case method as epidemiology to clinical diagnosis, and carries analogous political implications. As Julia Lathrop, first director of the U.S. Children's Bureau, argued, survey data tend to illuminate the environmental and structural, rather than personal and individual, origins of social problems. Discussion of the historical trajectories of the USCB and the CCCW will allow us to observe the dynamic relationships among social knowledge, social movements, and official policies. Before moving into that discussion, however, it is important to provide some historical background on the case and survey methods.

Casework is commonly defined as the study of "those processes which develop personality through adjustments consciously affected, individual by individual, between [people] and their social environment."[4] As such, the casework method originated in the charity organization movement in late nineteenth-century England. To the theorists of the charity organization movement, casework implemented a desire to understand poverty in terms of individual pathology, and to limit the distribution of material aid in favor of purely moral support and advice wherever possible. In the United States, medical analogies supplemented the case method because early American charity organization workers were frequently employed in hospitals: physicians provided attractive professional role models in part because they enjoyed legitimate powers of intervention in individual lives. The "medicalization" of discourse about poverty spread to Canada through the Montreal Charity Organization Society (COS), which hired many American workers and organizers.[5] In the twentieth century, of course, the medical model in casework has been supplemented further by an arsenal of therapeutic techniques that grew out of psychoanalysis.

The history of the survey method, while considerably longer and more complex, is also traceable to British antecedents. The closest ancestors of American social surveys were Charles Booth's survey of urban social conditions, *Life and Labour of the People in London,* published between 1889 and 1903, and B. S. Rowntree's similar, but more focused, study of York, *Poverty: A Study of Town Life,* published in 1901.[6] Both studies were concerned with assessing and accounting for poverty in late-Victorian Britain. Essentially they were exercises in enumeration; but despite their lack of sophisticated statistical techniques and systematic sampling, they made two major contributions: first, through detailed analysis of household budgets they were able to define the concept of the "poverty line" in fairly objective terms; and second, they derived consistent estimates of those living below it—around thirty percent in both studies. It is important to note that these early surveys were not the products of individual initiative alone. Rather they arose from, and were supported by, a broad social matrix of "wealthy philanthropists, charity workers, Marxists, single-taxers, trade unionists, Fabian socialists, liberals, workers of the new settlement houses, physicians and health workers, [and] evangelists of the new Salvation Army."[7] It is important to note the close connection between the settlement houses and the survey method: Shore observes that student residents of Toynbee Hall, the first settlement in England, worked on Booth's *Life and Labour.*[8]

The Booth and Rowntree studies were reported in a number of American magazines and professional journals, and they directly inspired a number of American imitators, the earliest of which were the Hull House survey of the Chicago slums in 1895, and W.E.B. DuBois's study of the black community in Philadelphia in 1896. The settlement movement was particularly receptive to the survey method, and while American and British social surveys shared a number of identifying characteristics—which included reliance on data drawn from the natural social world, focus on a bounded geographical domain, concern with detailed individual-level information, and use of at least some quantitative summaries—American settlement leaders gave the survey a unique spin by using it as a means of publicity and community mobilization.[9]

The "big bang" of the American social survey was a study of conditions in Pittsburgh directed by Paul U. Kellogg in 1907. Kellogg was a product of the settlement movement, and at that time he was managing editor of *Charities and the Commons*. This journal was formed in 1905 out of the merger of *Charities,* a journal concerned with philanthropy and casework published by the New York Charity Organization Society (COS), and *The Commons,* a settlement-oriented publication concerned with structural change and economic justice. Their merger symbolized the recent detente between the two movements. Seed money for the Pittsburgh survey was provided by the New York COS and the Pittsburgh Civic Association, and a large grant from the Russell Sage Foundation carried the project through.[10] According to Chambers, the study was "a truly pioneering adventure, the first major attempt to survey in depth the entire life of a single community by team research" using both quantitative data and data gained from individual depth interviews.[11]

The Pittsburgh survey had a number of important consequences. Locally, it generated conclusions about the causes of disability that encouraged the adoption of workmen's compensation legislation in Pennsylvania. It also spawned a number of imitators: surveys were soon conducted in Buffalo, Kentucky, Rhode Island, and New Jersey, and the Russell Sage Foundation set up its own department of Surveys and Exhibits in 1912. This wave of enthusiasm for social research seems, finally, to have influenced the development of the American social work profession. On the impetus of the Pittsburgh survey and with the support of the Russell Sage Foundation and private donors, *Charities and the Commons* soon became autonomous from the New York COS and changed its name to *The Survey;* its content then moved steadily away from social work practice toward more exclusive concern with structural issues. And while most social work training programs continued to focus on casework, the University of Chicago program proved an important exception due to its linkage with the settlements and their research orientation. The program was originally an outgrowth of Hull House, and even after its affiliation with the university in 1920, under the leadership of Julia Lathrop and Grace and Edith Abbott, it continued to stress research and social policy at the expense of casework. As we will see, Lathrop carried this emphasis directly into the program of the Children's Bureau.[12]

The reformist survey movement declined in the United States after the 1920s as the Depression dried up local funds and swamped local problems, and professional sociologists—such as Park and Burgess at Chicago—distanced themselves from reformist efforts and focused instead on a more neutral "human ecology" approach.[13] Canada never experienced a strong wave of American- or even British-style social surveys, mainly because of the lack of an indigenous settlement movement (or some equivalent). As we will see, however, the legacy of the survey method was a new vocabulary that was used by the Children's Bureau to redefine the problem of child welfare.

Policy Trajectories of the USCB and the CCCW

This section describes the historical development of the U.S. Children's Bureau and the Canadian Council on Child Welfare. I will discuss each agency in terms of (1) its origins and charter, (2) the research activities in which it engaged, and (3) the impacts it had on child welfare policy. My goal is not just to present historical summaries, but to construct a pair of analytically comparable natural histories. The point is to show how, in each case, decisive political choices informed working definitions of relevant social research, and ultimately set limits on the kinds of policies that could be promoted.

The Children's Bureau

The genesis of a national children's agency in the United States is due largely to the promotional activities of leaders in the settlement movement, who saw such an agency as a means of attacking child labor. Florence Kelley, a resident of Chicago's Hull House, first proposed a centralized clearinghouse of information on child labor in 1900; Lillian Wald, founder of the Henry Street Settlement in New York, specifically suggested a federal children's bureau in 1903.[14] Reformers' interest in federal action quickened after they failed repeatedly to get meaningful state-level child labor legislation. Thus in 1904, a coalition of settlement activists, including Kelley, Wald, and Jane Addams, joined by other prominent charity reformers, juvenile court judges, clergymen, and a few philanthropic industrialists, formed the National Child Labor Committee (NCLC). Their first assault on the problem failed when Congress voted down a national child labor bill in 1906. It was after this rebuff that the NCLC gave first priority to the children's bureau idea.

The next step in their endeavor was toward further coalition-building and national publicity. The NCLC had the ear of President Roosevelt, and in 1909 Wald organized the White House Conference on the Care of Dependent Children, and invited representatives not only from the settlement movement and the NCLC, but also from the charity organization movement and other reform groups. The conference ended with a petition to Congress calling for the creation of a children's bureau. Wald and Kelley drafted a proposed bill; Roosevelt endorsed it, conference members testified before Congress, and Jane Addams helped write a form letter sent out by the NCLC urging letters of support to congressmen. A bill was passed over significant opposition and signed by President Taft in 1912. Julia Lathrop, another Hull House resident, was named first chief of the Children's Bureau.[15]

Political pressures gave a conservative spin to the Bureau's activities from the outset. Enabling legislation gave the agency no administrative or enforcement authority; its emergent role was thus that of information gathering and education. Substantively, the bureau was chartered only in general terms to promote the "welfare of children." Thus, Lathrop's first task was to construct an agenda for the bureau, and to do so she turned to the source of her political strength, an extensive constituent network that connected the settlements, women's clubs, suffragists, charity organization societies and philanthropic agencies, academics (mainly at the University of Chicago), the American Medical Association (AMA), and lawyers concerned with the problems of children.[16] This network made up "the organization set of the liberal social welfare establishment."[17] She consulted this network for advice in setting up the bureau, and later used it as an informal pressure group in funding struggles with Congress.

Lathrop's dependence on this network affected the agency's early development in two ways. First, it cemented her commitment to reform through localism, gradualism, and cooperation among established elites. Second and more substantively, it encouraged an avoidance of politically dangerous social issues. In particular, some of the most important opposition to the Children's Bureau bill came from business interests fearful of an aggressive attack on child labor. In his communications with Lathrop, Homer Folks, the dean of American child welfare experts, advised her to focus the bureau's efforts on research into infant mortality and on the education of mothers. By de-emphasizing child labor, he argued, she would avoid political controversy, and demonstrate that the bureau was not simply an agent of the NCLC.[18]

Infant mortality became the first major issue taken up by the Children's

Bureau, and the methodology of the social survey became its distinctive claim to policy relevance. Survey work allowed Lathrop to use the expertise she had gained as director of research at the Chicago School of Civics and Philanthropy, and perhaps more important, it provided a means to define a unique turf for the bureau, differentiating it from, for example, the Bureau of Public Health. In requests for funds to conduct infant mortality studies, Lathrop emphasized the USCB's attributes as "the only child welfare agency in the federal government whose perspective is 'sociological' and whose method is statistical rather than clinical."[19] Politics aside, there was an important truth in this claim, and mortality studies led to critical conclusions. Carefully avoiding any inferences about the purely medical causes of infant mortality, Children's Bureau surveys found again and again that the most significant correlate of infant death was, quite simply, poverty, especially that which followed from unemployment and industrial accidents. This general agenda soon unfolded into two more specific campaigns that characterized the bureau's activities in its early decades. The first of these was the drive to promote a system of uniform birth registration among the states, as a means to generate a universe of useful mortality data; the second was a series of demonstration projects and health conferences designed to educate mothers in local communities. In both of these campaigns, Lathrop's network proved useful as a means of mobilizing state and local support, and both proved to be valuable experiments in federal-state cooperation in the area of child welfare.[20]

Our last step is to consider the bureau's impact on some major child welfare policy initiatives. Here it is readily apparent that Lathrop's emphasis on research and education not only constrained the agency's influence, but also provided a means to finesse some difficult political issues. One such policy initiative was mothers' pensions, a form of outdoor relief to families without a male breadwinner. After the first state pension law was enacted in 1911, the movement gained momentum from the growing conviction among child welfare experts that dependent children could be better maintained in their natural families than in institutions. The ideology of family preservation had been endorsed by the delegates at the White House Conference in 1909, and mothers' pension laws were promoted by the same coalition that had pushed for the creation of the Children's Bureau—most conspicuously, settlement workers and women's clubs, joined by juvenile court judges in the midwestern and western states. As might be expected, the Children's Bureau lent its support to the mothers' pension movement, but in a carefully oblique way. Pensions were, after all, a state legislative matter, and they met strong opposition from the private charity establishment. Thus the bureau, hewing to a strict interpretation of its legislative charter, approached the pension issue as a problem of research and publicity. In the 1910s and 1920s, the agency published comparative studies of mothers' pension laws in the American states and other nations, and cosponsored conferences on administrative standards with the National Conference of Social Work. Thus the bureau, while unable to offer direct support for the adoption of pension policies, at least implicitly encouraged the standardization of state and local policies; it may also have helped legitimize the idea of relief as an entitlement.[21]

Second, the bureau also played an important, though perhaps reluctant, role in American child labor policy. While Lathrop declined to use agency resources to attack this issue directly, the NCLC continued to press for federal child labor legislation. They were successful in 1916, when Congress passed the Wick's Bill, which prohibited some forms of child labor in interstate commerce. The law was not promoted by the USCB, and the statute itself did not mention the bureau. Administrative responsibility was given to an interagency board, and responsibility for enforcement was assigned to the Secretary of Labor. The Labor Secretary then passed enforcement duties to the Children's Bureau, which organized a new Child Labor Division in May 1917. The Wick's Bill was declared unconstitutional in 1917, but during the nine months it was in effect it appears that the bureau made a serious effort to fulfill its unsought mandate. Agents moved quickly in drawing up administrative regulations, soliciting state cooperation in the issuance of age certificates, and inspecting nearly seven hundred factories and twenty-eight mines. Indeed, the program can be seen as an early exemplar of state-federal cooperation: because of the bureau's emphasis on decentralization, it was able to run the program for significantly less than the budgeted appropriation. After the act was declared unconstitutional, the Child Labor Division continued to investigate workplaces under the bureau's general mandate, and in 1918 the division was chosen to enforce a new prohibition on child labor in government war contracts. Finally, the Child Labor Division was folded up in 1919 when the Treasury Department assumed responsibility for a federal child labor tax law passed that year. That bill, too, was declared unconstitutional in 1922. This litany of impediments tends to confirm Lathrop's political judgment: as Michael Katz has observed, the problem of child labor ultimately proved resistant to federal action.[22]

The third and arguably most successful policy legacy of the Children's Bureau was the Sheppard-Towner Maternity and Infancy Act of 1921. Sheppard-Towner was historically important because it was the only federal social welfare program enacted before the New Deal. For our more narrow purposes, it is important because it was actively promoted by the USCB, because it grew directly out of the bureau's main research activities, and because, in both its successes and failures, it clearly shows the imprint of the bureau's approach to social knowledge. Lathrop first proposed a federal grant-in-aid program aimed at lowering rates of infant and maternal mortality in her annual report to Congress in 1917. In support of her proposal, she brandished the results of the bureau's first series of infant mortality studies, all of which emphasized the preventability of a large proportion of infant deaths. To catalyze interest further, the bureau declared 1918 the Children's Year. Introduced to Congress in 1918, the Sheppard-Towner bill aimed to expand the USCB's program of birth and death registration, to disseminate information, and to establish clinics, health fairs, and visiting nurse programs. Lathrop's constituent network actively supported the bill, as did the labor movement and the Catholic child welfare establishment. Significantly, the American Medical Association took an equivocal position, with the general membership opposed, and the pediatrics section in support; in Congress, opposition was mounted on the usual states' rights grounds, with perhaps more than the usual amount of red-baiting apparent in debates. After a series of amendments that sharply limited the bureau's enforcement powers, Congress enacted Sheppard-Towner in 1921 on a limited five-year basis. Final passage, according to several writers, was strongly encouraged by the specter of the new and unpredictable female vote.[23]

To the Children's Bureau and its allies, Sheppard-Towner was significant for political reasons, beyond its potential impact on child health. The act promised to open up a whole new domain of preventive health care that defined special responsibilities for women, while at the same time leaving the traditional curative domain of the physician undisturbed. For the first time, it acknowledged that health and welfare were matters of concern to the national government, even while it was respectful of the prerogatives of state and local authority. To its most ambitious supporters, Sheppard-Towner was a Trojan horse that would, over the long run, mobilize support for a broader range of child welfare reforms by convincing mothers of the importance of "keeping the child in the school and out of the factory."[24] But the very fact that this agenda had to be disguised betrays a crucial weakness of the program, and perhaps of the Children's Bureau's more general strategy.

When the initial five-year funding period ended in 1927, Sheppard-Towner was effectively repealed, with only a two-year sunset extension. Some of the reasons for the act's demise are clearly external to the program itself: President Coolidge was less supportive than Harding had been; a shift in Congress decisively weakened the progressive coalition; and legislators no longer feared the women's vote. Meanwhile, the medical profession had shifted from ambivalence to opposition. Specialist obstetricians initially supported the program and participated in sponsored clinics because Children's Bureau administrators made room for them, deferred to their authority, and increased the flow of private patients by referring problem cases. Their support declined, however, as they came to define even routine pregnancy as a medical problem, and to see the preventive services of the clinics as a normal part of private practice.[25] But it is also apparent that the weaknesses of the Sheppard-Towner act, and the administrative timidity of the Children's Bureau, also contributed to the defeat of the initiative. Because of early political opposition, the act gave the bureau little leverage for enforcement, and the bureau itself was so deferential to state prerogatives that officials imposed almost no clear standards for compliance—hence, no barriers to the receipt of federal funds. Indeed, Sheila Katz Rothman argues that the Children's Bureau clinics effectively *taught* physicians to use such fundamental preventive techniques as regular physical examinations and patient case histories, which they then appropriated into their private practices.[26]

Rothman's argument about the fate of Sheppard-Towner can be expanded to cover the early career of the Children's Bureau. The bureau's careful adherence to a program of survey research and grassroots education, its reluctance to confront flammable issues head on, and its deference to established bureaucratic and professional turf doubtless helped it preserve a secure niche, but also blunted the agency's impact on policy. Most relevant to the concerns of this paper, the AMA's defeat of Sheppard-Towner had important implications for the link between knowledge production and policy. It represented a shift not only from public to private control of preventive health care, but also from a highly aggregated analysis of child welfare based on survey data to an individual-level analysis based on case histories. Hence, finally, it meant an inevitable de-emphasis of the effects of environmental conditions—such as unemployment and poverty—on child and maternal mortality, in favor of renewed attention to individual (and in some sense moral) factors.

The Canadian Council on Child Welfare

Our discussion of the CCCW will be considerably briefer than that of the Children's Bureau—in part, admittedly, because there are fewer sources on which to draw, and in part also because Canadian policies were conscious adaptations of those in the United States. Thus, in the interest of analytic clarity rather than national chauvinism, the discussion will treat the career of the CCCW primarily in terms of its deviation from the exemplar of the USCB.

Like the Children's Bureau, the Canadian Council on Child Welfare grew from an antecedent set of private voluntary associations. One feeder stream was the middle-class feminist movement in Canada, in particular the National Council of Women of Canada. The NCWC, formed in 1893, was an alliance of Canadian women's clubs that generally took a secular and moderate position on social problems. Thus the NCWC opposed restrictive employment legislation and supported female education, female suffrage, and mothers' pensions; they further recognized the need for trained professionals in social work. One of the council's major activities was a series of surveys on Canadian social problems in the period before World War I. It is important to note, however, that the organization's influence was sharply circumscribed in both class and ethnic terms: it generally ignored the problems of working women, and French Canadian women were notably underrepresented in its constituent groups.[27]

A second stream originated in the social gospel movement, a diffuse coalition of Protestant activists devoted to religiously based social reform. The movement took a secular turn in 1907 with the formation of the Moral and Social Reform Council, an alliance of Anglican and Protestant churches with the Labour Congress of Canada. Early on, the council was mainly concerned with issues of temperance and sabbatarianism, but gradually its focus turned to more purely secular reforms. In 1913, the MSRC changed its name to the Social Service Council of Canada. The SSC eventually became the dominant voice of Canadian social work, exerting an important influence on national legislation and providing a channel of communication with social workers in the United States. The NCWC and the SSC were allies on a number of issues, most notably in their advocacy of an advanced system of child welfare that emphasized prevention rather than institutional treatment. The 1914 Congress of the SSC brought together reformers from a broad range of voluntary associations with representatives of all levels of Canadian government, and endorsed a number of advanced social policies—among them, mothers' pensions and the creation of a federal children's agency on the model of the U.S. Children's Bureau.[28] This meeting represented the high-water mark of the coalition-building program that grew out of the social gospel movement, but the onset of World War I forestalled any immediate federal action. Partly as a result of the experience of the war, the Ottawa government established the Dominion Department of Health in 1919, and added a Children's Division in 1920. Reformers interested in a more broad-scale approach to child welfare were not satisfied with the narrow medical focus of the new agency, and in response to their continued pressure the Department of Health invited representatives of nearly two hundred groups to the first Dominion Child Welfare Conference in 1920. The Canadian Council on Child Welfare was founded on that occasion as "a voluntary agency, supported by federal subsidies and designated to serve as a national clearing-house for child welfare, to issue professional guidance materials, to inform public opinion, and to formulate briefs for legislation."[29] Thus while the charter of the CCCW was similar to that of the USCB, in structure and intent it was a different sort of compromise, designed as a bridge between public and private child welfare efforts.

The development of the CCCW's policy influence in the first twenty years of its history was powerfully constrained by the biases and ambitions of its leader for much of that time, Charlotte Whitton. Whitton came to the CCCW as a volunteer in 1920, after her initiation into social work with the Social Service Council. In 1922 she became the agency's first full-time chief executive, and she served in that position until 1941. Like Julia Lathrop, Whitton enjoyed the support of a network of voluntary groups, and she consciously sought to adapt the USCB's social research methodology to Canadian needs. But Whitton's vision of the CCCW's role was at the same time more ambitious and more parochial. She was not committed to the idea of a comprehensive program of child welfare—indeed, in the venerable tradition of the poor laws, she warned continually that public relief programs tended to encourage dependency and sloth. Rather, her considerable energies, and the resources of the CCCW, were devoted mainly to a zealous program of empire-building and professionalization.[30]

Whitton sought to construct an indigenous social work establishment as an extension of her personal network, which was strongest in Ontario. Since there were few professional social workers in Canada in the 1920s, her goal was to repatriate Canadians who were trained and working in the United States and place them in key positions throughout Canada, displacing or superseding untrained volunteers. To this end, the prestige of the CCCW and the mystique of the social survey were potent tools. Her strategy worked in the following way: using whatever personal connections she had, Whitton would approach community elites to sound out local opinion, wangle an invitation, and weaken potential opposition. The research team consisted of Whitton and a few personal aides; they used the investigation as a means to scrutinize the background and training of local volunteers, and typically to recommend replacements or new administrative leaders. In the course of the investigation, they strove to generate publicity that was favorable to their recommendations.[31] The CCCW's research was, by any reasonable standard, poor. The surveys it conducted were never taken seriously by leading academic social scientists in Canada, even those sympathetic with the organization's goals.[32] As far as I have been able to tell, the agency generated no new data on the problems of children, and offered no new insights on techniques for working with families. Instead it depended heavily on the Children's Bureau for many of the publications it distributed, as well as for "practical expertise and professional guidance."[33]

Because of the CCCW's ambiguous political status, its hollow research, and Whitton's almost exclusive concern with empire-building, the agency had no direct policy legacy comparable to Sheppard-Towner. It did, however, have an influence that lasted well into the Great Depression. One important outcome was the growing power of Whitton and the CCCW in all aspects of Canadian public welfare. Gradually the CCCW grew to monopolize not only child welfare, but national welfare policy generally. Whitton was increasingly able to use her position to control social welfare appointments in the provinces personally, encouraging officials to bypass, for example, the Canadian Association of Social Workers. Her personalistic attempt to professionalize child welfare did in fact create a number of new career opportunities for women, but largely by displacing experienced women volunteers. Eventually, as occurred in the United States, women were squeezed out of administrative positions in Canadian social work, ironically with Whitton's full encouragement. She disfavored not only women administrators, but also married women in any kind of career positions. Her attempt at building a monopoly was so successful that, in 1928, the Social Service Council officially transferred its research responsibilities to the CCCW. The CCCW added a Family Service Division in 1929, and in 1932 it assumed the functions of the Children's Division of the Dominion Department of Health; in 1935 it absorbed the Central Committee of Community Chests and Councils of Canada, and changed its name to the Canadian Welfare Council.[34] The agency's role gradually became hegemonic: "movie censorship, school attendance laws, youth employment, mental hygiene, 'social' diseases, unwed parenthood, mothers and family allowances, child legislation, delinquency, moral reform, drug and liquor traffic, birth control, immigration, housing, playgrounds, handicapped persons, and divorce all fell under its purview. The council acted as the moral watchdog over all aspects of child and family life."[35]

This statement is undoubtedly hyperbolic; even as the CCCW grew, other groups and some provincial governments continued to promote policies of which Whitton disapproved, and in these areas the major substantive influence of the CCCW was to make relief less available. Whitton imparted to the agency a stigmatizing view of poverty that can be traced back to the English charity organization societies. She used her official voice to criticize welfare polices in the Maritime Provinces as being too traditional and unprofessional, and those in the more progressive western provinces as being too bureaucratic and statist. The quasi-public structure of the CCCW exemplified her conviction, also derived from the charity organization movement, that public-private cooperation was a necessary antidote to the impersonalism of state control.[36] Thus, for example, when the mothers' pension movement gained impetus in Canada after World War I, the CCCW sought to influence pension policy at the margins rather than to oppose it categorically. The agency pushed hard for professional administration of pension programs as a means to limit relief to deserving mothers who fulfilled stringent residency requirements. On the basis of a CCCW survey, British Columbia cut back the rates of mothers' pension benefits in the midst of the Great Depression, and the council's recommendations also contributed to the failure of New Brunswick and Quebec to enact pension programs at all. Indeed the Depression was, for Whitton and the CCCW, a boom time. Whitton found a great deal to criticize as relief programs began to grow in an uncoordinated, stopgap fashion. In a series of surveys, she advocated more rigorous investigations and an overall cut in relief, even going so far as to advocate the closing of soup kitchens in Victoria. She formed alliances with influential local businessmen who feared ballooning relief costs and an ominous leftward trend in popular politics. One crowning salt of her efforts, in 1935, was a new federal policy that lowered the maximum relief amounts that Canadian provinces were allowed to disburse.[37]

Toward an Account of U.S.-Canadian Differences

At this point, we can summarize the salient differences in the political trajectories of the U.S. Children's Bureau and the Canadian Council on Child Welfare. The USCB proved to be a timid, but durable, presence in the American federal government. Its overall impact is summarized in the mixed success and failure of the Sheppard-Towner Act: on the one hand, the bureau eventually yielded the initiative to a medical conception of child welfare that was inimical to the sociological vision that originally animated the agency; on the other, during the brief heyday of Sheppard-Towner, child mortality rates were significantly decreased, a preventive model of child health was given broad legitimacy, and official statistical capacities in the area of health and welfare were permanently enhanced. Moreover, this early example of federal grant-in-aid programs laid the foundation for further attention to children under Title V of the Social Security Act. The CCCW made no lasting contribution to federal social policy in Canada, except in a negative sense. The agency came to monopolize many welfare efforts under an archaic mixture of public and private authority; it sabotaged more progressive provincial efforts concerning mothers' pensions, unemployment compensation, and other benefit programs; and, under the banner of professionalization and "scientific" philanthropy, it preserved the hegemony of a casework model of welfare long after it had outlived its usefulness.

In attempting to account for these differences, we begin with a small but salient literature that compares social policy outcomes in the United States and Canada. In a number of publications beginning over twenty years ago, Seymour Martin Lipset argued that major policy differences between the two countries are due in part to constitutional differences—specifically, Canada's parliamentary system may allow greater voice to representatives of the left—but mainly to differing value patterns around which the two societies are integrated.[38] Using Talcott Parsons's pattern-variable scheme as a template, Lipset argued that Canada veered closer to Britain than to the United States in its tendency toward elitism, recognition of ascribed status, and respect for law. These value differences, in turn, are accounted for by factors related to the founding and early histories of the two countries.[39] The United States, as a self-consciously revolutionary nation that expanded on an open frontier, emphasized individual initiative, encouraged religious pluralism, and rejected European-style statist policies in the conduct of its internal affairs. Canada, by contrast, absorbed American Tory elements, retained close ties with Britain, encouraged conformity to the established Anglican and French Catholic churches, and used federal authority to police the western frontier. Lipset's analysis is of limited value for our purposes because he does not address the issue of social policy directly. Yet we may tentatively infer that, based on these historically rooted value differences alone, Canada should have been more inclined toward centralized welfare programs of all kinds than the United Sates. While the United States, at least until World War I, saw itself as the more liberal of the two countries,[40] American liberalism was of a populist variety that was hostile both to centralized administration and to benefit programs that highlighted social class divisions. This prediction simply does not fit the case of child welfare policy.

A more recent analysis by Kudrle and Marmor attends more specifically to the issue of comparative social policies in North America. Their paper extends Lipset's concern with ideology and electoral representation, and examines also the differing patterns of federalism in the United States and Canada, to account for the development of four specific social policies: old age pensions, unemployment insurance, income maintenance programs, and health care. Based on arguments about ideology, electoral systems, and federalism, Kudrle and Marmor offer a series of empirical hypotheses: Canadian programs, they suggest, are likely to be enacted earlier, to be more advanced in form at any given time, to develop more steadily, and to be funded in a more egalitarian manner than their U.S. counterparts; policy innovations in the United States, moreover, are likely to appear only in response to social or economic "crisis."[41]

Kudrle and Marmor's analysis generally confirms these hypotheses, especially with regard to family assistance, the program that comes closest to our concern with child welfare. What is more telling, however, is their account of *why* Canada has overall been more progressive in the adoption of welfare initiatives. They argue that, of the three factors they considered, ideology—in the form of "general public as well as elite opinion"—was by far the most important. The next most important factor was federalism: the extraordinary autonomy of the Canadian provinces delayed enactment of some programs, but a highly institutionalized mechanism of "federal-provincial bargaining" smoothed the way for steady program development. Party and electoral differences seemed least significant. Kudrle and Marmor argue that the greater influence of left parties in Canada is due to the greater currency of socialist ideology among voters, not to the peculiarities of the parliamentary system.[42] These conclusions lead us back, with a fair degree of accuracy, to Lipset's basic argument: Canadian policies tend to be more statist than those in the United States because of historically rooted ideological differences. Given Kudrle and Marmor's broad and detailed survey of policy domains, American precocity in creating a federal children's bureau is an anomaly—not only in terms of policy differences between the two countries, but also in terms of the general course of policy differences between the two countries, but also in terms of the general course of policy development in the United States.

The problem in this section is to identify those factors that led child welfare to deviate from the pattern shown by a broader range of social programs. My strategy will be not to ignore arguments offered by Lipset and Kudrle and Marmor, but to specify them further by exploring in more detail the ways in which ideological and political resources were brought into play in this particular policy arena. The following discussion focuses on three overlapping and convergent sets of variables: first, historical residues that influenced prevailing ideologies and institutional responses to dependent children at the end of the nineteenth century; second, the role of social movements and professional entrepreneurs in generating pressures for change; and third, political and constitutional differences that constrained state responses.

Colonial Inheritances and Social Policy

A number of writers have followed Lipset's lead in emphasizing differing colonial histories—in particular, Canada's self-conscious identity as a "counterrevolutionary" state, its intimate and amicable ties to Britain, and its relatively late date of independence—in accounting for certain fundamental, stable differences in policy. To Dennis Guest, for example, local "colonial inheritances" were a major source of divergent social policies in the late nineteenth and early twentieth centuries both between and within the two nations. Following Louis Hartz's "fragmentation" thesis, Guest argues that while the United States took its welfare ideology from early bourgeois Britain, Canadian welfare ideology was inherited from two earlier sources, colonial British Toryism and prerevolutionary French feudalism. Despite their differences, both sources of Canadian thought emphasized hierarchy and paternalism, rather than the gospel of laissez-faire individualism that tended to prevail in the United States.[43]

This fact alone suggests that Canada would have moved more smoothly to a statist solution to the problem of dependency. In fact, as Guest argues, the main impact of Canada's relatively late date of confederation (in 1867) was the development of strikingly divergent policies among the provinces. While all Canadian provinces left great latitude to private charity, the mix of public and private authority varied in an east-west pattern that reflected the relative salience of the colonial experience. Thus, for example, the Maritimes adopted an Elizabethan poor law model that gave local government responsibility for the dependent poor, and ultimately encouraged the proliferation of almshouses. As was the case among the older states in the northeastern United States, the availability of almshouses inhibited the development of more centralized programs of outdoor relief. Ontario rejected the poor law model, and the absence of local government responsibility led to the growth of a dense network of private relief agencies. Late in the nineteenth century, Ontario borrowed some of the most advanced proposals for child welfare from American reformers, moving quickly to replace institutions with foster-care programs and adopting strong programs of government funding and regulation. Thus, ironically, Ontario combined private and public administration into one of the most highly centralized child welfare systems in either country. Quebec built upon its French heritage initially by letting all charitable responsibilities fall to the Catholic Church; as the English population increased, other private charities appeared as well. Quebec tended to resist the more liberal reformist trends that affected the rest of the country. The province was relatively slow to enact child-protection legislation, and clung to a purely private model of child welfare at least into the 1930s. Mothers' pensions were strongly opposed by Catholic rightists in Quebec, who viewed them as excessively secular and modernist. Finally, in the western provinces, provincial authority was unusually strong because of the small size and weakness of municipalities. The timing of mothers' pension legislation across the provinces reflects the relative salience of colonial archetypes: the western provinces moved first, with Manitoba enacting pensions in 1916, Saskatchewan in 1917, Alberta in 1919, and British Columbia in 1920; Ontario created a pension program in 1920, Nova Scotia in 1930, and Quebec in 1937; a pension law was passed in New Brunswick in 1930, but no funds were distributed until 1944.[44]

The United States showed a similar, but more moderate, pattern of east-west differences, and probably for reasons that had more to do with contemporary politics than colonial history. In the United States enthusiasm for state intervention was weakest in the eastern states, where politics tended to be seen as a corrupt enterprise, and strongest in newer states in the West and Midwest, where the state was seen more often as the "engine of progress." These were the states where mothers' pension laws were first enacted, but they spread throughout the nation much faster than in Canada.[45] The point here is that while institutionalized value patterns inherited from the colonial experience allowed some *provinces*—specifically, Ontario and, in different ways, those in the west—to move beyond the American states, the larger effect was to discourage concerted effort at the *national* level in Canada. There remains the question of how the United States was able to shake off its own commitment to laissez-faire individualism in the interest of a federal child welfare policy. To address this question, we turn to the role of activist social movements, and then to the structure of the state itself.

Social Movements and Professional Entrepreneurs

The second factor to discuss is a further specification of the kinds of ideological concerns raised by both Lipset and Kudrle and Marmor. Here I want to address ideology more precisely in terms of professional influence and social movement support. As I have already described, both the CCCW and the USCB grew from and relied upon networks of voluntary associations, particularly women's groups. At this point it is important to highlight some key differences in these networks. The first such difference is that, while the USCB was a direct outgrowth of the settlement movement, the CCCW is more closely tied to the charity organization movement.

Settlements originated in Britain, but flowered mainly around the major urban universities in the United States. The American wing of the movement consisted of a loosely linked set of organizations, typically located in poor urban neighborhoods, committed to research and the education and mobilization of the working class in support of large-scale political change.[46] Charity organization societies (COS), also founded in Britain, were seen as a means of coordinating the activities of private charity agencies. The first COS was established in the United States in the 1870s, and the COS model of welfare was institutionalized in the National Conference of Charities and Correction, founded in 1879. After the NCCC met in Toronto in 1898, Canadian charity officials, under the leadership of J. J. Kelso of Toronto, established their own branch of the conference. While Charlotte Whitton ultimately scorned Kelso's amateur approach to charity, her background with the Social Service Council places her much closer to the COS approach to poverty than that of the settlements, which had no Canadian equivalents.[47]

The charity organization and settlement movements espoused different models of poverty, showed different degrees of political sophistication, and were informed by very different forms of social knowledge: COS workers sought to uncover the causes of dependency through the compilation of detailed individual case histories, shunned direct relief in favor of family surveillance, and preferred to work through existing private charities rather than create publicly administered entitlement programs. The settlement movement, by contrast, was interested in the social and economic causes of poverty, overtly concerned with class relations, and committed to social and economic change. In short, the settlements were more radical, and less professional and "scientific" than the charity organization societies. In the United States, the two groups gradually moved from mutual hostility to detente, symbolized by Jane Addams's election to the presidency of the National Conference on Charities and Correction in 1909. One may speculate that this union contributed to the chronic ambivalence of the American social work profession about the relative merits of casework and structural reform. In any event, it appears that in Canada there was no effective counterweight to the COS approach to poverty.

Another source of ideological differences is the relative development of the social sciences in American and Canadian universities, and more generally, the relative opportunities for academics to participate in public policy debates. The settlements were established in the shadows of leading American universities, such as Chicago and Columbia, and Lathrop and the Children's Bureau drew sustenance from linkages to scholars engaged in ambitious programs of social and public policy research. Most of the American social science departments and professional associations were formed at the end of the nineteenth century, and many of this first generation of social scientists were "aggressive academic entrepreneurs" who "assumed they would advise and staff new government agencies with disinterested expertise."[48] Canadian universities tended to cling to a generalist-humanist model of scholarship, and were much slower to institutionalize the social sciences. In the 1890s, history was the major representative of the social sciences; political science and economics were not officially distinguished, psychology was taught in philosophy departments, and "anthropology, geography, and sociology had not made an appearance."[49] The situation had changed little by 1920. Only in the late 1920s did any self-conscious social scientists with specialized disciplinary orientations begin to emerge; even then, funding for large-scale research came from American sources such as the Social Science Research Council and the Rockefeller Foundation. As late as 1941, there were only 146 social scientists in Canada, out of a population of over 2,600 professors. Disciplinary associations were late in coming and tended to be dominated as much by amateurs and civil servants as by academics: the Canadian Historical Association was formed in 1923, the Canadian Political Science Association in 1929, and the Canadian Psychological Association in 1940.[50]

National differences also influenced the rate at which social work programs were founded and incorporated into the academic context. The first training program was founded in 1898 by the New York COS, and similar free-standing schools soon opened in other major cities. The trend, however, was toward affiliation with major universities, including Harvard (1904), Chicago (1920), and Columbia (around 1920). The first Canadian social work program was set up at the University of Toronto in 1914, with an American as director. McGill established a program in 1918; Manitoba began offering courses in 1920, and Montreal in 1921. At the beginning of the Depression, Canada still had only two schools of social work, and no well-organized corps of social workers.[51]

Canadian academics also faced a different set of expectations from the wider society, one that combined the English model of the amateur scholar with a sort of frontier anti-intellectualism common to the United States. The state expected little from the university: from the 1890s to the Depression there was no local or provincial funding for research, and the Dominion government funded only research in agriculture and natural resource management.[52] Perhaps more important, academic positions in Canada were precarious and poorly paid, and both university and public officials discouraged mixing politics and scholarship. The "ivory tower" self-image adopted by Canadian academics was, in a sense, protective coloration. Unlike the United States, the idea of academic freedom meant, primarily, not allowing politicians to influence university appointments, a practice that was common until reforms were enacted in 1906; it did not include any assurance of professors' rights as citizens. Academic tenure offered almost no protection to professors taking controversial positions until after World War II; leftist influences were particularly suspect before the Depression. As Michiel Horn has written,

> Left wing parties were proletarian and generally weak; they were unlikely to attract professorial support. In French Canadian universities, still dominated by the Roman Catholic Church, socialism was all too easily equated with atheism; in English Canadian institutions it was simply bad form. Socialists were not respectable, while Communists were quite beyond the pale of employment.[53]

Political and Constitutional Differences

The third factor to be discussed here is differences in the national political structures of the United States and Canada, especially those having to do with constitutional limitations on social policy and the role of parties. It is generally known that in the United States, the unclear division of responsibilities between state and federal governments in the Constitution has chronically inhibited the enactment and implementation of universalistic social policies. This tends to be more true of welfare programs for the disadvantaged and unemployed than of "entitlement" programs, such as

Social Security old-age benefits, that are aimed at the middle class. Thus from Sheppard-Towner to the present AFDC program, national welfare initiatives have been enacted in the form of grant-in-aid programs that are carefully deferential to state and local authority. In the Canadian case, however, constitutional limitations are even sharper. The British North America (BNA) Act gave the Dominion government broad and explicit powers over defense, trade, and economic development, but reserved health and welfare responsibilities to the provinces and municipalities. Thus, the national state aggressively sponsored programs of railroad building and industrial development, but—especially as the BNA Act was interpreted by a conservative judiciary—was for some time totally inactive in the area of child welfare. Indeed it appears that constitutional limitations contributed directly to the creation of the CCCW as a mixed public-private venture: Hareven writes that the Children's Division of the Dominion Department of Health would have played a role like that of the U.S. Children's Bureau but for the restrictive provisions of the BNA Act.[54]

Another aspect of political structure that deserves attention is the role of political parties, and, in particular, the distribution of patronage in the two countries. In the United States, party patronage was for some time a major source of redistributive benefits. Patronage flowed along party lines among all three levels of government, and while patterns of distribution were complex, it is fair to say that the two major national parties focused their efforts on distinct constituent groups. By gaining control over the Civil War pension program, for example, the Republicans sought disproportionately to mobilize native white citizens, while the Democrats had a stronger organization in the urban immigrant communities. Patronage was a target of self-styled progressive reformers, especially those concerned with the "defective, dependent, and delinquent classes" of society. Their goal was to professionalize and expand the administrative functions of the state. But the strength of the patronage system inhibited the enactment of more centralized, state-administered programs both by creating networks of vested interests outside the government, and by raising public skepticism about the efficiency and value of state action. In terms that are relevant to this study, my own research has shown that the salience of patronage influenced patterns of state policy directed at delinquent and dependent children in the United States: where interparty competition was strong, public institutions were weak and private agencies grew rapidly; where competition was low, public institutions flourished.[55]

Patronage was also an important element of the Canadian political system, but it was organized in a different fashion and played a different role than in the United States. Drawing on Gordon Stewart's account of patronage in Canada at the turn of the century, I would highlight three differences between the Canadian and U.S. systems. First, patronage appointments to public service positions were seen as a respectable route to social mobility for the professional middle classes in Canada. This view of patronage may in part be a residue of inherited Tory and feudal French political cultures; in part also it reflects the high prestige accorded the professional bourgeoisie in Canadian social life. As a result, patronage was a routine and respectable means of staffing positions at all levels of government. A second difference is that, while patronage appointments were nominally ratified by national party elites, crucial selection and screening decisions were made at the local level; indeed the major function of local party committees was to serve as an employment agency for party loyalists. In turn, the endurance of the system strengthened the localistic and parochial tendencies of Canadian politics. Third, the strength of the system varied little across the provinces; in particular, Stewart argues, French and English Canadian politics were more alike in this regard than is conventionally assumed. Given the lack of ethnic parties, potentially divisive national issues were fought out within the federal parties through a process of elite accommodation.[56]

Thus a key difference in U.S. and Canadian politics was the relative ascendancy of the professional bourgeoisie, and its place in the patronage system. In both countries, aspiring middle-class professionals were the carriers of reform ideals. In the United States, reform was a vehicle of status politics: professional entrepreneurs tended to promote statist, bureaucratic policies because they were excluded from the patronage system. They were only intermittently successful, but the Children's Bureau and various other state-level reforms must be counted among their achievements. In Canada, on the other hand, the professional bourgeoisie was the major beneficiary of patronage; as yet they had no competition either from an established industrial elite or an organized working class. Since patronage-based parties did not highlight, but rather absorbed, differences of class and ethnic status, reforms were worked out in a gentlemanly fashion. As a result, when agencies like the CCCW did appear, it was likely that they would be politically weak and deferential to local priorities.

The last political factor to be addressed here is that of the sequencing or timing of reform initiatives in relation to other political events. I have already mentioned the importance of relative dates of colonization and state formation: while the United States absorbed the liberal view of poverty and welfare that prevailed in eighteenth-century Britain, Canadian provinces inherited a much older and more paternalistic set of attitudes, and there was no national state capable of generating alternatives until 1867. I also mentioned that one of the important forces for change in the United States was female suffrage: legislators' apprehension of women's voting strength enhanced the power and prestige of organized women's groups, and contributed directly to the creation of the Children's Bureau;

when that apprehension faded, moreover, legislative enthusiasm for the bureau declined accordingly. Canada moved more slowly than the United States in expanding the franchise. Federal manhood suffrage was not enacted in Canada until 1889 (male suffrage was almost universal in the United States by 1845), and national female suffrage came only in the aftermath of World War I. Manitoba granted women the vote in provincial elections during the war, and by 1919 all provinces except Prince Edward Island and Quebec had followed suit; national suffrage was granted to women in 1920. The war encouraged female suffrage because of the increased civil status that accrued to women mobilized for wartime work, and suffrage, in turn, led to an improved climate for redistributive policies —in British Columbia, for example, a mothers' pension law was enacted in sessions immediately preceding the first election in which women were voters.[57] While I have found no direct evidence on this matter, it seems quite likely that the extension of national suffrage also encouraged the creation of the CCCW in the same year.

The war also had direct effects on policy, particularly by adding impetus to the drive for mothers' pensions: during the war the activities of radical movements increased, creating a perceived need for ameliorative measures; a program of wartime dependents' allowances provided a legitimate model of relief that could later be expanded; and more generally, the broad mobilization effort made it easier to see relief as a state obligation rather than as a matter of charity.[58] But in the end, the fact that it took the shock of World War I to catalyze even a limited interest in social policy reforms only highlights the immobility of the Canadian federal government up to that time, and its weakness for some time thereafter. That weakness was exemplified in its approach to the problem of child welfare, and more specifically in the retrograde influence of the CCCW.

Discussion: Social Knowledge and Child Welfare Policy

To this point, this chapter has made two arguments. First, focusing on the specific cases of the U.S. Children's Bureau and the Canadian Council on Child Welfare, the United States was relatively precocious in the federalization of child welfare policy. The discussion showed that the federal commitment in the United States was both precarious and incomplete; but given the conventional wisdom on this topic, the wonder is not that the USCB and the Sheppard-Towner Act were only partially successful, but that they existed at all. In the second, causal, argument, I attempted to account for these observed differences by extending and specifying the arguments offered by Lipset and Kudrle and Marmor. The analysis focused on three factors: differing ideological and institutional patterns that were informed by the colonial experience; the role of interest groups—including social movements, professional associations, and academic institutions—from which the two agencies drew their support; and differences in constitutional structure and party politics.

This argument is complex and overdetermined, perhaps too much so for this simple empirical case. But this approach has been useful in highlighting three issues. The first and most obvious of these is that the history of Canadian child welfare is not just a result of Charlotte Whitton's personal zeal, but of a unique institutional history that allowed someone like Whitton to achieve prominence. The second point concerns the issue of ideology, as invoked by earlier literature to account for U.S.-Canadian differences. It is simply not very helpful to invoke ideological differences to account for political variation among nation-states without describing the kinds of interest groups that act as ideological carriers and the linkages that tie them to each other and to the state. The Children's Bureau was not an outcome of some generalized societal concern for the welfare of children, but of a very specialized concern that was informed by the perspectives of the settlement movement; in the Canadian case, the major ideological agent was the charity organization societies. Third, the legacies of the USCB and the CCCW included not just substantive policies, but different and in some ways conflicting models of knowledge about social problems that became institutionalized in their respective domains.

By highlighting the political and ideological differences inherent in the case and survey methods, I have perhaps underemphasized an important transition that is exemplified in the career of the Children's Bureau. While the USCB did conduct a number of local surveys and, in the settlement tradition, used those surveys to publicize health and welfare issues, arguably its most lasting achievement was the popularization of uniform birth registration policies among the states. Birth registration, once enacted, produced a universe of *official* statistics that were generally regarded as definitive, and which could be used for both research and policymaking. As we noted in the case of the Sheppard-Towner Act, moreover, official statistics illuminate structural conditions that are correlated with poverty rather than individual moral states. Thus, I would argue, centralized (or uniform) data production tends to be linked to more centralized social policy.

This shift from social surveys to official statistics was not new or unique to twentieth-century America, however. As Lecuyer and Oberschall have noted, Booth's research in 1880s London was itself a "revival" of a tradition of systematically studying the poor that flourished in Britain between 1780 and 1840.[59] In both instances, the felt need for statistics was the product of a widespread perception of crisis in the social and economic orders, and reformist research eventually subsided as policy reforms were enacted and the state assumed responsibility for data collection. The recurrence of this pattern leads to a last comment on the issue of state capacities for creating "official" knowledge.

Paul Starr observes that the production of official "statistical systems" is tied to more general processes of state-building, but in complex ways. Thus, for example, authoritarian states might feel compelled to develop statistical capacities in order to enhance their control over the population, but they also tend to create incentives for secrecy and corruption that undermine the legitimacy of official data-collection efforts. Overall, he suggests, capitalist democracies are likely to be most amenable, because of the generally high value placed on methodical accounting, and the usefulness of statistics in allocating representation and factoring in interest groups.[60] I would complicate this further by suggesting that, even among democracies, statistical competency in specific substantive areas is likely to vary depending on the salience of corresponding social problems. Thus, while the United States pioneered the modern census, it appears that the Anglo-American democracies—Britain, the United States, and Canada—were slow relative to Continental states in developing both official statistics on poverty *and* welfare policies.[61]

The present study suggests that, in such "weak" states, the role of nonstate interest groups in framing and publicizing issues may be an important intervening variable. In the area of child welfare, the United States replicated a more general British model, in which reformist groups and private entrepreneurs inaugurated a drive for social research to highlight social problems. To the degree that these problems were officially recognized, the production of knowledge was institutionally bifurcated: the state developed the capacity for ongoing data collection in the service of policymaking and administration, and new research efforts were absorbed into professional academic settings. In Canada, by contrast, this model was skewed. In part because of the late emergence of the academic social sciences and the lack of an amateur social research tradition, the nineteenth-century moralism of the charity organization movement, preserved by the CCCW and perpetuated by the casework method, remained the reigning discourse on child welfare policy until the Second World War.

Notes to Chapter 6

1. John Boli-Bennet and John W. Meyer, "The Ideology of Childhood and the State: Rules Distinguishing Children in National Constitutions, 1870–1970." *American Sociological Review* 43 (1978): pp. 797–812; John Boli, Francisco O. Ramirez, and John W. Meyer, "Explaining the Origins and Expansion of Mass Education." *Comparative Education Review* 29 (1985): pp. 145–70.

2. Arnold J. Heidenheimer, "Education and Social Security Entitlements in Europe and America." In Peter Flora and Arnold J. Heidenheimer, eds., *The Development of Welfare States in Europe and America.* New Brunswick, NJ: Transaction Books, 1981, pp. 269–304; John R. Sutton, *Stubborn Children: Controlling Delinquency in the United States, 1640–1982.* Berkeley: University of California Press, 1988.

3. For a fuller discussion of this point, see John R. Sutton, "Therapeutic Justice: The Legal Construction of Deviant Persons." In Matilda White Riley, ed., *Social Structures and Human Lives.* Newbury Park, CA: Sage, 1988, pp. 63–82.

4. This definition is taken from Walter I. Trattner, *From Poor Law to Welfare State: A History of Social Welfare in America.* New York: Free Press, 1979, p. 193.

5. James Leiby, *Social Welfare and Social Work in the United States.* New York: Columbia University Press, 1978, pp. 113–14; Roy Lubove, *The Professional Altruist: The Emergence of Social Work as a Career.* Cambridge, MA: Harvard University Press, 1965, p. 158; Marlene Shore, *The Science of Social Redemption: McGill, the Chicago School, and the Origins of Social Research in Canada.* Toronto: University of Toronto Press, 1987, pp. 42–44.

6. Charles Booth, *Life and Labour of the People in London.* London: Macmillan and Co. Ltd., 1892; B. Seebohm Rowntree, *Poverty: A Study in Town Life.* London: Macmillan and Co. Ltd., 1901.

7. Jean M. Converse, *Survey Research in the United States.* Berkeley: University of California Press, 1987, p. 13.

8. Shore, *The Science of Social Redemption,* p. 48.

9. Converse, *Survey Research in the United States,* pp. 22–25.

10. Clarke A. Chambers, *Paul U. Kellogg and the Survey.* Minneapolis: University of Minnesota Press,, 1971, pp. 23–24, 33–34.

11. Ibid., pp. 36–37.

12. Ibid., pp. 39–40 and chap. 4; Converse, *Survey Research in the United States,* pp. 22–24; Trattner, *From Poor Law to Welfare State,* pp. 196–98.

13. Converse, *Survey Research in the United States,* p. 37.

14. Allen F. Davis, *Spearheads for Reform: The Social Settlements and the Progressive Movement, 1890–1914.* New York: Oxford University Press, 1967, p. 132.

15. Conference on the Care of Dependent Children, *Proceedings.* Washington, DC: U.S. Government Printing Office, 1909; Rochelle Beck, "The White House Conferences on Children: An Historical Perspective." *Harvard Education Review* 43 (1973): p. 665; Davis, *Spearheads for Reform,* pp. 130–33; Jacqueline K. Parker and Edward M. Carpenter, "Julia Lathrop and the Children's Bureau: The Emergence of an Institution." *Social Service Review* 55 (1981): p. 60.

16. Trattner, *From Poor Law to Welfare State,* p. 181; Michael Katz, *In the Shadow of the Poorhouse: A History of Social Welfare in America.* New York: Basic Books, 1986, p. 122.

17. Parker and Carpenter, "Julia Lathrop and the Children's Bureau," p. 62.

18. Trattner, *From Poor Law to Welfare State,* p. 179–80; Parker and Carpenter, "Julia Lathrop and the Children's Bureau," pp. 63–64.

19. Parker and Carpenter, "Julia Lathrop and the Children's Bureau," p. 65.

20. James Alner Tobey, *The Children's Bureau: Its History, Activities, and Organization.* Baltimore: John Hopkins University Press, 1925, pp. 3–19; Parker and Carpenter, "Julia Lathrop and the Children's Bureau," pp. 65–73.

21. Trattner, *From Poor Law to Welfare State,* pp. 184–88; Katz, *In the Shadow of the Poorhouse,* pp. 127–28; Tobey, *The Children's Bureau,* pp. 26–27.

22. Tobey, *The Children's Bureau,* pp. 5–7; Jane Perry Clark, *The Rise of a New Federalism: Federal-State Cooperation in the United States.* New York: Russell and Russell, 1965, pp. 95–97; Katz, *In the Shadow of the Poorhouse,* p. 134.

23. Joseph B. Chepaitis, "Federal Social Welfare Progressivism in the 1920s." *Social Service Review* 46 (1972): pp. 215–21; Katz, *In the Shadow of the Poorhouse,* p. 143; Trattner, *From Poor Law to Welfare State,* pp. 182–83.

24. Sheila Katz Rothman, *Woman's Proper Place: A History of Changing Ideals and Practices, 1870–1930.* New York: Basic Books, 1978, p. 137.

25. Chepaitis, "Federal Social Welfare Progressivism in the 1920s," pp. 222–23; Rothman, *Woman's Proper Place,* pp. 148–53; Katz, *In the Shadow of the Poorhouse,* p. 144.

26. Clark, *Rise of a New Federalism,* pp. 145–46, 207; Rothman, *Woman's Proper Place,* p. 144.

27. Veronica Strong-Boag, "The Roots of Modern Canadian Feminism: The National Council of Women, 1893–1929." *Canada* 3(2) (1975): pp. 22–33.

28. Tamara Hareven, "An Ambiguous Alliance: Some Aspects of American Influence on Canadian Social Welfare." *Histoire Sociale/Social History* 3 (1969): pp. 90–91; Dennis Guest, *The Emergence of Social Security in Canada.* Vancouver: University of British Columbia Press, 1985, p. 33.

29. Hareven, "Ambiguous Alliance," p. 92.

30. Patricia T. Rooke and R. L. Schnell, "'Making the Way More Comfortable': Charlotte Whitton's Child Welfare Career, 1920–48." *Journal of Canadian Studies* 17(4) (1982–83): 33–34.

31. Patricia T. Rooke and R. L. Schnell, "Child Welfare in English Canada, 1920–1948." *Social Service Review* 55 (1981): pp. 491–95.

32. Shore, *The Science of Social Redemption,* p. 171.

33. Hareven, "Ambiguous Alliance," p. 94.

34. James Struthers, "'Lord Give Us Men': Women and Social Work in English Canada, 1918 to 1953." *Historical Papers/Communications Historiques* (1983): pp. 96–112; Hareven, "Ambiguous Alliance," p. 92.

35. Rooke and Schnell, "Child Welfare in English Canada," p. 491.

36. Ibid., p. 492.

37. Ibid., pp. 487–92; Veronica Strong-Boag, "'Wages for Housework': Mothers' Allowances and the Beginnings of Social Security in Canada." *Journal of Canadian Studies* 14 (1979): pp. 27–28; Guest, *Emergence of Social Security in*

Canada, pp. 56–59; James Struthers, "A Profession in Crisis: Charlotte Whitton and Professional Social Work in the 1930s." *Canadian Historical Review* 62(2) (1979): pp. 174–85.

38. Seymour Martin Lipset, *Agrarian Socialism.* Garden City, NY: Doubleday, 1968, pp. xiii–xvii. In a later analysis of party politics, Lipset backed off of even his weak acknowledgment of the importance of parliamentary differences: see "Radicalism in North America: A Comparative View of the Party Systems in Canada and the United States." *Transactions of the Royal Society of Canada* 4 (v 14).

39. Seymour Martin Lipset, "The Value Patterns of Democracy: A Case Study in Comparative Analysis." *American Sociological Review* 28 (1963): pp. 515–31; idem, "Revolution and Counter-Revolution: The United States and Canada." In Thomas R. Ford, ed., *The Revolutionary Theme in Contemporary America.* Lexington: University Press of Kentucky, 1965, pp. 21–64.

40. Lipset, "Revolution and Counter-Revolution," pp. 53–57.

41. Robert T. Kudrle and Theodore R. Marmor, "The Development of Welfare States in North America." In Peter Flora and Arnold J. Heidenheimer, eds., *The Development of Welfare States in Europe and America.* New Brunswick, NJ: Transaction Books, 1981, pp. 81–121.

42. Ibid., pp. 111, 112.

43. Guest, *Emergence of Social Security in Canada,* chap. 2; Louis Hartz, *The Founding of New Societies.* New York: Harcourt, Brace, 1964.

44. Margaret Strong, *Public Welfare Administration in Canada.* Chicago: University of Chicago Press, 1930, pp. 200, 212–21, 227; Hareven, "Ambiguous Alliance," pp. 87–88; Strong-Boag, "'Wages for Housework,'" pp. 24–25; Guest, *Emergence of Social Security in Canada,* pp. 62–63.

45. Katz, *In The Shadow of the Poorhouse,* pp. 123, 128.

46. For general histories of the settlement movement, see Davis, *Spearheads for Reform,* and Trattner, *From Poor Law to Welfare State,* chap. 8.

47. On Kelso, see Hareven, "Ambiguous Alliance," p. 84. There is also evidence of U.S. influence on the founding of a charity organization society in Montreal: see Shore, *Science of Social Redemption,* p. 43. I have found evidence of only one settlement house established in Canada, and Shore suggests that the model here was different from both English and American precedents. The Women's University Settlement, set up by alumnae of McGill University, was intended as a setting where students could "learn the techniques of philanthropic organization, not as an arrangement whereby they threw in their lot with the dwellers of an underprivileged neighborhood" (p. 48).

48. Katz, *In the Shadow of the Poorhouse,* p. 123. See also Mary O. Furner, *Advocacy and Objectivity.* Lexington: University Press of Kentucky, 1975, and Thomas L. Haskell, *The Emergence of Professional Social Science.* Urbana: University of Illinois Press, 1977.

49. Robin S. Harris, *A History of Higher Education in Canada, 1663-1960.* Toronto: University of Toronto Press, 1976, p. 141.

50. On funding, see Shore, *Science of Social Redemption,* chaps. 5–6; on professional associations, see Harris, *History of Higher Education in Canada,* p. 187; Barry Ferguson and Doug Owram, "Social Scientists and Public Policy from the 1920s through World War II." *Journal of Canadian Studies* 15(4) (1980–81): pp. 5–6.

51. Katz, *In the Shadow of the Poorhouse,* p. 164; Trattner, *From Poor Law to Welfare State,* pp. 196–97; Harris, *History of Higher Education in Canada,* pp. 294–95; Struthers, "Profession in Crisis," p. 170.

52. Harris, *History of Higher Education in Canada,* pp. 194–96.

53. Michiel Horn, "Professors in the Public Eye: Canadian Universities, Academic Freedom, and the League for Social Reconstruction." *History of Education Quarterly* 20 (1980): p. 429.

54. Guest, *Emergence of Social Security in Canada,* pp. 5–8; Hareven, "Ambiguous Alliance," p. 91.

55. Theda Skocpol, *Protecting Soldiers and Mothers: The Political Origins of Social Policy in the United States.* Cambridge, MA: Belknap Press of Harvard University Press, 1992; Martin J. Schiesl, *The Politics of Efficiency.* Berkeley: University of California Press, 1977; Stephen Skowronek, *Building a New American State.* Cambridge: Cambridge University Press, 1982; John R. Sutton, "Bureaucrats and Entrepreneurs: Institutional Responses to Deviant Children in the United States, 1880–1920s." *American Journal of Sociology* 95 (1990): pp. 1367–1400.

56. Gordon T. Stewart, "Political Patronage Under MacDonald and Laurier 1878–1911." *American Review of Canadian Studies* 10 (1980): pp. 3–26.

57. Guest, *Emergence of Social Security in Canada,* p. 54.

58. Ibid., pp. 50–51.

59. Bernard Lecuyer and Anthony Oberschall, "The Early History of Social Research." *International Encyclopedia of the Social Sciences,* vol. 15. New York: Macmillan, 1968, pp. 41–44.

60. Paul Starr, "The Sociology of Official Statistics." In William Alonso and Paul Starr, eds., *The Politics of Numbers.* New York: Russell Sage Foundation, 1987, pp. 7–57.

61. See Lecuyer and Oberschall, "Early History of Social Research," for an overview of the relationship between statistical capacities and state-building in Britain, France, and Germany.

Part III

STATE MANAGERS AND THE USES OF SOCIAL KNOWLEDGE

7

International Modeling, States, and Statistics

SCANDINAVIAN SOCIAL SECURITY SOLUTIONS IN THE 1890s

STEIN KUHNLE

THE BEGINNING of the modern Scandinavian welfare states[1] can most meaningfully be traced to the last decades of the last century. As elsewhere in Europe, this development was at a general level associated with growing industrialization, but also with the political innovation of large-scale social insurance schemes introduced in the German *Reich* during the 1880s. Quite remarkably, the first major social insurance laws were passed at about the same time, in the course of three years (1891–94), in Denmark, Norway,[2] and Sweden. But just as noteworthy, the very first social insurance laws concerned different purposes across the three countries, and different institutional solutions were enacted.

Before the turn of the century, the following social insurance or income maintenance laws were passed in Denmark, Norway, and Sweden:

Denmark

1891: Old age pension law. Means-tested pensions for persons sixty years or older, financed by the state and communes through general taxation.

1892: Sickness insurance law. Public subsidies to recognized voluntary insurance funds.

1898: Employers' liability act. In order to ensure workers compensation in case of industrial accidents.

Norway

1894: Accident insurance law. Industrial workers compulsorily insured by employers, who were also to finance the scheme.

Sweden

1891: Sickness insurance law. Public subsidies to recognized insurance funds.

During the subsequent two decades, an employers' liability act (1901) and an old age and invalidity pension law (1913) were passed in Sweden; an unemployment insurance law (1906) with subsidies to voluntary insurance funds (trade union based) and a compulsory sickness insurance law for low-income earners and their families (1909) were enacted in Norway; and an unemployment insurance law (1907) with subsidies to voluntary funds was passed in Denmark.

Why is it that the first Scandinavian social insurance laws were introduced at about the same time? And why did Denmark introduce an *old age pension* law, Sweden a *sickness* insurance law, and Norway an *accident* insurance law in the first round of major social security legislation? Put differently, how do we account for the similarity in timing of the first laws and for the variations in priorities? I shall try to develop answers to these questions by reference to various explanatory arguments such as levels and processes of industrialization and democratization, the impact or role of international diffusion,[3] and by looking into the role of emerging state institutions and increasing state administrative capacity, such as the establishment of central statistical offices and the emergence and dissemination of new ideas about the role of the state.[4]

The Factors of Industrialization and Democratization

In their study of the historical development of welfare states in twelve West European countries, Flora and Alber (1981)[5] came to the conclusion that the variation in levels of socioeconomic development at the time of the establishment of social insurance systems is too great to allow any generalization about thresholds, except the obvious ones that predominantly agricultural societies probably will not adopt social insurance systems, and that highly industrialized and urbanized societies will have such schemes. The days of the logic-of-industrialism thesis are numbered also in several other historical studies.[6]

Among the Scandinavian countries, Denmark was definitely the most urbanized and industrialized. Norway clearly lagged behind Denmark, but was more developed than Sweden in terms of levels of urbanization and industrialization.[7] In a Scandinavian context, the simple logic-of-industrialism argument appears to hold at a general level: Denmark was a likely candidate to head the development of the modern welfare state, and it did. But what is the logic of being the *most* industrialized country and introducing an old age pension law (Denmark) and being *less* industrialized and introducing accident insurance for industrial workers (Norway)? The industrialism argument does not differentiate sufficiently the Scandinavian countries as to the timing of the first social insurance laws, nor does it reasonably account for the actual type of the first laws.

In general, various indicators of democratic development do not perform much better for the explanation of the early social legislation. Constitutional-dualistic monarchies tended to introduce social insurance schemes earlier (in chronological and developmental time) than parliamentary democracies, but among the subset of parliamentary democracies the extension of suffrage between 1880 and 1920 increased the propensity to introduce insurance schemes.[8] For the period we are interested in here, the timing of the first social insurance legislation in the 1890s, only Norway among the Scandinavian countries qualified as a parliamentary democracy. Denmark had the widest enfranchisement, the highest levels of electoral participation, and a somewhat more developed party system than both Norway and Sweden.[9] The democratization factor is multidimensional, and it is not obvious which dimension should logically be of greatest importance for social policy development. The overall variations in levels of democratization and the similarity in timing of the first laws reduce the explanatory power of the democratization argument. But the combined effect of socioeconomic development and a relatively politically mobilized electorate may to some extent account for the fact that Denmark on the whole was more active in the field of social policy legislation throughout the 1890s than her Scandinavian neighbors. Since this Scandinavian pattern does not hold in a broader European context, one should of course raise a cautious warning against the simple structural explanations of industrialization and democratization. Such an analysis can only take us a certain distance on the way to an understanding of the when, how, and for what purposes social legislation came about. One step ahead would be to look more into processes of decision making[10] and the role of international diffusion of the political innovation of social insurance.

The Impact and Role of Diffusion

Most writers trace the initiation of the welfare state, or at least the beginning of the present stage of development, to Bismarck's large-scale social insurance schemes of the last quarter of the nineteenth century.[11] This is, as others have pointed out,[12] only partly true since "social policy" (poor relief, health measures, education) was a fact of political life in some countries long before this period, and even social insurance was not an innovation of the 1880s. Guilds had introduced the principles and functions of (social or mutual) insurance during medieval times, and so had several state governments earlier in the nineteenth century. In a number of countries, accident, sickness or old age pension insurance, or pension schemes for limited groups of workers had been introduced or tried out in some form or other.[13] Almost all earlier schemes can hardly be labeled "national" because of their limited occupational scope. Bismarck's legislation attracted attention primarily because the coverage was actually nationwide, combined with a broader scope in terms of both functions and population. Besides, Bismarck revealed rather explicitly his nation- and regime-building motives for introducing social legislation. His measures were intended to serve the fight against both the radicalized socialist movement and the Church (*Kulturkampf*). On June 15, 1883, when Bismarck and his government obtained Reichstag approval of their proposal to establish a compulsory sickness insurance scheme for all industrial workers, soon to be followed up with broadly based accident insurance (1884) and old age and invalidity insurance (1889), the scope and intensity of state effort in the field of "social security policy" or "income maintenance policy" was such that it came to represent an innovation in state activity.[14] Whether we choose to look upon Bismarck's legislation as one of successfully catalyzing an idea that was already embryonically developed in many quarters of Europe, or as a true innovation, there can be no doubt that contemporary observers (intellectuals, government officials, parliamentarians) considered it what we today probably would call an "agenda-building" event. For better or worse, the German legislative actions provided the international community of state leaders, legislators, administrators, employers, workers, and academics with a model.[15] To what extent the German model helped accelerate social legislation in other countries has been put into question—sometimes with answers—by some writers. Thus, the British historian Asa Briggs has most emphatically attributed later social legislation to the German initiative: "German social insurance stimulated foreign imitation. Denmark, for example, copied all three German pension schemes between 1891 and 1898."[16] But a Danish scholar strongly advocates a contrasting assessment of the same nation:

> It has occurred that the modern social policy has been credited to Bismarck's policies in German. . . .Maybe one or two socialist-stricken Danes have thought "So ein Ding müssen wir auch haben." But there is no sign that Bismarck's policies have had any significant influence on Danish social policy of 1891–1892. . . .None of Bismarck's ideas were at the time taken over by Denmark.[17]

One may wonder how two competent scholars can reach such divergent conclusions concerning the same phenomenon. The answer can be said to lie in the degree to which the authors move from a broad historical overview to historically specific conditions. But closer analysis will indicate that both positions are overstated.

Early Danish Legislative Efforts[18]

In January 1862, the Danish Ministry of Interior in a circular recommended that free associations be created incorporating all masters and journeymen in towns to ensure support in cases of sickness, old age, and other debilitations.[19] The government initiative was the result of the anticipated effects of the Trade Act (passed in 1857, in effect from 1862), through which guilds with compulsory membership were prohibited. To support this initiative, the government had set up an official commission in November 1861 to establish rules for these associations, and generally worked to generate interest in the associations. Standard rules were established in February 1863, demanding, among other things, that the associations deliver standard information on their activity to the Statistical Bureau, so that the Ministry could work out a summary statistical overview. The first of these statistical tables came out in 1864 (for the year 1862), and thus a regular new series of public statistics of great significance for future governmental and legislative activity was introduced. The government role at this early date consisted of taking the initiative—or giving an official blessing legitimizing efforts—in the formation of voluntary insurance funds: to inform and assist in the establishment of such organizations; and to begin the systematic collection of statistics in order to monitor the development.

At this stage, no financial support from the state to the benefit of the associations or individuals was provided. But the relatively slow growth of voluntary associations soon gave rise to the question of more active state involvement. A second public commission was established by the government in February 1866 to discuss ways of promoting associations for mutual benefit in cases of sickness, old age, and death. This effort led to a law in June 1870 which facilitated voluntary old age insurance in a life insurance and relief institution guaranteed by the state. Also, the creation in 1872 of a joint municipal old age relief fund, which was to receive public subsidies, could be seen as a response to the commission's effort. A number of private proposals for the establishment of an old age insurance scheme were outlined in the early 1870s, and the Danish parliament set up another commission to look into this issue in 1874. Its report was submitted in 1875 but led to nothing in concrete terms, although it helped keep the topic alive, influencing the political agenda. Soon afterwards, in September 1875, the government set up a commission to study "the worker conditions in Denmark," with a particular mandate to consider sickness and invalidity assistance, old age relief, survivors' relief, and funeral benefits to workers. In October 1878, the commission proposed that the state establish an old age relief fund for persons without means. A majority proposed voluntary insurance, while a minority wanted compulsory insurance. But again, no legislation resulted, and several private and parliamentary proposals suffered the same fate in the years 1879 to 1883. With regard to sickness insurance, the commission proposed not to disturb the existing system of voluntary funds. A proposal by Finance Minister Estrup (later to become prime minister) in October 1883 to create an institution for "inexpensive" old age relief based on voluntary insurance and state subsidies came to nothing, nor did his revised proposal of November 1884. Yet another official commission to look into social insurance was appointed in July 1885 after the passage of the first two social insurance laws in Germany, and after the appointment of a similar committee in Sweden (see below). The commission's proposal of December 1887 ordained state subsidies to already established sickness funds based on voluntary insurance. This work came to have an impact upon a similar proposal later submitted by the Swedish commission. Actual legislation followed first in Sweden (May 1891), and subsequently by Denmark (April 1892).

The Danish 1885 commission also drew up plans for accident insurance clearly inspired by the German precedent. But as in Sweden, the proposal submitted in 1888 failed in parliament. A new commission, established in 1895, came up with different proposals for accident insurance in 1895 and 1896, finally rejecting the principle of compulsion, which was thought to lead to increasing numbers of accidents (with reference to official statistics for Germany and Austria), and a modified proposal of employers' liability was made into law in January 1898.

The first initiatives for old age relief with a financial role for the state originated with the 1875 commission, and a great number of proposals were discussed in and outside of parliament every year in the 1880s. An even higher intensity of proposals occurred in 1890–91, and finally, a proposal by ten members of the Danish Folketing for "Old Age Pensions for Respectable People Outside the Poor Relief System" was legislated in April 1891. It was a noncontributory pension scheme intended to support people above sixty years of age on a (local) means-tested basis with the state and municipalities sharing the cost (out of tax revenues) on equal terms. The social statistical basis for the law proposal was provided by two academic national economists, Westergaard and Rubin, who obtained public and private financial support between 1884 and 1890. Their data-collection project was spurred by a debate of the 1884 Estrup proposal in the association for national economists.[20] The Danish law bore no resemblance to the German law of 1889: its basic principles of financing, organization, and benefit entitlements were totally different. But it may be regarded as the first step toward the establishment of (universal) social rights. Given the prolonged and continuous public process of debating and dealing with the pension issue in Danish politics, the timing of the law enactment can hardly be related to the German effort in this field, and definitely not the contents of the law. If a sudden instigation to legislation can be said to have come from anywhere outside Denmark at all, it must have been from Iceland, whose parliament quickly passed a law along similar principles to the Danish one in July 1890.[21]

Early Norwegian Legislative Efforts

The Norwegian government took the first active steps to consider the introduction of social insurance in August 1885. With direct references to German and Swedish initiatives, a "workers commission" was established to study possible schemes for accident, sickness, and old age insurance. It seems that the government administration was little prepared for the huge task,[22] the commission openly admitted after a few years that it had no—or there existed no—administrative capacity to collect the necessary statistical material to assess schemes for old age pensions, even though the lack of provision for the elderly seems to have been perceived as the most serious social problem of the day[23]: "In order to solve social policy tasks of the range considered, the availability of current and timely social statistics is, among other things, required."[24]

The commission did collect an enormous amount of new statistics on industrial employment, industrial accidents, voluntary sickness insurance and/or funeral funds,[25] and proposals for factory inspection legislation and accident and sickness insurance laws were presented in 1887 and February 1890, respectively.

The laws on factory inspection and accident insurance—which closely followed the principles laid down in the German law of 1884—were passed in 1892 and 1894, respectively, while work on the sickness insurance proposal was taken up and completed by other public commissions through a prolonged and laborious process in the 1890s and 1900s.

The statistical basis for this policymaking effort was laid by the 1885 commission, which engaged an employee from the recently established Central Bureau of Statistics to investigate the extent of voluntary sickness funds and membership in these funds—a data-collection effort that was begun more than twenty years earlier in Denmark. The resulting overviews indicated that voluntary insurance existed to a far lesser degree in Norway than in Sweden and especially Denmark, and thus an early argument for the consideration of compulsory insurance (in contrast to the principles proposed and later adopted in Swedish and Danish legislation) was laid, since a voluntary subsidized insurance would have little effect. In March 1893, when the government proposed a law on workers' sickness insurance (a proposal that was never formally considered by the parliament),[26] it explicitly referred to collected statistics to argue for the greater utility of compulsory insurance.

Proposals for an old age pension scheme had surfaced in parliament as early as 1844, and again in 1851 and 1869, and a number of ideas and proposals appeared in the 1880s, but none were ever seriously considered or followed up by the parliament or the government. One suspects lack of investigative capacity or fear of anticipated financial consequences of the implementation of any proposal to be the reason for state inactivity on this issue, rather than lack of interest in the alleviation of an apparently large problem. The enormous waves of cross-Atlantic emigration in the late 1860s and during the first half of the 1880s can probably serve as indirect indicators of limited state capacity to tackle (increasing) social problems in this period. As discussed above, an unsuccessful attempt was made through the creation of the 1885 commission to lift the pension issue to a legislative agenda. But a serious assessment of the possibility of an old age and invalidity scheme was first made by the parliamentary workers' commission set up in 1894. Prolonged disagreement between political factions and parties, especially on the question of a premium versus tax-based pension scheme, held up a legislative decision until 1923, but only in 1937 did a somewhat modified law take effect.

Early Swedish Legislative Efforts

In Sweden the so-called "worker question" was frequently discussed in parliament during a thirty-year period prior to the German social insurance program, but no actual law proposals were initiated, and no public investigatory commissions were established to deal with the subject. It was with reference to the continuous Danish investigations of the social insurance issue and the German legislation of 1883, that a proposal by the Liberal parliamentary representative Adolf Hedin in the Lower House in May 1884 led the allegedly socially concerned Swedish king to set up the first investigatory committee in October 1884. The committee was specifically asked to study the German program and to propose legislation. Actual proposals followed in July 1888 (accident insurance); May 1889 (old age pension scheme); and October 1889 (sickness insurance). Also, a proposal for a law protecting the workers against industrial risks was set forth and immediately passed (1889). Among the proposals for social insurance, only the one on sickness insurance—which was similar to a Danish proposal to subsidize voluntary sickness funds—passed the test of parliament in May 1891.

Both the accident and old age insurance proposals were modeled after the German principle of compulsion (the Swedish pension proposal went much further in terms of population coverage), but none were approved by the parliament. A new governmental commission was appointed in September 1891 to outline new proposals, and a prolonged legislative process resulted finally in the enactment of an employers' liability law in 1901, based principally on the English Workman's Compensation Act of 1897 and the Danish law from 1898, and an old age and invalidity pension law in 1913, on a proposal from another official committee established in 1907.

As in the cases of Denmark and Norway, we observe that it took several years from the first public investigatory efforts to the passage of old age pension legislation. The old age pension was most likely considered the one issue, of the various ones dealt with, that would cause the heaviest financial burden on the state, and thus required a more thorough and concientious assessment before being put to decision.[27]

The Reach of the Diffusion Perspective

The first legislative initiatives for social insurance in Norway and Sweden were definitely triggered by the German legislation of the early 1880s, while one might argue that the prolonged and continuous efforts in Denmark from the beginning of the 1860s got a push ahead thanks to the German activity, and consequently through the establishment and work of the 1885 commission. But of the actual Scandinavian laws passed in the first round of social insurance legislation (i.e., during the 1890s), only one among the five, the Norwegian accident insurance law of 1894, was in any significant way modeled on the pioneering German law.

Cross-national diffusion of ideas and legislative models can naturally only lead to initiatives and lawmaking in the receiving countries if there are actors sufficiently interested, and if there exists a capacity in the states concerned to respond to ideas crossing the borders from outside. How were the Scandinavian nations in this sense prepared to act upon this intrusion of German ideas "sweeping across Europe as a contagion"[28] about a socially active role for the state? Decision-making elites were intellectually prepared, partly as a consequence of internal state-building processes and the institutionalization of new social knowledge production. By state-building processes, I mean the development of state administrative capacities and expertise, to which I return below. By institutionalization of new social knowledge production, I mean the firm establishment of national economics as a university discipline and the creation of associations for national economists in all three countries during the period 1872–83. Such associations for economists were established in Denmark in 1872, in

Sweden in 1877, and in Norway in 1883.[29] They were to be forums for political and policy debates for economists (scientific and amateur) active at the universities, in public administration, in politics, and in business. The associations achieved a central position in the public debate on economic and political issues. In particular, the combination of theoretical discussions and discussions of public policy proposals made them important.[30] As a university discipline, national or state economics was developed earlier in Denmark and Sweden than it was in Norway. The first professorship in Denmark was established at the University of Copenhagen in 1815,[31] and a political science degree with a strong component of economic subjects was introduced in 1848.[32] The first university position in *Statsoeconomiske Videnskaber* dates back to the year of independence from Denmark in Norway (1814), but the first "full" professorship was established as late as 1877.[33] Economics had been established as a university discipline in 1739 at Uppsala University in Sweden—the first country outside German areas to establish a chair in economics.[34] Anders Berch was appointed the first professor of economics in 1741.

The associations for economists became important links between the leading policy experts from various sectors of society. They played parallel roles in the three countries. They functioned as forums for scientifically based information and debates on topical economic and social issues. The influence of German academic development and debate is very clear and obvious. The very first speeches in both the Swedish and Norwegian associations were, for example, on the topic of catheder socialism (*Kathedersozialismus*) (Stockholm, March 12, 1877) and "The Theory of State Socialism" (Kristiania [Oslo], January 25, 1884).[35] The German "catheder socialism" was of great importance for the Norwegian debate on social and economic policies during the period 1870–90,[36] and social policy issues were often debated in the association. The Swedish association debated the German school of thought on several occasions (1883, 1885), and the social policies of Bismarck and the "German model" were also major topics for discussion.[37] The Danish association was, of course, similarly preoccupied with social issues and ideas stemming from her neighboring country, and debates in the association urged leading economists to collect data on the need for an old age pension scheme.[38]

The development of the science of economics at the universities and the establishment of associations for economists from all major sectors of society helped to create the institutional remedies to absorb and filter scientific and policy ideas coming from abroad during the 1870s and 1880s in Scandinavia. Not only the actual German social legislation, but the strong and continuous stream of ideas on political economy and social policy emanating from German universities—the most advanced system of higher education in the world[39]—during this period, influenced the political agenda in Scandinavia. The existence of national policy forums assumedly was conducive to the similarity in timing of the first social security legislation in the three countries, but the German ideas were not uniformly "decoded" and thus not transformed into similar priorities and institutional solutions.

General Acceptance of State Role in Social Policy

Social problems were not new in the Scandinavian countries of the 1880s, but the general recognition that the state could assist in solving them, was. The development of industrial life was viewed by the Swedish investigating official committee of 1884 as "creating greater uncertainties in the position of the working classes,"[40] but a clear need for better provision for the more persistent problem of old age relief was recognized in all three countries. The beginning industrialization of the Scandinavian countries gave rise to new needs for worker protection and income security. The emergence of a view that linked the recognition of social problems to a role for the state in solving them cannot necessarily be attributed to industrialization. In all three countries, the gradual incorporation of new social groups into political life through suffrage extension, the organization of mass parties, and representation in parliament must be assumed to have been of great direct and indirect importance for the emerging conception of the state as a political tool for alleviating social problems (and this process did occur before the anti-socialist laws in the bureaucratic-authoritarian Germany as well). Competition between parties presumably sharpened the awareness of the link between problems and solutions, and also structured political conflicts. But competition could theoretically (and empirically often does) concern the question of how to limit state expenditures rather than how to invent new purposes for outlays. It is well known that *Angst* for a growing socialist movement and reduction of the position of the Catholic Church were rather explicit and crucial motives for Bismarck's interest in state social insurance, but that this was a strong or prime motive for Scandinavian political efforts to introduce social insurance is less convincing, although a Norwegian historian[41] has referred to the Norwegian Ministry of Interior's remark to "keep the incipient [revolutionary] movement, also among our working folk, on a sound and sober course" as justification for legislating accident insurance to support such a view and in order to explain why accident insurance was legislated before an old age pension scheme. We should rather ask why it was that:

> from all sides, whichever party a person belonged to, we these days hear about worker friendliness, concern for the worker, and legislation for the workers is wanted everywhere[42]

and

> from the 1870s, and especially from the 1890s, all politically and socially interested people in Norway were concerned with the social question [and how it could be solved][43]

and why:

> views [in Sweden] diverged [only] on the best *means* to meet the problem of [old age relief]?[44]

The thought that the state should be "the strong arm of the weak" was particularly influential among Liberals,[45] "but also Conservatives supported the new ideas."[46] "To find new solutions to social problems was a common interest and a common goal. Disagreement centered around tempo and form,"[47] and a common view was that social policymaking was or ought to be lifted above the political (party) struggle in Norway.[48] "The entire human tendency of time has moved in the same direction [to prepare the great social political reforms of our times]."[49] Irrespective of party adherence, politicians met to work jointly for the implementation of social legislation, according to a contemporary analysis[50] of Norway.

An active role for the state in social affairs seems to have been an idea whose time had come.[51] How are we to understand this? Industrialization, democratization, and (limited) political radicalization are not sufficient factors of explanation. German ideas and legislation apparently influenced the actual timing of Scandinavian legislation, particularly in Norway and Sweden, and the actual institutional solution in the case of Norwegian accident insurance. The establishment and activity of the economists' associations for public information and debate helped structure the perception of problems and solutions. But why was the idea of state-legislated social insurance generally accepted? To what extent can we trace the general acceptance of state social insurance to elements in the development of the state itself—to its capacities to monitor and its capabilities to intervene in socioeconomic life? How was authoritative knowledge about social problems and needs developed, stored, and disseminated? In which sense was the state (in terms of administrative institutions) an actor?

If it is reasonable to assume, which I think it is, that "states may be sites of autonomous official action not reducible to the demands or preferences of any social group(s)" and that "the organizational structures of states indirectly influence meanings and methods of politics for all groups in society,"[52] then we should try to identify which important (new) state institutions developed during the period prior to the end of the 1880s, and what kind of knowledge, interests, and values they directly or indirectly represented. That the time had come for the social insurance idea—and why it had come—may be partly understood in the context of the development of official statistics, its organization, and its early orientation, which is particularly revealing in the Norwegian case.

Statistics, Expertise, and State Capabilities

The development of official statistics is closely linked to the process of state-building and the evolution of a specialized public bureaucracy.[53] Government interest in statistical information increased as a result of efforts to mobilize resources for the maintenance of a standing army and a professional public administration. The dominant view of the era of "mercantilism" of the 1600s to 1700s led to attempts to estimate population size and population movements in various countries. The size of the population was an indicator of the strength of the state as well as a basis for tax collection. In this early period, European governments were concerned with the collection of statistical information in order to further economic growth for political ends.[54] But efforts to collect statistics were often unsystematic, and the results were rarely published.[55]

The development of official statistics in Scandinavia was part of a general European development in the last century. The great breakthrough came after the July revolution in 1830: statistical offices were established in most European countries, and the period from 1830 to 1850 has been labeled "the era of enthusiasm" of the history of statistics.[56] From the 1850s, national official statistics and publications on various subjects stimulated international comparisons. Nine international meetings were held in the 1853–76 period under the auspices of the International Statistical Congress—with the purpose of advancing the professional organization of statistics and the cross-national comparability of data.[57] International networks of state-oriented statistical experts were firmly established during the latter half of the last century. In Scandinavia, the strengthening of constitutional life encouraged the publication of statistics, and the development was clearly interwoven with state-building processes.

Swedish Official Statistics

Sweden's modern civil service dates from the mid-seventeenth century, and the country was in this respect among the pioneers in Europe. Heclo[58] has stressed that the era of modern social policies in Sweden began with administrators in an accepted policymaking role, and he directs our attention to the seemingly paradoxical phenomenon that in the era popularly recognized as the heyday of laissez-faire in the nineteenth century, there was an unprecedented growth in state investigations. On the other hand, the paradox is less obvious if we take into consideration the historical role of local governments (*Kommunera*) in the formulation and execution of policies, and the role of the Church in public life since the Reformation. The expansion of governmental intelligence functions in the form of investigatory committees was determined less by a self-concious philosophy of government and more by the practical analytic needs of policymakers, according to Heclo: "The place of civil servants in the development of modern social policies has been crucial"[59] and

> between 1890 and 1913, Swedish administrators played a key and probably primary role in developing the basic analysis and exhaustive information which underlaid the construction of a Swedish pension policy. From the beginning, contributory insurance was seen to involve no serious burden on Sweden's relatively well-developed bureaucratic resources.[60]

Heclo gives high marks to the quality of research and analysis in the reports from the committee established in 1884 to study the question of worker insurance, and he refers to the solid statistical data basis provided (which stood out as a great contrast to similar investigative work in Britain at the time).[61]

Not only modern civil service, but also the development of official statistics has a long history in Sweden (and the two developments are probably closely interconnected). The oldest Swedish parish register containing demographic data originates from 1608, and the Church Law of 1686 demanded that the clergy register population movements within the parish of their domain. Such statistics collected and kept by clergymen (in their capacity as officials of the state) was, however, not seriously considered for utilization for state-administrative purposes until after the Great Northern War (1700–1721).[62] After a period of investigative preparatory work, a comprehensive bill for tabular records became law in 1748. This is reckoned as the birthday of the Swedish official statistics. The collection of population statistics for the year 1749 may be regarded as the oldest census report for a sovereign nation in Europe.[63] A royal commission for the tabular records was created in 1756, several decades earlier than in any other country. From the outset, however, the information gained from tabulations was regarded as a deep secret of the state.[64] But contemporary pressure for making statistics public came from the first Swedish professor of political economy, A. Berch of Uppsala, who claimed that "tables are not intended to be buried in archives,"[65] and the secretary, P. Wargentin of the Swedish Academy of Science. Less secrecy prevailed from the 1760s.

Gradually, the government accepted that more and more of the collected statistics might be made generally known, and gradually more and more types of statistics were collected: for example, more detailed demographic or vital statistics from the end of the eighteenth century; from 1804, data on the number of persons vaccinated; from 1811, agricultural statistics; from 1831, statistics on the economic conditions of childbearing women; from 1830, statistics on manufacture, commerce, and shipping; from 1851, hospital statistics. But the collection and publication of various kinds of statistics were a decentralized and uncoordinated undertaking. By 1850, Swedish statistics, with the exception of population statistics that were controlled by a separate scientifically trained institution, were wholly without plan. "The need of better statistics had long been recognized and to meet it, the government appointed a committee which reported its findings in 1856."[66]

The result of this investigation materialized in 1858 with, among other things, the creation of a department called the Central Bureau of Statistics with the duty of preparing population statistics and other branches of statistics. Although it was decided that all statistical reports were to be published uniformly under the common (and modest) title "Contributions to the Official Statistics of Sweden," the organization of the collection of statistics was substantially decentralized. A statistical journal was established, and from 1871 until 1913, the first issue of each volume was devoted to a summary of all the official statistics corresponding to the statistical yearbooks of other countries. A Swedish statistical yearbook has been published since 1914. Publication series on hygiene and hospitals began in 1861; on public education in 1868; on local government, poor relief, and finance in 1874; on salaries and pensions in 1881. The efforts to create a new branch of statistics, labor statistics, succeeded after many years of preparation to gain a place in the state administration in 1897.

The reforms of 1858 represented a major reorganization and consolidation of Swedish official statistics. The creation of the Central Bureau of Statistics must be seen as crucial for the development of greater state capacity to investigate social conditions and to provide the statistical basis often required by officials and politicians for policymaking purposes.

Danish Official Statistics

The history of official statistics is younger in Denmark. Somewhat unreliable population enumerations, entrusted by the government to private persons to carry out, took place in 1769 (and simultaneously in Norway, as part of the Danish kingdom) and 1787. "A steadily increasing demand for statistical information in which the question of taxes and tax-payers came strongly to the fore, and the desire that such data should appear regularly and at brief intervals"[67] led to the establishment of a Danish-Norwegian Tabulating Office in 1797. But it played an insignificant role and was abolished in 1819. An effort to reorganize the production of official statistics was made in 1834, when the government created the Tabular Commission whose members held high places in the central administration, "a circumstance which afforded them no small degree of independence."[68] The Tabular Commission successfully prepared the population enumerations of 1834, 1840, and 1845 and began, among other things, the collection of statistics on demographic changes; agricultural developments; shipping; trade; and criminal conditions. A plan for the establishment of an independent central statistical bureau was outlined and led to the creation of the Statistical Bureau in 1850. The establishment of an autonomous statistical office in Denmark must be seen as closely connected to the breakdown of absolutist rule and the demand by new representative institutions for information about societal conditions.[69] Its field of work was constantly enlarged. During the years 1869 to 1874 an annual series, "Summary of Statistical Information," appeared (later published at uneven intervals) and was continued in the Statistical Yearbook after 1895 when the bureau was reorganized and expanded. As outlined above, a certain amount of social statistics (potentially) relevant to efforts for state schemes for social insurance pensions, was collected from the early 1860s.

Norwegian Official Statistics

In Norway, which separated from Denmark in 1814 (but had to join a personal union with Sweden), a statistical office was first organized in 1832 as a tabular office in the Ministry of Finance (in 1846 it was moved to the newly created Ministry of Interior), but official statistical statements had been prepared long before this time,[70] especially in the fields of vital statistics, trade, and shipping. With the year 1838 the regular publication of official Statistical Tables for the Kingdom of Norway began. The first of five-year reports on the economic and social conditions of the nation covered the years 1836–40, and at about the same time came the first publications on agricultural statistics. Educational statistics had been collected by the Ecclesiastical and Education Ministry for 1827, 1840, and 1853, whereupon it was incorporated as a regular part of the official statistics of Norway. Statistics on hospitals and various diseases were published from the early 1870s. In 1861 a royal resolution ordered that all tabular statements and reports by different ministries should be published in a specific format and form a collection under the title, "The Official Statistics of Norway." The growing body of collected and published statistics led to the reorganization of the statistical office based on a report "in which the desirability of giving the office a more independent position was emphasized."[71] The government and parliament supported this, and an independent institution, the Central Bureau of Statistics, was established in 1876. Its field of work was to include the greater part of economic statistics, population enumerations, annual movements of the population, wages, and so on. A statistical handbook for the kingdom of Norway had been published in 1871 (by Kiær). In order to get the statistics "out to the people,"[72] a statistical yearbook was published from 1879 onward.[73] A. N. Kiær, the first director of the bureau (1876–1913), was a leading statistician with a great interest in statistics on income and wealth, social statistics, as well as data-collection methods. "Social questions came more and more into the foreground, a development which also left its mark on the statistics as data were continually sought for the purpose of shedding light on social conditions."[74]

Thus, from early on, Kiær built on the work done by a Norwegian self-made sociologist and statistician, E. Sundt (1827–75), who paved the way for social as well as for population statistics through his statistical investigations and great number of book publications from the 1850s onward on topics such as moral behavior, social and health conditions, hygiene, tramps and gypsies, urban and rural poor people, and alcohol consumption. Sundt carried out empirical sociological studies allegedly not undertaken in any other country at the time.[75] He definitely provided an important basis for the orientation of the Bureau of Statistics toward early emphasis on social statistics and the conditions of the working class. In the 1880s Kiær himself was much concerned about income statistics from a social point of view,[76] comparing income conditions in different classes and strata. Kiær played a prominent role in international statistical cooperation and was one of the founders of the International Statistical Institute in 1885. He took the initiative to establish regular, formal cooperation between Scandinavian statistical offices in 1889. He cooperated closely with the two chairs in national economics and statistics which the country [i.e., the university in Kristiania (Oslo)] had, and he influenced the extensive room for statistics in the study of economics.[77] From the very beginning as director of the Bureau of Statistics, Kiær was very interested in the use of statistics for the analysis of societal conditions and in the centralized organization of statistics, which put Norway much closer to the Danish than to the Swedish model of organization. The Norwegian Statistical Bureau was from the beginning (and until this date) much more oriented toward empirical social research and toward bridging this interest with practical policymaking. Kiær was crucial in this development. He became a member of the First Parliamentary Worker Commission of 1894 and later of the Social Insurance Committee of 1907. He was linked to these commissions in order to supply the necessary statistical data and research material.[78] Both Sundt, as the father of Norwegian sociology, and Kiær had a profound influence on the next generation of Norwegian statisticians. They gave a clear-cut social orientation to the work of the governmental statistical agency during the great surge of data production from about 1870 until 1914. This period represented the decisive takeoff for the production of statistics in Norway. These were years of rapid change in the structure of society:

> there was an acceleration of the rhythms of urbanization and industrialization, there was a series of waves of cultural, social and political mobilization, and the forces of opposition won out in Parliament against the regime of officials and patricians. The result was an extraordinary increase in the demand for statistics across all sectors of society.[79]

Administrative Capacity of Statistical Bureaus

In all three countries, the administrative capacity of the statistical bureaus was limited in the 1880s. The Danish Bureau had ten gainfully employed persons in 1880—of which seven had higher university degrees, and among these, three (including the director) had a degree in political science/national economics. The organization was small, and much concern about low organizational capacity was expressed in the Parliament in 1889 to 1890 when proposals for social insurance legislation were discussed. A law proposal to reorganize the statistical bureau was submitted seven times before finally being approved in 1895.[80] The request for industrial statistics at the beginning of the 1870s had to be considered in connection with the emergence of the "social question." But such statistics were not collected, nor were statistics on social issues (although population statistics contributed to social statistics). The Statistical Bureau stated in 1872 that it was impossible to collect complete industrial statistics, and that no other country had such statistics.[81] The Statistical Bureau in Denmark had nothing to do with the workers commissions appointed by the government in 1875 and 1885, or with their efforts to collect information. Statistical illumination of certain social issues was not followed up until the late 1890s. Sickness funds were obliged by law to send statistical data to the bureau from the early 1860s, and although statistics were incomplete, they were used as basis for the law on subsidies to sickness funds enacted in 1892.[82]

> Of course, the lack of statistical data on the conditions which social legislation was to deal with, was strongly felt, for example in the *Folketing* in 1889/90. Discussions in the *Folketing* led to a consensing view that the Statistical Bureau was not able to meet the rising demands for statistics given the way it was organized.[83]

There was a lack of capacity: the staff was considered too small and not sufficiently competent, and there existed great doubts about the possibility of collecting certain kinds of information from the population. Social and industrial statistics were collected only after the reorganization of the bureau in 1895. The link between the government, parliamentarians, and the statistical expertise of the state seems to have been much weaker in Denmark in this period than in Norway. The number of persons employed by the Norwegian Bureau of Statistics was also higher, with sixteen permanent staff members in 1879.[84] Also, the budget seems to have been bigger, and it increased significantly more rapidly in Norway in the period before the turn of the century.[85] The Central Bureau of Statistics in Sweden had a relatively small staff in 1879; one director, five actuarians, plus assistants.[86] But the more decentralized Swedish organization of official statistics makes it more difficult to estimate total administrative capacity.

The masses of statistics collected by various governmental agencies around mid-nineteenth century led to problems of coordination. A centralization of official statistical production and the systematization of statistical publications, as well as the creation of central statistical bureaus as relatively independent administrative institutions, occurred well before the period of Bismarckian social insurance legislation in the "old" nation-states (Denmark, 1850; Sweden, 1858), while the newer secession state, Norway, was relatively late (1876), but still ahead of the date of Bismarck's program. State capacity and capabilities in this field increased considerably in the decades after 1850, and from the 1870s these developments were coupled with the spread of a new conception of the role of the state in society, promoted particularly through the German Verein für Sozialpolitik, which was established in 1873. "Professorial socialism [*Catheder socialismus*] with its demand for the intervention of the state on behalf of the lower classes, was popular in the universities,"[87] and had an impact upon political economists beyond the German borders as exemplified by the creation of, and debates in, associations for economists.

Elite Interconnections

The professionalization of statistical expertise and—to some extent—social science analysis and the links between the scientific community (in Scandinavian countries very small), more or less independent government statistical agencies, and administrators and politicians helped bring social issues to the fore. The relatively autonomous organizations of central statistical bureaus, the development of national economic and statistical expertise, and the growing size of statistical administrations meant the creation of new influential administrative-scientific milieus. People with a background in national (or state) economics/statistics represented the empirically oriented social science of the day. These bureaus not only recorded data, but also developed analytical and research skills, were eager to expand the task of statistical investigations and data collection, and to inform the society about "the state of the nation," partly through the associations for economists. Premises for science-based and politically neutral opinion formation, political initiatives, and action were laid in this period. And governments and political representatives had an administrative-scientific tool viewed as useful and often necessary for policy and lawmaking. "The utility of statistics for lawmaking and the bureaucracy is now also generally recognized: it offers guidelines for such activity, and steps to be taken, and it controls their effects."[88] The increasing importance of social statistics in the last two decades of the nineteenth century was generally recognized. At a more general level, it is stated that

> [By the 1860s] statistics had entered into the everyday usage of elites and had successfully affirmed its social prestige and prerogatives as a specialized profession with international congresses. . . . [T]here can be little doubt that by the late nineteenth century statistics was absorbed into a mode of thought and argument in both the social sciences and public policy in all Western polities irrespective of their political diversity.[89]

In an assessment of the significance of statistics (and economics) in universities in nineteenth-century Europe, the Dane Holck[90] claims that university teachers were often self-evident members of statistical commissions and obvious candidates for the directorship of the government statistical office. Directors of statistical bureaus were frequently simultaneously professors of statistics,[91] and the first Danish director, Bergsøe (1850–54) is one Scandinavian example of this close interlinkage of the academic social science community and state administration.[92]

The preceding discussion has indicated that the Scandinavian states (institutions and actors) were ideologically, politically, and administratively prepared for state social insurance of some kind, although statistical-administrative preparedness (data-collection priorities and routines) and the capacity to undertake large-scale data-collection efforts on a short-term basis varied, when Bismarck's conception of state social insurance was exported from Germany.

Milieus representing empirical social-scientific knowledge developed within and outside relatively independent governmental statistical agencies. The conception of "social statistics" was formed. The availability, or not, of statistics was partly influenced by the data collecting capacity of relatively new statistical agencies, but probably also by the level and intensity of interest within the statistical bureaus for actually collecting various types of data. Availability of statistics, in its turn, affected policymaking alternatives in the area of social insurance.

Similarity in Timing of First Scandinavian Social Security Legislation

So, what made the Scandinavian countries pass their first social insurance laws at about the same time[93] in the beginning of the 1890s? Industrialization had started, and new social needs on top of old ones appeared. But industrialization levels differed. New strata were gradually being politically incorporated, and pressure for further suffrage extensions was evident in Norway and Sweden where enfranchisement was limited compared to Denmark. Political parties and mass political mobilization developed from the 1870s (Denmark) and the 1880s.[94] Formalized forums for public scientific and political debates had been created, bringing together prominent economic and other experts from many fields. Economics had been firmly established as a university discipline in all three countries. Within government administrations, relatively independent central statistical bureaus had been differentiated, agencies with an interest in and at least some capacity to produce and publish statistics on a wide field of topics, among these population movements and social conditions. Social problems were enumerated, and differences in living conditions began to be made statistically visible. A new empirically oriented social science expertise (if still of very limited size) developed. A new conception of the role of the state emerged and spread in official (state-building) circles, particularly from the early 1870s. Problems were increasingly registered, and there was a gradual acceptance in the same circles that the state had a role in solving them. The state interest as well as the general interest in doing or having something done with new and/or growing social needs were present in the 1880s—for human "self-evident" reasons as well as for various political reasons. It is difficult to find explicit views against a more active role for the state in social affairs. Social problems were widely recognized, and state-assisted solutions were welcome.

In 1884 to 1885, all three governments created committees with broad mandates to investigate the possibility for social insurance legislation. The availability of statistics varied as did the capacity to collect new statistics. But in all countries, new statistics were collected, and only when a statistical basis existed did legislation take place. The apparent importance of statistics (and consequently of state capacity to collect it) was such that one might argue that without it, legislation would not have happened. Industrialization was not a sufficient reason for legislation. Neither was political will to legislate (either positively defined or out of fear of a revolutionary socialist movement) a sufficient condition for legislation to take place. The availability of statistics was naturally not a sufficient condition for legislation, but it seems to have been a necessary condition.

Variations in Priorities

The Scandinavian countries all introduced their first social insurance/security laws in the early 1890s, but for various purposes and with different institutional solutions. The scope of Danish legislation was larger (three laws) in the 1890s than the Norwegian and Swedish (one law each). Denmark first legislated an old age relief scheme for needy, "respectable" people; Sweden, a scheme for state subsidies to voluntary sickness funds; Norway, a scheme for compulsory accident insurance for industrial workers.

That the scope of Danish legislation was larger than in the two other nations may tentatively be explained by much longer government attention to various social needs (since the early 1860s) and to a somewhat better statistical basis (with the exception of industrial accident statistics) for legislation as a result of this long-term concern. The most important statistical basis for the old age relief scheme of 1891 was, however, prepared by two private political economists, with public and private financial support, from 1884 to 1890. Solutions could more quickly be adapted in the Danish case. It was not self-evident that an old age pension scheme should come first, but a solution to the provision of old age relief had been considered for a very long time. A law on public (state and municipalities) subsidies to sickness insurance funds followed almost immediately (1892). The statistical basis necessary to legislate something for this purpose had been collected regularly since the 1860s. Statistics on industrial accidents had not, as far as I can establish, been collected earlier. Lack of this particular type of statistics seems to have been a consequence of relatively little political and/or professional interest and capacity. An explanation of why interest was modest cannot be offered here, except the partial and tentative one that policymakers and the Statistical Bureau were formally less strongly connected in Denmark during this period than in the two other countries—a proposition which in turn calls for an explanation (and especially since the Danish Bureau was the most centralized of them all). Industrial accident statistics seem to have been collected only after the reorganization of the Statistical Bureau (in order to increase its capacity) in 1895.

In Norway, the administrative capacity to collect statistics necessary for a political decision on an old age scheme was openly admitted to be lacking. Statistics on voluntary sickness funds were collected by the committee established in 1885, along with statistics on industrial working conditions and accidents. The modest development of voluntary sickness insurance in Norway (in absolute terms and relative to Denmark and Sweden[95]) made the Danish and Swedish solution with state/public subsidies to voluntary funds look less meaningful in Norway, because such a scheme would have little effect on the problem in the short run. Therefore, compulsory insurance in some form was considered, and such a solution would demand the consideration of more statistics as well as a substantial amount of state expenditure (also relative to the Danish and Swedish solution), unless one was prepared to let employers and/or the workers pay the full cost. In the Norwegian case, an early sickness insurance legislation was less likely than in the neighboring countries. Consequently, accident insurance for industrial workers was the most likely purpose (of the three under consideration) to be legislated first, and a law in Norway was passed in 1894.

In Sweden, proposals for all three schemes were forwarded in 1888–89 by the investigative committee. It was very likely that a solution with (very modest) state subsidies to voluntary sickness funds could be legislated early, and it was not surprising that it would take longer (as in Denmark) to contemplate the financial and other consequences of an old age pension scheme. But why an accident insurance law did not come earlier than 1901, and then in the form of an employers' liability act, is harder to explain. Statistics on industrial accidents were collected by the first workers insurance committee (established in 1884). The growing incidence of industrial accidents in Germany and Austria after the introduction of accident insurance may have been one factor working against a political consensus on the need for such insurance in Denmark and Sweden. But why did this German-Austrian development have no effect on Norwegian policymaking efforts? The answers must await more detailed studies of decision-making processes in the three countries.

The three countries were unequally prepared to introduce old age pension schemes when the German social insurance idea came on the agenda, and unequally prepared to legislate sickness insurance. In the first case, Denmark had a lead in terms of long-term investigations for a solution, while in the second case an organizational capacity outside the state existed in Denmark and Sweden, on which the state could build, but not in Norway to any considerable degree. Norway was forced to contemplate a more radical (and costly) solution than its neighbors. This difference in the strength and spread of a network of voluntary sickness funds thus helps to explain why Denmark and Sweden, on the one hand, and Norway, on the other, opted for crucially different institutional solutions in their first sickness insurance laws: state/public subsidized voluntary insurance in the two first countries; compulsory insurance in Norway (first law in 1909). That some form of a compulsory old age pension scheme (and the noncontributory scheme in Denmark must be considered of this kind) developed as a likely option in all three countries can be explained in terms of the argument above by the almost nonexistence of voluntary or private pension insurance (Sweden) and assumed (given the unavailability of statistics[96]) non- or limited existence in Denmark and Norway in the 1880s.

Summing up the argument on availability of statistics, we find that Denmark passed laws in the early 1890s on old age pension and sickness insurance, for both of which statistics had been collected, while not passing an employers' liability law until statistics on industrial accidents were collected after 1895. In Norway, statistics had been collected on industrial accidents, and a law on accident insurance was passed in 1894. Statistics necessary to estimate the costs of an old age pension scheme were not collected, and no law on such a scheme was passed. Statistics on voluntary sickness funds were collected but showed that very few were voluntarily insured, thus indicating a demand for a more comprehensive and costly state solution, which would reasonably require more time to consider and decide upon. In Sweden, statistics on voluntary sickness funds showed a relatively greater degree of coverage than in Norway, and a law on subsidies to voluntary insurance was passed. A statistical basis for the consideration of an old age pension scheme was provided, but in Sweden as in the other Scandinavian countries, it took quite a while before a law was enacted. Perhaps this was an area where more time to reach a decision was needed. Statistics are not neutral or self-explaining, and the availability of statistics is of course not a sufficient condition for political action. This fact was even more apparent in the case of statistics on industrial accidents in Sweden, but the lack of early Swedish legislation on accident insurance is the only surprising finding given propositions about the likely relationship between state administrative capacity, actual data collection, and social policy decisions in the 1890s in Scandinavia.

Conclusion

The explanation of the timing and type of the first social security legislation in the Scandinavian countries is a complex, multivariate affair. The first laws were enacted within a very short span of time during the first half of the 1890s. The three countries were all industrializing but varied substantially in levels of industrialization. Developments toward parliamentary mass democracies were under way, but only Norway was a parliamentary democracy in the 1890s, and the extension of suffrage varied considerably between Denmark at the top end and Sweden at the bottom. Democratization is not a unidimensional phenomenon, but the amount of variations on indicators of democratization suggests that such variables were important only in the very general sense that pressures for democratic change existed and that authorities and representatives had to take this factor into account when discussing and responding to demands for political action. Industrialization and democratization are not sufficient, and perhaps not even the most important variables, to account for the similarity in timing of the first social security laws (or the almost nonvariation in our dependent variable). I have also argued that the impetus gained from the politically innovative German social insurance legislation was not sufficient to induce Scandinavian legislation in the 1890s, but it probably represented an important factor. Domestic political initiatives to accelerate social legislation were motivated by German legislation. But the German legislation came at a time when the Scandinavian countries were politically and intellectually prepared for state social action. The social or worker question had been on the political agenda for some time, especially in Denmark. Associations for economists were created in all three countries during 1872–83, and their activities were much influenced by German academic development. Catheder socialism was an important and influential topic, and the idea of an active role for the state was generally accepted among elite groups from different sectors of the society. Economics of a positive or normative kind became firmly established as a university discipline. The associations for economists represented the leading forums for informed scientific and public, political debate. Parallel to, and interlinked with, this development of a positive social science, was the expansion of a state apparatus for the registration of social problems and collection of new social statistics. Central statistical bureaus were established in all three countries between 1850 and 1876. Both the interest in and the actual capacity to collect social data increased significantly during the latter half of the nineteenth century. The production of public and official statistics was firmly institutionalized. The directors of the statistical bureaus were major actors in the activities of the associations for economists.[97] I cannot assess the explanatory weight that each of these factors had for the similarity in timing of the first social security legislation in Scandinavia. They all worked together in a complex, interrelated way to produce an idea whose time had come and which made some kind of social legislation very likely.

The effort to explain why the three countries enacted social laws for different purposes and with different institutional solutions (principles of organization, principle of compulsory versus voluntary insurance) is more elaborate, and I shall only summarize my argument. One factor seems to have been the length of time a particular social problem or need had been under political surveillance, and some problems (and possible policy solutions) are bigger and more complicated than others. Thus, it seems that the problem of an old age pension or relief scheme took a long time from first being raised politically until some legislative action was, or could be, taken in all three countries, and only Denmark got a law in the 1890s (1891)—after twenty-five years of political and bureaucratic consideration of the issue. But my main argument is linked to the actual collection and use of relevant statistical data and the capacity to collect data. I have shown that the countries varied on these variables. Relevant data on coverage of voluntary sickness insurance were collected in all three countries and laid the basis for the sickness insurance laws in Denmark (1892) and Sweden (1891). The negligible coverage in Norway made the demand for compulsory insurance (to ensure an acceptable degree of coverage) more likely, but that required more time for consideration of a proper organizational and financial solution. Statistics on industrial accidents were collected in Norway and Sweden in the 1880s, but not until the mid-1890s in Denmark. Norway passed an accident insurance law in 1894, while no political decision was reached until 1901 in Sweden and 1898 in Denmark, after statistics had been collected. The delayed action in Sweden is the one which is most difficult to account for, and a more detailed study of the political process of decision making is needed. But although there is certainly no automatic link between availability of statistics and political decisions, it seems reasonable to conclude that without a statistical basis, legislation was not likely and that state capacity in the meaning of ability to provide statistics was important for legislative efforts. How do we account for the apparent fact the in the period under study, there seems to have been an odd correspondence between state interest and knowledge-producing groups? Perhaps this finding can be generalized across more countries than the three Scandinavian ones? Social legislation was in general more likely when certain kinds of statistics were available.

Further research should look into the question of how different kinds of statistics were interpreted and used for bureaucratic and political purposes, and of what role contemporary social scientists played in this political process.

Notes to Chapter 7

1. The concept of welfare state is not important here, but since many have been concerned about the date when the term was first used, it may be of interest to note that the Norwegian professor of economics, Hertzberg, used it in an article as early as 1884, with a negative connotation attached to it. See T. Bergh and T. Hanisch, *Vitenskap og politikk: Linjer i norsk sosialøkonomi gjennom 150 år* Oslo, Aschehoug, 1984, p. 94.

2. Norway enjoyed domestic independence in its union with Sweden (1814–1905).

3. This part represents an elaboration of research I have done earlier in S. Kuhnle, "The Growth of Social Insurance Programs in Scandinavia: Outside Influences and Internal Forces." In P. Flora and A. J. Heidenheimer, eds., *The Development of Welfare States in Europe and America.* New Brunswick, NJ and London, Transaction Books, 1981.

4. Subscribing to the view that "in the social sciences, changing questions and ways of seeking answers are just as important as accumulations of research findings," quoted from T. Skocpol and E. Amenta, "States and Social Policy." *Annual Review of Sociology* 12 (1981): pp. 131–57.

5. P. Flora and J. Alber, "Modernization, Democratization, and the Development of Welfare States in Western Europe." In Flora and Heidenheimer, *Development of Welfare States.*

6. For example, A. S. Orloff and T. Skocpol, "Why Not Equal Protection? Explaining the Politics of Public Social Spending in Britain 1900–11 and United States 1880s–1920s." *American Sociological Review* 49 (1984): pp. 726–50; D. Collier and R. Messick, "Prerequisites Versus Diffusion: Testing Alternative Explanations of Social Security Adoption." *American Political Science Review* 69 (1975): pp. 1299–1315.

7. Kuhnle, "Growth of Social Insurance Programs," p. 134.

8. Flora and Alber, "Modernization."

9. Kuhnle, "Growth of Social Insurance Programs."

10. The analytical path to be followed is in principle not very far from the one chosen by Peter Baldwin in his seminal, in-depth study of political struggles and processes leading up to early social policy legislation in Denmark, Sweden, Britain, France, and Germany; see Peter Baldwin, *The Politics of Social Solidarity: Class Bases of the European Welfare State 1875–1975.* Cambridge, Cambridge University Press, 1990. Baldwin does not include Norway in his analysis, and his study of the overall importance of agrarian interests in Scandinavia in the late nineteenth century and, more generally, economic interests of the middle class, does not really answer the more specific questions on similarities in timing and variations in early social policy priorities among the Scandinavian countries discussed in this chapter. Baldwin convincingly downplays the laborist interpretation of social policy development in Scandinavia, and he demonstrates the vital importance of economic (self-)interests and social risk assessments by various groups in accounting for policy development and policy contents. I propose that factors such as knowledge production and

linkages between knowledge-bearing groups and policymakers were also important independent of both structural factors, such as levels of industrialization and democratization, and the crude economic self-interest of various social groups in accounting for the type of social legislation that was likely to come first in different nations.

11. For example, Flora and Alber, "Modernization." G. Perrin, "Reflections on Fifty Years of Social Security." *International Labour Review*, 99(3) (1969), H. Heclo, *Modern Social Politics in Britain and Sweden*. New Haven, Yale University Press, 1974; G. V. Rimlinger, *Welfare Policy and Industrialization in Europe, America, and Russia*. (New York, John Wiley and Sons, 1971).

12. C. Jones, *Patterns of Social Policy*. London, Tavistock Publications, 1985.

13. State legislation pertaining to accident insurance or employers' liability for limited groups prior to the German legislation of 1883 had been introduced in Prussia (1838); Norway (1842, 1869); Austria (1854); Belgium (1868); Germany (1871); Switzerland (1877); Great Britain (1880). Similarly limited legislation pertaining to sickness had been enacted in Belgium (1844, 1851); France (1852); Prussia (1854); Austria (1854); Russia (1866); Sachsen (1868); Bavaria (1869); and legislation pertaining to old age/invalidity in France (1791, 1856); Belgium (1844); Austria (1854); and Italy (1861). For more extensive information and sources, see S. Kuhnle, *Velferdsstatens utvikling: Norge i komparativt perspektiv*. Bergen, Universitetsforlaget, 1983.

14. The active role of central government authorities in the introduction of social insurance in Germany was, however, not reflected in the actual organization of social insurance. The central government played a modest role in terms of financing, and also in terms of organization of social insurance schemes; see E. Rieger, *Die Institutionalisierung des Wohlfahrtsstaates*. Opladen, Westdeutscher Verlag, 1992.

15. "This German measure created attention all over the civilized world, and Germany was for many years characterized as the motherland of social insurance." M. Ormestad, *De sosiale trygder: Historisk og grunnprinsipper*. Oslo, Sem & Stenersen, 1948, p. 18; And similarly, ". . . a completely new period in the history of worker insurance was initiated." Aa. Sørensen, "Tysk og dansk Arbejderforsikring," *Nationaløkonomisk tidsskrift*, Tredje Rækkes 12. Bd. (Copenhagen, 1904): p. 209. (Both quotations in this note are translated into English by this chapter's author.)

16. A. Briggs, "The Welfare State in Historical Perspective." *Archives Europeennes de Sociologie* II (1961): p. 147.

17. K. Philip, *Staten og fattigdommen*. Copenhagen, Jul Gellerups forlag, 1947, p. 71. (Author's translation.)

18. This and subsequent parts on Norway and Sweden are primarily based on Dr. Zacher, *Die Arbeiterversicherung im Auslande*, vol. 3: *Die Arbeiterversicherung in Norwegen* (1898); ibid, vol. 2, *Die Arbeiterversicherung in Sweden* (1898); ibid. vol. 1, *Die Arbeiterversicherung in Dänemark* (1900). Berlin, Verlag der Arbeiter-Versorgung; *Handwörterbuch der Staatswissenschaften* (1909); Betænkning, Invaliditets- og *Alderdomsforsikringskommisjonen*. Copenhagen, 1915; H. E. Berner, "Arbeiderforsikringen i de nordiske lande," *Statsøkonomisk tidsskrift* (1894, [Kristiania] Oslo); A. Elmer, "Danmark i den svenske folkepensionsdebatten." In *Festskrift til Frederik Zeuthen*. Copenhagen, Nationalökonomisk forlag, 1958.

19. Batænkning, Invaliditets- og *Alderdomsforsikringskommisjonen.*

20. M. Rubin, *Om Alderdomsforsørgelsen.* Copenhagen, P. G. Philipsens forlag, 1891, p. 4.

21. Berner, "Arbeiderforsikringen i de nordiske lande."

22. Ibid.

23. A. Hatland, *The Future of Norwegian Social Insurance.* Oslo, Norwegian University Press, 1984.

24. Berner, "Arbeiderforsikringen i de nordiske lande." p. 138. (Author's translation.)

25. S. Ringen, "Arbeiderkommisjonene av 1885, 1894 og 1900." *Arbeidsnotat* 41 (1974), Levekårsundersøkelsen, Bergen.

26. M. Ormestad, *De sosiale trygder,* p. 30.

27. The case of Iceland (mentioned earlier in the text), where a decision seems to have been reached in a short time, should be viewed as an exceptional case. The Icelandic population was, and is, very small (78,000 inhabitants in 1901).

28. The viewpoint was expressed by the Swedish ex-Minister of Finance, Forsell, in 1884. Here quoted and translated from Elmér, "Danmark," p. 57.

29. Nationaløkonomisk forening (Denmark), Statsøkonomisk forening (Norway), Nationalekonomiska föreningen (Sweden).

30. Bergh and Hanisch, *Vitenskap og politikk; Nationalekonomiska føreningen 1877–1927, Minneskrift.* Stockholm: P. A. Norstedt & Söner, 1927.

31. Ibid., p. 16.

32. Ibid., p. 55; K. T. von Inama-Sternegg, "Der Statistische Unterricht." In Georg von Mayr, *Allgemeines Statistisches Archiv.* Tübingen, Jahrgang 1890, p. 12.

33. The Chair was established by the *Parliament,* not as a result of demand from the (only) university. Bergh and Hanisch, *Vitenskap og politikk,* p. 54.

34. S.-E. Liedman, *Den synliga handen.* Stockholm Arbetarkultur, 1986, pp. 12–69.

35. *Nationalekonomiska føreningen 1877–1927, Minneskrift;* Bergh & Hanisch, *Vitenskop og politikk.*

36. Ibid., p. 52.

37. Ibid., p. 35.

38. M. Rubin, *Om Alderdomsforsørgelsen.*

39. Bernard Lecuyer and Anthony Oberschall, "The Early History of Social Research," *International Encyclopedia of the Social Sciences* 15 (1968): pp. 36–53.

40. H. Heclo, *Modern Social Politics,* p. 182.

41. E. Bull, "Velferdsstaten i historisk perspektiv." In S. Stjernø, ed., *Velferd eller nød?* Oslo, Pax, 1982.

42. (Translated from Danish.) As expressed in the late 1880s by the Danish social democrats, P. Holm and H. Hansen, "Den nye Drøftelse af sociale Spørgsmaal 1890–94." In P. Engelstoft and H. Jensen, eds. *Sociale Studier i Dansk Historie efter 1857.* Copenhagen, Nordisk forlag, 1930.

43. A. L. Seip, *Sosialhjelpstaten blir til.* Oslo, Gyldendal, 1984, p. 281.

44. H. Heclo, *Modern Social Politics,* p. 181.

45. Seip, *Sosialhjelpstaten,* p. 89; H. Heclo, *Modern Social Politics,* p. 181.

46. Seip, *Sosialhjelpstaten.*

47. (Translated from Norwegian.) Seip, *Sosialhjelpstaten,* p. 281.

48. Ibid., p. 281.

49. H. E. Berner, "Arbeiderforsikringen i Tyskland," p. 41.

50. Ibid.

51. "The phrase captures a fundamental reality about an irresistable movement that sweeps over our politics and our society, pushing aside everything that might stand in its path," quoted from J. W. Kingdon, *Agendas, Alternatives and Public Policy.* Canada, Little Brown & Co., 1984, p. 1. An idea whose time had come "can be recognized by signs like sustained and marked changes in public opinion, repeated mobilization of people with intensely held preferences, and bandwagons onto which politicians of all persuasions climb" (ibid.). Perhaps European and Scandinavian social insurance in the last decades of the nineteenth century was an example of such an idea?

52. A. S. Orloff and T. Skocpol, "Why Not Equal Protection?"

53. P. Flora, "Quantitative Historical Sociology." *Current Sociology* XXIII (2) (1975).

54. D. S. Landes, "Statistics as a Source for the History of Economic Development in Western Europe: The Protostatical Era." In V. R. Lorwin and J. M. Price, eds., *The Dimensions of the Past.* New Haven, Yale University Press, 1972.

55. P. Flora, "Quantitative Historical Sociology."

56. H. Westergaard, *Contributions to the History of Statistics.* London, P. S. King & Son, 1932.

57. Norway and Sweden were not represented at the first international congress in Brussels in 1853, but participated in all subsequent congresses according to the Swedish *Statistisk tidsskrift,* vol. I. 1860–62, p. 290.

58. Heclo, *Modern Social Politics,* p. 42.

59. Ibid., p. 301.

60. Ibid., p. 302.

61. Ibid., pp. 181–82.

62. E. Arosenius, "The History and Origin of Swedish Official Statistics." In J. Koren, ed., *The History of Statistics: Their Development and Progress in Many Countries.* New York, Macmillan, 1918, p. 538.

63. Iceland, at that time part of Denmark, carried out the first complete "nationwide" census in 1703. See S. Kuhnle, "Statistikkens historie i Norden," *Norden förr och nu.* Stockholm, 1989.

64. Arosenius, "History and Origin," p. 542.

65. Ibid., p. 544.

66. Ibid., p. 553.

67. A. Jensen, "The History and Development of Statistics in Denmark." In Koren, *The History of Statistics,* p. 201.

68. Ibid., p. 202.

69. B. Odén, "Historisk statistikk." in B. Schiller and B. Odén, *Statistik for historiker.* Stockholm, Almqvist & Wiksell, 1970.

70. A. N. Kiær, "The History and Development of Statistics in Norway." In Koren *History of Statistics,* p. 447.

71. Ibid., p. 452.

72. NOS, ser. 11, no. 65. *Statistisk sentralbyrå gjennom 75 år.* Oslo, 1951.

73. The first volume was published in French and could not have reached much beyond elite groups.

74. Kiær, "History and Development," p. 455.

75. N. Rygg, "Statistikken," *Festschrift*. Published on the occasion of the hundredth anniversary of Det Kgl. Fredriks University, Kristiania (Oslo).

76. Seip, *Sosialhjelpstaten.*

77. SØOS 59, *Economy, Population Issues and Statistics.* Oslo, Statistick Sentralbyrå, 1985.

78. I. Thomsen, "Anders Nikolai Kiær—statistiker og samfunnsforsker." In *Statistisk sett,* anniversary publication. Oslo, Norwegian Statistical Association 1936–1986, 1986.

79. S. Rokkan, "The Production, Linkup, and Communication of Social Science Data: A Survey of Developments in Norway." University of Bergen, unpublished manuscript, 1977.

80. *Statistisk Bureaus Historie.* København, Statens Statistiske Bureau, 1899.

81. *Samfundet og statistiken. Et historisk rids 1769–1950.* Stat. Medd. 4. Række, 139 Bd., 1. Hæfte. København, 1949, p. 23.

82. *Statistisk Bureaus Historie,* pp. 112–14 (translated from Danish).

83. *Samfundet og statistiken,* p. 26 (translated from Danish).

84. SØS no. 28, *Statistisk Sentralbyrå 100 år, 1876–1976.* Oslo, Statistisk Sentralbyrå, 1976, p. 122.

85. *Statistisk Bureaus Historie,*; SØS no. 28.

86. SOU, *Bilaga till statistiksakkunnigas betänkande.* Stockholm: (SOU = Statens offentliga utredningar,) 1922, pp. 50–51.

87. H. Westergaard, *Economic Development in Denmark.* Oxford, Clarendon Press, 1922, p. 30.

88. SØS no. 28, on the history of the first thirty-five years (1876–1911) of the Norwegian Central Bureau of Statistics.

89. S. Woolf, "Statistics and the Modern State." *Society for Comparative Study of Society and History* (1989): pp. 601–4.

90. A. Holck, *Dansk statistisk historie 1800–1850.* Copenhagen: Statens statistiske Bureau, 1901, p. 16.

91. Inama-Sternegg, "Der Statistische Unterricht," pp. 23–24.

92. *Statistisk Bureaus Historie.*

93. "About the same time" is a sufficiently precise formulation for my query. If the purpose had been, for example, to perform a precise test of diffusion theory, the expression would, of course, be meaningless.

94. S. Kuhnle, *Patterns of Social and Political Mobilization. A Historical Analysis of the Nordic Countries.* Contemporary Political Sociology Series. London/Beverly Hills, Sage Publications, 1975.

95. Kuhnle, "Growth of Social Insurance Programs."

96. Ibid.

97. In the Norwegian case, hardly a year went by without the director A. N. Kiær being one of the invited speakers and among the contributors to the journal (as of 1887) of the association for economists. Bergh and Hanisch, *Vitenskap og Politikk,* p. 75.

8

Social Knowledge and the State in the Industrial Relations of Japan (1882–1940) and Great Britain (1870–1914)

SHELDON GARON

IN her introduction to *Bringing the State Back In,* Theda Skocpol criticized the tendency of many social scientists, whether pluralists or classical Marxists, to play down the role of the state as an independent actor.[1] Together with other state-centered theorists, she instead called for more discussion of the "autonomy" or "relative autonomy" of states vis-à-vis interest groups and dominant classes within civil society. Students of Japanese history and politics were interested, but not shocked. No one, of course, had to bring the Japanese state back in. Japanese Marxists themselves had long insisted on the centrality of the pre-1945 "absolutist state" or "emperor-system state," whose repressive bureaucracy, police, and military held the upper hand in a coalition with the bourgeoisie and landlords.[2] In a more positive vein, many Western scholars have portrayed the Japanese state as the engine of rapid modernization following the Meiji Restoration of 1868. Chalmers Johnson's influential study similarly highlighted the dynamic role of Ministry of International Trade and Industry officials in the postwar "economic miracle."[3]

Much less work has been done on the Japanese state's relationship to labor questions over the past century. This is unfortunate, for labor-management relations are in many respects an acid test for any government, forcing officials to choose sides or to define an independent position. Only recently have historians described the innovative labor policies during the 1920s and 1930s of a group of higher civil servants whom I have elsewhere called the "social bureaucrats."[4] Based in the Home Ministry's newly created Social Bureau, these officials took the lead in formulating and promoting legislation that would establish conciliation machinery for resolving labor disputes, repeal previous antistrike regulations, and above all guarantee the right of workers to organize unions by means of a

Note to readers: Following East Asian practice, Japanese surnames precede given names, excepting those of Japanese whose English-language works have been cited.

labor union law. Contemporary assessments of the social bureaucrats varied considerably. They themselves claimed to be acting autonomously in the interests of the state—interests which stood above those of any one class. Yet they were frequently denounced by industrialists for being the "pinkish" allies of militant labor unionism. Within the labor movement, moderate leaders praised the progressive qualities of the Social Bureau's officials, whereas left-wing activists condemned the bureau's labor legislation as a subtle means of fragmenting and controlling the unions.

The issue of state initiatives concerning labor raises a number of comparative questions that transcend Japanese history. Recent studies of the United States and European nations have similarly demonstrated the activist roles of civil servants in the development of industrial relations and welfare policies.[5] What we need now is a comparative framework that allows us to examine variations in the conditions giving rise to relatively autonomous state policies, in the methods of official intervention in industrial relations, and in the outcomes of such interventions.

Toward that end, I offer a comparison of Japan before World War II and Great Britain from roughly 1870 to 1914. The choice may seem odd in light of the two nations' very different political traditions and patterns of industrial relations. Nonetheless, the two cases yield suggestive comparisons and contrasts. As in Japan, increased industrial unrest in Britain during the 1890s aroused public awareness of a pressing "labor problem," prompting widespread calls for governmental solutions. Just as Japanese officials in the Social Bureau seized the initiative to sponsor labor reforms, a number of progressive civil servants surfaced in the Board of Trade's new Labor Department (established in 1893). They, too, worked to strengthen the bargaining power of labor by urging employers to recognize trade unions and by campaigning for a more pro-labor trade union law between 1901 and 1905. Labor Department officials also played an increasingly forceful role in settling labor disputes under the Conciliation Act of 1896.[6] In terms of social policy, it was civil servants in the Board of Trade—and not labor leaders—who proposed the path-breaking social legislation that resulted in the Trade Boards Act and Labour Exchanges Act in 1909 and the Unemployment Insurance Act in 1911.[7]

Comparisons between Japan and Britain are valid for another reason. State intervention in both nations was related to the emergence of the modern social sciences and new thinking about how best to ameliorate social problems. As officials and later scholars argued in each case, the civil servants innovated successfully in part because they enjoyed greater access to the latest in "social knowledge" than their competitors in civil society. Whether they came by their knowledge of social problems by previous study and experience or on the job, these officials became known for their expertise in the complexities of labor policy. Japanese civil servants, in particular, benefited from the diffusion of social knowledge from other nations. Indeed, to the reformist bureaucrats and liberal politicians of interwar Japan, British labor legislation served as the leading model in their attempts to establish a system of industrial relations predicted on legally protected trade unionism. I have compared the Japanese labor administration of the 1920s with Whitehall's policies *before* World War I because Japanese reformers, confronting widespread strikes and unionization for the first time, were themselves more interested in the British government's initial efforts to define roles for the trade unions and the state than in the mature system of the interwar years.

Nevertheless, for all the similarities, the outcomes of state intervention in industrial relations differed significantly in Japan and Britain. Although British trade unions experienced some setbacks in the subsequent period between the two world wars, the trend toward the state's integration of organized labor continued. In contrast, the Japanese government's movements toward a more liberal labor policy during the 1920s did not reach fruition. The government thrice failed to have its labor union bills enacted by the Diet (parliament) between 1926 and 1931. State officials, including several erstwhile social bureaucrats, subsequently played the central role in the dissolution of the nation's labor unions between 1938 and 1940.

This chapter is concerned with elucidating how bureaucratic innovation and the application of social knowledge could produce such contrasting results. The state's exposure to differing types of social knowledge, I will argue, significantly affected the policy outcomes. In addition, we must place the state's utilization of social knowledge within a broader social and political context, rather than treat the production of knowledge as an independent variable. Accordingly, this chapter first considers contextual differences in (1) conditions within each civil society (that is, relations between workers and employers); (2) each state's relationships with organized labor and employers; and (3) societal attitudes toward state intervention.

Labor Movements and Industrial Relations

A meaningful comparison of state policies toward labor necessarily begins with an examination of the labor movement and system of industrial relations within each society. Put simply, the British government's increasing accommodation of trade unionism from the mid-nineteenth century was related to the rise of a large and powerful labor movement. The Trades Union Congress counted 1.2 million members as early as 1874, and total union membership in the nation in 1892–94 has been estimated at

1,550,000. That figure rose to more than 4 million in 1913, or nearly one-fourth of the nonagricultural workforce.[8] By contrast, Japanese officials during the interwar era devised labor policies in a nation where total union membership peaked at a mere 420,000 in 1936 and where organized workers did not amount to more than eight percent of the labor force at any time before 1945. Yet as adherents of state-centered explanations rightly warn, measures of working-class strength cannot by themselves explain cross-national differences in policy.[9] The German Social Democratic Party's free trade unions rivaled British Labour in terms of national levels of unionization during the decade preceding World War I, but such strength did not lead to comparably favorable industrial relations legislation.[10] Rather than dwell on differences in working-class strength, we would do better to assess the degree of integration of each labor movement into the economy, society, and polity.

Britain

Trade unions and collective bargaining became integral parts of British industrial relations long before the state established a positive legal framework in the form of trade union acts (1871, 1875, 1906, and 1913). Combinations of journeymen existed in most craft trades by the mid-eighteenth century, and workers grew adept in the use of collective action against employers. The trade unions of the nineteenth century also inherited strong craft traditions that allowed them to regulate the labor market and the labor process more effectively than in later-industrializing societies. The emerging trade unions proved strong enough to weather the 1799–1800 Combination Acts, which codified criminal penalties against workers who formed combinations. It is noteworthy that the labor movement rapidly expanded between 1825 and 1871, despite numerous court judgments against unions. District and national federations arose to impose central control over locals. In 1868, most of the nation's unions joined together to form the Trades Union Congress, which has remained the unrivaled national labor center to this day.[11]

By adopting relatively tolerant attitudes toward unions, British employers also had a hand in furthering the integration of organized labor at the shop-floor level. Although many employers initially resented workers' combinations, growing numbers recognized the advantages of dealing with disciplined organizations that could regulate the labor market and represent workers in an orderly system of collective bargaining. According to Alan Fox, employers from the time of the original Combination Acts further "lacked the stomach, the resources and the unity for any attempt at the total destruction of worker combinations."[12] In contrast to the early unification of labor movement, management did not organize a central association until World War I, and it was a rather weak one at that. Most remarkable, even when some employers' organizations committed themselves to weakening the trade unions in the wake of the Taff Vale judgment of 1901, the majority of the nation's employers eschewed the opportunity to smash unions at the height of the depression of 1902–5. By the 1880s, most employers preferred to engage in collective bargaining with the trade unions, in return for the unions' commitments to obey the law, avoid "political" strikes, and recognize principles of ownership.[13] In short, any state intervention in British industrial relations by the 1890s had to contend with a well-functioning system of voluntary collective bargaining.

Japan

Japanese civil servants, on the other hand, formulated labor union and conciliation legislation during the 1920s when unions were just beginning to appear on a widespread basis. The relative weakness of the Japanese labor movement had much to do with the nature of Japan's industrial revolution, which did not commence until the late 1880s. A majority of the workforce consisted of young female textile operatives until the 1930s; for various reasons, including the short tenure of their employment, few were organized. Also, unlike the British trade unions, Japanese organizations suffered from a lack of craft traditions. The introduction of Western technologies following the Meiji Restoration of 1868 created entirely new trades. In the late 1890s, the first craft unions quickly folded, in part as a result of pressures from the government and employers, but primarily because they were unable to impose control over their members and the labor market.[14]

The last years of World War I witnessed the unprecedented outbreak of strikes and the organization of labor unions in Japan's rapidly expanding heavy industries and other sectors employing large numbers of skilled male workers. From less than 50,000 in 1918, the total number of unionized workers grew to more than 400,000 by the mid-1930s. The first postwar year of 1919 was filled with predictions that Japanese industrial relations were following the British path and that labor unions were there to stay. As in Britain, employers divided over strategies toward the new unions. Whereas the most powerful employers' organization remained opposed to recognizing labor unions, other influential business associations and strike-weary owners favored recognition of craft unions, at the very least, in order to establish orderly labor-management relations.[15]

As it turned out, Japanese unions did not succeed in placing themselves and collective bargaining at the center of industrial relations. During the recession years of the 1920s, most large, privately owned companies managed either to keep unions out or to oust the few that had gained footholds. Not only were the big firms able to weather strikes and lockouts, they also lured workers away from labor unions with improved benefits and job security or by organizing company unions and works councils.[16] The labor movement found itself confined to small and medium-sized firms and government-owned and public enterprises. Employers played upon the divisions within organized labor to weaken the unions further. Labor suffered a series of schisms during the 1920s, as left-wing unions withdrew from the social democratic General Federation of Labor (Sōdōmei) to protest the leadership's cautious economic unionism.

Needless to say, Japanese unions made relatively little progress in institutionalizing collective bargaining. Employers effectively blocked the labor movement's drive to establish the "right" to bargain collectively in the early 1920s. Fear of left-wing unions persuaded several companies after 1924 to conclude collective agreements with the moderate General Federation of Labor. The General Federation made further inroads during the mid-1930s, when affiliated unions negotiated a series of agreements with trade associations of small producers. However, the General Federation's collective agreements covered only 10,780 workers at their peak in 1937.[17] In Britain, by comparison, national collective agreements covered some three million workers in 1913.[18]

Given the weakness of Japanese unions and collective bargaining, Japanese bureaucrats confronted a problem not faced by their British counterparts. Industry continued to be rocked by labor disputes between 1920 and 1937, but workers and managers in most plants lacked formalized mechanisms for resolving them. As we shall see, such conditions encouraged Japanese officials to play a more interventionist role while aggressively seeking knowledge of various models of labor organization and state policy.

Political Integration of Labor and Attitudes Toward State Intervention

Britain

Governmental labor policies in both nations were affected not only by the reality of shop-floor relations, but also by the degree of labor's *political* integration vis-à-vis management. Great Britain was not the only country with a sizable labor movement by 1900, yet in few other societies did the unions achieve such a prominent position in the policymaking process. Parliamentary committees had recognized the nascent trade unions as spokesmen for local workmen as early as the 1830s and 1840s during the investigations of factory conditions.[19] Following the enfranchisement of the upper strata of workmen in 1867 and 1885, labor leaders increasingly won election to Parliament as Lib-Labs within the Liberal Party. In 1886, Henry Broadstreet, a leader of the Trades Union Congress, became the first working-class unionist to be appointed to high office (undersecretary to the Home Office), and John Burns served in the Liberal cabinet of 1906.[20]

Political inclusion was accompanied by the trade unions' participation in the state's knowledge-gathering and administrative organs. Several union leaders sat on the authoritative Royal Commission on Labour (1891–94), together with employers, politicians, and lawyers. In 1911, the Liberal government sought to institutionalize tripartite conciliation and policy formation by establishing the Industrial Council, chaired by the chief industrial commissioner and consisting of thirteen representatives each from the unions and employers.[21] Equally remarkable was the recruitment of trade unionists into the civil service itself. Of the thirteen senior labor officials in the Board of Trade between 1886 and 1914, seven had been associated with the trade unions. One, John Burnett, held the post of chief labor correspondent for over a decade, and many other union men served as local labor correspondents, factory inspectors, and justices of the peace. The Liberal governments' introduction of innovative welfare reforms between 1906 and 1914 accelerated the process of integration as large numbers of ambitious union officers became salaried administrators of trade boards, superintendents of labor exchanges, and labor advisors to the Home Office.[22]

Historians have offered several explanations for the political inclusion of the British working class. Most revolve around the willingness of the state and ruling classes to accommodate working-class demands and the labor movement's corresponding belief in the efficacy of parliamentary means to advance its interests. Compared to powerful early modern regimes in France and Prussia, the British state lacked the resources to suppress workers' combinations and popular protest. Fearing monarchical absolutism, the gentry succeeded in blocking the emergence of a national police and large standing army. The passage of the Combination Acts in 1799 and 1800 notwithstanding, the Home Office proved reluctant to prosecute trade unionists, in part because officials were loath to provoke working-class protest that they could not contain. To be sure, the central authorities occasionally gave their blessings to savage repressions of working-class associations by local magistrates, militia, and regular army units—notably in the infamous Peterloo massacre of 1819. Also, until 1871 trade unions remained vulnerable to official sanctions against making demands on employers that were backed with threats of coordinated strikes. By the middle of the nineteenth century, however, many in the ruling groups believed that the legalization of trade unions and the enfranchisement of the upper strata of workmen offered the only effective means of maintaining social stability. Most trade unionists, for their part, eagerly sought political integration, in contrast to syndicalist comrades in some other societies. By the 1860s, the trade unions were actively campaigning for the franchise, as well as lobbying Parliament for favorable legislation.[23]

The historical weakness of the bureaucratic state also helps to explain how British labor became so influential in the policymaking process. As Heclo noted, Britain stands out as a nation in which a historically strong parliament and "electorally competitive parties" after 1832 preceded the development of a modern civil service in latter half of the nineteenth century.[24] In their quest for workers' votes, Liberals and Conservatives competed to expand the franchise and sponsor labor legislation. By 1900, businessmen had lost much of their former power in the Liberal Party, replaced by Lib-Labs and an assertive group of "social radicals" who pressed later Liberal governments to support the demands of the labor movement.[25] There were, to be sure, some instances of progressive civil servants promoting health and social security policies in advance of the Labour and Liberal parties. Within the realm of industrial relations legislation, however, the state generally responded to pressures from the unions and their supporters in Parliament. In the cases of both the Trade Union Act of 1871 and the Trade Disputes Act of 1906, Parliament granted the unions significantly greater concessions than those recommended by either the preliminary royal commissions or the civil servants who drafted the legislation.[26]

Lastly, it should be noted that the British working class distinguished between Parliament and "the state." Although labor leaders made every effort to influence public policy, they by no means viewed the state as the protector of their interests vis-à-vis employers. Regarding themselves as "free-born Englishmen," workers since the eighteenth century instead claimed certain "liberties" or "immunities" from the monarchical state. The trade unions neither demanded nor did governments sponsor a comprehensive trade union act by which the state would punish employers who denied workers the right to organize unions.[27] The British labor movement generally conceived of parliamentary action as a means of *limiting* anti-union interventions by other segments of the state—that is, the judiciary, the police, and the House of Lords. The Trade Union Act of 1871 and the Conspiracy and Protection of Property Act of 1875 stopped the courts from applying common-law injunctions against criminal conspiracy and "restraint of trade" to the acts of trade union activity and peaceful picketing. After several courts and the House of Lords ruled in the 1901 Taff Vale judgment that unions were liable for claims for damages resulting from actions of their officers and members, Parliament enacted the Trade Disputes Act of 1906, which conferred total immunity upon unions engaging in industrial actions. The Trade Union Act of 1913 similarly aimed to weaken the House of Lord's Osborne judgment, which had prevented trade unions from using members' dues for political purposes. The state's role, as viewed by the mainstream of the labor movement, was simply to guarantee that the trade unions be allowed to compete, legally unimpaired, with employers in the process of collective bargaining.

Organized labor was equally wary about the introduction of compulsory arbitration and conciliation of industrial disputes by the government. It is true that a few of the weaker unions—notably Ben Tillet's dockworkers and the railway employees—consistently favored state intervention in wage determination from the 1890s because they had failed to secure employers' recognition and collective bargaining agreements on their own. In their desire to curb rank-and-file militancy, some craft union leaders also called for a law to enforce wage agreements resulting from collective bargaining. Stronger unions in the Trades Union Congress, on the other hand, easily defeated a resolution proposing compulsory arbitration in 1906 for the eighth year in a row.[28] Although trade union leaders increasingly supported mediation and arbitration efforts by Board of Trade officials after 1905, the Trades Union Congress and most Labour Party politicians between 1910 and 1914 opposed proposals to enforce "cooling-off" periods or to make agreements legally binding. They feared that such compulsion would inhibit the spread of collective bargaining.[29]

Nor were the majority of British industrialists eager for unilateral intervention by Board of Trade officials, whom they regarded as friends of labor. Suspicions of state compulsion by both labor and management were decisive in the making of the Conciliation Act of 1896, which pointedly rejected proposals for obligatory mediation and binding arbitration.[30] Amid the strike wave of 1910–13, many employers did advocate compulsory arbitration or curbs on the right to strike, but the Board of Trade refused to impose penal sanctions against dispute actions to avoid inflaming the labor movement.[31] In sum, a politically potent labor movement and the aversion to state intervention on the part of both labor and employers severely constrained truly autonomous actions by the British state.

Japan

The Japanese state's more intrusive role in industrial relations during the 1920s and 1930s reflected both Japanese society's greater acceptance of state initiatives and organized labor's inability to gain more than marginal political influence. Unlike their British counterparts in the 1830s and

1840s, the Japanese officials charged with drafting a factory law systematically consulted business associations between 1882 and 1911 while pointedly ignoring the early unions. The government did not invite any labor union leaders to sit on its two Higher Councils on Agriculture, Commerce, and Industry, which considered factory legislation in 1896 and 1898. The councils consisted solely of representatives from business, the bureaucracy, and the academic community. Nor were unionists permitted to testify before the special committee that put the finishing touches on the government's Factory Law of 1911.[32]

With the franchise confined to less than three percent of the population before 1919, workers remained effectively excluded from the Diet as well. In 1900, the Home Ministry drafted and the Diet overwhelmingly approved the Police Law (Chian Keisatsuhō), whose Article 17 prohibited the act of "instigating or inciting" others to strike, join unions, or engage in collective bargaining. Unlike Britain's Combination Acts, Article 17 did not outlaw unions per se, but the police extensively employed the provision and other laws against striking workers over the next two decades. The following year a group of labor leaders and intellectuals founded the Social Democratic Party, whose moderate reformist platform was influenced by the German Social Democratic Party and the American social gospel. The party survived a mere half day before the home minister ordered its dissolution.[33] The state further denied workers permission to form producers' cooperatives under the 1899 Industrial Cooperatives Law, even though conservative governments in nineteenth-century Europe sometimes encouraged producers' cooperatives as an alternative to socialist associations. The Meiji-era regime, observed one prewar scholar, apparently feared that any "such working-class organization might lead to the spreading of the socialist ideal in Japan."[34]

During the period between the world wars, higher civil servants and bourgeois politicians took steps to incorporate the expanding labor movement. The Home Ministry's progressive officials championed measures for universal manhood suffrage, a labor union law, and the abolition of the repressive Article 17. The government granted labor unions official recognition in 1924, when it agreed that Japan's workers' delegate to the annual conferences of the International Labor Organization be elected solely by the large labor unions, not by unorganized workers as before. Beginning in 1923, the Social Bureau of the Home Ministry formally consulted labor unions when drafting legislation and the ordinances that implemented statutes, and in 1930 Abe Isoo became the first social democratic politician to be appointed to an official commission on social policy.[35]

The enactment of universal manhood suffrage in 1925 introduced the possibility of a "Lib-Lab" alliance as a means of integrating labor into the political order. One of the two major bourgeois parties, the Kenseikai (later reorganized as the Minseitō), had been courting the working class since 1920 with a program that included manhood suffrage, a labor union bill, and workers' health insurance. In 1926, a Kenseikai cabinet joined with Social Bureau officials to repeal Article 17 and to enact the Labor Disputes Conciliation Law. Kenseikai and Minseitō governments also tried but failed to secure parliamentary approval for a labor union law in 1926, 1927, and 1931. In the first parliamentary election held under universal manhood suffrage in 1928, many working-class voters apparently preferred the reformist Minseitō to the fledgling socialist parties. Only eight labor and socialist candidates from three different "proletarian parties" won election to the Lower House. Within the Diet, the Minseitō promoted labor and social legislation in alliance with the recently founded Social Democratic Party, which represented most of the nation's labor unions.[36]

By 1938, however, it was clear that the Japanese labor movement had not become effectively incorporated into either the bourgeois parliamentary order or the state structure. A brief comparison with the British experience helps to illustrate why. The difference between the two states is central. Whereas the relatively weak British state accommodated working-class assertiveness in the absence of a potent police force, the newly centralized Japanese state after 1868 rapidly established a French-style national police, which it freely used to suppress popular movements.[37] At their most repressive, Britain's Combination Acts and court decisions placed nonviolent trade union activities in the category of conspiracies ("in restraint of trade"). By contrast, the antilabor provisions of Japan's Police Law were part of a law that proscribed numerous "threats" to the entire social order—including the mere attendance at political meetings by women and minors. Although the Home Ministry (which controlled the police) adopted a more accommodating labor policy after 1919, officials continued to harass and occasionally disband labor unions that they regarded as anarcho-syndicalist or associated with the outlawed Communist Party. If, as some suggest, the British labor movement's avoidance of radical ideologies was in response to the tolerant attitudes of the ruling classes, the fragmentation of Japanese labor during the 1920s into potent anarcho-syndicalist and Communist blocs, as well as a social democratic group, conversely was related to the state's policies of blatantly repressing radical activists while patronizing the moderates.

The strength of the Japanese state also accounts in part for why the surviving labor moderates during the 1930s looked to the bureaucracy for integration, rather than to the relatively liberal Minseitō party. In terms of historical sequence, the Japanese case was the inverse of the British. A powerful, knowledgeable civil service had emerged in late-nineteenth-century Japan *before* the formation of cohesive parliamentary parties in

1900–1913 and well before the introduction of universal manhood suffrage after 1925. Government officials first proposed factory legislation nearly a decade before the establishment of the Diet in 1890, and the nascent bourgeois parties could not form cabinets of their own until 1918. Moreover, the bureaucracy succeeded in remaining relatively insulated from infiltration by the parties. Civil service regulations severely restricted the appointments of those outside the civil service, requiring that even bureau chiefs and administrative vice-ministers be selected from the ranks of career bureaucrats.[38]

As a result, key posts in Japan's labor agencies were closed not only to the parties' experts, but also to the type of moderate union leader recruited by governing parties in Britain. I have argued elsewhere that the parties possessed some degree of policy expertise and innovation in the persons of former civil servants, professors, and journalists—as witnessed by the Kenseikai's formulation of labor legislation while in opposition in 1920.[39] Once in power, however, the Kenseikai and Minseitō largely deferred to the initiatives of the Social Bureau, which proposed stronger measures to protect the rights to organize and bargain collectively.

The British Liberal Party, it will be remembered, went beyond the recommendations of Board of Trade officials in enacting the 1906 Trade Disputes Act to please its working-class supporters. The Kenseikai/Minseitō, on the other hand, significantly weakened the Social Bureau's progressive draft labor union bills in both 1925 and 1931, hoping to placate the business community. Japanese employers enjoyed much greater influence within the major bourgeois parties (Kenseikai/Minseitō and Seiyūkai) than their British comrades. In 1931, employers united into a central association, the National Federation of Industrial Organizations (Zensanren). Their nationwide campaign resulted in the defeat of the Minseitō cabinet's labor union bill in the House of Peers that year. Employers' associations also stopped the Minseitō cabinet from instituting a system of tripartite consultation, modeled after Britain's 1928 Mond-Turner talks, which would have involved equal numbers of labor and managerial representatives.[40]

Faced with hostile employers and an undependable liberal party, most interwar Japanese unions placed an extraordinary degree of trust in the bureaucratic state's capacity to protect them. Whereas British workers shared the public's suspicions of "positive government," Japan's mainstream labor leaders echoed the rest of society's convictions that higher civil servants were more knowledgeable and "progressive" than the other elites.[41] Rather than demanding piecemeal immunities from state actions, the labor movement sought a comprehensive labor union law by which the government would prevent employers from denying workers the right to organize and would also enforce the provisions of collective agreements.

The Japanese unions' reliance on state intervention was most apparent in their support of official mediation and arbitration of industrial disputes. To be sure, most labor federations, like their British counterparts, opposed the enactment of a labor disputes conciliation law in 1926 because it required a cooling-off period in public-sector disputes. Once the conciliation machinery was put in place, however, the General Federation of Labor and other moderate unions increasingly regarded the government's conciliation officers and ordinary policemen as sympathetic allies, particularly as unions proved incapable of defending themselves. In practice, workers and unions more commonly requested mediation than did employers.[42] By the 1930s, labor leaders so welcomed state intervention that they proposed amendments to the Labor Disputes Conciliation Law that would grant authorities the power to order conciliation proceedings and to arbitrate in any dispute, not only those in public enterprises.[43] Most employers, on the other hand, opposed compulsory conciliation and arbitration, although some employers' associations did favor a total ban on strikes in response to labor unrest in 1919–20 and 1930–31. During the 1930s, businessmen repeatedly complained about the alleged pro-labor bias of officials as the police intervened with greater frequency to settle disputes.[44]

To sum up, bureaucratic innovation may occur in any society, yet its impact is most significant in a nation like Japan where groups outside the bureaucracy—unions, employers, and political parties—seem incapable of solving a social problem. It is in such circumstances that social knowledge plays a substantial role in altering past policies and restructuring relationships in civil society.

Bureaucratic Innovation and Social Knowledge

A comparison of the Japanese and British cases demonstrates significant variations in the relation of social knowledge and state actions. Ironically, scholars have studied this theme in greater depth for Britain, where bureaucratic innovation before 1914 was the exception, than in the case of Japan, which boasted a powerful higher civil service.

Britain

Several recent studies invoke the concept of social knowledge to explain why Britain's Board of Trade played an innovative role in industrial relations and social security policies between 1886 and 1916. They further ponder why the Home Office and the Local Government Board did so little. Prior to 1886, the Board of Trade held few responsibilities for labor matters, while the Home Office oversaw industrial relations and factory inspection and the Local Government Board dealt with unemployment and poor relief. Roger Davidson and others have pointed to three factors in the rise of the Board of Trade. First, they assert that

> the correlation between innovation and recruitment patterns in late Victorian and Edwardian social administration closely conforms to that posited by organisational theorists. At the Board of Trade, labour officials were receptive to new functions and the formulation of fresh policy initiatives rather than a passive adherence to precedent. They were problem-orientated rather than career-orientated.[45]

The Home Office and the Local Government Board recruited their social administrators by open competitive examinations and tended to hire the "generalist" graduates of Oxbridge—the majority of whom arrived without specialized knowledge of social problems. On the other hand, the Board of Trade's senior labor officials were not appointed by examination, but were laterally recruited, usually from outside the government, for their expertise in industrial relations, social statistics, unemployment, or investigation of working conditions.

Second, the recruitment of specialists exposed the Board of Trade to new ideas of reform then current in British universities and among social workers and industrial relations experts. Most senior labor officials in the Board of Trade had been influenced by such thinkers as T. H. Green, Alfred Marshall, and Stanley Jevons, who challenged the tenets of orthodox economics. Rebelling against prevailing British beliefs in limited government, these civil servants advocated greater state intervention in improving the conditions of the working class and the poor. Several had been active in assisting the trade unions and had participated in Charles Booth's famous surveys of poverty, the "new Oxford movement" of the 1880s, the University Settlement Movement, or the radical wing of the Liberal Party. Hubert Llewellyn Smith, who served as the first commissioner of labor (1893–1907), was a dynamic case in point.[46]

Lastly, Davidson and Heclo (concerning the Boards of Trade in both Britain and Sweden) make the case for the innovative role of social statistics.[47] In their view, the Board of Trade became the leading labor office after 1886 because it already possessed the finest statistical and research department in the British government. In 1885, the Board's statisticians allied with the Royal Statistical Society to lobby for an agency that would compile accurate statistics on the state of trade, wages, and labor supply so that the government could "form sound judgements as to the relative claims of capital and labour."[48] The Board's statistically oriented Labour Bureau was established in 1886, followed by a full-fledged Labour Department in 1893. It was on the basis of their agency's superior labor statistics and intelligence gathering, concludes this argument, that the Labour Department's progressive statisticians—led by Llewellyn Smith—persuaded the public of their "impartiality" and "objectivity" in intervening in industrial relations.[49]

Japan

Davidson and Lowe may have noted a strong correlation between innovation and recruitment patterns in the British case, but the Japanese bureaucracy's acquisition of social knowledge raises serious questions about the causal nature of this relationship. The Home Ministry's reformist "social bureaucrats" were the very type of generalists that British scholars and organizational theorists have assumed would not be innovative. In the Home Ministry, as in most Japanese agencies, higher civil servants were usually recruited straight out of the two leading national universities, Tokyo and Kyoto Imperial Universities, on the basis of competitive civil service examinations in administration. The most able young men thereupon rose within the ministry as generalist administrative officers (*jimukan*). Such a system depended on the expertise of numerous lower-ranking "technical officers" (*gijutsukan*) and part-time "commissioned officers" (*shokutaku*), who were usually appointed because of outside experience. Yet these specialists were seldom promoted to the influential policymaking position of section or bureau chief.[50]

In terms of educational training, rarely did the higher civil servants come to their posts with any specialized knowledge of labor or social problems. Nearly to the man, the elite bureaucrats who championed new labor policies in the 1920s had graduated from Tokyo University's Faculty of Law with concentrations in either law or politics. Economics was but a minor part of their studies. Indeed, the higher civil service examination system played a prominent role in retarding the development of the social sciences in Japanese universities. As explained by Robert Spaulding, the government in the 1880s adopted the German model of civil service, in which higher examinations "produced officials whose specialty was administering the law."[51] At the same time, Tokyo University—followed by most other imperial and private colleges—subordinated the teaching of economics by placing the field in the Faculty of Law. The economics curriculum stagnated as "students of law and political science took only survey courses in economics since the Higher Examinations required nothing more."[52] In 1919, Tokyo University established an autonomous Faculty of Economics, which soon became a center for the study of social statistics and Marxist theory.[53] However, few of its graduates entered the Home Ministry or other ministries. If anything, the weight of economics in the training of bureaucrats decreased after the economists moved to their own department. Some aspiring candidates within the Faculty of Law did take courses on social policy (*shakai seisaku*), but as late as the 1930s social policy was merely an elective in the politics curriculum and not a part of the law curriculum.[54]

Furthermore, unlike the British Board of Trade, the Home Ministry was probably the *least* specialized agency—functioning more as a general staff for domestic administration. Once in the Home Ministry, higher civil servants, including the labor officials of the Social Bureau, regularly transferred to posts in other bureaus handling the administration of the police, local government, public health, State Shinto shrines, and public works. Only one administrative officer, Kitaoka Juitsu, a long-time chief of the factory inspection section, served continuously within the Labor Division of the Social Bureau from 1922 to 1938.[55]

Nevertheless, several of the Home Ministry's elite generalists rapidly acquired expertise in industrial relations, whether in the Social Bureau or the police. One historian has called the government's earlier proponents of the 1911 Factory Law "bureaucrat-intellectuals," and the label applies equally well to their interwar successors.[56] These were men who might publish massive tomes on labor policy, as well as numerous essays in erudite journals of social policy and public administration.[57] Their success in gaining social knowledge was not only pivotal in rising to the top ranks of the Home Ministry, it also enhanced their influence vis-à-vis employers, labor leaders, and members of parliament. The prewar Diet, it should be noted, lacked standing committees that might have rivaled the expertise of the bureaucracy. Its special committees were confined to a single parliamentary session, and they seldom launched independent investigations. In Britain, on the other hand, parliamentary select committees mushroomed in the first half of the nineteenth century, contributing to an "unprecedented increase in governmental investigation."[58]

Counterintuitive as it may seem, the social bureaucrats' expertise in labor policy derived in part from their general training in law. Although the higher civil servants analyzed results of social surveys and frequently met with representatives of employers and workers, their primary response to rising labor problems was to draft new laws to govern industrial relations. The drafting of the Home Ministry's first labor union bill in 1919 illustrated their profound faith in the transformative powers of legal knowledge. Charged with drawing up the legislation, Nambara Shigeru, a twenty-nine-year-old administrative official in the Police Bureau, proceeded to do what Japanese bureaucrats did best. He surveyed the ministry's newest graduates from Tokyo University, deliberately selecting three who had studied English, German, and French law, respectively. The team intensively researched the leading labor statutes of the world before completing their own union bill.[59]

Nambara's story also demonstrates how growing knowledge among the social bureaucrats owed much to their greater access to transnational information and models. Toward the end of World War I, the Home Ministry institutionalized the practice of sending its brightest young officials on one- to two-year tours to study social and police administration in Europe and the United States. There, they gravitated toward surveying labor unions, social welfare, electoral reforms, and police tactics toward labor movements and leftist organizations. Upon returning, several became powerful advocates of recognizing labor unions, granting manhood suffrage, and improving welfare services.[60] In addition, during the 1920s the Social Bureau and the semigovernmental Kyōchōkai (Harmonization Society) built up excellent libraries of up-to-date materials on labor issues. The Kyōchōkai devoted a large share of its resources to statistics gathering, detailed surveys of social and labor conditions at home and abroad, and translations of works by Western scholars.[61]

The systematic incorporation of Western legislative models unquestionably propelled Japanese labor policy in a more coherent, and during the 1920s in a more liberal, direction than would have otherwise been the case. Social Bureau officials drew heavily on the British model when drafting their labor union bills. A rising young official named Yasui Eiji made a thorough investigation of arbitration laws in New Zealand and Australia. In the end he framed the 1926 Labor Disputes Conciliation Law on the basis of Canada's Industrial Disputes Investigation Act (1907) because the latter gave the state the power to order conciliation and a cooling-off period in disputes affecting the public interest.[62] The social bureaucrats' eagerness to formulate policies based on transnational knowledge contrasts with the general reluctance of British Board of Trade officials to adopt features of Australasian and Canadian conciliation laws between 1896 and 1914.[63]

Few of the reformist bureaucrats learned much about labor questions in the course of higher education, yet once in their posts they benefited from institutional and sometimes personal associations with academic specialists. The long struggle to enact the Factory Law of 1911 received critical support from the emerging social sciences. Despite the subordination of economics to law at Tokyo University, two economics professors, Kanai Noburu and Kuwata Kumazō, established the field of social policy in the Faculty of Law during the 1890s. They self-consciously espoused the ideas of Germany's "young historical school" with its emphasis on *Sozialpolitik*. Like the German scholars, Kanai's group rejected the Manchester school's doctrine of laissez-faire, positing the obligation of the "social state" to protect workers and the rest of society's weak from the ravages of industrialization. In 1897, Kanai, Kuwata, and like-minded economists at other institutions founded the Japanese Social Policy Association (Nihon Shakai

Seisaku Gakkai), which was modeled after Germany's Verein für Sozialpolitik. The association lobbied vigorously for the passage of a factory law and during the 1910s called on the state to recognize the rights of workers to organize themselves.[64]

Not many higher civil servants were willing to recognize unions before 1919, but officials increasingly relied on the professors of social policy for advice on labor questions. The Ministry of Agriculture and Commerce invited Kanai Noburu to serve on a commission examining factory legislation in 1898, and his forceful arguments helped firm the ministry's resolve to promote a measure that more fully protected workers. Kuwata Kumazō began participating in the Home Ministry's poor relief campaigns as a salaried employee in 1908, and he was an active member of nearly every governmental deliberative commission on labor legislation in the 1910s and 1920s.[65] He also briefly served as an executive director of the semi-governmental Kyōchōkai foundation. A small, yet influential, group of bureaucrats strengthened its ties to the scholars by attending and occasionally presenting papers at the Social Policy Association's annual conferences. Oka Minoru, a member of the association and the bureau chief responsible for framing the Factory Law, highlighted the alliance between officials and the professors in the early advancement of social knowledge:

> Our nation's Factory Law was championed almost exclusively by the government and academic experts. It did not result from bargaining with workers or their organizations. Nor did the parties ever deal with it as a political problem. It was purely a question of the protection of labor.[66]

The close relationships between the bureaucrats and academic experts are hardly surprising. The Japanese state played a powerful role in organizing social knowledge before 1945, and the first generation of social policy experts looked to the government for funding and sometimes employment. Tokyo University and the other imperial universities were originally established "to teach the sciences and the arts and to probe their mysteries in accordance with the needs of the state."[67] Decisions to expand the teaching of social policy or to create a separate faculty of economics ultimately rested with the Ministry of Education. In the 1920s and 1930s, the Kyōchōkai's journal, *Shakai seisaku jihō* (Social policy review), was the largest of its type, patronizing the nation's social policy scholars in order to provide the government with the latest information on labor questions both at home and abroad.

The state similarly dominated in the realm of social surveys. Whereas the great surveys of the urban working class in Britain were privately sponsored by individuals like Charles Booth and Henry Mayhew, the government commissioned most comparable investigations in Japan. The Ministry of Agriculture and Commerce employed such outside specialists as Professor Kuwata Kumazō and the investigative reporter Yokoyama Gennosuke to produce the comprehensive survey, *Shokkō jijō* (The condition of factory workers), in 1903.[68] The Home Ministry's Bureau of Hygiene hired a crusading physician, Ishihara Osamu, who hastened the passage of the Factory Law with the findings of his study, *Jokō to kekka* (Factory women and tuberculosis, 1913).[69] In October 1918, the home minister recruited Takano Iwasaburō, a social statistician at Tokyo University, to direct a major survey of a working-class neighborhood, even though Takano was one of the most ardent proponents of labor unions in the Social Policy Association.[70]

The partnership between the social policy experts and the bureaucrats underwent major changes after 1920. Leading scholars in the Social Policy Association divided so sharply over the questions of working with the government, and especially over how to deal with the burgeoning labor movement, that the society ceased to function in 1924. Under the growing influence of Marxism following the Bolshevik Revolution, many younger faculty members and students began to challenge the state's near monopoly over social knowledge. Yet Marxist ideology was not the only stimulus. Public consciousness of the "labor question" after World War I coincided with a general pluralization of organized knowledge in the form of numerous private study groups and research institutions.[71] The larger labor federations and unions employed professionals to survey local working conditions and study the methods of successful Western unions, while powerful, newly formed federations of employers funded research on American and European personnel policies.[72] Many specialists emerged outside the government's networks as journalism expanded, private universities proliferated, and the parliamentary parties sought out policy experts with the advent of party-led cabinets in 1918.

The state's largest rival in the investigation of labor problems was the Ōhara Institute for Social Problems Research (Ōhara Shakai Mondai Kenkyūjo). Founded in 1919 by the textile magnate and Christian philanthropist Ōhara Magosaburō, the institute became a bastion for Marxian social scientists under the direction of Takano Iwasaburō. Professor Takano formalized his break with the government's social policy establishment in 1920 by resigning from Tokyo University. Several younger members of the Faculty of Economics followed their mentor into the institute—notably Morito Tatsuo and Ōuchi Hyōe. Drawing on the services of numerous university-trained research associates, the Ōhara Institute specialized in reporting on labor unions and working conditions, publishing the authoritative *Nihon rōdō nenkan* (Japan labor yearbook). The organization also competed with the Social Bureau and Kyōchōkai in its huge collection of foreign books and by regularly sending personnel to study Western labor conditions.

Generally critical of the Home Ministry's labor programs, the Ōhara Institute's relations with state officials were at times marked by extreme antagonism. In 1920, the government pressured Morito Tatsuo to resign from Tokyo University after charging and then convicting him and his publisher Ōuchi Hyōe for printing an essay on the anarchist ideas of Kropotkin. In addition, Takano and other institute members supported the Japan Labor-Farmer Party and the left-center wing of the union movement, prompting the police to investigate and harass Ōhara Institute members for alleged ties to the outlawed Communist Party in 1928 and thereafter.[73]

Some have argued that academic influence in labor policymaking substantially declined after 1920 because of ideological cleavages and the rise of nongovernmental centers of social knowledge; the social bureaucrats had, moreover, grown more knowledgeable and had less reason to deputize professors than had their predecessors.[74] Yet the borders between the state and the academic specialists remained porous. The essentially generalist administrative officials continued to rely on expertise in the universities, and many scholars, for their part, spent considerable time trying to influence policy formation through formal and informal channels. The bureaucracy's lines of communication with leftist and liberal scholars were not totally severed, even after the Ministry of Justice successfully prosecuted Morito Tatsuo and Ōuchi Hyōe in 1920. While the case was on appeal, the two, plus some eight other progressive economists, invited the Home Ministry's Nambara Shigeru to the Tokyo University faculty club to discuss the Nambara's draft labor union bill. According to Nambara, the scholars welcomed both the measure and the enlightened spirit sweeping the Home Ministry.[75]

Home Ministry officials continued to employ the services of older, more conservative professors, such as Kuwata Kumazō, who looked to the state to encourage the development of "sound," nonmilitant unions. But the Social Bureau also consulted some of the most outspoken advocates of rights for labor unions. The bureau's advisory council (*sanyokai*) functioned as the most direct conduit, comprised of high-ranking officials from the relevant ministries and roughly equal numbers of employers and scholars. The council's academic specialists during the 1920s and early 1930s included not only Kuwata, but also two prominent left-liberal professors, the economist Fukuda Tokuzō (Tokyo Higher Commercial School), and the labor law scholar Suehiro Izutarō (Tokyo University). Though not formally empowered, the advisory council frequently revised the Social Bureau's draft legislation and killed a few measures outright.[76] The panel's scholars played a dual role in making bills more favorable to workers and in allying with progressive officials to overcome the opposition of the employers' delegates, notably to the Social Bureau's liberal draft union bills in

1925 and 1929. In the relatively pluralistic setting of the 1920s, professors like Suehiro Izutarō sought to influence governmental policy both as "insiders" and "outsiders."[77] When the Kenseikai party's cabinet weakened the Social Bureau's draft union bill in 1926, Suehiro went public in the liberal daily, the *Tōkyō asahi shimbun,* with a serialized critique of what he bitterly termed "the bill to control labor unions."[78] The legal scholar nonetheless retained his paid position on the advisory council, and a cabinet led by the same party appointed him to serve on the Commission on Social Policy, which recommended a progressive union bill in 1929.

Although the social bureaucrats shared the rest of the government's hostility toward Communism, they often exchanged knowledge with experts considered to be Marxists. One former assistant factory inspector recalled that the Social Bureau and the Ōhara Institute for Social Problems Research routinely put aside ideological differences to share labor statistics.[79] Following the dissolution of the Japanese Social Policy Association, Takano Iwasaburō of the Ōhara Institute cofounded the International Labor Association (Kokusai Rōdō Kyōkai) in 1925 to support the work of the International Labor Organization and to lobby for labor legislation. Later renamed the Social Legislation Association (Shakai Rippō Kyōkai), the group functioned much like the earlier Social Policy Association, periodically bringing together several social bureaucrats, academic specialists, union leaders, socialist politicians, and a few industrialists.[80] The Social Bureau's substantial exposure to academic expertise unquestionably contributed to the agency's progressive orientation during the interwar era.

Types of Social Knowledge: Economics versus Police Knowledge

Most analyses of social knowledge have taken Britain, the United States, or Sweden as their subjects, and they tend to assume that the actual content of the knowledge acquired by the state does not significantly differ from society to society. However, this comparison of Japan and Britain makes clear that the policy outcomes vary considerably according to (1) the nature of the knowledge applied and (2) the type of state agency that seeks to innovate.

In Britain, the United States, and several other nations, specialized labor offices originated in those agencies dealing with labor matters as questions of economics or commerce and industry. Senior labor officials in Britain were also responsible for the Board of Trade's commercial and industrial administration, and they invariably considered the wage demands of the trade unions in light of the overall economy, the labor market, and the return on capital. Not surprisingly, British labor bureaucrats were selected for their expertise in economics or statistics. Moreover, in enforcing the 1896 Conciliation Act, the understaffed Labour Department relied on a small handpicked group of umpires and conciliators, primarily drawn from the professional and middle classes. They were generally appointed for their knowledge of the state of trade, wage differentials, productivity statistics, and the costs and profit margins of companies. With an eye toward maintaining British competitiveness, the Board of Trade informally communicated wage guidelines to these mediators. As Davidson noted, Board of Trade officials might have been critics of orthodox economics, but they were hardly socialists. Their training in economics led them to maintain faith in the primacy of market forces and the economic (versus the social) determination of wages.[81]

In the cases of interwar Japan and tsarist Russia, on the other hand, labor administration was handled almost entirely by agencies associated with the police.[82] Once again, Japan appears to be the inverse of Britain. Whereas the British Home Office, a law enforcement department, had been the primary labor agency during most of the nineteenth century, in Japan the Ministry of Agriculture and Commerce, which promoted industrial development, originally held responsibility for labor policy before World War I. Curiously enough, the Ministry of Agriculture and Commerce lost control over labor policy to the Home Ministry in 1920–22 because Japanese leaders believed that the labor question could no longer be confronted from the narrow perspective of industry and economics.

The Home Ministry's takeover of labor administration represented in a very real sense the triumph of "social" over "economic" knowledge, for its claims rested on the agency's experience in maintaining social order, safeguarding the general welfare, and shaping the public's values. In his case against the Ministry of Agriculture and Commerce's rival draft labor union bill in 1920, the chief of the Police Bureau explained that his Home Ministry could enforce controls over legally recognized unions more effectively than Agriculture and Commerce. He also insisted that Home Ministry officials, unlike their economically oriented rivals, understood the demands of workers "to be recognized as human beings" who required betterment "not only materially, but spiritually."[83] As one liberal newspaper noted approvingly, the Home Ministry approached the labor question in "human terms as a Social Problem in which laborers are the same as labor," whereas the Ministry of Commerce and Industry (successor to Agriculture and Commerce) viewed labor "industrially as one element in production."[84]

Significantly, middle-ranking police officials from the Police Bureau were the first to recommend and draft progressive labor union legislation shortly after World War I, and several veterans of the Social Bureau went on to high-level positions in the police agencies. The postwar surge in labor organization and popular protest convinced many police administrators that maintaining the indiscriminate repression of the past would tax their undermanned forces and antagonize the working class. They also argued that the demands of employers, if left unchecked by the state, would so radicalize the workers as to conflict with the Home Ministry's ultimate responsibility for preserving social order. The strategy of tolerating and occasionally encouraging labor unions and social democratic parties instead offered the possibility of converting workers into supporters of the existing order.[85]

The differing influences of economics versus law-enforcement knowledge are best seen in the operation of each nation's conciliation and arbitration machinery. In contrast to the British case, knowledge of statistics and economics played little role in mediation efforts by the Japanese state. Official mediation during the interwar period was generally performed by regular police officers and after 1926 by full-time conciliation officers, who had also been trained as policemen. During the two decades before the Home Ministry took control of labor administration, the task of gathering detailed statistics on wages and working conditions rested with the Ministry of Agriculture and Commerce and statistical agencies under the cabinet. The government placed a statistics section in the newly created Social Bureau, but it compiled labor statistics for less than two years before its functions reverted to the Cabinet Statistical Bureau and the Ministry of Commerce and Industry in 1925. From the 1890s to 1945, the Home Ministry specialized in gathering only those labor statistics that would appeal to an interventionist police—that is, the counting and classifying of labor disputes and labor unions.[86] The Home Ministry's directives to prefectural conciliation officers rarely mentioned guidelines for wage determination nor urged coordination with the government's statistical and commercial agencies.

Japanese police mediators instead emphasized considerations of social peace in their settlement of disputes. This might mean heavy-handed harassment of allegedly Communist union organizers and fellow travelers, yet it just as often involved official pressure on employers to rehire laid-off workers or grant reasonable severance pay. From the time of the Great Depression in 1930–31, the Home Ministry utilized police arbitration as a major program against unemployment. By the mid-1930s, police reports commonly linked the resolution of labor disputes to the companies' provision of retirement or severance pay and other welfare benefits. Ordinary policemen—rather than professional conciliation officers—mediated in a majority of the labor disputes settled by conciliation in 1935 and 1936, intervening in most cases without requests from either side.[87] Japanese scholars have aptly termed such practices "saber mediation."

Policy Outcomes and Conclusions

Try as they might, studies of social knowledge in Britain, the United States, and Sweden have allowed a certain whiggishness to slip in. The organizers of one such project on the state and social investigation recently concluded:

> In retrospect, the most important institutional legacy of social empiricism in both Britain and the United States was the creation of new state capacities, embodied in public agencies . . . , which were charged with monitoring the conditions of various segments of the populace, recommending preventive or protective legislation, and eventually administering social welfare legislation.[88]

Indeed, it may be difficult to avoid the conclusion that interrelationships between the social sciences and the state have led to improved social welfare and more stable industrial relations in these societies. The present volume confines itself to the origins of modern social polices before the 1930s, but would such a conclusion remain valid if we also included the cases of authoritarian Japan (1932–45), Fascist Italy, Nazi Germany, and Vichy France?

I have argued that the state's access to social knowledge in Britain was one of several factors explaining the direction of governmental labor policy between 1870 and 1914. Although the Board of Trade's Labour Department unquestionably advanced a set of innovative programs, its policies nonetheless supported general trends within British industrial relations toward collective bargaining between organized workers and employers. Neither employers nor most trade unionists expected the state to restructure industrial relations or to protect them from their adversaries. The economic and statistical nature of the Board of Trade's social knowledge further supported an existing capitalist order predicated on market forces and the maintenance of managerial prerogatives. When we consider that Japan's "generalist" administrative officers played an equally or perhaps more innovative role than the Board of Trade's "specialists," the specialized training and previous experience of civil servants may be a less important explanatory variable for bureaucratic reformism than the sociopolitical context and the content of the social knowledge applied.

In the Japan of the 1930s, we witness a case of what can happen when relatively autonomous bureaucrats deal with crises by relying on social knowledge that is divorced from actual conditions in civil society. The Home Ministry's social bureaucrats faced the problem of stabilizing industrial relations in lieu of a well-integrated labor movement. Weak political parties, societal acceptance of state interventions, and unusually good access to the transnational diffusion of social knowledge led to the state's bold search for new forms of industrial relations. During the 1920s, the social bureaucrats turned to British and other liberal models for the purposes of drafting labor legislation, but they assigned the state a greater role in encouraging the growth of labor unions, collective bargaining, and conciliation machinery.

These efforts had clearly failed by the mid-1930s, and the bureaucrats confronted the problem of how to prevent labor unrest, which they believed was impairing Japan's mobilization for war in Manchuria and China. In retrospect, circumstances hardly justified a major departure from the loose system of industrial relations that had evolved over the past fifteen years. Up to 1936, Social Bureau officials relied on a variety of workers' organizations, from genuine labor unions to labor-management works councils and mutual aid societies, to resolve workers' grievances. Their colleagues in the police had already eliminated those unions and labor leaders associated with the Communist Party and left-wing socialists, and the remaining "realistic" labor unions eagerly proclaimed their patriotism and willingness to assist in the war effort. There was no reason why the Japanese government, like the British in the two world wars, could not have placed these cooperative union leaders, together with employers, on boards charged with settling strikes, determining wages, and allocating manpower. Instead, the state—led by some of the most prominent social bureaucrats—chose to dissolve the nation's labor unions between 1938 and 1940, reorganizing all workers into an ineffectual Industrial Patriotic Association.

The Industrial Patriotic Association marked the triumph of bureaucratic autonomy and runaway social knowledge. Employers were not much more enthusiastic than social democratic labor leaders about permitting the state to establish labor-management "discussion councils" in every plant. Industrialists appeared satisfied with a status quo that permitted gradual union busting with a minimum of interference from the authorities. The real initiative behind the Industrial Patriotic movement came from a group of labor specialists and social bureaucrats who had become fascinated by the newest Western model—that of Nazi labor policy and the German Labor Front.[89]

Ironically, at no other time in Japanese history before 1945 did so many experts from outside the government participate in policymaking as in the authoritarian 1930s. A mere handful of scholars, mostly from Tokyo University, had served as liaisons between the government and the pioneering Social Policy Association before 1920, whereas the emerging authoritarian order drew in specialists from a large variety of private study groups, research foundations, and institutions of higher learning. In response to the national "state of emergency," the government created new investigative organs designed to overcome ministerial sectionalism and incorporate nonbureaucratic knowledge. The most prominent was the Cabinet Research

Bureau (Naikaku Chōsakyoku), which later became the Planning Board (Kikakuin). The movement for an authoritarian "New Order" was also centrally supported by Prime Minister Konoe Fumimaro's brain trust, the Shōwa Research Association. This latter group included a number of academic labor specialists who looked to Nazi models. Prominent among them was Ryū Shintarō, a key figure in the left-wing Ōhara Institute.[90]

Contemporary Japanese also compared their New Order with the New Deal in the United States. In both cases, widespread perceptions of crisis called forth radically new solutions and elevated the power of ideas. Yet the results of applying the new knowledge could not have been more different. Whatever the source of its ideas, the New Deal's labor program succeeded because it rested on firm bases of support among the electorate and a fairly sizable labor union movement (the Wagner Act itself originated in the office of a senator in the Democratic Party).[91] In Japan, by contrast, the restructuring of labor relations *from above* not only failed to ease social tensions, but was catastrophic for Japan's industrial mobilization during World War II. Deprived of their unions and angered by Nazi-style measures intended to curb labor mobility, workers responded with sabotage, low productivity, and widespread absenteeism.[92]

It may strike some as ahistorical to evaluate the role of social knowledge in Japan during the 1920s through the glasses of the illiberal 1930s, yet developments in the latter era raise the troubling question of the relation between social knowledge and democracy. I have concentrated on elucidating how states acquire the knowledge to deal with labor problems, but we should also ask how states affect the production of nongovernmental knowledge. In Britain, the social sciences, whether refined in the universities or the settlement houses, developed rather autonomously from the state and in many cases before the emergence of an activist bureaucracy. For the specialist in industrial relations, government service was but one option, along with employment in educational institutions, political parties, labor unions, companies, or philanthropic organizations. In the Japanese case, the state imposed a high degree of management over the production of social knowledge from the 1880s to 1945. This was possible in large part because of sequence (the development of a strong bureaucratic state before the advent of modern social sciences), centralized control of higher education, and the weakness of competing bodies within civil society—that is, labor unions, parties, and truly private social work organizations.

Also, let us not underestimate the power of the police and judiciary to constrain and reshape knowledge in societies with serious limits on the freedom of expression. The imperial Japanese state made it attractive for experts to cooperate with the bureaucracy, while brandishing the stick at those who did not. Even at the height of prewar democratization in the late 1920s, specialists associated with militant unions or the Ōhara Institute had to walk a fine line between engaging in Marxist scholarship and criticism of the government's policies—which were permitted—and the illegal act of affiliating with organizations that allegedly advocated the overthrow of the "national polity" (*kokutai*) and the system of private property. The selective arrests and forced resignations of prominent scholars sent a clear message to the rest of the social policy community.[93] The new European doctrines of national socialism and fascism thus offered a solution to many marginalized, persecuted specialists in Japan during the 1930s. Armed with the newfound support of the bureaucratic state, the social scientists resumed their quest to apply knowledge to the radical transformation of society.

The author wishes to thank Andrew Gordon for sharing his research, and Howell J. Harris, Arno Mayer, and Byron K. Marshall for their helpful comments.

Notes to Chapter 8

1. Theda Skocpol, "Bringing the State Back In: Strategies of Analysis in Current Research." In Peter B. Evans, Dietrich Rueschemeyer, and Theda Skocpol, eds., *Bringing the State Back In*. Cambridge: Cambridge University Press, 1985, pp. 3–43.

2. Inoue Kiyoshi, *Tennōsei*. Tokyo: Tōkyō daigaku shuppankai, 1958.

3. Cyril E. Black et al., *The Modernization of Japan and Russia*. New York: Free Press, 1975; Chalmers Johnson, *MITI and the Japanese Miracle: The Growth of Industrial Policy, 1925–1975*. Stanford: Stanford University Press, 1982.

4. Hayashi Hirofumi, *Kindai Nihon kokka no rōdōsha tōgō: Naimushō shakaikyoku rōdō seisaku no kenkyū*. Tokyo: Aoki shoten, 1986; Sheldon Garon, *The State and Labor in Modern Japan*. Berkeley: University of California Press, 1987; Andrew Gordon, "Business and the Corporate State: The Business Lobby and Bureaucrats on Labor, 1911–1941." In William D. Wray, ed., *Managing Industrial Enterprise: Cases from Japan's Prewar Experience*. Cambridge: Council on East Asian Studies, Harvard University, 1989, pp. 53–85; W. Dean Kinzley, *Industrial Harmony in Modern Japan: The Invention of a Tradition*. London: Routledge, 1991.

5. Howell J. Harris, "The Snares of Liberalism? Politicians, Bureaucrats, and the Shaping of Federal Labour Relations Policy in the United States, ca. 1915–47." In Steven Tolliday and Jonathan Zeitlin, eds., *Shop Floor Bargaining and the State*. Cambridge: Cambridge University Press, 1985, pp. 148–91; in the case of welfare reforms, see Hugh Heclo, *Modern Social Politics in Britain and Sweden*. New Haven: Yale University Press, 1974.

6. Roger Davidson, "The Board of Trade and Industrial Relations 1896–1914." *The Historical Journal* 21 (September 1978): pp. 573, 576.

7. Roger Davidson, "Llewellyn Smith, the Labour Department and Government Growth 1886–1909." In Gillian Sutherland, ed., *Studies in the Growth of Nineteenth-century Government*. London: Routledge & Kegan Paul, 1972, p. 227.

8. Henry Pelling, "The Working Class and the Origins of the Welfare State." In his *Popular Politics and Society in Late Victorian Britain*. London: Macmillan, 1968, p. 72; Gary Marks, *Unions in Politics: Britain, Germany, and the United States in the Nineteenth and Early Twentieth Centuries*. Princeton: Princeton University Press, 1989, pp. 83–84.

9. Margaret Weir and Theda Skocpol, "State Structures and the Possibilities for 'Keynesian' Responses to the Great Depression in Sweden, Britain, and the United States." In Peter Evans, *Bringing the State Back In*, p. 112.

10. Marks, *Unions in Politics*, pp. 62–63, 84–86.

11. Alan Fox, *History and Heritage: The Social Origins of the British Industrial Relations System*. London: George Allen & Unwin, 1985, pp. 62–64, 76–77, 87, 99, 117, 129.

12. Ibid., pp. 77–78.

13. Ibid., pp. 174, 188–91.

14. Andrew Gordon, *The Evolution of Labor Relations in Modern Japan: Heavy Industry, 1853–1955*. Cambridge: Council on East Asian Studies, Harvard University, 1985, pp. 22–24, 47–49.

15. Garon, *State and Labor,* pp. 44–47.

16. Thomas C. Smith, "The Right to Benevolence: Dignity and Japanese Workers, 1890–1920." *Comparative Studies in Society and History* 26 (October 1984): p. 613; Gordon, *Evolution of Labor Relations,* pp. 207–8, 211–35.

17. Garon, *State and Labor,* pp. 116, 195; see also George O. Totten, "Collective Bargaining and Works Councils as Innovations in Industrial Relations in Japan during the 1920s." In R. P. Dore, ed., *Aspects of Social Change in Modern Japan.* Princeton: Princeton University Press, 1970, pp. 210–25.

18. H. V. Emy, *Liberals, Radicals and Social Politics, 1892–1914.* Cambridge: Cambridge University Press, 1973, p. 264.

19. Gerald Abrahams, *Trade Unions and the Law.* London: Cassell, 1968, pp. 28–29.

20. Rodney Lowe, *Adjusting to Democracy: The Role of the Ministry of Labour in British Politics, 1916–1939.* Oxford: Clarendon Press, 1986, p. 16.

21. Fox, *History and Heritage,* pp. 252, 260.

22. R. Davidson and R. Lowe, "Bureaucracy and Innovation in British Welfare Policy 1870–1945." In W. J. Mommsen, ed., *The Emergence of the Welfare State in Britain and Germany, 1850–1950.* London: Croom Helm, 1981, pp. 266–67, 274; Fox, *History and Heritage,* pp. 247, 266–68.

23. Fox, *History and Heritage,* pp. 35–42, 75, 115, 124, 139, 165; E. P. Thompson, *The Making of the English Working Class.* New York: Vintage Books, 1966, pp. 81–82, 683–66; Marks, *Unions in Politics,* pp. 63–64.

24. Heclo, *Modern Social Politics,* pp. 39–42.

25. Emy, *Liberals,* pp. 100–103.

26. Pelling, "Working Class," pp. 71–72; Davidson, "Board of Trade," pp. 583–84; Fox, *History and Heritage,* pp. 151–53.

27. Fox, *History and Heritage,* pp. 16, 41, 162–64.

28. E. H. Phelps-Brown, *The Growth of British Industrial Relations.* London: Macmillan, 1959, p. 187; Roger Davidson, "Social Conflict and Social Administration: The Conciliation Act in British Industrial Relations." In T. C. Smout, ed., *The Search for Wealth and Stability.* London: Macmillan, 1979, pp. 177–78.

29. Emy, *Liberals,* p. 264.

30. Davidson, "Social Conflict," pp. 177–80.

31. Roger Davidson, *Whitehall and the Labour Problem in Late-Victorian and Edwardian Britain: A Study in Official Statistics and Social Control.* London: Croom Helm, 1985, p. 263; Emy, *Liberals,* pp. 265, 268.

32. Sumiya Mikio, "Kōjōhō taisei to rōshi kankei." In his *Nihon rōshi kankei shi ron.* Tokyo: Tōkyō daigaku shuppankai, 1977, pp. 23–24; Garon, *State and Labor,* p. 20.

33. Garon, *State and Labor,* pp. 30–31.

34. Kiyoshi Ogata, *The Co-operative Movement in Japan.* London: P. S. King & Son, 1923, pp. 316, 89–91.

35. See Garon, *State and Labor,* pp. 106–7, 113–14, 164.

36. Ibid., pp. 140–43, 149, 152.

37. D. Eleanor Westney, *Imitation and Innovation: The Transfer of Western Organizational Patterns to Meiji Japan.* Cambridge: Harvard University Press, 1987, pp. 40–51, 94–99.

38. Robert M. Spaulding, Jr., *Imperial Japan's Higher Civil Service Examinations*. Princeton: Princeton University Press, 1967, pp. 115–17.

39. Garon, *State and Labor*, pp. 56–57, 59, 139–40, 143–49, 161.

40. Ibid., pp. 167–76, 180–84.

41. For example, Nishio Suehiro, *Taishū to tomo ni*. Tokyo: Sekaisha, 1951, p. 273; Akamatsu Katsumaro, *Nihon shakai undō shi*. Tokyo: Tsūshin kyōiku shinkōkai, 1949, p. 312.

42. Naimushō shakaikyoku rōdōbu, *Rōdō undō nempō*, 1926. Reprint, Tokyo: Meiji bunken, 1971, pp. 73, 431–32.

43. Saitō Ken'ichi, "Jiji kaisetsu: sōgi chōteihō no kaisei." *Rōdō* 279 (October 1934): pp. 12–13.

44. Garon, *State and Labor*, pp. 169, 206–7.

45. Davidson and Lowe, "Bureaucracy and Innovation," pp. 265–66, also 268.

46. Roger Davidson, "Llewellyn Smith," pp. 239–45.

47. Davidson, *Whitehall*, pp. 79–84; Heclo, *Modern Social Politics*, p. 84.

48. Quoted in Davidson, *Whitehall*, p. 82.

49. Fox, *History and Heritage*, pp. 248–49.

50. Spaulding, *Imperial Japan's Higher Civil Serivice Examinations*, pp. 166, 316–18; Endō Kōichi, "'Shokutaku' to shite no Tomeoka Kōsuke—Naimu gyōsei to jizen jigyō." *Meiji Gakuin ronsō*, nos. 352–53: *Shakaigaku, shakai fukushigaku kenkyū*, nos. 65–66 (March 1984): pp. 243–310.

51. Spaulding, *Imperial Japan's Higher Civil Service Examinations*, pp. 163–64.

52. Ibid., pp. 165–66.

53. Byron K. Marshall, *Academic Freedom and the Japanese Imperial University, 1868–1939*. Berkeley: University of California Press, 1992, pp. 98–105.

54. Spaulding, *Imperial Japan's Higher Civil Service Examinations*, pp. 166, 171.

55. Kitaoka Juitsu, "Kyū-shakaikyoku no omoide." In *Rōdō gyōsei shi yoroku*, supp. to vol. 1 of Rōdōshō, *Rōdō gyōsei shi*. Tokyo: Rōdō hōrei kyōkai, 1961, p. 1.

56. Kenneth Pyle, "Advantages of Followership: German Economics and Japanese Bureaucrats, 1890–1925." *Journal of Japanese Studies* 1 (Autumn 1974): p. 151.

57. For example, Yasui Eiji, *Rōdō undō no kenkyū*. Tokyo: Nihon daigaku, 1923; or the bureaucrat-turned-professor, Kawai Eijirō, *Rōdō mondai kenkyū*. Tokyo: Iwanami shoten, 1920.

58. Heclo, *Modern Social Politics*, p. 44.

59. Nambara Shigeru, "Naimushō rōdō kumiai hōan no koto nado." In *Rōdō gyōsei yoroku*, p. 28.

60. Garon, *State and Labor*, pp. 83–86.

61. Kinzley, *Industrial Harmony*, pp. 95–96; Garon, *State and Labor*, pp. 51–53, 108–10; for a list of its major publications, see "Kyōchōkai" kaiwakai, ed., *Kyōchōkai shi—Kyōchōkai sanjūnen no ayumi*. "Kyōchōkai" kaiwakai, 1965, pp. 169–78.

62. Yasui, *Rōdō undō*, pp. 139–54.

63. Davidson, *Whitehall*, pp. 262–63.

64. Garon, *State and Labor*, pp. 25–26, 32–33; Pyle, pp. 127–64.

65. Including the Commission to Investigate Relief Work (Kyūsai Jigyō Chōsakai, 1918–19), Extraordinary Commission to Investigate Industry (Rinji Sangyō

Chōsakai, 1920), and the Commission on Social Policy (Shakai Seisaku Shingikai, 1929).

66. Oka Minoru, *Kōjōhō ron,* rev. ed. Tokyo: Yūhikaku, 1917, pp. 136–37.

67. Article I of Tokyo Imperial University's University Ordinance of 1886, cited by Andrew E. Barshay, *The State and Intellectual in Imperial Japan*. Berkeley: University of California Press, 1988, p. 39.

68. Garon, *State and Labor,* p. 27.

69. Kagoyama Takashi, "Kōjōhō no seiritsu to jisshi ni okeru kanryōgun." In Takahashi Kōhachirō, ed., *Nihon kindaika no kenkyū*. Tokyo: Tōkyō daigaku shuppankai, 1973, 2:84–85.

70. Andrew Gordon, *Labor and Imperial Democracy in Prewar Japan*. Berkeley: University of California Press, 1991, p. 152.

71. Sharon H. Nolte, *Liberalism in Modern Japan: Ishibashi Tanzan and His Teachers, 1905–1960*. Berkeley: University of California Press, 1986, pp. 191–94.

72. See Kyōchōkai, *Saikin no shakai undō*. Tokyo: Kyōchōkai, 1929, pp. 734–37, 1003; Hiroshi Hazama, "Japanese Labor-Management Relations and Uno Riemon." *Journal of Japanese Studies* 5 (Winter 1976): pp. 71–106.

73. Hōsei daigaku Ōhara shakai mondai kenkyūjo, ed., *Ōhara shakai mondai kenkyūjo 50 nen shi*. Tokyo: Hōsei daigaku shuppankyoku, 1971, pp. 10, 19–20, 24–30, 59, 66–69.

74. Marshall, *Academic Freedom,* pp. 92–94.

75. Nambara, "Naimushō rōdō kumiai hōan," p. 29.

76. On the liberal revision of the labor disputes conciliation bill, see Yano Tatsuo, "taishō-ki rōdō rippō no ichidammen—rōdō sōgi chōteihō no seiritsu katei." *Hōseishi kenkyū* 27 (1977): p. 120, n. 44; for veto of the seamen's insurance bill, see *Tōkyō asahi shimbun,* 21 Sept. 1928, p. 3.

77. Andrew Barshay analyzes these two types of "public men" in *State and Intellectual in Imperial Japan*.

78. *Tōkyō asahi shimbun,* pp. 10–14, 17, 19 February 1926, p. 2.

79. Interview with Tanino Setsu, Tokyo, 6 October 1988.

80. Iwao F. Ayusawa, *Industrial Conditions and Labour Legislation in Japan*. Studies and Reports, ser. B. (Economic Conditions), no. 16. Geneva: International Labor Office, 1926, pp. 10–11; in July 1930, the Social Legislation Association's general council included the Social Bureau's section ochiefs—Kitaoka Juitsu, Kimishima Kiyokichi, and Kawanishi Jitsuzō—plus a former official attached to the ILO office, Maeda Tamon. Shakai rippō kyōkai, *Shakai rippō kyōkai nempō,* 1930. Tokyo: Shakai rippō kyōkai, 1931, pp. 9–12.

81. Davidson, "Conciliation Act," pp. 185–87; idem, "Board of Trade," pp. 584–85.

82. See Jeremiah Schneiderman, *Sergei Zubatov and Revolutionary Marxism: The Struggle for the Working Class in Tsarist Russia*. Ithaca: Cornell University Press, 1976.

83. Kawamura Takeji, Sanjikan gijiroku, 31 March 1920, Records of the Rinji sangyō chōsakai (Extraordinary commission to investigate industry), National Archives, Tokyo.

84. *Tōkyō asahi shimbun,* 6 August 1925 (evening), p. 1.

85. Garon, *State and Labor,* pp. 87–89, 103.

86. Rōdōshō, *Rōdō gyōsei shi,* 1:194–95; Rōdō undō shiryō iinkai, ed., *Nihon rōdō undō shiryō.* Tokyo: Chūō kōron shuppan, 1959, 10:276, 289, 440.

87. Nishinarita Yutaka, *Kindai Nihon rōshi kankei shi no kenkyū.* Tokyo: Tōkyō daigaku shuppankai, 1988, pp. 232–34, 361; Gordon, *Labor and Imperial Democracy,* pp. 247–48, 308–9.

88. Michael J. Lacey and Mary O. Furner, "Social Investigation, Social Knowledge, and the State: An Introduction," In Michael J. Lacey and Mary O. Furner, eds., *The State and Social Investigation in Britain and the United States.* Washington, D.C.: Woodrow Wilson Center Press, 1993, p. 30; for a discussion of the twentieth-century state as the promoter of "social progress," see Gianfranco Poggi, "the Modern State and the Idea of Progress." In Gabriel A. Almond, Marvin Chodorow, and Roy Harvey Pearce, eds., *Progress and Its Discontents.* Berkeley: University of California Press, 1982, p. 351.

89. See Garon, *State and Labor,* chap. 6.

90. See William Miles Fletcher, III, *The Search for a New Order: Intellectuals and Fascism in Prewar Japan.* Chapel Hill: University of North Carolina Press, 1982; Itō Takashi, "'Kyokoku itchi' naikaku-ki no seikai saihensei mondai—Shōwa sanjūnen Konoe shintō mondai kenkyū no tame ni." *Shakai kagaku kenkyū* 24 (August 1972): pp. 56–129; Shōwa kenkyūkai, *Rōdō shintaisei kenkyū.* Tokyo: Tōyō keizai shuppanbu, 1941.

91. See Harris, "Snares of Liberalism," pp. 164–68.

92. Gordon, *Evolution of Labor Relations,* pp. 266–73, 275, 314–24.

93. For an analysis of these episodes, see Marshall, *Academic Freedom,* chaps. 5–6.

Conclusion

DIETRICH RUESCHEMEYER
AND THEDA SKOCPOL

How has the development of social knowledge been spurred by, and contributed to, the emergence of modern states and social policies? Contributors to this volume have grappled with this broad question, proceeding at a level of analysis in between grand overviews of the evolution of the modern state and detailed studies of the "utilization" of theories or data in episodes of policy formulation. By analyzing developments over long stretches of time, and by making comparisons across different national contexts, the chapters in this volume have revealed and explored such broader and more indirect ways in which social knowledge—and groups making knowledge claims—have historically influenced the social policies devised by modern national states. Moreover, by examining issues historically and comparatively, the chapters have highlighted ways in which the modern social sciences themselves were not just given as objective knowledge, but evolved intellectually and institutionally in different ways in various countries.

In this concluding chapter, we offer a series of generalizations that seem to us to follow from the chapters assembled in this volume considered along with other studies that have arrived at complementary conclusions.[1] Although our tone is somewhat declarative, our purpose is to offer hypotheses that can inform further research. We begin with the macrohistorical transformations that lay behind the emergence of modern social knowledge and helped to established its authority. Then we examine the class interests, state structures, and actions as influences on the content and deployment of social knowledge. Finally, we pull together thoughts about states and the relevance of social knowledge to policymaking.

The Emergence of Secular Social Knowledge

A number of developments in industrializing nations worked together to promote the increasing use of knowledge for governmental policymaking, the growth of institutions concerned with producing knowledge, and the enhanced influence of elites deploying secular knowledge claims.

The first and perhaps most obvious facilitating developments were centered in the economy. Production shifted from agriculture toward industry, and techniques of production became subject to more rapid and strategic innovation. These changes were driven by competitive pressures and made possible by the growing power and autonomy of capital owners. As economic transformations and competitiveness intensified, governments, businesses, and scholarly institutions alike sought new knowledge about economic conditions and techniques, including socially relevant knowledge about consumption and the wage-labor process.

Nevertheless, the interests of modern states were probably more pertinent than those of capitalists to the emergence of modern social knowledge. The leaders of national states sought to develop good citizens, and governmental agencies sought to recruit loyal and trained officials. Such needs spurred the development of primary and secondary schooling, and of university-level education with its obvious potential to create self-conscious official status groups. The desire of public officials to act in "the national interest" in increasingly complex socioeconomic settings created growing demands both for general theories of how economies or societies functioned, and for reliable information on particular issues that seemed problematic—such as the living conditions and the likely responses of the lower classes. More than just the production needs of the economy (which primarily tended to spur research in science and engineering), state interests stimulated the growth and systemization of social inquiry. In fact, where state apparatuses were well developed and active, as they often were in many nations on the European continent, it was their knowledge needs that instigated the early development of social science. As a number of the contributions to this volume have detailed, this is reflected in the very labels used to describe nascent kinds of systematic social knowledge: "statistics," "political economy," "police (i.e., policy) science," and "*Staatswissenschaften*."

Public officials needed social theories and statistical data, and often they developed their own intragovernmental capacities to meet such needs, at least in part. Stein Kuhnle's chapter on Scandinavia, as well as Sheldon Garon's on Britain and Japan, detailed important instances of the creation of governmental investigative agencies. However, demands and supply for social knowledge also came from politically active individuals and groups and from economic enterprises. This was especially true in liberal-democratic societies, but it happened as well in the more statist political economies. With important differences from country to country, the rise of the modern "public sphere," in which private groups and institutions proposed ameliorative measures in the collective interest or in their own interest, fueled the search for information and analysis of social problems. Such information and analysis, in turn, encouraged demands for governmental interventions—or abstentions!—to improve social welfare. The government's interventions and abstentions themselves generated more problems and, directly or indirectly, more needs for social knowledge to help officials and politically active groups to set things right.

The nineteenth century also saw a complementary hunger for information and understanding at the grassroots level. Craftsmen, workers, and farmers, as well as professionals and businessmen engaged in self-education, created reading and study groups, and used private and public libraries to advance their understanding of social change and social reform. The directions of these undertakings in continuing education were variously determined—sometimes in fairly autonomous fashion by the participants, often by religious bodies and their authorities, and also by reformist elites interested in spreading certain ideas or disciplines. All of the intellectual groups involved in social policy debates engaged in at least some efforts at popular education and mobilization. This was true even of the professorial "academic socialists" of Germany, as we learned in the chapter by Dietrich Rueschemeyer and Ronan Van Rossem.

Further impetus to the application of knowledge to policymaking came from institutions for the creation and transmission of knowledge that were built or rebuilt from the eighteenth century onward. Modern universities emerged during roughly the same era when the capitalist transformation of economy and society was reflected in public consciousness. In France and Prussia, the reform of higher education and research came early and received its main impetus from the political sphere, from the French Revolution and the Napoleonic Wars. In England and the United States, similar transformations occurred later and more closely in tandem with economic transformations. The chapters by Björn Wittrock and Peter Wagner, Libby Schweber, and Dietrich Rueschemeyer and Ronan Van Rossem explored nationally varying patterns by which universities were modernized and social science professions established, showing the considerable effects of different patterns of industrialization, status arrangements, and the structures and actions of states. Yet emerging universities and professions were not only influenced by economic, social, and state arrangements; they became reciprocally influential. As established or newly created knowledge-bearing institutions responded to new demands for systematic social knowledge by governments, citizenries, and economic enterprises, members of the knowledge-bearing institutions developed a vested interest in systematic intellectual innovation, and in championing the social relevance of their knowledge products. The existence of universities and other knowledge-bearing institutions stimulated further demand for their ideas, information, interpretations, and predictions.

Establishing the Authority of Social Knowledge

All knowledge, except for truly firsthand information, has to be taken on trust—its reception and impact are secured by intellectual authority. Establishing such authority and trust is inevitably a social process and not only a matter of intellectual validation. Communities of scholars organized in networks of academies and universities, as well as in specialized disciplines, solve part of this problem by institutionalizing a social system of mutual intellectual validation, recognition, and reputation.[2] But even for established scholarly communities there is still the question of achieving and sustaining a broader authority that reaches beyond the circle of mutual validation.

Both the validity of a given set of ideas and their pragmatic relevance are matters that become established in society at large only through complex processes that are largely political, social, and cultural in character. They are thus subject to criteria that are exterior to the internal, intellectual standards of judgment.[3] Western societies nowadays take the prestige and authority of established institutions of knowledge for granted. That these institutions enjoy such standing is indeed a partial solution of the problem of a societywide intellectual authority. But we must not overlook that the modern standing of schools and universities developed under very specific conditions. We must also recognize that the resultant authority is subject to considerable variation across the countries, types of institutions, and disciplines involved.

A major historic development strengthening the authority of secular knowledge was the Enlightenment's fusion of "scientific" knowledge with a compelling vision of progress. Intellectual movements promised social and human improvement through a knowledge freed of prejudice and tradition. As these claims became broadly accepted and embedded in common assumptions, secular knowledge and its spokesmen gained status and more credibility.

The late Joseph Ben-David contrasted this legitimation of science through progressive movements in England and especially in France with the quite different legitimation through government sponsorship in the more backward sovereignties of central Europe.[4] Paradoxically, it was in the German states that scientific research first became fully institutionalized. Traditional monarchies, as their powers were enhanced economically and politically by bureaucratizing state apparatuses, did much to institutionalize science—more than the sheer presence of Enlightenment ideas could do. Under these conditions, too, scholarly knowledge and its elites gained substantially in authority. But this new authority for science in central Europe was initially closely fused with the existing status order, and thus shared much more in the political authority of established states and social elites than was the case in Western Europe and North America.

What Kinds of Knowledge Mattered, and How?

We have stressed so far that even empirical and scientific knowledge comes to be accepted in society as true and relevant only by way of complex sociopolitical processes. Even so, various types of knowledge face quite distinctive problems in claiming validity and relevance. What we consider "knowledge" covers a wide range of phenomena indeed. It includes knowledge claims based on a wide variety of methodologies. It includes conceptual formulations and reformulations that make the same information appear quite differently. It ranges from anecdotal information illustrating an idea to the most systematic treatments of a subject.

In the broadest conception, knowledge includes both cognitive ideas about "what is the case," and prescriptive, normative ideas about "what should be the case" and "what should be done." Values and prescriptions can be differentiated to some extent from description and theoretical analysis, but the latter can never be completely cut off from normative ideas.[5] In addition, knowledge relevant to policymaking is inevitably implicated in the interest-ridden world of politics. This was especially true of knowledge claims made in connection with early social policies.

Sheer statistical information may be needed for estimating the cost of a pension program, as Stein Kuhnle pointed out in his discussion of policy innovations in Denmark. With elementary institutional precautions securing nonpartisan professional procedures of authoritative data collection, there may seem to be few issues of political or moral distortion displayed in an instance such as this. But we know from many historical and contemporary experiences that apparently "nonpartisan" factual claims are not always accepted. Glaring denials of available information underline that factual descriptions, if publicly accepted, can have a decisive political and moral impact. Suffering and injustice, even if merely described, stand out as morally or politically unacceptable—especially when they are presented against a background of shared values that are both challenged and reinforced by the descriptive information. Describing such conditions, then, amounts to making a moral and political statement. Sheer factual description can become a tool of political agenda setting. Several chapters in this collection offered examples of such politically strategic descriptions of problems.

Competent description of issues of broad interest also can be influential in an indirect fashion. Such description establishes the authors as experts and lends authority to their views. This authority is rarely confined just to the factual information and analysis; it typically spills over to cover broader ideas, conceptions, and policy proposals presented along with the "facts." Thus Gustav Schmoller, the leader of German academic proponents of social reform who sought to change the outlook and basic assumptions of economics and government studies, consciously adopted a strategy of doing detailed empirical investigations. He advocated this strategy rather than what might be considered the more direct road of presenting ideological and philosophical argument. The latter in isolation, he reasoned, would be easily rejected, whereas facts could establish the authority of related ideological and philosophical arguments. This strategy was successful. Schmoller and his associates established their distinctive outlook—in contrast to both free-market and socialist ideas—as hegemonic in the social sciences from 1870s to the turn of the century. Social analysts with different values could readily see what Schmoller's strategy had achieved. As Rosa Luxemburg commented angrily in 1903: "In the one hundred and three volumes of the Verein für Sozialpolitik [the real issues of] social science rest in a deep grave under an enormous sand pile of social knowledge."[6]

If the most straightforward kind of cognitive authority—that involved in the presentation of descriptive information—cannot easily be separated from contending interests and moral or political commitments, other ideas and types of "knowledge" are intertwined in even more obvious and complex ways with interests and values. This is apparent in the case of prediction. Given the quite limited fund of secure predictive knowledge about economic and social change, predictions tend to be at best plausible and are inevitably subject to ideological contest whenever serious interests or value commitments are at stake. This is not to say that social analyses and predictions—for instance, of the explosive potential of class division—would fail to influence public discussion if the underlying theories were too weak. In fact, such predictions did become influential in public discussion—but they did so largely for "external" social and political reasons, rather than for purely "internal" cognitive ones.

Even mere shifts in the way issues or facts are conceptualized—something not in itself involving claims of truth or falsehood—can acquire compelling force and transform the way problems as well as potential solutions are seen. Describing developments in France, Anson Rabinbach discussed changing ideas about responsibility for accidents. This involved a conceptualization that is perhaps best known from the central place it found in Durkheim's thought, the idea that rates of events in different populations—events such as marriages, suicides, or accidents—can be seen as attributes of these collectivities and that may be indicative of social rather than merely individual causal factors. Such a conceptualization played a decisive role in the development of early social policy. It not only facilitated a shift toward social responsibility for events previously seen in individual terms, but—at a more practical level—it also constituted the rationale for a collective, social insurance system based on stable aggregate probabilities.

Early social analysts often sought to buttress their authority with the claim of being "scientific," capitalizing on the achievements of astronomy and other natural sciences that had transformed the conception of nature and the world. In the course of the nineteenth century, this claim was quite thoroughly diluted (though not necessarily rendered ineffective) as it was invoked for Saint-Simonianism and Comte's "positivism," for economic liberalism as well as for Marx's scientific socialism and, in the German academic world, for all of the humanities, for law, and even for theology. In nineteenth-century Germany, any systematic scholarly undertaking was considered "science." Similarly surprising is nineteenth-century American use of the label: philanthropic practices that were well organized and effective were considered "scientific."

The ubiquitous claim to scientific status may on its face suggest that in the nineteenth century strong distinctions were made between different kinds of "knowledge," separating speculating from empirical investigation, methodically controlled research from other work, and normative from cognitive argument. But as many of the essays in this volume have documented, that inference would be mistaken. Nineteenth-century social thought slowly moved toward some of the distinctions we now take for granted in academic discourse, but that movement was slow indeed. Even Durkheim, now known as a founder of empiricist sociology, originally hoped that sociology could provide the normative blueprint for the modern good society.

The advocates of early social policies identified new societal problems; they simultaneously had little normative hesitation in arguing for new and controversial policy measures, including nationwide governmental interventions aiming to ameliorate problematic social and economic conditions. Such projects created the need for radically new kinds of information and knowledge.

The implications of this can perhaps best be appreciated if we contrast the new knowledge required to two other kinds of information systems that were previously well established: the knowledge underlying local action to help the poor; and the information that expresses itself in market prices. Commonsense understandings of local leaders and groups traditionally guided the treatment of the poor, who in early modern European societies were typically in the care of local institutions. Market prices understood as a system of signals—the "invisible voice" that belongs to Adam Smith's invisible hand—similarly reflected and then aggregated the decentralized intelligence of socioeconomic actors. Market signals (then and now) inform about people's preferences as well as about the costs and scarcities of goods and services.

Seen from a conventional point of view, community knowledge and market signals may not have much in common at all. Yet as information systems, they share some remarkable features. Both were decentralized in character. Both were available without special action seeking information and understanding. Both can be seen as parts of self-regulating systems—of the market guided by an invisible hand toward its inherent equilibrium, and of the local community reproducing its established hierarchies, relations, values, and understandings. Both were thoroughly "naturalized," close to common sense, by-products of normal living. Both therefore were widely considered as trustworthy beyond much question.

Crystallizing especially in the nineteenth and early twentieth centuries, new knowledge claims centering around the "social questions" associated with the effects of capitalist industrialization challenged the adequacy of local common sense and market signals to provide information on the needs, wants, and situations of national populations. The problems faced by the industrial working class as well as a host of other, related social dilemmas, arose from structural conditions extending beyond the local community. In rapidly growing cities even local problems were no longer amenable to commonsense understanding. Market information proved equally inadequate, for it was insensitive to needs and wants not backed up by disposable economic resources. This was true even as market dynamics increasingly transformed employment relations in antagonistic directions. The market not only failed to articulate the problems of the subordinate classes; it both camouflaged and worsened them at the same time. Rather than the market, political protest and an increasing incidence of large-scale, organized collective action gave voice to the new issues involved in "the social question." Yet elites found information derived from such forms of voice very threatening. They wanted other ways to learn about problematic societal conditions.

New knowledge claims associated with social reform initiatives, especially those emanating from above, thus had to bypass and contradict both local common sense and market signals. New forms of social knowledge sought to describe and to diagnose societywide structural problems. In this they could not rely on "naturalized" forms of decentralized intelligence, but had to build on new, specially collected information and more abstract modes of analysis. "Artificial" by comparison to market signals and common sense, and inherently more controversial, the new types of knowledge at the same time tackled formidable vested interests associated with the information patterns of communities and markets.

Social policy initiatives furthermore required more than descriptive information. They also called for analytic knowledge that would allow for the prediction of the outcomes of alternative courses of public policy. If sheer information about whole classes and economic sectors is hard to obtain and hard to make trustworthy, the authority of predictive knowledge, as noted before, is even harder to establish, especially if it is inevitably intertwined with conflicting interests and values. Small wonder that the new knowledge claims were often contested. In fact, we may wonder why social theories about industrialism and the consequences of various policy interventions (or noninterventions) gained as much authority as they did.

There were, to be sure, pressing demands for supralocal knowledge that would displace, or at least complement, community knowledge and the signal system of the market. Many groups, organizations, and institutions offered relevant information and claimed new interpretations—workers' mutual aid societies, political clubs and parties, churches and church organizations, state institutions and, last but not least, social scientists, both amateur-generalists and professional scholars in established institutions and emerging specialist disciplines.

Knowledge claims of one sort or another gained acceptance in very different degrees. Providing new information and interpretations was often only part of these projects. While some institutions and groups did confine themselves to that, most had more far-reaching aims, involving the identification and public acknowledgment of new problems and proposals for redressing them. As nicely exemplified by the Verein für Sozialpolitik in Germany, the Fabian Society in Britain, the American Association for Labor Legislation, and other groups of early social scientists discussed in chapters in this volume, the formulators of new social knowledge often saw themselves as simultaneously advancing new findings about societal problems *and* logical recommendations for reorientations of public policy.

As such knowledge groups combined the collection of factual data with advocacy of new moral-political outlooks and new public policies, their authority had to be built on more than information and analysis considered competent by immediate audiences. Competent information and analysis were the entering wedges for projects of moral and political influence that required much more—such as the building of institutions, the establishment of new associations, the stimulation of new audiences, and the deployment of fresh channels of communication.

For these broader endeavors, "external" noncognitive assets and liabilities mattered much more than intellectual competence. Especially important were the linkages and relations that emerging knowledge-bearers enjoyed with recognized and established institutions of social knowledge, as well as with groups highly placed in overall societal status structures. Locations within arenas of competing political groups also mattered, as did the access that particular groups of social scientists gained to powerful parts of the apparatuses of their respective national states. The knowledge-bearing and policy advocacy groups examined in the various chapters of this volume differed considerably—and in very instructive ways—in their enjoyment of the sorts of relationships and resources it took to achieve far-reaching intellectual authority in their respective national contexts. Consequently, they also differed in degrees of kinds of influence over policymaking, and in their capacities to persuade powerholders and defend against opponents determined to question their credibility or relevance.

Social Knowledge and Class Interests

Class conflicts greatly influenced the development of modern social knowledge and social policies. Without the divisive issues of class that intensified during early capitalist industrialization, public social policies would probably not have been instituted. More fundamentally, the fact that knowledge claims about social policy issues were made in the context of class conflict gave questions about intellectual authority a peculiarly sharp edge—a point especially well illustrated in the chapter by Anson Rabinbach. Issues of intellectual authority became intensely political as well as academic. Wherever it came to actual struggles about the intellectual authority of a given position in social policy disputes, particular standpoints derived their meaning and importance, in part, from underlying class tensions. Consequently, the social and political bases of intellectual authority for social policymaking became even more relevant than they may have been for other sorts of applications of knowledge to policy, and others uses of social knowledge.

Politically active advocates of new ideas about social reality often used an interesting argument to parry worries (including their own) about the basis of their authority to speak on controversial issues. They extended the universalistic ideals of the search for knowledge to a different kind of universalism: a claim to represent the interests of society as a whole rather than factional interests. This assertion was strictly analagous to the claim of the state to represent the common good. Insisting that their position was not identified with either capitalist or worker, landlord or farmhand, knowledge elites sought to add to their intellectual authority a recognized claim to social objectivity.[7] We must not reject such claims in a simplistic way. All conceptions of the common good are socially constructed, all are inherently contestable, but not all necessarily represent the partial interests of any one class.

However, whether knowledge elites could in historical reality successfully claim such a moral and political authority based on transcendent social objectivity depended on conditions that were very particular to each nation. In some national contexts—arguably more so in Prussia/Germany and Scandinavia—close ties to an authoritative state may have helped knowledge elites make such claims credible, at least for a time. In other contexts—the United States especially comes to mind—"nonpartisan" universities and academic disciplines offered more promising institutional terrains from which to make credible claims of objectivity and ability to serve interests of the whole society.

Paradoxically, the very recognition of classes, class division, and class conflict was in large part an achievement of knowledge creating and articulating elites. This is not to say that workers, entrepreneurs, farmers, and landowners had to be told that they had conflicting interests. It is to maintain that the public recognition of "the social question" among the dominant and the educated classes reflected to a large extent the efforts of intellectuals and scholars, and was not a self-evident acknowledgment of objective reality. Conflicting interests can, after all, be experienced and discussed in many ways, not only in terms of "class."

It is important not to look only at knowledge-bearing groups that supported social policy reform measures. This would give our analysis an unwarranted whiggish character. All sides in the conflicts between classes—as well as in the debates over social policy measures—created or used new ideas, information, and analysis. As Rabinbach's chapter revealed, the skepticism of doctors in France about the seriousness of reported accidents after the insurance principle was introduced was as important an application of "social knowledge" to disputes over policy as were the counterarguments that ultimately prevailed. A similar point can be made juxtaposing the "Manchester liberalism" of the heirs of classical economics to the more interventionist conclusions of German historical and institutional economics. Social scientists, then as now, could deploy theories and facts to argue either for or against possible state interventions.

Degrees of unanimity about ideas and information are critical for an understanding of their political impact. Division of opinion within the academy can undercut the claims of knowledge elites to speak with authority about controversial issues. Since the problems of social reform in the latter nineteenth and early twentieth centuries developed in the context of class conflict, as well as in the context of far-ranging disagreements among politically active groups about what the state should do, or even how the state should be organized, disagreements among even the most "ivory tower" scholars took on potentially conflictual implications. At the same time, there were quite a few occasions where certain ideas gained overwhelming acceptance, and these will be of special interest for our inquiry into intellectual authority under conditions of conflict.

If conflicting class interests often interacted with academic discussions and caused serious divisions of opinion and judgment, we must also ask another question: Did academic divisions of opinion reflect the major contradictions of the structure of interests in capitalist political economies? Clearly there is no one answer to this question that holds across the diverse and historically changing relations of the academy to the class tensions and conflicts in different countries. Yet for most debates about social policy around the late nineteenth century it seems fair to say that the interests of the subordinate classes were only weakly represented. If they were at all directly acknowledged, they typically entered the discussion through the understandings of them held by well-meaning members of scholarly establishments. Only when the subordinate classes became quite well organized, particularly through moderate social democratic parties, did the public articulation of their interests and problems by "third-party" voices become effectively complemented and partly superseded by more direct forms of expression. At that point, intellectuals associated with the moderate social democratic parties became recognized spokespersons for organized "working-class" demands.

States and the Relevance of Social Knowledge to Policymaking

Finally, we turn to the state as an actor and institutional influence in public policy formation, exploring how social knowledge feeds into official decision making. At the start, we can rule out some widely held but overly simplified conceptions. Social knowledge does not serve as a straightforward instrumentality of neutral bureaucrats and value-oriented politicians. It is not adequate to say that technically efficient knowledge merely helps to sort out optimal courses of action, providing a basis for officials to choose rationally among alternative possible policies.

There are several interrelated reasons for the inadequacy of this "instrumental" conception. For one thing, as we have just seen, social scientists often claim much more than the possession of instrumentally relevant knowledge. They offer ideas about the good society and are hardly ever politically neutral. Even sheer description can have a political impact—identifying problems and assessing their urgency (underlining or deflating it) and thus shaping the political agenda. In addition, much of information actually needed for policy implementation will be gathered routinely by government agencies themselves. They can then tailor the process more precisely to their requirements than if they relied on outside research.

Another reason for the inadequacy of an instrumental conception is that social science had in the nineteenth century little actual predictive capacity of any precision. On many issues social science operated at a level not much elevated above the "amateur knowledge" of civil servants and politicians. Especially where there were competing claims, there often was little difference in authority between the common sense of political decision makers, the claims of amateur social investigators, and the claims of the nascent professional social scientists.

Perhaps most decisive historically and now, political decisions are inherently the decisions of generalists. Information, predictions, and considerations of feasibility all have to be condensed and fused with political considerations, before they can help determine policy outcomes. As research on bureaucracies since Max Weber has put it, the top of an organization, the arena of policy setting, is bound to be nonbureaucratic in character. Nor is there any neat division of labor between decision makers and purveyors of information and ideas outside the official arenas of authoritative decision making.

Thus it is not astonishing that several of the chapters in this volume come to the same conclusion, showing that social science had a greater effect on the background assumptions of policymaking than it did on the instrumental delineation of means for politically determined ends. In spite of claims to offer solid, empirically based findings, social science often had a more direct impact on ideology and the premises of public discourse about social policy than on the factual assumptions of policy makers.[8] This observation makes sense of the surprising finding by Libby Schweber that amateur social research could play such an important role in the formulation of English early social policies.

"Bureaucratic administration means fundamentally domination through knowledge." This insight of Max Weber has two corollaries important for our inquiry. First, we too often overlook the tremendous knowledge-gathering and processing capacity of the bureaucratic state. Second—a point apparently contradictory but in fact complementary to the first—it is the bureaucratic character of the state that makes it especially receptive to inputs from social knowledge generated "outside" the state.

Not only do government agencies often gather themselves the statistical information that is of immediate relevance to their operations; Weber's proposition implies much more. Bureaucratic administration means rule by trained experts. Their professional education may be more or less specialized, and their official activities may entail the application of specialized expertise or a more generalized administrative competence. National states, and within them particular agencies, differ considerably. But whatever the degree and the pattern of specialization among officials, the body of higher civil servants tends to be professionally educated and as capable of independent interpretation and analysis of information. They are likely to come to judgments of their own and have an interest in controlling the political agenda at least as it pertains to their own agencies.

An agency's place in the flow of policy-relevant knowledge depends not just on its personnel. Equally relevant is its organizational capacity to generate and assess pertinent knowledge. An organization with the most able officials is not necessarily able to gather and analyze large bodies of policy-relevant knowledge with technical expertise. Such a capacity has to be built up over a considerable period of time. On this issue, Sheldon Garon's portrait of Japanese officials stands at one extreme of variations across countries. Here we encounter a bureaucratic knowledge elite that at the same time was the decisive political elite within the state apparatus. In Imperial Germany, the knowledge elite in the social sciences was more strongly differentiated from the state apparatus and located in the universities; but top civil servants were well informed, and the members of the higher civil service had a solid and fairly homogeneous professional training. Much of the influence of the academic social scientists ran, on the one hand, through personal contact at the apex of the state apparatus and, on the other, through shaping the outlook of the corps of higher civil servants trained at the universities. In fact the German Verein für Sozialpolitik, though led by professors, included many civil servants among its members.

The generation of policy-relevant knowledge within the state is not only found in such well-established and fairly autonomous state apparatuses as the German and Japanese states of the late nineteenth and early twentieth century. John Sutton described a U.S. federal agency, the Children's Bureau, established by female reformers in 1912, which represented a consolidation of initiatives of the social settlement movement in a governmental agency. This interesting bureau initially had few operative functions, but it had important capacities to gather data and communicate it relatively authoritatively not only to the U.S. Congress but also to local voluntary groups of American women who played a vital role in public discussions of social policy issues during the early twentieth century in the United States.

How open or closed governmental agencies are to outside information and ideas depends on many factors, and we have seen quite different patterns in the studies collected in this volume. Receptivity and its absence depend on such features of the state itself as the character of its officials and organizational capacities of state agencies for gathering knowledge as well as for devising social policy interventions. Yet relations between state and society are equally consequential, including such factors as the compatibility (or noncompatibility) in outlook between officials and groups in society that advance knowledge claims potentially relevant to policy formulation.

In general, the more bureaucratically rationalized a state's administration, the more it will rely on systematic information, professionally assessed and interpreted. Even an agency that is deeply involved in knowledge creation on its own is likely to generate demand for outside input. In fact, it may generate a greater demand of this kind than an agency that is less oriented toward securing an adequate supply of information and analysis. The role of extra-bureaucratically generated knowledge may then be complementary rather than simply an alternative to knowledge generated by officials themselves.

Closing Thoughts

Much recent research on the way the social sciences and public policy operate treats social science as rationally instrumental. But it is not valid to assume that social knowledge simply develops in its own terms and then operates as a means for designing effective state interventions. As we have seen in the chapters collected here, social knowledge is historically embedded and has mostly had more indirect reverberations in politics and policymaking.

After as well as before the emergence of the modern social sciences, social knowledge and its bearers primarily helped to identify and characterize the "social problems" on which states could act, and helped to rule in or out conceivable sorts of policy responses. Social knowledge influenced the very framing of issues, reflecting broad cultural predispositions, status connections, and the interests of some politically relevant groups rather than others. In turn, states and their policies influenced the development of the social sciences, both intellectually and institutionally, thus affecting the possibilities for experts to influence the further course of politics and policy in and across modern nations.

States, social knowledge, and social policies have indeed been intimately intertwined in their historical development. This collection has explored some of these intertwinings for a formative epoch. It has certainly not exhausted agendas for research or theorizing. Yet this book will have achieved its objective if it stimulates further research and debate about the sociocultural and institutional groundings of social knowledge and its uses in public policymaking, past and present. Many insights remain to be developed, going to the heart of how scholars and citizens know about their societies, and deploy that knowledge to perceive and influence political possibilities in the modern world.

Notes to Conclusion

1. In thinking about the interrelations of state action and social knowledge, we have also drawn upon other excellent studies, including the books by Peter A. Hall and Robert Wuthnow cited in the Introduction, along with *The State and Economic Knowledge,* edited by Mary O. Furner and Barry Supply. Washington, DC: Woodrow Wilson Center, and Cambridge: Cambridge University Press, 1990; Dorothy Ross, *The Origins of American Social Science.* Cambridge: Cambridge University Press, 1989; *Social Science and Modern States,* edited by Peter Wagner et. al. Cambridge: Cambridge University Press, 1991; Charles E. Lindblom and David K. Cohen, *Usable Knowledge.* New Haven, CT: Yale University Press, 1979; Charles E. Lindblom, *Inquiry and Change: The Troubled Attempt to Understand and Shape Society.* New Haven, CT: Yale University Press, and New York: Russell Sage Foundation, 1990; and *The European and American University Since 1800,* edited by Sheldon Rothblatt and Björn Wittrock. Cambridge and New York: Cambridge University Press, 1993.

2. Karl Popper has argued that the sociology of knowledge as advanced by Karl Mannheim and others missed this most important phenomenon. That social processes involved in the generation and consolidation of knowledge claims, rather than inherently distorting and relativizing knowledge, are actually constitutive of the cumulative creation of valid knowledge ought, he insisted, to be central to any sociology of knowledge. See *The Open Society and Its Enemies,* 5th ed. London: Routledge and Kegan Paul, 1966.

3. See Dietrich Rueschemeyer, *Power and the Division of Labour.* Cambridge: Polity Press, and Stanford: Stanford University Press, 1986, chap. 6.

4. Joseph Ben-David, *The Scientist's Role in Society.* Englewood Cliffs, NJ: Prentice Hall, 1971.

5. It is important to note that while these categories are most familiar from discussions of scientific logic and the philosophy of knowledge, we use them here for a different purpose. In the present context they are of interest only because they affect the social acceptance of ideas as valid and pragmatically relevant, and not as they pertain to a normative discourse on the validity of ideas.

6. Dieter Lindenlaub, *Richtungskämpfe im Verein für Sozialpolitik.* Wiesbaden: F. Steiner, 1967, p. 284.

7. The German reformers of the Verein für Sozialpolitik again serve as a prominent example. Haskell discusses similar claims of R. H. Tawney, Émile Durkheim, and C. S. Pierce in terms of a contrast of "professionalism versus capitalism." He dismisses this position because the professions and their institutions ultimately "blended frictionlessly into the capitalist landscape"; though they place "a modest premium on certain non-pecuniary dimensions of human performance . . . (they were) finally cut from the same cloth of universal competition and rationalization as the market itself." See Thomas L. Haskell, ed., *The Authority of Experts.* Bloomington, IN: Indiana University Press, 1984, p. xx, introduction. This is sound judgment; but it is not sufficient also to reject the related but separate claim of social scientists to represent a position on collective interests different from the main class positions.

8. This point is also made in Lindblom and Cohen, *Usable Knowledge* and in Lindblom, *Inquiry and Change*. Björn Wittrock systematically examines different patterns of the knowledge-policy nexus in “Social Knowledge and Public Policy: Eight Models of Interaction.” In Wagner et al., *Social Sciences and Modern States,* pp. 333–53.

Notes on the Contributors

Sheldon Garon is Associate Professor of History and East Asian Studies at Princeton University. He is the author of *The State and Labor in Modern Japan* (Berkeley: University of California Press, 1987), for which he won the American Historical Association's John K. Fairbank Prize in 1988. A longtime student of state–society relations in modern Japan, he has recently published articles on the regulation of prostitution, control of popular religions, and relations between women's groups and the state. In addition to examining welfare policies, these essays form the core of his current research on "social management" in twentieth-century Japan. He has also begun a historical study of Japanese savings and frugality campaigns.

Ira Katznelson, who has taught at the University of Chicago and the New School for Social Research, is Ruggles Professor of Political Science and Professor of History at Columbia University. His books on American political development, cities, and the comparative analysis of race, class, and ethnicity include *City Trenches: Urban Politics and the Patterning of Class in the United States* (New York: Pantheon, 1981); *Schooling for All: Class, Race, and the Decline of the Democratic Ideal* (with Margaret Weir); (New York: Basic Books, 1985); *Working-Class Formation: Nineteenth-Century Patterns in Western Europe and the United States* (edited with Aristide Zolberg) (Princeton: Princeton University Press, 1986); *Marxism and the City* (Oxford: Clarendon Press, 1992); and *Paths of Emancipation: Jews within States and Citizenship* (edited with Pierre Birnbaum) (Princeton: Princeton University Press, 1995). Currently, he is finishing a book on postwar American liberalism.

Stein Kuhnle has been Professor of Comparative Politics at the University of Bergen, Norway, since 1982. Since 1988, he has also served as one of three directors of the Welfare State Research Program of the Norwegian Research Council for Applied Social Research. He has written extensively on the Norwegian and Scandinavian welfare states, social and political mobilization in Norway, and political science in Norway. A recent publication is *Government and Voluntary Organizations: A Relational Perspective* (Avebury, Aldershot, 1992), coedited with Per Selle.

Anson Rabinbach is Professor of Modern European History at The Cooper Union for the Advancement of Science and Art. He is an editor of *New German Critique* and has written extensively on European labor and working-class history. His most recent book is *The Human Motor: Energy,*

Fatigue, and the Origins of Modernity (Berkeley: University of California Press, 1993).

DIETRICH RUESCHEMEYER teaches sociology at Brown University and directs Brown's Center for the Comparative Study of Development. His doctoral dissertation at the University of Cologne dealt with theories in the sociology of knowledge. Among his recent publications are *Power and the Division of Labour* (Cambridge, MA: Polity Press, 1986); *Bringing the State Back In* (coedited with Peter B. Evans and Theda Skocpol) (New York: Cambridge University Press, 1985); and *Capitalist Development and Democracy* (coauthored with Evelyne H. Stephens and John D. Stephens) (Cambridge, MA: Polity Press, 1992), which won the Outstanding Book Award of the Political Sociology Section of the American Sociological Association.

LIBBY SCHWEBER is a graduate student at Princeton University in sociology and at the Ecole des Hautes Etudes en Sciences Sociales in history. She is in the process of completing a thesis on the mapping of the social sciences in France and Britain through a study of the institutionalization of demography.

THEDA SKOCPOL is currently Professor of Government and Sociology at Harvard University. Her first book, *States and Social Revolutions: A Comparative Analysis of France, Russia, and China* (Cambridge University Press, 1979), won the 1979 C. Wright Mills Award and the 1980 American Sociological Association Award for a Distinguished Contribution to Scholarship. For the past decade, Skocpol has been doing research on U.S. politics and public policies in comparative and historical perspective. Her book *Protecting Soldiers and Mothers: The Political Origins of Social Policy in the United States* was published in 1992 by the Belknap Press of Harvard University Press. It won five scholarly awards: the J. David Greenstone Award of the Politics and History Section of the American Political Science Association; the Best Book Award of the Political Sociology Section of the American Sociology Association; the 1993 Woodrow Wilson Foundation Award of the American Political Science Association, given annually for "the best book published in the United States during the prior year on government, politics or international affairs"; the 1993 Allan Sharlin Memorial Award of the Social Science History Association; and the 1993 Ralph Waldo Emerson Award of Phi Beta Kappa, given to honor a comprehensive study that contributes significantly to "historical, philosophical, or religious interpretations of the human condition."

JOHN R. SUTTON is an associate professor in the sociology department at the University of California, Santa Barbara. Most of his research is concerned with the politics of social control; his book *Stubborn Children*

(Berkeley: University of California Press, 1988) on the history of delinquency policy in the United States, received the C. Wright Mills Award in 1989. He is currently involved in a comparative study of prisons, mental hospitals, and welfare policies in Western industrial democracies since 1955.

RONAN VAN ROSSEM recently graduated in sociology from Columbia University and is a research scientist at the New York State Psychiatric Institute. Although most of his research is now concentrated in the area of adolescent mental health, he also has a strong interest in comparative development and political processes, especially state formation and collective action.

PETER WAGNER, a sociologist and political scientist, is research fellow at the Wissenschaftszentrum Berlin für Sozialforschung. His main research interests are in political sociology and the sociology of science and technology. His publications include *Sozialwissenschaften und Staat* (1990), *Discourses on Society* (coeditor, 1991), and *A Sociology of Modernity, Liberty and Discipline* (1993).

BJÖRN WITTROCK is professor of political science at the University of Stockholm and director of the Swedish Collegium for Advanced Study in the Social Sciences at Uppsala. His major research interests are in the fields of comparative and historical studies of societal institutions and discourses on society. His most recent volumes are *Social Sciences and Modern States* (coeditor) (Cambridge: Cambridge University Press, 1991), *Discourses on Society* (coeditor) (Norwell, MA: Kluwer, 1991), *The European and American University Since 1800* (coeditor) (Cambridge: Cambridge University Press, 1993), and *Social Theory and Human Agency* (editor) (Newbury Park, CA: Sage, forthcoming).

Index